C000193307

SOCIAL MOVEMENTS
AND
SOCIAL CLASSES

SOCIAL MOVEMENTS
AND
SOCIAL CLASSES

The Future of Collective Action

edited by
Louis Maheu

SAGE Studies in International Sociology 46
Sponsored by the
International Sociological Association/ISA

First published 1995

 SAGE Publications Ltd
6 Bonhill Street
London EC2A 4PU

SAGE Publications Inc
2455 Teller Road
Thousand Oaks, California 91320

SAGE Publications India Pvt Ltd
32, M-Block Market
Greater Kailash – I
New Delhi 110 048

British Library Cataloguing in Publication data

A catalogue record for this book is
available from the British Library.

ISBN 0 8039 7952 5
ISBN 0 8039 7953 3 (pbk)

Library of Congress catalog card number 94–074041

Typeset by The Word Shop, Bury, Lancashire
Printed in Great Britain by Biddles Ltd, Guildford, Surrey

Contents

Notes on Contributors   vii

Introduction *Louis Maheu*   1

Part I: Foundations for Collective Action

Introduction   18

1 Does Social Class Matter in the Study of Social
Movements? A Theory of Middle-class Radicalism
Klaus Eder   21

2 Social Movements and Class: The Decline of the
Marxist Paradigm *Jan Pakulski*   55

3 Racism and Social Movements *Michel Wieviorka*   87

4 The New Social Movements Revisited:
Reflections on a Sociological Misunderstanding
Alberto Melucci   107

Part II: Space, Power and Collective Action

Introduction   120

5 Social Movements in the Transition from
State Socialism: Convergence or Divergence?
Chris Pickvance   123

6 Social Movements and the Challenge of Urban Politics
Henri Lustiger-Thaler and Louis Maheu   151

7 Rethinking Class *John Urry*   169

Part III: Collective Action: From Politics to Democracy

Introduction   182

8 Rethinking Citizenship and Social Movements:
Themes in Contemporary Sociology and
Neoconservative Ideology *Maurice Roche*   186

9 A New Class? The Higher Educated and
the New Politics *Chris Rootes*   220

10   Collective Action and the Paradigm of Individualism   236
     Pierre Hamel

11   Democracy: From a Politics of Citizenship to a
     Politics of Recognition *Alain Touraine*   258

Index   276

Notes on Contributors

Klaus Eder is a professor of sociology at Humboldt-Universität, Berlin. He has written many articles and books, and his recent publications include *The New Politics of Class: Social Movements and Cultural Dynamics in Advanced Societies* (Sage, 1993).

Pierre Hamel is a professor at L'Institut d'urbanisme of the Faculté de l'aménagement at Université de Montréal. His recent publications include, *Action collective et démocratie locale: les mouvements urbains montréalais* (Les Presses de l'Université de Montréal, 1991). He also edited, with G. Boismenu and G. Labica, *Les Formes modernes de la démocratie* (L'Harmattan and Les Presses de l'Université de Montréal, 1992).

Henri Lustiger-Thaler is a professor of sociology at Ramapo College of New Jersey (USA). He is editor of *Political Arrangements: Power and the City* (Black Rose Books, 1992), and, with V. Amit-Talai, of *Urban Lives: Fragmentation and Resistance* (McLelland and Stewart, 1994).

Louis Maheu is a professor of sociology and Vice-Dean of the Faculté des études supérieures at Université de Montréal. He is editor, with A. Sales, of *La Recomposition du politique* (L'Harmattan and Les Presses de l'Université de Montréal, 1991); and, with J. Hamel, of *Hommage à Marcel Rioux: sociologie critique, création artistique et société contemporaine* (Éditions Saint-Martin, 1992).

Alberto Melucci is a professor of sociology and clinical psychology at the University of Milan, Italy. He has written many books and articles on social movements. Among his works published in English is *Nomads of the Present: Social Movements and Individual Needs in Contemporary Society* (Temple University Press, 1989). His latest book in Italian is *Passagio d'epoca* (Feltrinelli, 1994).

Jan Pakulski is a professor of sociology at the University of Tasmania at Hobart, Australia. He is the author of *Social Movements: The Politics of Moral Protest* (Longman Cheshire, 1991), and co-authored, with Stephen Crook and Malcolm Waters, *Postmodernization: Change in Advanced Society* (Sage, 1992).

Chris Pickvance is a professor of urban studies and Director of the Urban and Regional Studies Unit at the University of Kent at Canterbury. He is a founding member of the Editorial Board of the International Journal of Urban and Regional Research. He is co-editor, with M. Gottdiener, of *Urban Life in Transition* (Sage, 1991), with M. Harloe and J. Urry, of *Place, Policy and Politics: Do Localities Matter?* (Unwin Hyman, 1990), and, with E. Preteceille, of *State Restructuring and Local Power: A Comparative Perspective* (Pinter Publishers, 1991).

Maurice Roche is a senior lecturer in the Department of Sociological Studies at the University of Sheffield, England. He has published extensively on the sociology of the politics of citizenship. His most recent book is *Rethinking Citizenship: Welfare, Ideology and Change in Modern Society* (Polity Press, 1992).

Chris Rootes is a senior lecturer in sociology and Director of the Centre for the Study of Social and Political Movements, Eliot College, University of Kent at Canterbury. Most recently he has edited, with D. Richardson, *The Green Challenge: The Development of Green Parties in Europe* (Routledge, 1995); and, with H. Davis, *Social Change and Political Transformation: A New Europe?* (UCL Press and Taylor & Francis, 1994).

Alain Touraine is a professor at l'École des Hautes Études en Sciences Sociales, Paris, and has been the founding director of the Centre d'analyse et d'intervention sociologiques, Paris. Among his works translated into English are *Return of the Actor* (University of Minnesota Press, 1988); and with M. Wieviorka and F. Dubet, *The Workers' Movement* (Cambridge University Press, 1987). His most recent books are *Critique of Modernity* (Blackwell, 1995) and *Qu'est-ce que la démocratie?* (Fayard, 1994).

John Urry is a professor of sociology at Lancaster University. His recent works include *The Tourist Gaze: Leisure and Travel in Contemporary Societies* (Sage, 1990); *Restructuring Place* (Routledge, 1995) and, with Scott Lash, *Economies of Signs and Space* (Sage, 1994).

Michel Wieviorka is a professor at l'École des Hautes Études en Sciences Sociales, Paris, and acting director of the Centre d'analyse et d'intervention sociologiques, Paris. He is the author of *The Making of Terrorism* (University of Chicago Press, 1993), *La France Raciste* (Seuil, 1992), and, with A. Touraine and F. Dubet, *The Workers' Movement* (Cambridge University Press, 1987).

Introduction

Louis Maheu

Social movement theories have travelled a qualitative distance in the last two decades. To varying degrees, from the 1960s and 1970s onwards, Western societies have been the centre of a seemingly endless train of collective actions and social movements. The student movement, from its base on university campuses, soon gravitated to larger global issues and struggles. The civil rights movement became an important foundation for later protests around a wide range of socioeconomic and political issues, related to the struggles of visible minorities. More recently, environmental and ecological conflicts have contributed to the ongoing cycle of protest and social change through social movements. This has certainly been the case regarding controversies surrounding the appropriate uses of technology, particularly those related to military and nuclear industries. The global peace movement has also grown in its close relationship with all these forms of collective action.

Another form of collective action threading its way through these movements is mobilization around gender issues and sexuality, which has acquired its full expression in the many areas of conflict that today characterize the feminist movement. We could also mention the diversity and dynamism of modern sexual preference movements, both gay and lesbian, in their close yet conflict-laden relationship to the women's movement and more generally global transformations in society.

It would be an understatement to say that the many recent forms of collective action and concrete social movements are connected to one another. Indeed, they represent a self-sustaining chain of historically convergent events, hard-won political lessons and – from the perspective of social movement analysis – a vastly rich object of investigation.

Collective action in search of a model of analysis

These issues are echoed in the many nodes and convergences of the broader literature of the social sciences. Can these epistemological convergences give added meaning to the array of social movements listed above? A quick perusal of the literature leads to the conclusion that it is less comprehensive than we once thought or even hoped. A growing scholarly opinion suggests that once reigning model and paradigms have not distilled the essence of collective action. Kuechler and Dalton, for example, argue that collective action must visibly explain 'a collectivity of people united by common belief (ideology) and a determination to challenge the existing order in the pursuit of these beliefs outside institutionalized channels of interest intermediation' (1990:278). Furthermore, current sociological theory is confronted with relatively new expressions of collective action, or at the very least new contexts for action. These conjuncturally led activities inject a sense of ambivalence into the very core of collective action, unsettling our understandings of social transformation (Maheu, 1994). But is this the first appearance on the stage of history for at least some of these activities? Most likely not. These conflicts only appear to be 'new' because they insert contemporary meanings and forms of significa-tion into cumulative and ongoing systems of knowledge, as well as having a structural impact on the social fabric.

Following the many trajectories of social change has not always been a self-evident enterprise in sociology. We must acknowledge that current sociological knowledge was (and perhaps still is) show-ing signs of a general malaise regarding explanations of social transformation. The quality of our dominant models of analysis left much to be desired.

Indeed, the classical approach of collective behaviour gave too much explanatory power to 'breakdown theories'. According to this discourse, actors, after a period of intense stress and social tension, reappear on the stage of history as ruptured collective agents. The model of collective action defended by 'breakdown theories' is one in which the world of social relations is composed, in the last instance, by chaotic and unstructured media.

This seems far removed from the types of social relations and social conducts animating contemporary forms of protest. It tells us little about the broader functioning of a social system. More critically, it is not particularly informative about patterns of domination and exploitation experienced in everyday life.

Conventional Marxist models identify principal agents through their *a priori* material interests. They do this by underscoring the tumultuous effects of structural contradictions in capitalist societies. With daily reminders of ethnic strife occurring throughout the world, especially in the former 'places' of 'actually existing socialism', the disappoint-ing social legacy of this century stands out clearly. At the very least, the passage from a state of unbridled consciousness, or a 'class in itself', to a 'class for itself', is enigmatic and deeply problematical.

We are certainly at the point, historically, of admitting that the collective actor cannot be subsumed in the interplay of structural contradictions or the mode of production. As an added problem, new social conflicts and social movements seem to be fragmenting the traditional identity of social classes, or at least undermining the structural media that have been attributed to them. Furthermore, the new movements are not concerned, as a first order of activity, with the traditional issues of industrialization, the motor propelling social action in the late nineteenth and early twentieth centuries.

We are also increasingly questioning the explanatory power of 'relative deprivation' theories. It is impossible to condense the very essence of protest movements to the simple dictum of an 'us against them' relationship. It is equally impossible to reduce all forms of social action to social groups that are objectively confronted with a widening gap between what they expect and what they will eventually receive. It is more difficult than ever to make a causal or even purposeful link between dissatisfied groups and their participation in protest movements.

It should be pointed out, however, that simply *because* many collective agents come from relatively privileged sectors of the population is *not* reason enough to doubt deprivation theories. The inadequacy of these theories, rather, is that they do not explain why the social conditions of relative deprivation have failed to mobilize larger sectors of the population. Environmental questions, for example, do not in and of themselves ignite mass mobilization. The theory does not explain, when indeed mobilization does take place, why its principal actors turn out to be those *least* exposed to the actual experience of deprivation.

Theoretical models of relative deprivation are confronted with a 'black box' packed with unsolved inquiries about how a collective grievance becomes an instance of mobilization. Other models of analysis have an abundance of problems too. Rational choice approaches, for example, have been receiving their fair share of critical salvos. Rational choice models shed light on certain dimensions of contemporary collective action, but their explanations of the social characteristics of collective action were not totally convincing.

The model of rational self-interest is perhaps the most radical wing in this school of thought, inspired by the classic contribution of Mancur Olson. This model is most compelling when used to examine selective criteria of an economic or visibly finite nature. Filtered, as it is, through a rational cost-benefit analysis, it cannot explain the deeper motivations for engaging in a collective process. The dilemma presented by the 'free rider' phenomenon, moreover, adds little to the analysis of collective action. The waves of protest that occurred throughout the 1960s and 1970s were indicative of substantive intersubjective dimensions around issues of ideology, race and generation, perhaps the first moments of what we have come to call, in the 1980s and early 1990s, 'identity politics'.

But collective rational choice is a model that points to how collective actors, often with great difficulty, develop organizational strategies. It explains how collective actors conceive interests and mobilize to defend them. The model cannot be confined to its algebraic explanations: it mirrors a social practice. Social agents are the masters of an instrumental rationality that is present at the very core of collective action.

However, over and above cognitive qualities that one might associate with rational choice models, the *meaning* of a collective action cannot be discounted, since it is linked to expressive and subjective characteristics. This dimension in particular has contributed to how we understand relations between agents, and the conflict-laden contexts within which they interact.

Most scholars of collective action would readily agree that the current state of knowledge about social movements is ruled by two schools of thought which remain more or less polarized in their own sectarian corners. In the social movement literature, controversy usually surrounds which approach emerges as the more promising: resource mobilization theory, on the one hand, or new social movement approaches, on the other.

Resource mobilization theory offers a broad analytical framework within which to 'site' collective rational choice issues. But it goes significantly further in its overall vision of collective action by suggesting that grievances and conflicts are not the primary elements to take into account when looking at social movements. More critical are the form a social movement takes, and how it inscribes itself in various politico-institutional mechanisms. The accent here is on organizational displays of collective action and on the material or ideological resources that prove useful in maintaining an open channel for collective mobilization to take place. Political opportunity structures and sociopolitical conditions are also considered important in this model. Collective action hence becomes part of a complex web of institutional social processes, structured by access to political systems and public opinion.

In contrast to resource mobilization theory, 'new social movements' approaches, as some authors have proposed, take as their critical point of inquiry the 'why' behind collective action as opposed to the 'how' of it. The goal of this theory is to explain meanings linked to structural factors behind a collective action. The emphasis is placed on collective and conflicting world views, or *Weltanschauungen*, which subjectivize and filter social factors into forms of collective action.

An important work by Klandermans and Tarrow (1988) focuses on these two approaches. These authors link the first to American social movement theory, and the second to European intellectual traditions. Klandermans and Tarrow point to the polarization of the two schools of thought and insist upon the need for a more sustained dialogue, exchange and debate. A more recent book by Rucht (1991) also accords special attention to these two currents of analyses, highlighting their intrinsic duality. These authors take up a challenge outlined some years earlier by Jean Cohen. In a 1985 issue of *Social Research* devoted to social movements, Cohen contrasts these two prevalent schools. She juxtaposes the paradigm of rational strategic action and 'new social movement' approaches, creating what she refers to as an 'identity paradigm'.

It is doubtful however that one can, or should, regroup distinct epistemological perspectives, and their varying analyses of social movements, under the rubric of an 'identity paradigm' (Maheu, 1991). The putative duality of these two approaches requires more critical reflection and debate. Before we construct our new *orienting strategies* for the growth of theory, as Berger and Zelditch (1993) have described them (multiplying the realm of analytical interrelations), we should have a clearer idea of what exactly is being sought out in this fusion. What is the nature of collective action?

Collective action: beyond the mobilization of resources and new social movements

Collective action is at the heart of this book. In the following chapters the authors define their understanding of collective action, social movements and class action. Many divergences appear, as one might imagine. I have asked the contributors, as much as possible, to enter into a dialogue with one another.

These chapters, regardless of their divergences, share what Wittgenstein has so aptly referred to as 'family resemblances', in so far as collective action is concerned. The authors are careful not to impoverish the notion of collective action. Hence, they refer to social movements with a fair measure of analytical and empirical reserve. Most would argue that in order to move beyond a nominal definition of collective action, a more restrained notion is necessary. This notion must, however, be sensitive to the complex play of social factors and the various repertoires of collective action.

We can say that a collective action is found in various forms of protest and claims-making, through which actors define their identity. Through a mix of non-institutional and institutional channels, their protest movements simultaneously work with, and oppose, the established order. This intersubjective and 'critical-institutional' *modus operandi* of collective action is linked to another notion: collective action creates a 'structural space', a force-field of stratification processes and social divisions. It is a space for the articulation of various modes of domination, buttressed by modes of consumption, cultural productions and global interrelations which threaten the well-being of the planet. More critically, this space contains the will for social change, for personal and collective emancipation: the capacity to 'do otherwise'. It therefore contains defensive and offensive struggles, progressive as well as non-progressive movements, addressing issues that are constitutive of the social fabric. In many of the contributions in this book these fundamental characteristics of collective action appear over and over again. Understood in this manner, collective action becomes a general conceptual notion. And it can materialize in the context of a class action or as a practice of social movements.

In terms of establishing a standpoint from which to view issues of collective action, this book does not, unlike the readers discussed above, start from the premise of an obvious duality between resource mobilization theory and new social movements perspectives. The obvious preoccupation with these dual approaches has, however, brought us face to face with some very important characteristics of modern types of collective action. As noted above, the American literature on social movements abundantly exploits resource mobilization theory. In so doing, it adds to our general knowledge of the complex organizations in which social movements navigate. Contextualizing this for us, Margit Mayer (1991) has argued that this strain of analysis owes much to structural characteristics, notably the political system of interest mediation present in the American body politic. The new social movement perspective, of course, in part finds its bearings in the European tradition, inspired by Marx and Weber. Here collective action – the praxis of social movements – emerges more as an indicator of structural conflicts, conflicts indicative of the transformation of modern societies.

This notion of duality, when applied to these approaches, does con-tain some ingrained difficulties (Neidhardt and Rucht, 1991: 437–43). Resource mobilization theory and new social movement approaches are in fact internally varied. This is certainly true of the resource mobilization variant. Aside from its close relation to rational choice models, it has an equal resonance with notions of political opportunity structures, as well as with organizational assets and entrepreneurial functions (Morris and Herring, 1987; Kitschelt, 1989). Many of the studies in this latter tradition clearly point to more macro- and meso-structural dimensions of collective behaviour. This is evident in the attention these studies pay to the linkages between social movements and the functioning of 'the political' in its more objective characteristics.

Certainly the prominence, within the American literature, given to resource mobilization obscures other types of analysis of collective action. Numerous American studies have examined the cultural dimensions of collective action. The notions of identity and the self, or technologies of the self, inspired by the works of Foucault and Habermas, have characterized recent American contributions to social movement analysis. Approaches in the field of cultural studies, for example, have examined youth protests, sexual preference communities, the women's movement, aesthetic movements and national movements, to name but a few. In sociology and political science, the volume edited by Dalton and Kuechler (1990) includes many contributions by American writers, working from a new social movements perspective.

The new social movement paradigm cannot claim to be a cohesive wing of this stated duality any more than resource mobilization approaches can. New social movement theory is anything but homogeneous: like any school, it has internal complexity. The chapters in this book allow a close examination of its diverse characteristics in the works of Alberto Melucci, Klaus Eder and Alain Touraine. It is difficult to accept Neidhardt and Rucht's (1991: 441) proposition that these authors can be gathered together under the rubrics of cultural struggle and social reproduction.

The purported duality of new social movement and resource mobilization approaches is thus too arbitrary to be of real analytical use. At best it enables us to differentiate authors and analytical perspectives, but other criteria must be used to distinguish the analytical trends in the literature. We will be introducing some of these in this book, in order to underscore its contribution to debates in the collective action literature.

Sectorial sociology or global sociology?

For certain authors, collective action constitutes a defining rubric, a sectorial sociology. In the same manner as there are sectorial sociologies of the family, leisure and religion, there is a sectorial sociology of collective action. The collective behaviour approach is a good example of a sectorial sociology: it contrasts collective action with a backdrop of more or less institutionalized patterns of action which remain contiguous with the norms and values inherent in a given system of social relations.

But the lingering residual of a sectorial sociology is also present in a wide array of analytical frameworks in today's prevailing models and approaches. Collective action and social movements emerge from this school of thought as 'ideal types', collective practices uncoupled from structures. By isolating collective action from larger conflict-laden issues and structural grievances, these approaches are unfortunately reviving a sectorial sociology of collective action.

In other approaches, collective action is much wider, more generalized and horizontally structured: it is seen as part of the extended family of critical processes, such as the social division of labour and/or forms of domination and rationalization that mark us as moderns. As such, it fits comfortably within a framework of Grand Theory, addressing the relations between agents and systems. From this perspective, collective action presents problems of a global nature.

It is because of this broad impact of social movements on the constitution of the social that several writers have insisted that collective action, in the halcyon days of the 1960s and 1970s, was closely linked to qualitative societal changes and transformations. It should be said, as well, that collective action as a horizontal process is *not* necessarily synonymous with social change. It is often better defined as a key process of structuration, a synchronic element of social life.

The cleavage between notions of collective action as sectorial rubric and collective action as a global process embedded in the structuration of social life parallels the division between micro- and macro-perspectives discussed by McAdam et al. (1988). Having said this, however, the importance one ascribes to collective action as a social process remains controversial. Is collective action completely integrative, covering all forms of social relations? Is it specifically useful as an integrative theory of new social movements? Can it explain structural issues related to subsystems of social relations, such as the problem of social regulation and political order?

The standpoint from which collective action emerges as a general process does not necessarily bring us any closer to affirming its link to qualitative transformations in the social structure. As many of our contributors argue, there is no obvious point of transition between transformations in social structure and the emergence of new action repertoires.

Collective action and the problem of totality: social movements or social classes?

It is these types of inquiry that thread their way through this volume, particularly in Part I, which looks at the structural foundations of social movements. These preoccupations link the notion of collective action to a more general process of social structuration, opening the door to discussion of collective action's integrative capacities, and its global impact on social life. These questions urge us towards a more careful examination of global theories of collective action and social movements. Another 'family resemblance' emerges from this forest of questions: the Western Marxian notion of totality (Jay, 1984), and how revising a theory about collective action brings us to reconsider it anew.

In the Marxian problematic, collective action and its class subjects were at the very core of the concept of totality. In terms of a late twentieth-century reformulation of a theory of collective action, and after the detritus of postmodernism, would we do well to reconsider the notion of totality? If we do so, what then of the relationship between social classes and social movements?

Surprisingly, these questions have been virtually absent from modern debates about collective action and social movements. This book is distinguished by the constant juxtapositions of collective action and the problem of totality, as well as class issues and social movements – indeed, for several chapters such juxtapositions become the central theme. This type of debate cannot avoid the postmodern disclaimer about the limits of holistic metanarratives. The pluralistic and fragmented character of modern societies, and the drastically transformed nature of class identities, have consequences that are nothing less than socially overwhelming. One contributor, Jan Pakulski, proposes thinking about contemporary collective action through channels other than the production and reproduction of global identities. In Chapter 9, Chris Rootes suggests that this line of reasoning exposes the relations between social movements and social classes to a substantive critique.

In short, many authors argue for a specific paradigm of social movements uncoupled from their class context. They would insist that these movements exhibit, in and of themselves, a sufficient density and social composition, as well as adequate organizational forms of action. They are therefore capable of framing claims and confronting structural barriers, and their actions do not need to be linked to any social class whatsoever.

This position would no doubt affirm that social movements contribute to the constitution of specific sites of social stratification, the 'structural spaces' of collective action referred to earlier. These spaces may be distinct from those of class capacities and their social locations. They find expression in relations of opposition and conflict, in confrontation with specific institutions and established orders of powers. Social movements can therefore welcome highly volatile circumstances, destabilizing or reinforcing social systems and structures. Their internal composition and structural effects make them agents of a new system of stratification, which encompasses cultural, political and private life. The chapters by Alberto Melucci, Maurice Roche and Pierre Hamel espouse this particular viewpoint.

But yet again, social movements in particular historical circumstances have been linked to specific types of class relations. The structural and strategic features of social movements have proven at times to be highly contingent factors in the relationships between classes. Social movements can be seen as instances in the ongoing frictional relations between social classes. A good case in point is the type of struggle associated with the ecology movement and its contingent impact on the social and technical division of labour. Such struggles have introduced a considerable tension within the sphere of class relations. Similar examples could be drawn from collective action about housing issues, urban development, the particularities of local political networks and scenes, or questions of social space, as illustrated in the chapters by Chris Pickvance, John Urry, Henri Lustiger-Thaler and Louis Maheu.

Yet, depending on factors of time, space and place, social movements may even be necessary and central to the formation of certain classes or class practices. Some authors have even suggested that certain types of collective action associated with social movements do constitute the founding categories of a rejuvenated class theory: namely the conflict-laden products of identity and their links to the new middle classes. The chapter by Klaus Eder argues precisely this. The collective action of class must also be rethought in ways that address and reorder spatial problems in the context of new causal powers and factors, a case put forward by John Urry.

As mentioned earlier, this book raises the question of linkages between the type of collective action associated with social movements and a reinvigorated notion of totality. We can fruitfully recall Touraine's admonition that social movements are the main agents of the emerging post-industrial society. Touraine's point is that they participate in a 'central conflict'. The notions of totality and historicity are at the core of his understanding of how social movements constitute the social basis of society, or the transformed class foundation of the post-industrial epoch.

Another facet in the emergence of the post-industrial society parallels what George Ross referred to as the 'dramatic deflation in the integrative capacities of the great ideological and organizational complexes that began to emerge in the late nineteenth century' (1992: 532). Michel Wieviorka, in his chapter, explores what Ross sees as the subtle link between this structural deflation and social movements, or their antithesis in anti-social movements.

Collective action: analytical constructs or movement actors?

The chapters of this book caution against seeing movements simply as concrete collective actors, or as givens in the panoply of mobilizations that make up everyday life. Social movements are not spontaneously constituted. Neither are they necessarily the starting point of an analysis. They are more the end result, the fruit of a labour of theoretical construction and analytical demonstrations. The groundwork is set for a much stronger assertion that collective action and social movements are constituted through wide and encompassing processes. This condition brings attention to their structural conditions of existence as well as their ongoing significa-tion in everyday life.

Social movements are in this regard overlapping conceptual 'constructs', addressing structural exigencies and strategic dimen-sions of action, putting into motion a process of collective agency: a social movement cycle (Scott, 1991). They are composed of resources, values and ideologies and they are carriers of meaning about the constitution of action. These processes are part of the ongoing 'framing of action', as a praxis of protest movements. They translate conflictual issues and structural grievances into patterns of social action.

A more rigorous use of the notion of collective action would allow us to move beyond movement-centred analyses. Collective action certainly contains a discourse and a practice about resources and strategies. These dimensions of action cannot however be treated in an isolated manner. Collective action is inherently dialogical, bringing together systems and actors. No collective actor is self-constituted.

This is even more reason to support a paradigm of collective action that underscores conflict-laden relations between agency and the structures of domination. Movement-centred and system-centred analyses are *de facto* the situational and structural contexts for a model of collective action and collective agency. This however does present a challenge in terms of maintaining an analytical equilibrium between system-centred and movement-centred modes of analysis, allowing the pendulum to rest in the centre. Collective action as an analytical construct, in the hands of macro-theoreticians like Alain Touraine, or constructionists like Alberto Melucci, must face some hard questions regarding the ongoing evolution of collective action. Do these approaches sufficiently capture new emerging patterns of institutionalization that require an intimate knowledge of the 'movement as an actor' and its multiple insertions within institutions?

Clearly, the ecological, peace and sexual preference movements, amongst others, have taken the form of socially constituted collective agents through these mechanisms. But these are agents that generally do not show signs of conventional processes of integration. They have emerged through the venue of anti-systemic actions directed against the general process of regulation, unequal social exchanges and issues of domination. In a contesting and unconventional manner, they have gradually penetrated varying levels of institutional life, as well as a wide variety of public opinion networks and culturally prescribed markets.

As a result, these movements have become public, semi-public and private media that socially construct collective actors. They have become social venues where the experiences of struggle and identity fuse in the recesses of public and individual consciousness. The collective action of these agents becomes reflexively institutionalized by their insertion into a public sphere and the many threads of the social fabric. This is certainly a different view of institutionalization, one constituted, at least partially, as a practice of social movements.

Beyond the institutionalization of collective action

We truly have come a long way! In the last 20–25 years the repertoire of collective action has dramatically changed. So have our understandings and representations of these processes. Yet the multi-dimensional and conflict-laden institutional dynamic of collective action still requires imaginative theory building, ongoing debate and, most importantly, concrete research.

Up to now, the institutional characteristics of social movements have been mainly broached in the literature in the following two ways. First, some have argued that institutional dimensions of action tend to be normatively based. Institutions in this regard have a crystallizing impact on normative dimensions of action, through an accumulative and cognitive process, re-embedding systems of knowledge and representation. Social movements through their various repertoires of action emerge as producers of cognitive constructs with a considerable symbolic and cultural density. It is in this way that they institutionalize *themselves* by 'framing' cultural understandings of their world, as well as those of their adversaries. Movements are hence reconstituted as alternative sources of information and identity for a wide array of agents: ideological signposts in a 'post-corporatist order' (Eder, 1993).

What needs emphasis here is the conflictual dimension of this normative and cognitive institutional process. Social movements are actors in conflict-laden cultural fields. It is within these fields that global cultural models of rationalization, risk and subjectivation emerge as part of the construction of late modernity. Social movements share a common, but also very different, cultural and cognitive field from those of other social forces and/or dominant elites.

Secondly, social movements invade the political terrain of social claims and interest mediation by raising issues directly related to the political order and its crisis of legitimacy. By so doing they institutionalize *themselves as political forces*. This process, to which we will return, is not to be dissociated from ideological and cultural struggles central to the cognitive order of modernity, but its density is such, and the importance given it in the literature is so pronounced, that it tends to be seen as a more or less parallel process.

There is still another important sense of institutionalization that emerges from the overlapping effects of the two phenomena described above. Curiously it often escapes detection. All institutions have to be seen as systems of action, through which actors construct their world. Rationalization, risk and subjectivation, as social products, are therefore immanent features of modernity: their very foundations reflexively materialized within the web of institutions.

Institutions as such constitute conflict-laden spaces for experiencing modernity. It is within institutions that collective actors and social movements find reflexive sources of rationalization and subjectivation. Quite often, these are also the very forces and processes they oppose. Agents bring rational and expressive ideologies, experiential forms of subjectivation and collective identities into formal institutions, building relations with Others, and thus heightening their own powers of reflexivity. The effects of this can be seen in the differential approaches and ideologies which coexist in the health sector, caring institutions, education and local economic development, to name but a few. Movements have a need to gesture in two directions at once (Lustiger-Thaler, 1994). This hitherto unconsidered dimension of institutionalization, in its anti-functionalist framing, is discussed by Lustiger-Thaler and Maheu in Chapter 6 of this book.

The problem of institutions and social movements remains central to the literature, but with a focus mainly on the production of a legitimate institutional and political order. Neidhardt and Rucht, for example, argue that the emergence of social movements is 'related to dysfunctions and deficits of interest mediation by means of parties and pressure groups' (1991:448–9). At a meso-level, social movements complete the functioning of these institutions. They assure a mediating space between functionally specialized systems and the lifeworld of the general population.

Kuechler and Dalton, for their part, focus attention on ideological forms of contestation, opening the door to a new social paradigm (1990: 277–8). But they are still very concerned with the way these groups confront the political order. Kuechler and Dalton argue that the determining impact of new social movements on modern societies could very well be the 'unintended consequence of securing the long-term stability of the political order' (1990:298). An analogous observation can be made from a more constructionist approach, in which social movements expose power structures which systems of politico-institutional regulation tend to camouflage (Melucci, 1985).

These perspectives offer, if very implicitly, a structural-functionalist view of social life. The dysfunctional deficits of the system, particularly its instability and/or invisible efficiency, are ultimately corrected as a prelude, more or less, to the reproduction of the established political order. This perspective suggests that the functional differentiation of subsystems circulates social products in a sort of homeostatic game, finally reaching a point of social equilibrium. Social movements emerge as functionally instrumental rather than as ongoing reflexive practices around the contingencies of human agency, as shared conflictual instances of rationalization and subjectivization.

Yet, regardless of their individual standpoints, contributors to this book share a common concern to explain conflict and its regulation. The chapters by Maurice Roche, Chris Pickvance, and Henry Lustiger-Thaler and Louis Maheu point to the gulf between contestation and regulation, and how their borders are often very thin and insecure. A movement's social practices are composed of contestations and mediations, and its venture into institutions, political as well as social, is conditioned by the tensions they ignite around structural factors of domination and inequality. These same movements are however also pregnant with struggles over issues that affirm modes of subjectivation and rationalization, within a condi-tion of mounting structural complexity.

Securing the future

The unsteady world of relations between contemporary politics and the activities of social movements should compel us to emphasize these modes of subjectivation and rationalization. This is as true of patterns of authenticity as of threats and risks which affect our relationship to one another, our demo-cratic future and the earth's very survival as a planet. Historically, the hallmark of social movements has been the exposure of systems of domination and the construction of social relationships. We must count on their collective prescience to do the same today. This applies to those issues constitutive of our modern condition but not yet fully acknowledged in the institutional mêlée of cultural practices and political agendas.

The insight of Kuechler and Dalton remains pertinent here: the collective action of social movements does shed light on the real 'threats to the future of the human race' (1990:280). These authors have underlined the essential challenge of contemporary social movements. Social movements can and must contribute to human survival.

Nowadays, issues of stratification and social domination are key structuring forces that are entirely pertinent to that understanding. These are issues that challenge the very potential of human capacities. They also challenge the future of democracy. They eventually do this by exposing institutional expressions of collective action to struggles about the cognitive order of modernity, as well as conflictual issues embedded within its experiential/institutional networks. These issues underscore a recentring of the problem of legitimacy, one composed of subjects mastering their modes of subjectivation and rationalization. It is in this sense that this book ultimately invokes the question of democracy and the way it is rooted in the unfolding of processes of collective action.

This book presents reflections and critical data which explain the complex universe of social domination that has become so charac-teristic of late modernity, where little can be taken for granted. Gaining further insights is essential in understanding the old, new and hidden forms of domination that collective action captures in its multi-faceted view of society. As this tumultuous and often tragic century comes to an end and a new one commences, part of the challenge is to comprehend the way social movements negotiate the plural spaces of the social and the political.

The contributions to this reader have been collected into three thematic parts. Part I is composed of four chapters underlining general analytical models of collective action. These texts discuss the foundations of collective action through a critical evaluation of existing models of analysis. This is done with an eye towards securing a base for empirical generalizations about modern action repertoires. Klaus Eder, Jan Pakulski, Michel Wieviorka and

Alberto Melucci dialogue with each other as well as with authors who treat different facets of collective action in the second and third parts of this book.

Political and economic power structures, most notably local power structures, are the themes which run through Part II. The chapters by Chris Pickvance, Henri Lustiger-Thaler and Louis Maheu and John Urry point to the articulation of collective action with power structures and issues of space. These issues of space in turn cannot escape larger questions about analytical models of collective action: they are not sheltered from questions regarding the very nature of the political raised throughout this book.

The contributors to Part III, Maurice Roche, Chris Rootes, Pierre Hamel and Alain Touraine, address the relationship between the political sphere and collective action. Many facets of this relationship are examined, concerning the politics of social movements, the treatment of social claims within state systems and the diverse mediations between new citizenship rights and the realm of everyday politics. Part III also underlines questions about the limits of politics and how its frontiers are inscribed within the social fabric, raising challenges for democracy.

The book itself is the product of discussions and debates associated with an international network of researchers and scholars belonging to the Social Movements and Social Classes Research Committee of the International Sociological Association (ISA). The group received the status of a Research Committee (no.47) in 1993. The majority of the texts gathered here were first presented at the meetings of this group in Madrid at the ISA World Congress in the summer of 1990. In the following years, new discussions, conferences and the circulation of papers have updated, sharpened and transformed these initial presentations. The result has been a far-reaching series of contributions to collective action theories.

Finally, and perhaps most importantly, this book has retained the sense of a collective project that first animated it – authors in dialogue with each other. This is very much in the spirit of the Research Committee, a purpose that bodes well for the future study of collective action and social movements.

Note

Henri Lustiger-Thaler translated the General and Section Introductions for this book. I would also like to thank him for his invaluable suggestions, comments, and criticisms.

References

Berger, J. and Zelditch, M. (1993) *Theoretical Research Programs: Studies in the Growth of Theory*. Stanford: Stanford University Press.

Cohen, J. (1985) 'Strategy or identity: new theoretical paradigms and contemporary social movements', *Social Research*, 52(4): 663–716.

Dalton, R. J. and Kuechler, M. (1990) *Challenging the Political Order: New Social and Political Movements in Western Democracies*. Cambridge: Polity Press.

Eder, K. (1993) 'Negotiating a postcorporatist order in advanced societies. An institutional analysis of environmentalism'. Florence, European University Institute, Project No. 42, Research paper No. 8.

Jay, M. (1984) *Marxism and Totality: The Adventures of a Concept from Lukács to Habermas*. Berkeley: University of California Press.

Kitschelt, H. (1989) 'Explaining contemporary social movements: an exploration in the comparison of theories'. Paper delivered at the 1989 Annual Meeting of the American Political Science Association, Atlanta, Georgia.

Klandermans, B. and Tarrow, S. (1988) 'Mobilization into social movements: synthesizing European and American approaches', in B. Klandermans, H. Kriesi and S. Tarrow, *International Social Movement Research, Vol. 1: From Structure to Action: Comparing Social Movement Research across Cultures*. Greenwich, CT: JAI Press.

Kuechler, M. and Dalton, R.J. (1990) 'New social movements and the political order: inducing change for long-term stability?' in R.J. Dalton and M. Kuechler (eds), *Challenging the Political Order*. New York: Oxford University Press.

Lustiger-Thaler, H. (1994) 'Community and the contingency of everyday life', in Vered Amit-Talai and Henri Lustiger-Thaler (eds), *Urban Lives: Fragmentation and Resistance*. Toronto: McLelland & Stewart.

McAdam, D., McCarthy, J. D. and Zald, M. N. (1988) 'Social movements', in N. J. Smelser (ed.), *Handbook of Sociology*. Newbury Park: Sage. pp. 695–737.

Maheu, L. (1991) 'Identité et enjeux du politique', in L. Maheu and A. Sales (eds), *Recomposition du politique*. Paris: L'Harmattan; Montreal: Presses de l'Université de Montréal.

Maheu, L. with the collaboration of H. Lustiger-Thaler (1995) 'Les mouvements sociaux: plaidoyer pour une sociologie de l'ambivalence', in F. Dubet and M. Wieviorka (eds), *Penser le sujet*. Paris: Fayard.

Mayer, M. (1991) 'Social movement research and social movement practice: the US pattern', in D. Rucht (ed.), *Research on Social Movements: The State of the Art in Western Europe and the USA*. Boulder, CO: Westview Press.

Melucci, A. (1985) 'The symbolic challenge of contemporary movements', *Social Research*, 52(4): 789–816.

Morris, A. and Herring, C. (1987) 'Theory and research in social movements: a critical review', in S. Long (ed.), *Annual Review of Political Behavior*. Boulder, CO: Westview Press.

Neidhardt, F. and Rucht, D. (1991) 'The state of the art and some perspectives on further research', in D. Rucht (ed.), *Research on Social Movements: The State of the Art in Western Europe and the USA.*. Boulder, CO: Westview Press.

Ross, G. (1992) Review of Dalton and Kuechler (1990) *Challenging the Political Order*, in *Social Forces*, 71(2): 530–2.

Rucht, D. (ed.) (1991) *Research on Social Movements: The State of the Art in Western Europe and the USA*. Boulder, CO: Westview Press.

Scott, A. (1991) *Ideology and the New Social Movements*. London: Hutchinson.

PART I
FOUNDATIONS
FOR COLLECTIVE ACTION

Introduction

It has become a truism to say that modern repertoires around collective action are mostly about social conflicts. We know that these have a determining effect upon the very construction of established orders, their intrinsic forms of power, and the ethical foundation of society and politics. At first glance, both these statements appear self-evident. But what deeper sense can we derive from them? Which conflicts are we speaking of? What type of relations, issues and social agents do they bring onto the modern stage of human struggles and collective actions?

We might also ask what would be the most appropriate model for the study of new forms of collective action? Once we set up the epistemological parameters for framing the above question, how vigilantly should we hold to the linkages between social movements, collective actions and social classes? There is no unanimity in the literature on these points of inquiry.

These questions do, however, present grids for the themes and issues discussed in the first four chapters. These contributions debate the foundations of collective action in their empirical and analytical forms and expressions. They purposefully unpack the many differences which have come to characterize social conflicts and modern collective action. These chapters also adopt what should be viewed as a 'theory of discontinuity', in the form of a radical critique of modernity. This suggests that contemporary collective actions are far removed from the cardinal principles of industrial societies, and their discursive positions and modernist global ideologies. Most importantly, these chapters point to a break, an analytical rupture with traditional notions of class location and its principal agents of transformation.

For authors such as Jan Pakulski, the problem of discontinuity is linked to the central tenets of postmodernism. Contemporary societies are too fragmented to produce central actors such as social classes. Pakulski refers to the problem of discontinuity to challenge the Marxist understanding of class. He argues that the constitution and transformation of postmodern societies have rendered the influence of class agents more or less obsolete. Protest movements, Pakulski insists, with all their antinomies and contradictions, emerge as moments of resistance. Most importantly, they contain a determining cultural density, grafted on to a value-relational world.

The importance of protest movements cannot be grasped through singular references to class. Nor is an appeal to Grand Theory particularly helpful. More pertinent are questions related to the role of generations as a criterion of movement composition. This generational dimension contributes to the creation of social sites (situs). As such, generational actors of the post-1960s era share a common degree of mobility, life chances and relations of autonomy to the labour process. They figure greatly in the composition of modern social movements.

Discontinuity in social conflicts is also at the heart of Alberto Melucci's contribution to this book. In the same vein as Pakulski, Melucci argues that class is too discursively and practically embedded in the history of industrial society to properly account for contemporary collective actions. The paradigm of new social movements has a purchase beyond classes. New social movement theories have thus drawn considerable attention, yet they are now more often criticized by scholars of different theoretical backgrounds. Chris Pickvance debates these perspectives in Part II.

Melucci makes a plea in favour of an analytical position that does not take new social movements as empirical givens, or as practices that are already socially constituted. Social movements, he argues, are complex and composite action systems. As such they are the products of resources as well as of the limits and constituents of conflictual discourses. Most importantly for him, however, are the symbolic and cultural challenges they present. These challenges underscore the following critical question for the social movement analyst: are complex societies grounded in antagonistic social relations around the production and consumption of informational resources? Analyses of social movements would be abundantly richer if we found innovative ways to raise this kind of question.

Most contributors to Part I share such a point of view, but it is particularly evident in Klaus Eder's chapter. Eder also adopts, to a certain extent, the thesis of discontinuity, emphasizing important cultural dimensions of identity formation and change. In so doing, he offers an approach that prises open the door for a constructionist version of class theory.

In this light, new social movements are very closely tied to the radicalism of the new middle classes. These classes offer social movements immense opportunities for framing collective action, because of their ambiguous class locations. These 'opportunities' are first and foremost designed and configured by the cultural characteristics and contradictions of middle-class radicalism. Collective action is in this regard a motor force behind new forms of social relations. New social movements, through their identity struggles, produce class antagonisms. They are deeply embedded in the social relations of class, around the control and production of the means of cultural expression.

Michel Wieviorka in Chapter 3 bases his argument on Touraine's understanding of social movements. From Touraine's standpoint, social movements represent an ensemble of struggles between adversaries. These conflicts produce not only situational agents, but actors that possess a certain degree of 'historicity' or are central participants in the principal arrangements of society. Wieviorka uses Touraine's model to explain several conjunctural elements of collective action, arguing that the transition to post-industrial society is critical in the formation of new social movements. This transition reconstitutes fundamental social relations, but also presages the historic decline of former social movements and their practices. Collective action, he argues, is not always conducive to the building of movements.

Wieviorka reflects on why certain forms of collective action do not succeed in securing the social and cultural outlets which would allow them to reconstitute themselves as movements. In this problematical context, racism, ethnic intolerance, discrimination and exclusion emerge on the battered human landscape as anti-movements. Such collective action, according to Wieviorka, is an expression of social forces that are incapable of universalizing their conflicts towards a horizon that holds greater promise for equality, liberty and justice.

1

Does Social Class Matter in the Study of Social Movements? A Theory of Middle-class Radicalism

Klaus Eder

Does social class matter?

Why should class matter at all?

The concern with class in social movement theory and analysis seems to raise old questions that have been surpassed by the evolution of modern society. Class no longer plays a role in the diagnostic discourses of advanced modern societies. It has even become fashionable to perform critical diagnoses of modern societies beyond and against the discourse of class. The fall of communist regimes and the rise of nationalism have given an additional impetus to arguments against the obsolescence of class analysis for modern societies. Class has to do with industrial society and its ideologies, and since these societies and their ideologies no longer exist, we should free ourselves from the old conceptions and analytical tools used to understand modern society.

We will follow a strategy that is altogether opposite. We are interested in knowing to what extent the new social movements are indicators of new and deep social cleavages or antagonisms in modern society. The new social movements have been given credit for introducing new issues, being carriers of a new paradigm of social existence, and pointing toward new social cleavages in modern societies besides the traditional religious and ethnic ones. The new cleavages introduced by these groups are then perceived as replacing the old cleavage based on class, the cleavage between capital and labour. This argument usually implies that with the institutionalization of class conflict, the notion of class no longer applies.

This argument confounds a historical and a structural explanation. The historical argument of institutionalization can be true; but this does not necessarily imply that we have to accept the structural argument. It may be that industrial class conflict no longer dominates class conflicts. We even accept the idea that this type of class conflict is diminishing in importance, but we will argue against the idea that class conflict is vanishing with the disappearance of its first embodiment: class conflict organized around the contradiction of capital and labour.[1]

Why then do we retain class as a structural element in explaining social movements? The conceptual and theoretical option for the concept of class has to do with the way modern society is organized. When analysing the arenas of social movements in societies based upon an egalitarian and libertarian culture, we are left with two arenas: political rights and industrial relations. We then analyse either the struggle for the extension of universal rights or the struggle between classes of people whose interests, norms and values are incommensurable. The logic of political rights is the universal inclusion of every human being into structures that guarantee these rights; the logic of industrial relations is relating antagonistic classes of people to each other. Which of the two is chosen in constituting collective action varies empirically. The labour movement combined both aspects; whether the new social movements do so as well, or whether they are predominantly collective actions of the first type, is also an empirical question. We assume that like the old movement, the new social movements contain both elements. They are movements which strive for more justice, for more rights and freedom; and they are simultaneously movements which oppose categories of people to other categories,[2] thus creating a conflict arena over issues in which the gains of some are necessarily coupled with the losses of others.[3] Thus the rationale for sticking to the concept of class has to do, first, with the assumption that the new social movements cannot be reduced to movements demanding universal inclusion. We want to find out whether these movements (defined as issue-movements) reveal antagonistic and even incommensurable interests, norms and values at stake in an issue. The second rationale is that we want to conceptualize new social movements in a way that does not exclude beforehand the possibility of their being part of emerging new social antagonisms.

Conceptual clarifications

The question of whether social classes matter in the analysis of social movements cannot be answered without discussing the problems that underlie class analysis and movement analysis. Within class analysis there is the problem of whether classes, in the sense of shared characteristics of social existence, still do exist; whereas within social movement analysis the problem lies in whether movements can still be seen as mobilized classes in the sense of class-conscious historical actors. In taking the extremist versions of each, we have class analysis as an analysis of objective conditions of existence of social groups on the one hand, and movement analysis as an analysis of the collective and creative practices of groups of social actors on the other. How can both perspectives be brought together?

It could, for example, be asked to what extent social class is an independent variable that explains the rise and fall of social movements. Such a question presupposes that we have an idea of what a *class* is. We must define some criteria that constitute class as an independent variable. We could ask to what extent the concept of class can be applied to characterize specific social groups in modern societies, and we could then analyse the economic, political or cultural status of such groups.[4] Class is thus seen as external to the collective practice of social movement actors, and this is what makes it an independent variable in the explanation of mobilizing practices. Such a perspective also implies that we can define *social movements* as independent of class, and conceptualize them in terms of a theory of collective action. Social movements are defined as collective practices within which rational interests, norms and values determine the outcome of collective action. These criteria are not imposed as structural constraints upon action, but are seen as options in the course of collective action.

The theoretical construction of the two variables leaves out, by the very conceptualization, the problem of their interrelationship. We could solve this question – as is usually done – through methodological considerations of probability. For instance, we would ask how probable it is that indicators of class have to do with indicators of mobilization, and conclude that there is some interrelationship between the phenomena observed from the probability of covariance. The question of whether mobilization can be attributed to class is thus resolved by looking at co-occurrences in space or time. However, such co-occurrences do not allow for a causal explanation. One of the reasons is simply that to the extent that a causal explanation would work, the grounds for further causality of the same set of conditions are destroyed. The idea of a structural determination of courses of action has a paradoxical effect: the more social structures produce courses of action that have effects upon structures, that even create structures, the less this structure has a determining effect. The paradoxical property of class theory is that its empirical realization destroys the conditions of its empirical adequacy. To resolve this paradox by simply giving up structural analysis and explanation leads to an individualistic agency theory and a return to the principles of methodological individualism. We will defend, in opposition to such reductionist strategies, a 'structuralist' theory of agency. The idea is that we must analyse collective action as a type of action whose collective nature is constituted by structural features of society. Class is such a feature. Collective action is embedded not only politically, but also socially. Therefore the general question is: *To what extent does collective action reproduce traditional forms of class conflict, and to what extent does collective action contribute to its reorganization and eventually to new forms of class conflict?*

This basic question allows us to differentiate between two types of effect that emerge in the interplay of class and collective action. The first effect is the traditional one of class 'determining' collective action. The second is the effect of collective action upon class. This latter effect is less visible because it only becomes manifest when (traditional!) class no longer has effects on collective action. If we show that the first effect does not exist, we are not yet allowed to conclude that class does not play a role. There is still the possibility that social movements give collective action a new meaning that not only manifests itself in, but even contributes to, the redefinition of the class structure and the traditional class conflict tied to it.

As long as we only look for an answer to the first part of the above question, we do not have to take into account the structural conditions of the 'creative' aspect of social movement analysis. But as soon as we do, a second structural feature has to be introduced: culture as the repertoire of making sense of collective action. In a historical situation where an old class structure loses its meaning for collective action, redefinitions of the social situation become a central part of movement action. Collective action has to make sense of itself, has to invent a meaning, but is restricted in such sense-making by the cultural repertoire of possible meanings. The first effect, as described above, works without culture; culture can be reduced to an ideology reproducing a given class structure. The second effect cannot be described without reference to culture. Our interest then shifts towards the possibilities contained in these new meanings of identifying and referring to a new class conflict beyond the political, religious or cultural cleavages that abound in any society. Class, we conclude, matters in the study of social movements in two very different ways, and it is the second effect that is our main concern. Therefore, we have to look at the 'new' cultural meanings ascribed to collective actions which lead to diverse social conflicts, to 'mobilization' and 'counter-mobilization' outside traditional class relationships. Whether these new meanings dissolve it by reducing it to mere political cleavages that can be handled by institutionalizing procedures of conflict resolution is the subject-matter of a controversial debate. Our hypothesis is that the new social movements, seen from the 'creative' side of collective action, create meanings that no longer relate to traditional class conflict.

We take this theoretical proposition as a starting point for a reinterpretation of the link between class and movement. We conceptualize the 'creative' activity in the new social movements as an interaction of action and culture and will grapple with the 'creative' character of collective action through analysing the interests, norms and values that orient it. To include class as a variable, we postulate that there are different ways of relating movements with social class: either class-character of collective action or cultural definition of class relationships. The model for explaining these different links of class and the generation and reproduction of movement mobilization can be represented as follows:

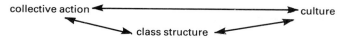

The theoretical implication for class theory is that class has two effects. It has a determining effect which is the 'conservative' test of the role of class. It has explanatory relevance and power because we claim that anchoring protest practices in class-specific social positions allows for explaining the specific strength and durability of these practices. The first effect of class, then, is to serve as a 'social opportunity structure' for collective action. This is what we described as the first type of relationship between class and movement. However, the class structure is not invariant; it can be redefined by collective action. This second effect implies that given class structures no longer determine collective action and that culture can no longer be reduced to a class-specific ideology. Collective action thus gains a 'creative' aspect. It creates an arena of social conflicts within which the principles of separating and opposing classes of people are redefined. Our model therefore contains a feedback loop within which culture works as the mediating variable between collective action and class, allowing for a dynamics of the class structure in the course of collective action itself.

From this arises a simple and basic question: do the social movements produce practices and meanings of these practices that allow us to describe them as part of a new class cleavage in modern societies? Or do these practices produce meanings that can be dealt with within the system of institutionalized dispute resolution? To test such questions, the theory is proposed that the new social movements are forms of middle-class radicalism and middle-class protest which are characterized by two structural features that indicate such new antagonistic practices and meaning. The first is that the new social movements carry *identity projects* with them that cannot be made the object of political forms of conflict resolution. The second is that the new social movements are concerned with *issues that are non-negotiable* within existing institutional frameworks. In the following we will show how a revised conception of class can shed light on emerging structural features of the relationship between middle classes and social movements seen as an expression of class-bound collective action.

Middle classes in class theory: the need for a new conceptual frame

The history of the middle classes and traditional class theory

The traditional notion of class has been used to realize two different normative intentions. The first has been to identify those who are exploited as a class. Class in this sense has become nearly synonymous with exploitation.[5] The other normative interest has been the identification of the exploiters, of people who are in a structurally advantaged position or who possess direct personal power over others, such as the capitalist class, as the embodiment of the structurally advantaged. This class model has been generalized into a model of power. Classes are related to each other in terms of power or lack of it: the powerless are those who have no control of the material conditions of their existence; they are simply the poor. On the other hand, we have classes of people with economic, social or even cultural power; the so-called 'new class'[6] is the embodiment of such political and cultural domination.

Between both normative motivations for identifying classes, there has never been a systematic place for the *middle classes*.[7] They simply could not mobilize theoretical attention except in derogatory formulas such as 'petit-bourgeois classes', 'labour aristocracy' or 'small property owners'.[8] There has been no normative concern to deal with these groups, who only posed difficulties for traditional class theories (which did not contribute to an adequate understanding of them). The first systematic concern has also been motivated by a negative experience: the role of the middle classes in the rise of Fascism. It was only in the 1970s that the middle classes again gained theoretical attention,[9] and this was the first time that they had been seen in a non-derogatory light – the reason is the role of the middle classes in the rise of what has been called the new social movements. The middle classes were seen as a social class that had become a historical actor, thereby developing a consciousness that had innovating effects on society and significant effects on the institutional framework of modern societies.[10] This explains the renaissance of interest in the middle classes, which, of course, has given support to the assumption that the lower class and its embeddedness in industrial class conflict can no longer serve as the model for an understanding of the emerging middle class.

I will argue that the term 'middle class' makes sense historically within the context of a class relationship defined by the working class and the capitalist class.[11] Its intermediate position explains the specific reaction and movements of social groups that have not become a class. It is the exclusion from a class relationship, the non-class existence of the middle classes, which proves to have explanatory power regarding collective action: middle-class radicalism can be explained by its tendency to avoid being identified with the lower classes and their failure to become a dominant class. This situation of the middle classes, however, changes with the rise of the 'new' middle class. To clarify this new situation, we will turn to the controversial assumption of the 'new middle class' as the class base of the 'new social movements'.

The concept of a 'new middle class' raises the problem of whether it can be seen in continuity or in discontinuity with the old middle classes. The central argument for discontinuity has been that the loss of a working-class culture has led to a non-class culture of protest and private retreatism. There are two versions of this, one claiming the emergence of a universal mass culture, another claiming the emergence of cultural differences that dissolve culture into highly individualized cultures.[12] Both developments, contradictory as they are, have one thing in common: they deny the possibility of a culture that is related to class conflicts and class relationships as had been characteristic of the working class. The new middle class has – like its historical predecessor, the old middle class – developed its culture outside the dominating class relationship; but with the rise of the new social movements it has become a constitutive element of an emerging new class structure. The 'old' class structure has excluded the middle classes systematically and viewed them as borderline groups. We see the new social movements as the mechanism creating a new class structure in modern societies, giving these middle classes a central role in the restructuring of class relationships in modern societies.

The middle class in the nineteenth century was not very

numerous, but it had key roles in the social structure in that those who belonged to it controlled the flow of everyday communication in society. Merchants and artisans offered social settings where people met and exchanged ideas. Teachers and functionaries whose socializing function is constitutive of their professional role had everyday contact with people.[13] Structurally, the middle classes have been defined by their structural location in the service sector. This sector has increased since then, to include the non-proletarianized craftsmen and tradesmen, the emerging white-collar groups since the beginning of the twentieth century, and ultimately professional groups in the social service industries that have increased in number over the last four decades.[14] The development of the middle classes as a culture shows, however, an erratic profile. These groups have been defined in recent discussions as sharing the habitus of the 'petit bourgeois'. This label originally referred more to the culture of small property owners (in opposition to the large property holders, the capitalists and traditional landowning classes) than to their exact class position. This term, originally restricted to small property owners (craftsmen and tradesmen), has been extended to other non-production groups, and ultimately to middle-class groups in general. Between the world wars these groups had been described as a class based on conspicuous consumption[15] and as being politically reactionary.[16]

It suffices to note that, regarding the term 'middle classes', the existing definitions signal the non-classifiability of these groups within the class relationship tied to industrial capitalist society. They are alien to traditional class theory. Moreover, this discussion shows that the description of the middle classes in class terms contains a fundamental ambivalence. There is no consensus in the discussion of whether the middle classes should be seen as a dominating or a dominated class. Interpretations of the new middle class diverge radically: for some they are the new proletariat, for others a new dominating class.[17] This basic ambivalence is not due to bad theory, but to the phenomenon itself. Instead of motivating us to give up the use of class as an explanatory concept, we claim that both conceptualizations are correct. The middle classes are made up – *within* the traditional class structure – of both dominant and dominated classes; they contain in themselves relationships of domination as a latent social relationship. The theoretical ambivalence can be taken as an indicator of an unresolved puzzle, the puzzle being that the theoretical construction of the middle classes tries to assimilate the phenomenon of the middle classes to the model of class characteristic of traditional class relationships.[18]

This puzzle has to be solved today for two reasons: first, using a model of class analysis where the majority of the population falls in between the classes[19] obviously undermines the relevance of the traditional class structure; secondly, the middle classes have become the most dynamic element in the modernization of modern society – they have proven to be an important carrier of collective mobilization, thereby fulfilling a social role ascribed to the lower classes by traditional theory. Both reasons leave us with two options: either give up class-theoretical explanations, or revise the class-theoretical approach. Our proposal is a 'revisionist' one: to take into account the change in modern society that has shifted the locus of class relationships from industrial relations to other fields. To argue in favour of such a case, we will have a closer look at the 'new' middle class. We suspect that the new middle class has attracted attention primarily not because of its class location, but because of its specific culture. We see in this predominance of cultural analysis an implicit way of dealing with what we have called the creative effect of culture upon class. But the middle classes, socially anchored within neither class relationships nor a culture of universal inclusion (a civil society), have so far been unsuccessful in defining their role and their identity in these terms. Their culture has been one of permanent failure. They failed when engaging in the conflicts over universal inclusion and, when joining class conflicts, they ended up on the side of the dominant class.[20] Our central theoretical assumption is that with the mobilized new middle classes, this history of political and cultural failures has come to an end.

Operationalizing class: toward a constructionist notion of class

The historical analysis of the middle classes lays the ground for a discussion of the changes that have been brought about by the emergence of the new middle class and by the mobilization of the new middle class in the new social movements. However, it has left out systematic methodological questioning. The advancement of a revised theory of class in general, and of the middle class in particular, obviously forces us to avoid the methodological procedure generally used to prove a class base in social movements. Therefore it is imperative to lay some methodological ground for the theory to advance.

In the search for measures of a class base, some researchers have resorted to analysing the social composition of the activists of a given movement. These researchers have actually defended the idea that a class consists of activists. The same strategy has been followed regarding the social composition of supporters (defined as those who identify with goals taken up by a movement), but neither is an indicator of the class character of mobilizations. What would happen if we applied this argument to the working class? The existence of labour activists or supporters of the labour movement would have become the criterion of the existence of a working class. It is obvious that there is much more to the labour movement than its activists or its supporters. They are – and this is the systematic place of such analyses – parts of what has been called the 'social opportunity structure' for the making of a class. They tell where the people who engage in protest action come from, but they do not tell why the actions of these people should be regarded as an element of class. One's class origin is no guarantee that one's action is class action.

A second step in the analysis would be to investigate more intensively the dimensions of the protest culture emerging among mobilized middle-class people. Shared symbolic properties add to social-structural characteristics the dimension of a cultural unity of middle-class radicalism. This is not yet a measure of class; it allows, however, the addition of a second series of necessary conditions for class to emerge.[21] The criterion is a certain cultural unity emerging from collective action that can be generalized across and beyond mobilized groups. Within the classic Marxian and Weberian perspective, such shared characteristics can be divided into *interests, norms* and *values.*

Shared interests are an elementary definitional criterion of movement culture. This criterion is itself variable, depending upon interpretations of what one's interests are. Historically, the interests of the proletarians shared the frame of injustice,[22] and within such a frame they have been able to define their interests. Whether this frame is universal is an open question (except for hard-core rational choice theorists). Given the dominance of the injustice frame, at least for modern Western societies up to the present, we can define shared interests as the calculation that we get less than we should. This frame has been dominant so far in the transition from traditional to modern society and modernization.[23]

Shared norms are a second aspect of a movement culture. Thus the definitional criterion of class becomes dependent upon given institutional frameworks. This applies to the notion of 'blue' and 'white' collar, which is primarily a legal definition. Norms differentiate between types of citizens and create a sense of community based upon norms which define a citizen's status. Such normative definitions do not necessarily coincide with the criterion of shared interests. But the normative definition of what belongs together certainly has the effect of creating a wider circle of cultural belonging, thus transforming the culture of protest into a more encompassing group culture.[24]

A third mechanism for transforming and normalizing a movement culture is shared values. This has been the object of the 'social psychology of class' and has been used in traditional stratification research to prove and disprove the existence of classes in terms of shared values.[25] This criterion again measures to what degree people have been socialized into a culture, something that is not necessarily an aspect of class. It gives us information about the degree to which people classify social reality in evaluative terms and the degree to which they are capable of giving answers within this classification system. We are ultimately left with an indicator of the degree to which society is integrated on the level of value orientations.

Attempts to construct a notion of class simply by adding the social-structural and cultural dimension of constituting social groups of actors have proven meaningless. The procedure of looking for correlations between occupational positions and attitudes, of correlating the new arational, non-rational or neo-rational lifestyles to traditional class differences (mainly measured by father's occupation), does not measure what it is supposed to, which is class. In order to identify the effects of emerging protest cultures on redefining the field of class conflict, we have to define class in a way that goes beyond demographic and cultural criteria.[26] So one of the difficulties in operationalizing the relationship between movement and class is methodological: the procedure chosen for its proof can easily be made representative and reliable, but it is not necessarily valid. It measures the extent to which this culture is able to extend to other classes. This turns the way of measuring class action upside down: what has been taken as manifesting class is nothing more than a measure of the degree to which a class culture can produce the image of its classlessness.

Methodological problems may lead to new theories. Therefore, we will propose a framework that lays the ground for a class theory within which the middle class can be seen as taking over the role the working class had in the class theory of industrial society. This theory of class (upon which we will later on base our theory of middle-class radicalism) is basically a constructionist version of class theory.[27] This constructionism presupposes two elements: *agency* and *context* within which and upon which agency is situated. There is a third element, the *structural outcome* of acting within and upon a culturally defined situation, which ranges from the internalization of conflict into the subject through the institutionalization of social and political cleavages to class conflict. This third element is the variable that must still be explained.

Agency has to do with the capacity of social groups to define and redefine the interests, norms and values that separate them beyond demographic differentiation from other social groups. We locate agency in the specific capacity to generate – through collective mobilization – collective definitions of interests, norms and values. Every mobilization has or creates its own culture. Agency is thus intricately related to the cultural space that it creates and draws upon in order to constitute and reproduce itself as a collective capacity for action. However, the relationship between culture and mobilization has remained an open problem. The culture of mobilization has been analysed by using middle-range theories of mass psychology, relative deprivation or resource mobilization to account for collective mobilization.[28] Grand Theory has taken whatever fashionable thesis was available to make sweeping generalizations about the culture that underlies mobilization in social movements: post-materialism, lifeworld colonization and individualization are examples of such approaches.[29] These theories assume that the culture they measure in different ways is already given. Post-materialism, for example, has been explicit on this assumption. Lifeworld theories assume some communitarian mode of existence prior to society. Individualization theories assume a modern culture of individualism as a general cultural orientation in modern societies. Rational choice theories simply presuppose a shared culture of interests, norms and values, within which collective actors behave on the basis of calculating their available resources and the possible gains to be made given their 'preference structure'.[30] In opposition to such approaches, the *construction of such cultures in the process of collective action* has to be stressed, which reduces these theories to mere hypotheses on alternative organizing principles of emerging cultures of mobilization.[31]

The second element engages the context, that is the arena of social conflicts in which new social movements situate themselves. These are first of all cultural movements which transcend the field of industrial relations. The terms used to define the new field of social conflicts are identity, expressivity and the good life.[32] Defining the field of agency in this way implies types and rationalities of action beyond the utilitarian calculus constitutive of the model of industrial relations and industrial class conflict. Defining a new field of social conflict does not necessarily imply that this field is no longer connected to possible class conflict and thus to a new type of class structure. This conclusion has dominated the theoretical idea of 'individualization' in modern societies (Beck, 1992; Melucci, Chapter 4 in this volume). The alternative is to look at the new boundaries created in the process of individualization.

Contrary to the image of a society of highly individualized people distinct from each other and engaged in marking such distinctions, we will defend the image of a society organized around the attempt to re-establish such a society that no longer uses exclusion from the means of production as the dichotomizing criterion. The social dichotomy that is invented and ultimately defended is one in which the exclusion from a society allowing for identity and expressive individualism is the dominant criterion. The culture of the new social movements contains an element of dichotomizing social reality, namely the idea of *exclusion from the social means of realizing identity*.

We can now specify our explanatory goal: does the mobilization of a new protest culture beyond the industrial protest culture have an effect on the class structure? We can also specify a basic assumption of our theory, which is that the people in different social classes who are mobilized into social movements (as activists), or who identify at least with the goals of social movements (as bystanders), do so because they identify with cultural values and not because they experience a class-specific powerlessness (whether in economic, political or cultural terms). The mobilization mechanism appears in response not to class differentiation and class emulation but to the desire to take action on matters that are of concern to people. In doing so, such action creates a sense of collective identity between social groups. It defines who belongs to the action and its goals and who doesn't. In so far as such a setting of boundaries, such a creation of a collective identity, can be related to social positions (to 'status', whether occupational, educational or political), this will change the class structure, both in its differentiation and in the forms of class emulation. Thus, the answer to our question will be: that *classes do matter in the study of social movements, not only as causes of mobilization, but also as the effects of mobilization*. Social movements also create class relations. Class is not a social fact, but is – beyond being a theoretical construction – a social construction. This forces the abandonment of any idea of the natural existence of class. There are no lower, middle and dominant classes as such.

This constructionist approach to class, however, has limits which are set by the 'social opportunity structure' of advanced modern societies. Social opportunity structure is understood to be the social-structural processes (occupational differentiation, educational differentiation, income differentiation, lifestyle differentiation etc.) that open up the social space for class differentiation and class relations. The capacity of the new middle class to redefine the field of class conflict is dependent upon the objective situation of this middle class in terms of occupation and educational attainment. Countervailing processes on the level of institutions also have to be taken into account. The theory of the institutionalization of class conflict argues that institutions, above all institutionalized political regulation, define the boundaries between classes and shape class relationships. This theory has been especially successful in relation to the institutionalization of industrial class conflict in modern Western societies. Whether it has an explanatory value regarding a post-industrial class conflict has yet to be seen. The conditions that limit the effectiveness of collective action have to be integrated as contextual conditions into the theoretical framework. Our theory nevertheless states that the mobilization of collective action is the basic mechanism that changes the boundaries between classes and shapes class relation-ships.[33] This theory will now serve us in reformulating the theory of middle-class radicalism and in transforming it into a new theory of the 'new social movements'.

Middle classes and social movements: a theory of class radicalism

New social movements and the new middle classes: a critique of Pakulski

Is a class account of contemporary protest a futile theoretical endeavour? This is the point of view forcefully defended by Pakulski,[34] who argues that the new social movements have a social base that cross-cuts class lines. It is generation, situs and mobility which are characteristic of the groups of people engaging or sympathizing with the politics of new social movements. A second argument which explains the lack of correlation between class and movements has to do with their cultural and thus non-social orientation. The new social movements are value-laden movements which do not directly link with social-structural characteristics related to social inequality,[35] so their social composition will not follow social cleavages that have to do with social inequalities, but cleavages that have to do with cultural conflicts (such as generational conflicts and local conflicts).

The counter-theory has been that it is the 'petit-bourgeois habitus' (Bourdieu, 1984) that serves as a link between the new middle classes of advanced modern societies and the new social movements.[36] Our assumption is that they are still more than that. They are the most visible part of an emerging new type of class antagonism centred on issues beyond exploitation and injustice. This leads to the following questions: are the new social movements capable of making their cultural orientations the basis for a new class conflict? Or are they groups defined by ascriptive criteria which contribute to a cycle of protest in the history of modern middle-class protest? We would like to follow the former explanatory strategy and argue that contemporary middle-class radicalism is not a manifestation of cycles of protest, but a moment in the making of a new class relationship for the analysis of which the 'middle' class is the key. Arguments in favour of a cyclical interpretation have been used in recent research in social stratification.[37] The argument is that the return to demographic normality, that is to 'normal' social stratification after the initial levelling effects of educational expansion since the 1970s, will lead to a cultural normality in the sense of a return to a normal level of protest in society, a lessening of unconventional forms of political behaviour and a lessening of hedonist lifestyles. Our argument against theories that deduce cultural cycles from demographic ones will be based on the distinction between the 'triggering causes' and 'structural effects' of such demographic changes in the mobilization potential for protest behaviour. With regard to the triggering causes, we will take up the argument that the post-war generation is transitory in its social-structural characteristics: it has experienced the reorganization of social differences in the social structure due to educational expansion, postponement of marriage, and new life-course patterns. It is also taken for granted that a re-equilibration of social structure along the lines of traditional forms of inequality has taken place. Social structure has become 'normalized'. The generation following the protest generation will again live in a system characterized by modern stratification patterns; the difference between the lower, middle and upper classes will again become normal forms of modern social life (except for one factor – migration – whose effects on social structure cannot be calculated). We thus accept the argument that mobilization was tied to this 'exceptional' generation, but add the qualifying remark that this exceptionality has had a triggering effect on mobilization. As soon as this effect has been triggered, the consequences become independent of the causes.[38]

Against the methodologically sophisticated but theoretically mechanical interpretation which affirms that the movements will rise and fall with the social-structural reshuffling of these groups, a sociocultural interpretation would argue that this generation succeeded in freeing traditional middle-class cultures from their historical cultural bonds, cultural cage and traditional ideological dependence upon the state. The exceptional generation of the 1960s and 1970s has been the promoter of a change in the culture of middle-class groups, creating the 'new social movement culture' which has entered economic, political and cultural, and even religious life. This cultural effect can be traced back to a demographically atypical generation. But atypicality does not explain why this generation produced the cultural effects it did. This has to do with the specific culture created in the mobilization of these structurally defined groups.

We see two main implications of this effect. First, the new social movements have reshaped the institutional system of modern societies.[39] They have – at least partially – introduced additional political cleavages. Secondly, they are drawing new social boundaries in modern societies, thereby redefining the old class relations. The role of the new social movements in the process of democratization, and the intended as well as unintended consequences, have been the object of extensive discussion.[40] But the question as to what extent the culture of the new social movements has succeeded in redrawing not only political but also social boundaries in modern societies has not been seriously addressed. The question itself, along with its theoretical foundation, was posed a long time ago in the seminal work of Touraine. Touraine's hypothesis is that the new social movements no longer identify with natural forces but with social forces (Touraine, 1981). Traditionally, the working class has been tied to natural forces, the forces of production. The idea of the working class carried a fundamental ambivalence: it was at the same time a natural as well as a social phenomenon. The concept of class inherited from this tradition is a concept suited to a society that is itself still bound to naturalized forms. Defining modernity as denaturalization of social reality, industrial society appears as a 'semi-modern' society. Dissolving the naturalized view of social reality means realizing modernity. The theoretical critique of Historical Materialism as a naturalistic theory of society is an indicator of this 'modernization'. The new social movements are its concrete social indicator, and their common denominator is that they distance themselves from the naturalism underlying the world of the labour movement and the working class.[41] The denaturalization of the semi-modern industrial society forces us to define the arena and object of social conflicts and the classes of actors involved in a way that is not naturalistic but genuinely social. This means that the field of class conflict is not a given, but is itself produced in social practices, and that the collective actors involved are not predefined collectives (which is implied in the idea of a class 'in itself'), but are constituting themselves as a class through their collective action.

Regarding the first aspect, the social definition of the field of class conflict, the new social movements have contributed to its genuinely *social* definition. They have transformed the field of class conflict into 'arenas' that are created by these movements through their action. The concept of an 'arena' indicates the shift of emphasis away from a historically (and even world-historically) given field of class conflict to fluid arenas of social conflicts.[42] Regarding the second aspect, the notion of class, these new social movements no longer refer to class as defining their collective identity. Collective identity is sought outside prefabricated patterns of identity that have been carried within the semi-modern notion of class. Therefore we can no longer use the traditional model of class and class conflict with regard to the new social movements. Does it then still make sense to talk about the middle-class basis of the new social movements?

I claim that it does. The concept of the middle class is an ideal case study for the modernization of collective action taking place in the context of the evolution of the labour movement and the rise of the new social movements. It allows us to develop a systematic critique of the concept of class and of its naturalization in the Marxist and socialist tradition. As soon as we conceive of class in a non-naturalistic way, we have to define class independently of naturalistic criteria. This will lead us in the following pages neither to the reduction of the class concept to a compound demographic variable, nor to its elimination. Instead, we will try to develop a concept of class that corresponds to a society that has crossed its semi-modern phase, and we will try to show that the concept of social movement is paramount to this endeavour.

A class-theoretical account of the new social movements: a critique of Melucci

The conclusion that has been drawn from this coincidence is that the two (class and social movements) are interrelated. According to traditional class analysis we would simply check whether the 'members' (activists, supporters, protest voters etc.) of the new social movements are recruited from the new middle class (and/or other fractions of the middle class), defining middle class in terms of social-structural characteristics.[43] This explains why specific demographic processes (especially educational expansion and a changing occupational structure) provide opportunities for mobilization. But we can explain such phenomena equally well without the concept of class (see Pakulski, Chapter 2 in this volume). We know that a social group, having had the experience of cultural upward mobility in terms of education and being active in the social service sector, is prone to greater mobilization in this conflictual field. The discussion of middle-class radicalism to which we refer demonstrates that there is a social opportunity structure for the 'making of a class'. These middle-class groups are those engaged in qualified production and service occupations, that is, those with an educational training which distinguishes them from working-class culture, and those who produce and reproduce the cultural resources in modern societies.

So far we have discussed the elements provided by a social opportunity structure for the construction of a social class. It is an open problem to what extent these elements lead to a unified whole, to more than an aggregation of individual traits. To look for additional factors that make a class I propose to look at the cultural space within which these groups of people make sense of themselves.[44] Our historical analysis has shown that the history of the middle classes and their social-structural position between the working class and the capitalist class within the old class relationship have left the problem of *identity* as a central concern for the middle classes. Middle classes live with a traditional notion of the good life, with consensual social relations playing a prominent role. Thus we complement the idea of a social opportunity structure with the idea of a specific 'cultural opportunity structure'. The definition of a new conflictual field, centred on the social means of realizing identity, allows us to bring together the 'new social movements' and the 'new middle class'.[45]

Among the semantic resources available in this cultural opportunity structure, two concepts are of central importance: the concept of *good life* and the related ideas of community and lifeworld; and the concept of *consensual social relations*, which has to be seen together with the concept of communication. The first concept, good life, has been the quest of the middle classes for over a century. It is above all a religious notion: the good life is led by good people. Religious groups are based upon such goodness – and these religious notions have survived neither in the lower nor in the upper class, making it a middle-class phenomenon by elimination. Young people's search for alternatives to the greed, materialism and violence of the older generation is an expression of the inner dynamic of middle-class culture that never escaped its search for the good life. Outrage against middle-class values expressed itself in sexual freedom, opposition to the Vietnam war, and so on. Today, the middle classes are obsessed with personal aggrandizement, autonomy and competition. This is the cultural basis upon which new social movements were built, and from which they drew their motivational and ideational sources.[46] The culture of good life is more than a philosophical idea: it is the expression of a class-specific lifestyle.[47] We can apply such an idea to contemporary social protest and unrest relating mainly to environmental issues: environmental risks and damage are exactly those things that most threaten a good life because they threaten the physical and increasingly the psychic world.

The second concept, consensual social relations, fosters the idea of an authentic lifestyle where people interact as equals and as free persons. Communication is a central feature of the middle-class life-style. From didactic matters (how to educate children) to personal affairs (how to solve conflicts with your partners), this culture of communication has started to serve as an integrating code of middle-class culture.[48] The lower classes were traditionally and objectively bound to negate the primacy of communication (they simply were not able to communicate in the way the other classes could). The communication of the dominating classes on the other hand had to be exclusive (so they engaged in ritualized and specialized codes of communication). Risk communication seems to be the newest version of the rise of middle-class culture in protest and collective mobilization.[49] It seems that all this has given to consensual social relations the role the early bourgeois ascribed to it 200 years ago.

But the theory, we propose, goes one step further by adding a third element beyond the social and the cultural opportunity structure. It claims that the new social movements contain more than specific social-structural and historical-cultural characteristics. Rather, it interprets these movements within the class structure of an emerging type of society. To the extent that class theory has been applied to these movements, it turns out to be an application that is dominated by the class model of the old industrial society. The 'orthodox' theory is to associate the new middle class with the traditional class relationship by extending the dominated class beyond the traditional working class. Then the new social move-ments are simply variations of the class conflict based 'ultimately' on the working class. The 'heterodox' theory is to define middle classes as falling outside of or in between social classes. Then these movements appear in a negative way; they are concerned with issues that are kept out of traditional class conflicts; they are concerned with non-class issues; instead of struggling for a share in societal resources, they 'defend' a lifeworld.[50] Against such ortho-dox and heterodox class theories of the new social movements we will propose the theory that the new middle class is an element of a new type of class relationship.

This theory argues that there is a new emerging class relationship which has its own and different logic, but does not deny the existence of non-class relationships outside these middle classes. Certainly, gender and ethnicity are alternative and competing forms of social relationship and social conflict, but these are collectivities socially constructed on the basis of 'natural symbols'. Classes, on the contrary, exist as social facts, that is, as collectivities socially constructed on the basis of socially defined symbols. This is the basic difference between class and any other criterion identifying collectivities. The middle classes are related to each other no longer by objective conditions of existence, but by their collective practices to define a mode of social existence. The fundamental antagonism underlying this mode of existence is, as argued above, the conflict over the means of an 'identitarian' existence. Furthermore, this conflict does not resolve the question of what the identity is. The middle-class-specific form of experiencing and perceiving the world is – as already stated – characterized by using two key and favourite concepts: *good life* and *consensual social relations*. What gives the middle classes the status of a potential class is not their history, which ties them to an old class conflict, but their direct insertion into a new antagonistic social relationship which is defined by control over the means of creating an identity, an identitarian lifestyle. This conflict has a class character because there is no other solution to this antagonism other than by structural changes in the distribution of power. Because identity is a good that is indivisible, the conflict over identity cannot be litigated; the conflict is structurally inscribed into the problem and the groups involved in it.

Our theory thus consists of three elements. The first is the social opportunity structure that has developed out of the class conflicts of the period preceding contemporary forms of mobilization and conflict. Within this social opportunity structure, the middle classes are defined merely by their specific location in traditional class relationships. This middle position continues to provide for a specific type of experiencing and perceiving the world that makes these groups prone to engage in issues beyond the traditional class issues. The second element consists of the cultural themes characteristic of the history of middle-class radicalism that are intricately related to the social-structural location of the middle classes. The third – and decisive – element of our theory is that a new class relationship is to be based on the criterion of the control of the means of an 'identitarian' social existence in the sense of guaranteeing identity and expressive social relations. These means of social existence are no longer described as means of production, but as means of cultural expression. Power differences refer to the way in which the chance of realizing identity is defined and its assets are unevenly distributed. These three elements have contributed to a form of mobilization that has succeeded in redefining social reality in dichotomic terms. This makes the middle-class groups that have so far been defined as a problematic case in traditional class theory the unproblematic centre of a new class relationship. We have argued that the 'middle classes' are potential classes, and we must identify the specific conditions under which class will dominate the contemporary struggles over an identitarian existence.

Social class does matter

Our original question can then be answered with a clear 'yes': social class does matter. Class is a social construction which puts together social categories in order to form a more encompassing whole. This presupposes a collective praxis. We have analysed the praxis of the middle classes as such a collective and creative praxis; we have identified in it the social construction of the field of class conflict as well as the social construction of a collective identity as a social class beyond natural and naturalized determinants of social existence. Class turned out to become the variable in need of explanation. The main result of our theory is a radical change in the research question. This question is: what are the factors that contribute to the capacity of collective agency in order to define its characteristics in terms of structural conflicts or antagonisms? Here we identified social-structural variables (the rise of middle-class groups within the traditional class structure) and cultural variables (a history of middle-class concerns as expressed in the diverse forms of middle-class radicalism). We ultimately added a third variable in order to distinguish social conflicts and antagonisms that can become the field of class relationships from those that cannot. The theoretical proposition is to define as an element of a new emerging class relationship any conflict that has to do with the exclusion from the means of an 'identitarian' social existence. The new social movements concerned with the realization of an 'identitarian' existence are therefore those that foster the construction of new class relationships. In this sense class does matter in the new social movements.

The question of whether the new social movements cut across class lines or whether they manifest new emerging class cleavages in advanced industrial societies has led to the competing hypotheses of 'middle-class radicalism' versus 'individualized protest behaviour'. An analysis of the history of petit-bourgeois radicalism allowed for the identification of some developmental continuities with actual forms of protest. Additional variables are located in changes in social structure (in the emergence and internal differentiation of the non-proletarian social groups). The argument for a class perspective has further been backed up by a methodological critique of the 'anti-class' literature on social movements, showing that the anti-class assumption is the product of individualistic methodological presuppositions in actual social movement research. The new social movements are certainly not a class movement in the traditional nineteenth-century sense. They can, however, be seen as a manifestation of a new type of class relationship within which the 'making of the middle class' in advanced modern societies takes place.

Notes

1. This question has again been raised by Clark and Lipset (1991) who argue in favour of the theory that classes are dying out. This claim has been weakened in Clark et al. (1993), which reduces it to the declining *political* significance of class. Pakulski's answer is in line with the idea proposed in the following: that such hypotheses and theories might be due to a traditionalist notion of class (Pakulski, 1993). I will add an additional argument to that debate by claiming that the link between structural determination and collective action is much more complex than what can be represented by the idea of a 'correlation' between class and action.

2. The term 'category' still leaves open the question of whether we are dealing with classes or not. To be able to identify categories of people is not a sufficient, but is a necessary condition for the existence of class. The second condition to be introduced is the symbolic world within which a society interprets the categorical differences existing in a society. This second element is historically variable, and this is the reason why the idea of 'economically' determined classes is a culturally and historically specific interpretation of categorical differences among people.

3. The environmental movement is a good example. Its universality consists of the plea for an integration of nature into society, for a gradual extension of rights of humans to rights of nature. Its class character is grounded in the fact that environmentalist action will produce categories of people with gains (those with an interest in an ecologically modernized economy) and categories of people with losses (those who are excluded from nature as an aesthetically rewarding lifeworld). The environment is a field of class struggle as well as a field of demands for more political rights up to rights for animals or nature as a whole.

4. This also excludes the reduction of classes to groups sharing a specific 'habitus'. By defining classes in relational and not in substantial terms, we will be better equipped to see the antagonisms that separate social classes. Our theory, like that of Bourdieu (1984), puts the emphasis on the difference between a theoretical construction of class in terms of social antagonisms, and the empirical reality of class (Bourdieu, 1987). However, it deviates from his proposition regarding the empirical indicators of class, which in Bourdieu are ultimately identical with socio-psychological traits of status groups.

5. This is basic to the Marxist conception of class, above all in its socialist variant. The communist variant was oriented more towards the structural determination of the powerful (which by the way might explain the real effects of this type of thinking!).

6. This generalized notion of class underlies the analyses of the poor as a powerless class (Piven and Cloward, 1972). The interest in class as a power elite has been put forward by Mills (1956). There are also conservative versions of class as a power elite. Not only are the classic theories of dominant classes (Mosca and others) good examples, but so are the more recent theories on the 'new class' (Schelsky, 1975; Gouldner, 1979). For a good discussion of such assumptions see McAdams (1987).

7. The middle classes are composed of at least three different groups: the old and new self-employed, the office employees and the new middle class (those working in the culture industry and in the health business). For this distinction see Bourdieu (1984). Data on the new self-employed (the least known among these three groups) are given by Steinmetz and Wright (1989). For data on Germany see Bögenhold (1985) and with a more historical perspective, Winkler (1983). For an empirical analysis of old and new middle class in Germany see Pappi (1981).

8. These terms can be found in Marx, where they also had a political function.

This ideological and political loading is another indicator of the troubling effect these groups have had for traditional class theory. A good overview of the discussion of the middle class with special reference to the new middle class is given by Burris (1986).

9. This is due mainly to Bourdieu, whose work is sometimes seen as a treatise on the middle class. This is at least true of his most famous book, *The Distinction* (Bourdieu, 1984), even given the fact that he sticks to the traditional negative image of the middle class. A more positive view of middle-class radicalism has played an important role within the discussion of the environmental movement and the peace movement. See Parkin (1968) as an early figure, as well as the work of Cotgrove and Duff (1980, 1981), Kann (1986), Brand (1990) and Offe (1985c). See also Eder (1993: 141ff.).

10. This 'new class' version of this hypothesis can be found in ideas expressed by Ehrenreich (1989). She argues that those who 'discover' other classes – professionals, media personnel, managers and intellectuals – are a middle class with an enormous power over our culture and our very self-image as a people. Her analysis does not deal with class relations, but with the inner life of this class, with the class cues that make this class recognizable to its members.

11. I speak of middle classes in spite of the fact that they are social groups defined by their exclusion from a class relationship. This is terminologically inconsequent, but we stick to it because we have become used to describing these groups as middle classes. The use of the plural is thought to be sufficient to indicate the specific nature of the middle classes being a class.

12. A sophisticated version of the latter explanation can be found in Pakulski (1988, 1991). He argues for a non-class interpretation using the concepts of 'generation', 'situs' and 'mobility' to account for the social basis of the new social movements. But such variables do not replace a class analysis; they simply indicate that there is a time dimension, an institutional dimension and a social dimension to the phenomenon of new social movements. Not every generation is equally affected, and this therefore points to historical conjunctures. Not every autonomous situs in an institutional environment leads to mobilization; those of the rentier class of the nineteenth and early twentieth centuries lived without being mobilized in their institutional niches. And mobility towards the city does not necessarily lead to movement action; deviant action is obviously a functional equivalent. The interesting question is under what conditions such factors really lead to movement action. The claim here is that these conditions have to do with their role and function within class relationships.

13. This phenomenon is extensively treated in Eder (1985). The literature on the emerging public space in the late eighteenth and nineteenth centuries is pertinent here.

14. This has been the object of studies of an emerging service sector and even service class society. The discussion ranges from Touraine (1969) through Gershuny (1978, 1983) to Esping-Andersen (1993).

15. See, for example, Kracauer (1985). Similar arguments can be found in Lederer (1912, 1979) and Dreyfuss (1933).

16. See Winkler (1971, 1972, 1978, 1979), who has done extensive research on these groups. He argues that this group has become – at least in Germany – the carrier of what has been called the 'refeudalization' of the bourgeois classes that explains their specific social and political habitus. Countervailing tendencies, having to do with processes of trade unionization, are analysed by Prinz (1981) and by

Kocka and Prinz (1983). The middle classes were also held responsible for the rise of Fascism. There is controversial literature on the question of to what extent Fascism was a mobilization of middle classes and a manifestation of middle-class culture. This argument has been put forward by Speier (1977) and by Hamilton (1982) and has been heavily criticized by Falter (1982, 1984).

17. The new middle class is often regarded as a new technological and cultural elite because of its greater conceptual ability, better knowledge and increased opportunity to become involved in politics (Baker et al.,1981: 10–11; Alber, 1985). Lipset (1988) also argues in favour of the latter. For more sweeping claims see Schelsky (1975), Gouldner (1979) and Konrad and Szelenyi (1979). A well argued point in favour of such a position is found in Lash and Urry (1987: 161ff.). See also Abercrombie and Urry (1988) and Carter (1985). For the alternative interpretation referring to a new service proletariat see Esping-Andersen (1993: 7ff.).

18. The term 'middle class' is already revealing: it implies the attempt to find a location for social groups in a class relationship which is no location at all. The paradox produced by the term 'middle class' is that there are classes and that there are groups that are not part of the class relationship defined by these classes and at the same time defined in terms of exactly this relationship. Important in this context is the Marxist discussion on middle classes. See Bechhofer et al. (1978), Bechhofer and Elliott (1981, 1985). For a critique see Goldthorpe (1978). Further accounts in a Marxist framework are found in Burris (1980); Wright (1985, 1986, 1990); Johnson (1982); Abercrombie and Urry (1988).

19. Hamilton and Wright (1986) even simply talk of the 'masses'. For the vagaries of the discourse on the middle class in America see DeMott (1990).

20. The middle classes have often contributed to the modern pathology of universalism. Being the carrier of modern forms of anti-universalist forms of citizenship (i.e. nationalistic, populist or even racist forms) they blocked themselves from becoming a historical force in realizing a civil society.

21. They also, by the way, allow the embedding of group formation in cultural history. This is important in the case of middle-class radicalism that can be understood only within historical contexts.

22. Here the greatly neglected historical work of Moore (1978) on injustice frames as a basis of disobedience and revolt is pertinent.

23. This does not mean that further modernization will still rely upon such interest. The ecological discussion, at least, raises doubts concerning the continuing dominance of this interest. For the classic discussion see Hirschman (1977, 1982). A revival of these discussions takes place in what has been called 'Analytical Marxism' (Roemer, 1986). The point throughout these discussions remains the same: interests play an important role, but without contextualizing interests in norms and values, they do not work. For a plea to introduce norms in an interest-based theoretical framework see Elster (1989). For an analogous attempt to do so with values see Hechter (1989, 1990, 1991).

24. We avoid the term 'class' in this context which is reserved for a level of analysis beyond real groups of people. But in the literature the term 'class' is loosely used. The institutional definitions considered above have normally been discussed in the context of class (see the contributions in Clegg, 1989). An interesting example of the role of institutional norms in defining occupational groups as a class is the study of the formation of the 'cadres' in France (Boltanski, 1982). An application of normative regulations of citizenship and its effects on the differentiation of 'classes' of citizens can be found in Lockwood (1987).

25. The classic piece of work is that of Centers (1949), who discussed class in terms of attitudes and value orientations. Values have become prominent in sociology during the dominance of Parsonian sociology. An important work in this tradition is Kluckhohn and Strodtbeck (1961). Since then it has only been with Inglehart (1977, 1990a) that the role of values has received renewed attention. See also the negative answer to the question 'Should values be written out of the social scientists' lexicon?' given by Hechter (1991).

26. The demographic reduction of the concept of class is characteristic of most stratification and mobility research. For a recent discussion on the role of class theory in quantitative stratification research, see Sørensen (1991). He maintains that we do not need class theory in order to explain inequality in the labour market or income differences. Such an irrelevance would even support our claim for a class-theoretical perspective. Class theory is not a theory of the working of the labour market, but of the social construction of conflictual fields of action. The argument in the following will be that the demographic dimensions are presocial categories, that occupation, educational level and household characteristics gain their structuring force not in themselves, but by the meaning given to them by the actors, the institutions and the existing culture.

27. This theory is opposed to the one that views the problem of social order as the basic problem of a theory of society. This does not imply that the problem of social order is irrelevant; it only states that it is a secondary problem arising out of the capacity to act upon existing social orders. These orders are even defined in different ways: as equilibria of interests, normative orders or orders based upon shared values. The sociological tradition did not agree on which was the central aspect of social order. We simply see this as three different ways of creating social order, which implies that the theory has to explain why actors choose one of them. A theoretical primacy of the problem of agency is over the problem of order. This argument can draw upon theoretical arguments put forward, for example, by Giddens (1973, 1987) and Touraine (1981).

28. For an overview see Eder (1993: 42ff.). For a discussion of the mass psychology argument see Moscovici (1985); for the theory of relative deprivation Gurr (1970); and for resource mobilization theory Zald and McCarthy (1979, 1987).

29. In particular I refer to Inglehart (1977, 1990a), Habermas (1984, 1987) and Beck (1992). Melucci also defends a radical individualist programme, centring the problem of collective mobilization around the problem of subjectivity. See Chapter 4 in this volume.

30. This idea has been taken up to reformulate the old theory of class relations in a new conceptual scheme. The work of the 'Analytical Marxists' is central here; see Roemer (1982, 1986) and Elster (1982, 1985b). For a discussion see Offe (1985a). The differential rationalist logic underlying the industrial class conflict has been shown very well in terms of the 'two logics' of collective action representing the two traditional classes; see Offe and Wiesenthal (1980). The paradoxical effect is that as soon as we argue in game-theoretic terms, the traditional image of class relations reappears; this theory makes sense of class relations characteristic of industrial relations, which points to an implicit culture contained even in such 'culture-free' theories.

31. A further problem has to do with the methodological individualism underlying survey research on collective beliefs and opinions. Methodological individualism gives people equal status: everybody has an opinion (with some marginal cases who never have an opinion) and it is enough to look at the distribution of such opinions.

Everybody has resources (to have an opinion is just one of them) in order to indicate differences and even changes in culture. Post-materialist values can be combined with old and new values in different ways, but they do not necessarily covary with ecological concerns; they have different impacts upon the capacity and potential of collective action, depending upon their action-relevance, which can vary considerably. Thus we only have indicators that need extensive interpretation in order to be relevant for explaining cultures of mobilization.

32. The return of the problem of identity in the modern public discourse and its role in shaping social relationships is already proof of the power that such elements have in society. It is also a signal that the traditional class relations no longer play an important role in the struggles characterizing modern societies. The shift in sociological theory towards the symbolic realm, towards a dramaturgical notion of social action, is also signficant. See for example Gusfield's introduction to the work of Kenneth Burke (1990).

33. Touraine (1985a, 1985b) sometimes argues in a way that comes close to such a theory, but he remains basically unclear about the status of class theory within his action theory.

34. See Chapter 2 in this volume. However, his position is slightly less radical considering his arguments regarding the Clark and Lipset thesis of a dying of class (Clark and Lipset, 1991). Pakulski argues that classes are locked within a framework (the Marxist one) which forecloses the possibility of seeing them in the emerging post-industrial world. See Pakulski (1993). This is also the argument here: classes exist, and some of the old theoretical models no longer allow us to see them. We have to test new class theories in order to check whether they allow us to see more.

35. This hypothesis has already been defended by Cohen (1985), Offe (1985c) and most explicitly by Melucci (1985, 1988, 1989). See also the discussion in Olofsson (1988), who claims that the new social movements are cultural movements; but he relativizes the role of these movements, arguing that they are not – like the old movements – necessarily linked to societal changes. This latter argument allows for a 'weak' class-theoretical explanation.

36. This is a recapitulation of a thesis formulated by Lederer in 1913! See Lederer (1979). See also my discussion in Eder (1989).

37. For such arguments see, among many others, Bürklin (1984, 1987), and recently Blossfeld and Shavit (1993). Bürklin has consequently turned to cyclical theories to explain the rise and fall of mobilization and protest assuming a latent stability of institutions over the vicissitudes of protest. Blossfeld and Shavit radicalize this approach by assuming a latent conservatism in social structure and social stratification, which takes protest as manifestations of a re-equilibration of social structures, as a transitory phenomenon in the self-organization of social structures.

38. This again points to the self-defeating types of class analysis that have been used in the discussion of class and social movements. They adhere to a deterministic idea of class which negates sociocultural properties emerging from the relations between classes by redefining the interests, norms and values which are at stake. It is obvious that a reductionist sociology, explaining social phenomena by their social-structural and even demographic characteristics, has had no problems in pointing out the lack of complexity of traditional class theory. See the revealing article by Sørensen (1991) in this context. These emergent effects, we will claim below, can be accounted for within a class theoretical framework that defines classes as collective actors creating arenas for social struggles and contributing to class differentiation along lines that are different from those that have dominated industrial society so far.

39. I refrain from ascribing a historical role to these movements. The effect is a change in the traditional political structures and institutional procedures of decision-making that as a result of the class compromise with the working class have dominated modern societies so far. This institutional system is put into question, and we have to analyse the ways this reorganization is going to be effected.

40. Discussion of the new social movements is mainly centred – implicitly and even explicitly – on this question, from Habermas (1984, 1987) and Touraine (1985a) to the more empirically oriented movement research (Rucht, 1991).

41. This, after all, remains the basic criterion of the 'newness' of the new social movements: that they conceive themselves as practices for which there exists no historical (= necessary = natural) reason to exist; rather, nature is seen as something to be created (or defended through practice). In this sense, the ecological movement is the most radical anti-naturalist movement that can be conceived of, for it takes nature not as a determinant of social action, but as a goal of action, which completely reverses the naturalism characteristic of the dominant social movements of the nineteenth and first half of the twentieth centuries (Eder, 1988, 1993).

42. The increasing importance of 'public discourse' as a mechanism for creating such arenas is reflected in the turn that research in mass communication and public discourse analysis has taken in recent years. See as a prominent example the work of Gamson (1988, 1992) and Gamson and Modigliani (1987, 1989).

43. For such attempts see Bürklin (1984), Kriesi (1987) and Hulsberg (1988). Kriesi (1989) argues in an empirical study of Dutch new social movements that the middle class is itself split, the most enthusiastic supporters being the younger generation of 'social and cultural specialists' which includes professionals and semi-professionals in teaching, social and medical services, the arts and journalism. For a sophisticated analysis on the basis of such a theory regarding the German case see Vester (1983, 1989).

44. Instead of idealizing the public space as the realm of discourse, a realistic account looks at public space as embedded within social class. For an attempt to take up the Habermasian notion of public space in a critical anti-illusionary perspective see Eder (1992).

45. This is contrary to the idea of Melucci (Chapter 4 in this volume) who argues that the new public spaces create the opportunity for a self-reflexive, global type of collective action which is to be seen as decoupled from social structure. He replaces the metaphysics of the collective actor simply with a voluntaristic notion (or 'agency' notion) of the collective actor which forbids us to see identity claims as socially rooted and determined.

46. There are two very different books relating to this topic: Baritz (1989) and Bourdieu (1984).

47. One of the interesting hypotheses is by Featherstone (1989), who argues that the new middle class has an effect on the rise of postmodernism. A general theory of middle-class positions and middle-class cultures is contained in Bourdieu (1984). See also Gans (1988) for an attempt to extend the idea of 'individualism' as a basic cultural orientation to the middle class as a whole.

48. This holds true above all for the new middle class; but it is also an important aspect of the other middle-class groups which use communicative competence to mark their difference from the lower classes. It has a mirror in the classic social-scientific discussion of restricted and elaborated codes as underlying lower-class and middle-class lifestyles.

49. Risk communication is intricately entwined in the culture of the middle

48   *Foundations for Collective Action*

classes. Historically seen, middle-class life has been risky, because of the impact of the capitalist economy. The middle classes' alignment with the state has sensitized them to problems of the lifeworld as such, above all in today's environmental risks.

50. For 'heterodox' attempts to integrate the class perspective into a broader macro-sociological and sociohistorical framework see Habermas (1987), Offe (1985b, 1985c), Luke (1989) and Brand (1990), who try to combine the 'European' type of explanation of new social movements with class analysis.

References

Abercrombie, N. and Urry, J. (1988) *Capital, Labour and the Middle Classes*. London: Allen & Unwin.

Alber, J. (1985) 'Modernisierung, neue Spannungslinien und die politischen Chancen der Grünen', *Politische Vierteljahreschrift*, 3: 211–26.

Baker, K. L., Dalton, R. J. and Hildebrandt, K. (1981) *Germany Transformed: Political Culture and the New Politics*. Cambridge, MA: Harvard University Press.

Baritz, L. (1989) *The Good Life. The Meaning of Success for the American Middle Class*. New York: Knopf.

Bechhofer, F. and Elliott, B. (eds) (1981) *The Petite Bourgeoisie. Comparative Studies of the Uneasy Stratum*. New York: St Martin's Press.

Bechhofer, F. and Elliott, B. (1985) 'The petite bourgeoisie in late capitalism', *Annual Review of Sociology*, 11: 181–207.

Bechhofer, F., Elliott, B. and McCrone, D. (1978) 'Structure, consciousness and action: a sociological profile of the British middle class', *British Journal of Sociology*, 29: 410–36.

Beck, U. (1992) *Risk Society*. London: Sage.

Blossfeld, H. P. and Shavit, Y. (1993) 'Persisting barriers: changes in educational opportunities in thirteen countries', in Y. Shavit and H. P. Blossfeld (eds), *Persistent Inequality*. Boulder, CO: Westview Press. pp. 1–24.

Bögenhold, D. (1985) *Die Selbständigen. Zur Soziologie dezentraler Produktion*. Frankfurt: Campus.

Boltanski, L. (1982) *Les cadres. La formation d'un groupe social*. Paris: Minuit.

Bourdieu, P. (1984) *The Distinction. A Social Critique of the Judgment of Taste*. Cambridge, MA: Harvard University Press.

Bourdieu, P. (1987) 'What makes a social class? On the theoretical and practical existence of groups', *Berkeley Journal of Sociology*, 32: 1–17.

Brand, K. W. (1990) 'Cyclical aspects of new social movements: waves of cultural criticism and mobilization cycles of new middle-class radicalism', in R. J. Dalton and M. Kuechler (eds), *Challenging the Political Order. New Social and Political Movements in Western Democracies*. Cambridge: Polity Press. pp. 23–42.

Burke, K. (1990) *On Symbols and Society*, edited and with an Introduction by Joseph R. Gusfield. Chicago: University of Chicago Press.

Bürklin, W. P. (1984) 'Ansatzpunkte einer sozialstrukturellen Verankerung der neuen sozialen Bewegungen', in J. Falter et al. (eds), *Politische Willensbildung und Interessenvermittlung*. Opladen: Westdeutscher Verlag. pp. 566–79.

Bürklin, W. P. (1987) 'Governing left parties frustrating the radical non-established left: the rise and inevitable decline of the Greens', *European Sociological Review*, 3: 109–26.

Burris, V. (1980) 'Class formation and transformation in advanced capitalist societies: a comparative analysis', *Social Praxis*, 7: 147–79.

Burris, V. (1986) 'The discovery of the new middle class', *Theory and Society*, 15: 317–49.

Carter, R. (1985) *Capitalism, Class Conflict and the New Middle Class*. London: Routledge & Kegan Paul.

Centers, R. (1949) *The Psychology of Classes. A Study of Class Consciousness*. New York: Russell & Russell.

Clark, T. N. and Lipset, S. M. (1991) 'Are social classes dying?', *International Sociology*, 6: 397–410.

Clark, T. N., Lipset, S. M. and Rempel, M. (1993) 'The declining political significance of class', *International Sociology*, 8: 293–316.

Clegg, S. R. (ed.) (1989) *Organization Theory and Class Analysis. New Approaches and New Issues*. Berlin and New York: de Gruyter.

Cohen, J. L. (1985) 'Strategy or identity: new theoretical paradigms and contemporary social movements', *Social Research*, 52–4: 663–716.

Cotgrove, S. and Duff, A. (1980) 'Environmentalism, middle-class radicalism and politics', *Sociological Review*, 28: 333–51.

Cotgrove, S. and Duff, A. (1981) 'Environmentalism, values, and social change', *British Journal of Sociology*, 32: 92–110.

DeMott, B. (1990) *The Imperial Middle: Why Americans Can't Think Straight About Class*. New York: Morrow.

Dreyfuss, C. (1933) *Beruf und Ideologie der Angestellten*. Munich and Leipzig: Duncker & Humblot.

Eder, K. (1985) *Geschichte als Lernprozess? Zur Pathogenese politischer Modernität in Deutschland*. Frankfurt: Suhrkamp.

Eder, K. (1988) *Die Vergesellschaftung der Natur. Studien zur sozialen Evolution der praktischen Vernunft*. Frankfurt: Suhrkamp.

Eder, K. (1989) 'Jenseits der nivellierten Mittelstandsgesellschaft. Das Kleinbürgertum als Schlüssel zu einer Klassenanalyse fortgeschrittener Industriegesellschaften', in K. Eder (ed.), *Klassenlage, Lebensstil und kulturelle Praxis*. Frankfurt: Suhrkamp. pp. 341–93.

Eder, K. (1992) 'Politics and culture: on the sociocultural analysis of political participation', in A. Honneth, T. McCarthy, C. Offe and A. Wellmer (eds), *Cultural-Political Interventions in the Unfinished Project of Enlightenment*. Cambridge, MA: MIT Press. pp. 95–120.

Eder, K. (1993) *The New Politics of Class. Social Movements and Cultural Dynamics in Advanced Societies*. London: Sage.

Ehrenreich, B. (1989) *The Fear of Falling: The Inner Life of the Middle Class*. New York: Pantheon.

Elster, J. (1982) 'Marxism, functionalism, and game theory. The case for methodological individualism', *Theory and Society*, 11: 453–82.

Elster, J. (1985a) 'Drei Kritiken am Klassenbegriff', in N. Luhmann (ed.), *Soziale Differenzierung. Zur Geschichte einer Idee*. Opladen: Westdeutscher Verlag. pp. 96–118.

Elster, J. (1985b) *Making Sense of Marx*. Cambridge: Cambridge University Press.

Elster, J. (1989a) *Solomonic Judgments: Studies in the Limitations of Rationality*. New York: Cambridge University Press.

50   Foundations for Collective Action

Elster, J. (1989b) *The Cement of Society. A Study of Social Order.* New York: Cambridge University Press.

Esping-Andersen, G. (ed.) (1993) *Changing Classes. Stratification and Mobility in Post-Industrial Societies.* London: Sage.

Falter, J. W. (1982) 'Radikalisierung des Mittelstandes oder Mobilisierung der Unpolitischen? Die Theorien von Seymour Martin Lipset und Reinhard Bendix über die Wählerschaft der NSDAP im Lichte neuerer Forschungsergebnisse', in P. Steinbach (ed.), *Probleme politischer Partizipation im Modernisierungsprozess.* Stuttgart: Klett-Cotta. pp. 438–69.

Falter, J. W. (1984) 'Die Wähler der NSDAP 1928–1933: Sozialstruktur und parteipolitische Herkunft', in W. Michalka (ed.), *Die nationalsozialistische Machtergreifung.* Paderborn: Schöningh. pp. 47–59.

Featherstone, M. (1989) 'Towards a sociology of postmodern culture', in H. Haferkamp (ed.), *Social Structure and Culture.* Berlin: Walter de Gruyter. pp. 147–74.

Gamson, W. A. (1988) 'Political discourse and collective action', in B. Klandermans, H. Kriesi and S. Tarrow (eds), *From Structure to Action: Comparing Social Movement Research across Cultures* (Vol. 1, International Social Movement Research). Greenwich, CT: JAI Press. pp. 219–44.

Gamson, W. A. (1992) *Talking Politics.* Boston, MA: MIT Press.

Gamson, W. A. and Modigliani, A. (1987) 'The changing culture of affirmative action', in R. D. Braungart and M. M. Braungart (eds), *Research in Political Sociology,* Vol. 3. Greenwich, CT: JAI Press. pp. 137–77.

Gamson, W. A. and Modigliani, A. (1989) 'Media discourse and public opinion on nuclear power: a constructionist approach', *American Journal of Sociology,* 95: 1–38.

Gans, H. J. (1988) *Middle American Individualism.* New York: Free Press.

Gershuny, J. I. (1978) *After Industrial Society? The Emerging Self-Service Economy.* London: Macmillan.

Gershuny, J. I. (1983) *The New Service Economy. The Transformation of Employment in Industrial Societies.* London: Pinter.

Giddens, A. (1973) *The Class Structure of Advanced Societies.* London: Hutchinson.

Giddens, A. (1987) *Social Theory and Modern Sociology.* Cambridge: Polity Press.

Goldthorpe, J. H. (1978) 'Comment on: F. Bechhofer et al., *Structure, Consciousness and Action. A Sociological Profile of the British Middle Class'*, *British Journal of Sociology,* 29: 436–8.

Gouldner, A. W. (1979) *The Future of the Intellectuals and the Rise of the New Class.* New York: Seabury.

Gurr, T. R. (1970) *Why Men Rebel.* Princeton, NJ: Princeton University Press.

Habermas, J. (1984) *The Theory of Communicative Action: Reason and the Rationalization of Society. Volume I.* Boston, MA: Beacon Press.

Habermas, J. (1987) *The Theory of Communicative Action. Lifeworld and System. A Critique of Functionalist Reason. Volume II.* Boston, MA: Beacon Press.

Hamilton, R. F. (1982) *Who Voted for Hitler?* Princeton, NJ: Princeton University Press.

Hamilton, R. F. and Wright, J. D. (1986) *The State of the Masses.* New York: Aldine.

Hechter, M. (1989) *Principles of Group Solidarity.* Berkeley and Los Angeles: University of California Press.

Hechter, M. (1990) 'The emergence of cooperative social institutions', in M.

Hechter, K. D. Opp and R. Wippler (eds), *Social Institutions. Their Emergence, Maintenance and Effects*. New York: Aldine de Gruyter. pp. 13–34.

Hechter, M. (1991) 'Should values be written out of the social scientists' lexicon?' Stanford University, unpublished manuscript.

Hirschman, A. O. (1977) *The Passions and the Interests. Political Arguments for Capitalism*. Princeton, NJ: Princeton University Press.

Hirschman, A. O. (1982) *Shifting Involvements: Private Interests and Public Action*. Princeton, NJ: Princeton University Press.

Hulsberg, W. (1988) *The German Greens: A Social and Political Profile*. London: Verso.

Inglehart, R. (1977) *The Silent Revolution. Changing Values and Political Styles among Western Publics*. Princeton, NJ: Princeton University Press.

Inglehart, R. (1990a) *Culture Shift in Advanced Industrial Societies*. Princeton, NJ: Princeton University Press.

Inglehart, R. (1990b) 'Values, ideology, and cognitive mobilization in new social movements', in R. J. Dalton and M. Kuechler (eds), *Challenging the Political Order. New Social and Political Movements in Western Democracies*. Cambridge: Polity Press. pp. 43–66.

Johnson, D. L. (ed.) (1982) *Class and Social Development: A New Theory of the Middle Class*. Beverly Hills: Sage.

Kann, M. E. (1986) *Middle Class Radicalism in Santa Monica*. Philadelphia, PA: Temple University Press.

Kluckhohn, F. R. and Strodtbeck, F. L. (1961) *Variations in Value Orientations*. Westport, CT: Greenwood Press.

Kocka, J. and Prinz, M. (1983) 'Vom "neuen Mittelstand" zum angestellten Arbeitnehmer. Kontinuität und Wandel der deutschen Angestellten seit der Weimarer Republik', in W. Conze and R. M. Lepsius (eds), *Sozialgeschichte der Bundesrepublik Deutschland*. Stuttgart: Klett. pp. 210–55.

Konrad, G. and Szelenyi, I. (1979) *The Intellectuals on the Road to Class Power*. New York: Harcourt Brace Jovanovich.

Kracauer, S. (1985) *Die Angestellten. Aus dem neuesten Deutschland*. Frankfurt: Suhrkamp.

Kriesi, H. (1987) 'Neue soziale Bewegungen: Auf der Suche nach ihrem gemeinsamen Nenner', *Politische Vierteljahresschrift*, 28: 315–34.

Kriesi, H. (1989) 'New social movements and the new class in the Netherlands', *American Journal of Sociology*, 94: 1078–117.

Lash, S. and Urry, J. (1987) *The End of Organized Capitalism*. Cambridge: Polity Press.

Lederer, E. (1912) *Die Privatangestellten in der modernen Wirtschaftsentwicklung*. Tübingen: Mohr.

Lederer, E. (1979) 'Die Gesellschaft der Unselbständigen. Zum sozialpsychologischen Habitus der Gegenwart (1913/19)', in J. Kocka (ed.), *Kapitalismus, Klassenstruktur und Probleme der Demokratie in Deutschland 1910–1940. Ausgewählte Aufsätze von Emil Lederer*. Göttingen: Vandenhoeck & Ruprecht. pp. 14–32.

Lipset, S. M. (1988) *Revolution and Counterrevolution*, revised edn. New Brunswick, NJ: Transaction Books.

Lockwood, D. (1987) 'Staatsbürgerliche Ungleichheit', in B. Giesen and H. Haferkamp (eds), *Soziologie der sozialen Ungleichheit*. Opladen: Westdeutscher Verlag. pp. 31–48.

Luke, T. W. (1989) *Screens of Power. Ideology, Domination, and Resistance in Informational Society*. Urbana: University of Illinois Press.

McAdams, J. (1987) 'Testing the theory of the new class', *Sociological Quarterly*, 28: 23–49.

Melucci, A. (1985) 'The symbolic challenge of contemporary movements', *Social Research*, 52: 789–816.

Melucci, A. (1988) 'Getting involved: identity and mobilization in social movements', in B. Klandermans, H. Kriesi and S. Tarrow (eds), *From Structure to Action: Comparing Social Movement Research across Cultures* (Vol. 1, International Social Movement Research). Greenwich, CT: JAI Press. pp. 329–48.

Melucci, A. (1989) *Nomads of the Present. Social Movements and Individual Needs in Contemporary Society*, ed. John Keane and Paul Mier. London: Hutchinson Radius.

Mills, C. W. (1956) *The Power Elite*. London: Oxford University Press.

Moore, B. (1978) *Injustice: The Social Bases of Obedience and Revolt*. White Plains, NY: Sharpe.

Moscovici, S. (1985) *L'âge des Foules. Un traité historique de psychologie des masses*. Brussels: Editions Complexe.

Offe, C. (1985a) 'Bemerkungen zur spieltheoretischen Neufassung des Klassenbegriffs bei Wright und Elster', *Prokla*, 15: 83–8.

Offe, C. (1985b) *Disorganized Capitalism. Contemporary Transformations of Work and Politics*. Cambridge: Polity Press.

Offe, C. (1985c) 'New social movements: challenging the boundaries of institutional politics', *Social Research*, 52: 817–68.

Offe, C. and Wiesenthal, H. (1980) 'Two logics of collective action: theoretical notes on social class and organizational form', in M. Zeitlin (ed.), *Political Power and Social Theory*, Vol. 1. Greenwich, CT: JAI Press. pp. 67–115.

Olofsson, G. (1988) 'After the working-class movement? An essay on what's "new" and what's "social" in the new social movements', *Acta Sociologica*, 31: 15–34.

Pakulski, J. (1988) 'Social movements in comparative perspective', in L. Kriesberg (ed.), *Research in Social Movements, Conflicts and Change*, Vol. 10. Greenwood, CT: JAI Press. pp. 247–67.

Pakulski, J. (1991) *Social Movements. The Politics of Moral Protest*. Melbourne: Longman Cheshire.

Pakulski, J. (1993) 'The dying of class or of Marxist class theory?', *International Sociology*, 8: 279–92.

Pappi, F. U. (1981) 'The petite bourgeoisie and the new middle class. Differentiation and homogenisation of the middle strata in Germany', in F. Bechhofer and B. Elliott (eds), *The Petite Bourgeoisie. Comparative Studies of the Uneasy Stratum*. New York: St Martin's Press. pp. 105–20.

Parkin, F. (1968) *Middle Class Radicalism*. Manchester: Manchester University Press.

Piven, F. F. and Cloward, R. A. (1972) *Regulating the Poor. The Function of Public Welfare*. London: Tavistock.

Prinz, M. (1981) 'Das Ende der Standespolitik. Voraussetzungen und Konsequenzen mittelständischer Interessenpolitik in der Weimarer Republik am Beispiel des Deutschnationalen Handlungsgehilfenverbandes', in J. Kocka (ed.), *Angestellte im europäischen Vergleich. Die Herausbildung angestellter Mittelschichten seit dem späten 19. Jahrhundert*. Göttingen: Vandenhoeck & Ruprecht. pp. 313–53.

Roemer, J. E. (1982) *A General Theory of Exploitation and Class*. Cambridge, MA: Harvard University Press.

Roemer, J. E. (ed.) (1986) *Analytical Marxism*. Cambridge: Cambridge University Press; Paris: Editions de la Maison des sciences de l'homme.

Rucht, D. (ed.) (1991) *Research on Social Movements. The State of the Art in Western Europe and the USA*. Frankfurt: Campus.

Schelsky, H. (1975) *Die Arbeit tun die Anderen*. Opladen: Westdeutscher Verlag.

Sørensen, A.B. (1991) 'On the usefulness of class analysis in research on social mobility and socioeconomic inequality', *Acta Sociologica*, 34: 71–87.

Speier, H. (1977) *Die Angestellten vor dem Nationalsozialismus. Ein Beitrag zum Verständnis der deutschen Sozialstruktur 1918–1933*. Göttingen: Vandenhoeck & Ruprecht.

Steinmetz, G. and Wright, E. O. (1989) 'The fall and rise of the petty bourgeoisie: changing patterns of self-employment in the postwar United States', *American Journal of Sociology*, 94: 973–1019.

Thompson, M., Ellis, R. and Wildavsky, A. (1990) *Cultural Theory, or, Why All That is Permanent is Bias*. Boulder, CO: Westview Press.

Touraine, A. (1969) *La société postindustrielle*. Paris: Denoël.

Touraine, A. (1981) *The Voice and the Eye*. New York: Cambridge University Press.

Touraine, A. (1985a) 'An Introduction to the Study of Social Movements', *Social Research*, 52: 4: 749–88.

Touraine, A. (1985b) 'Klassen, soziale Bewegungen und soziale Schichtung in einer nachindustriellen Gesellschaft', in H. Strasser and J. H. Goldthorpe (eds), *Die Analyse sozialer Ungleichheit*. Opladen: Westdeutscher Verlag. pp. 324–38.

Vester, M. (1983) 'Die "Neuen Plebejer": Thesen zur Klassen- und Schichtstruktur und zu den Entwicklungsperspektiven der neuen sozialen Bewegungen', in H. H. Hartwich (ed.), *Gesellschaftliche Probleme als Anstoss und Folge von Politik*. Opladen: Westdeutscher Verlag. pp. 213–24.

Vester, M. (1989) 'Neue soziale Bewegungen und soziale Schichten', in U. C. Wasmuht (ed.), *Alternativen zur alten Politik? Neue soziale Bewegungen in der Diskussion*. Darmstadt: Wissenschaftliche Buchgesellschaft. pp. 38–63.

Winkler, H. A. (1971) 'Der rückversicherte Mittelstand: Die Interessenverbände von Handwerk und Kleinhandel im deutschen Kaiserreich', in W. Rüegg and O. Neuloh (eds), *Zur soziologischen Theorie und Analyse des 19. Jahrhunderts*. Göttingen: Vandenhoeck & Ruprecht. pp. 163–79.

Winkler, H. A. (1972) *Mittelstand, Demokratie und Nationalsozialismus. Die politische Entwicklung von Handwerk und Kleinhandel in der Weimarer Republik*. Köln: Kiepenhauer and Witsch.

Winkler, H. A. (1978) 'Vom Sozialprotektionismus zum Nationalsozialismus. Die Bewegung des gewerblichen Mittelstandes in Deutschland im Vergleich', in H. G. Haupt (ed.), *'Bourgeois und Volk zugleich?' Zur Geschichte des Kleinbürgertums im 19. und 20. Jahrhundert*. Frankfurt: Campus. pp. 143–61.

Winkler, H. A. (1979) 'Extremismus der Mitte? Sozialgeschichtliche Aspekte der nationalsozialistischen Machtergreifung', in H. A. Winkler, *Liberalismus und Antiliberalismus. Studien zur politischen Sozialgeschichte des 19. und 20. Jahrhunderts*. Göttingen: Vandenhoeck & Ruprecht. pp. 205–17.

Winkler, H. A. (1983) 'Stabilisierung durch Schrumpfung: Der gewerbliche Mittelstand in der Bundesrepublik', in W. Conze and M. R. Lepsius (eds), *Sozialgeschichte der Bundesrepublik Deutschland. Beiträge zum Kontinuitätsproblem*. Stuttgart: Klett-Cotta. pp. 187–209.

Wright, E. O. (1985) *Classes*. London: NLB.

Wright, E. O. (1986) 'What is middle about the middle class?', in J. Roemer (ed.),

Analytical Marxism. Cambridge: Cambridge University Press. pp. 114–40.

Wright, E. O. (1990) 'A general framework for the analysis of class structure', in E. O. Wright (ed.), *The Debate on Classes*. London: Verso. pp. 3–43.

Zald, M. N. and McCarthy, J. D. (eds) (1979) *The Dynamics of Social Movements*. Cambridge: Winthrop.

Zald, M. N. and McCarthy, J. D. (eds) (1987) *Social Movements in an Organizational Society*. New Brunswick and Oxford: Transaction Books.

2

Social Movements and Class: The Decline of the Marxist Paradigm

Jan Pakulski

Class interpretations of social movements have a long and disting-uished history. For Karl Marx, the key source of 'history-making' conflict and the principal propellant of collective action were material interests engendered in class position. He associated contemporary protests and movements with the articulation of class interests and class outlooks by the principal 'challenging classes', first the bourgeoisie and subsequently the proletariat. Marx saw workers' protests as structurally determined and historically central: they were the key engine of social change.

This interpretation remained unchallenged throughout the late nineteenth and early twentieth centuries. Werner Sombart, for example, defined social movements as 'attempts at emancipation on the part of the proletariat', and many authors who presented the Russian Revolution saw it as a workers' and peasants' movement.[1] The dissenting view of Max Weber – who linked social movements, especially the prophetic ones such as the Protestant Reformation, with charisma and status groups – never gained wide currency.

However, the eruption of nationalist movements, especially European Fascism in the 1920s and 1930s, posed serious problems for advocates of the class interpretation. Some of the most prominent analysts (e.g. Arendt) explained Fascist movements as a symptom of massification and atomization, a consequence of the collapse of class boundaries and identities. This resulted in 'atomized', unorganized masses of people who became vulnerable to totalitarian mobilizations and responded to nationalistic Nazi appeals.[2] By contrast, advocates of the Marxist approach insisted on linking Fascist movements either with the interests of the major propertied classes or with the defensive responses of the 'middle classes', mainly the petite bourgeoisie.[3] The debate between the two continued in the post-war period.

A modified version of class interpretation was adopted by Seymour M. Lipset in *Political Man* (1959, 1981). Fascist, authoritarian,

Peronist and communist movements, according to Lipset, reflected the extremist (rather than mainstream) class politics of the marginalized sections of the major classes. This line of argument, minus the negative assessment of mass movements as 'extremist politics', inspired some later theorists of 'new' movements in the West.[4]

Since the 1970s, the class interpretation has been in steady decline. Studies of the American civil rights movements, West European ecological and anti-nuclear (eco-pax, green) mobilizations, fundamentalist movements in Iran and the Middle East, and the more recent wave of anti-partocratic movements in Eastern Europe, have prompted further critical revisions of the class interpretation. Neither the social composition and identities of the actors nor their key concerns could adequately be accounted for in class terms. The shortcomings of class accounts became particularly apparent to students of 'new social movements', especially the Green and feminist movements. The universalistic, non-economistic and 'lifestyle' concerns articulated in these movements, combined with status- and generation-specific rather than class-specific social composition, added to the doubts about the validity and utility of the class interpretation. Only recently have the protagonists of class analysis mounted a vigorous defence: Touraine (1981, 1985) outlined a highly original version of 'class-action' interpretation, and Eder (1993) proposed a 'culturalist' class account of the West European new social movements.

The debate these publications have triggered is not likely to be easily settled. 'Conceptual stretch' made the key concepts – those of 'class' and 'social movement' – extremely elastic and vague. Ideological considerations also frequently colour movement analyses, and a myopic focus on the new Western movements hinders attempts at a broad comparative assessment. A serious test of the validity and utility of the class interpretation would therefore require an elucidation of key concepts and a broadening of the research horizons by incorporating a wider and more diverse range of contemporary mass movements into the analysis.

Movement and class

There is no agreement among social theorists as to what constitutes a social movement. The term has been blurred and stretched, so that everything from a local vigil to a major revolution has been called a movement, prompting one researcher to comment that everything that moves is a movement.[5] There is no agreement on the constitutive 'units' (groups, events, concerns), supporters (participants, sympathizers, all concerned people), location of boundaries, or historical roots of such movements.

A necessary first step is an awareness of the broad variety of meanings hidden behind the label 'social movement', combined with a commitment to explicit and clear definitions of the key concepts. Here, I suggest a sociological definition which sees a social movement as a recurrent pattern of polymorphous and value-charged protest activities.[6] Recurrence and polymorphism distinguish movements from occasional protests, organized political groups (e.g. mass parties) and regimes. Strong value orientations separate them from the predominantly instrumental orientations of parties and interest groups.

The concept of class is even more ambiguous and stretched. In the mainstream Marxist tradition, it is deployed mainly in the context of analyses of social conflict and change. Class refers to both the structural sources of social tensions generated by opposed interests of labour and capital, and to social categories (with varying degrees of consciousness and organization) articulating these tensions. Analyses using such a generative concept of class treat the issues of class membership and boundaries as relatively unimportant. The Marxist aim is not a hierarchical classification of occupational categories, but the identification of (allegedly objective and oppositional) class interests, which are then causally linked with observable social conflicts and the groups articulating them.

In the mainstream Weberian tradition, however, class serves as more of a categorical concept referring to market-generated hierarchical patterns of inequality in life chances (differential access to goods and services). Neo-Weberians reject the polarity of classes, emphasize the importance of authority relations and social mobility in social class formation, and contrast class conflicts with status group and party political conflicts. 'Class structuration' occurs not only through the differential distribution of property, skills and disposition of labour power, but also through the division of labour and authority relations.

This distinction cross-cuts another: between class concepts which focus on such objective aspects of social location as property/occupational status, and concepts which stress subjective class identification plus consciousness. In objectivist interpretations class membership is determined independently of consciousness, identities and orientations of class members, and these aspects are seen as variable. Subjectivist concepts of class, by contrast, take consciousness and identity as bases and the key indicators of the articulation of a class-actor.[7]

This diversity makes the class interpretation immune to criticism.

Almost any refutation can be questioned from another 'class position'. In order to avoid such a sterile game, I limit my critical comment to class interpretations based on objective socioeconomic notions of class, that is, those that equate class with large social categories sharing a similar location in the processes of production (property and/or market relations) and therefore similar interests attributable to this socioeconomic location. Thus defined, class is not the only possible structural basis of collective action, and not the only possible social framework of action. The class character of social movements is a matter of degree, and it may be analysed in terms of social composition (to what extent they attract support of a class), identity (to what extent movement activists and supporters see themselves as class-actors), and in terms of the logical and historical fit between class interests and key concerns articulated in the movement. Also, in line with the Marxist analysis, class interests may be attributed to the general orientations of movement supporters and/or to the unintended consequences and outcomes of their actions (who benefits). In the latter case, the attribution can be made independently of the consciousness of movement supporters on the basis of an abstract model of what the 'objective class interests' are.

Problems with class interpretations

While difficulties with class interpretations of mass movements prompt some theorists to reject the class paradigm, others have modified it and redefined the nature of movement–class links. Three such modifications will be briefly examined: the interpretations of Nazi/Fascist movements in Germany and Italy as defensive 'middle-class' mobilizations; accounts of Polish Solidarity as a 'working-class' or 'new-class' (socialist middle-class) movement; and interpretations of Western eco-pax movements as articulations of the styles and interests of an altogether 'new' class.

Fascist movements and the middle class

According to Salvatorelli, 'Fascism represents the class struggle of the petty bourgeoisie which is placed between big business and the proletariat, like the third man between the two fighters'.[8] This classical middle-class interpretation was reformulated by Lipset, who linked the extremist forms of political expression (Fascist movements) with the 'disgruntled and the psychologically homeless' sections of the middle class (1959: 175). Economic and political crises, as well as general historical change (industrialization), triggered insecurity among these 'marginal' categories and led to mass mobilizations which were defensive and class-expressive in their social bases, forms and references.[9] Fascism represented an extremist movement of shopkeepers, white-collar and professional workers threatened by economic depression, revolutionary upheavals and the collapse of liberal politics. Lipset characterized Fascism as a defensive and reactionary (anti-modernist) movement that mobilized the most threatened and authoritarian segments of the middle class 'found among the small entrepreneurs who live in small communities or on farms'. The ideology of the movement was hostile to its class 'competitors' at both ends of the spectrum: the communists and 'big unions' on one end, and 'big business' on the other. Fascism glorified the virtues of the 'little man' and elevated the petite-bourgeoisie ethos to the role of a universal ethical code.

The first problem in such accounts is the fuzziness of key concepts. 'Middle class' includes almost everybody who is not a manual worker: from upper-white-collar through routine clerical to lower supervisory, plus (most importantly) the petite bourgeoisie: peasants, shopkeepers, small employers and craft workers. 'Class' is used as a socioeconomic category – people distinguished in terms of property relations – and also as a sociocultural (status) category – people who maintain certain 'middle-class' lifestyles, consumption patterns and/or identifications. Because of this vagueness and inclusiveness, almost any large-scale social process may be accurately attributed to middle class(es) of one sort or another. Moreover, Lipset's interpretation oscillates between the 'class' and 'declassé' (mass) accounts. In the second edition, he approvingly quotes Sauer's statement that 'Fascism is a revolt of the declassés' (1981: 490), and Zetkin's observation that 'fascism appealed to the socially displaced of all strata' (1981:494). A few pages later Lipset notes that 'analyses of the social base of the [Fascist] parties in both Italy and Germany indicate that their supporters were pre-dominantly drawn from pre-industrial strata, farmers, artisans, and small business people' and that '[e]ach movement was a reaction in a part to a sense that a particular nation was denied its proper place in the sun' (1981:496–7).

It must also be stressed that Lipset does not clearly distinguish Fascism as a radical mass movement from Fascism as a mono-party regime. Data on early movement supporters, as well as data on voters for the Fascist parties in power, are scrutinized together in his reviews of the social bases of Fascist support. This, as argued later, may blur some important differences in the constituencies of Fascist movements and Fascist regimes.

Even though he clearly links Fascism (and other mass movements) with social marginality, Lipset nevertheless stresses the explanatory centrality of class. He insists that his aim is 'to explain the propensity of the middle strata to support a certain kind of extremist political movement, namely, classical fascism' (1981:493). These propensities, however, are analysed not in terms of intrinsic class characteristics, i.e. characteristics derived from socio-economic location, but in terms of incidental (in relation to class) characteristics, such as economic insecurity, the lack of political sophistication, decline in status, threat to values and low integration into democratic institutions, all of which – according to Lipset – happened to affect 'certain sections of the middle classes' more than other classes.

This alleged affinity, however, is not well scrutinized. It is not altogether clear why 'certain sections of the middle classes' should be more affected and more threatened by the process of modernization, economic crises and political instability than, say, the working class or the dominant propertied classes. [10] Nor is it clear why the 'middle classes' – threatened or not – should be more inclined than the other classes to embrace the nationalistic 'populist idiom', and destroy liberal democracy. If, as Lipset suggests, Fascism represents a class 'reaction' rather than 'class action', a sort of knee-jerk response by a class but not necessarily in its own interests, the very irrationality of such a response would make it difficult to explain it by reference to *any* socio-structural category or class, middle or other. The problematic nature of such middle-class attribution is particularly striking in the light of Lipset's earlier discussion of working-class authoritarianism. He endorses mainstream social theory which links 'middle-class' sociopolitical interests, orientations and inclinations with conventional liberal democratic politics – the very type of politics that the allegedly 'middle-class' Fascist movements attacked and destroyed. [11]

There are also other interpretive problems. As Lipset and other advocates of the 'middle-class interpretation' acknowledge, class identification (middle or any other) was conspicuously absent among Fascist supporters. Fascist movements not only stressed the importance of national (and racial, in the case of the German Nazis) identity, but also actively opposed any notion of intra-national division or identity, especially of Marxist origin. Class identity, in other words, could be seen as totally incompatible with Fascism's own identifications and ideological orientations.

Even if one takes the 'middle-class basis' as referring merely to the occupational composition of movement supporters, and not the identities, goals and orientations of the movement, the doubts remain. First, a 'middle-class' composition was not a distinctive feature of the movement. The problem is not with attributing predominantly 'middle-class' status to Fascist/Nazi activists, but in attributing uniqueness to this fact. Supporters and activists of non-Fascist and anti-Fascist political groups and parties were also predominantly 'middle class'.[12] All political activism – Left and Right, extremist and conventional – has been the domain of loosely defined 'middle classes'.

Secondly, the middle-class interpretation does not square well with the apparent social heterogeneity of movement constituencies. The German and Italian movements, for example, did receive strong support from manual workers, including ex-communists and ex-socialists. They also attracted a disproportionately high percentage of professionals, managers and intellectuals, as well as such non-class categories as students, the unemployed and ex-service pensioners.[13] Above all, however, the class interpretation ignores such strikingly distinctive features of Fascist supporters as age and gender. In the initial stage of mobilization, the movement attracted mainly young and able-bodied males. The social composition of the early supporters – those who joined the PNF before the 'March on Rome' and who joined the NSDAP before 1933 – leaves no doubt as to the salience of generational location and gender. About 80 per cent of adult members were young male veterans. Studies of SA stormtroopers and Italian *squadristi* have concluded that at the centre of the movement were young males who were born in the first decade of this century and who experienced the First World War.[14]

Thirdly, the 'middle-class' interpretations tend to gloss over those changes in social composition that occurred between the early (mobilization) and the late (takeover) stages of the movement. The so called 'fascists of the first hour' represented different social types and occupational categories than later Fascist voters, mainly as a result of takeovers by Fascist parties, mass recruitment drives, mergers with centre-right parties, and the bandwagon effect. While Fascist movements transformed into mass parties and regimes, Fascist parties gradually became catch-all political parties attracting all cohorts and classes, and both genders. This shift was associated with changes in programmes and orientations: oppositional slogans and idealistic commitments were played down and gradually disappeared, giving way to calls for discipline and pragmatism.[15]

The Solidarity movement, the 'working class' and the 'new socialist middle class'

The popular image of Solidarity as a 'working-class movement' requires revision. Even if one accepts that the notion of class is applicable to a non-capitalist society (such as Polish society in the

1980s), Solidarity can hardly be seen as a movement of the working class or any other class. It is true that the movement was dominated by 'workers', but such a 'worker' category included both manual and non-manual labourers: skilled tradesmen, 'professionals' and intellectuals. The strongest support for the movement came, in fact, from both skilled industrial workers and 'professionals' (engineers and doctors, as well as students), while the most under-represented among the supporters were unskilled workers, routine white-collar and, to a lesser extent, rural workers. In political-organizational terms, the strongest backing for the movement came from non-party members, while the strongest opposition to the movement came, quite understandably, from the higher echelons of the partocratic apparata.[16]

It is also difficult to link Solidarity movement issues and concerns with any consistent model of class interests, class concerns or class styles. The movement focused on the issues of political freedom and democracy, national sovereignty, human rights and dignity, justice, citizenship and constitutional legalism, as well as the traditional 'class issues' of wages and working conditions. Class was, however, clearly overshadowed by the other issues. There were few signs of class identity and 'class consciousness' among supporters of the movement. If anything, movement participants overwhelmingly adopted national identity and stressed national solidarity.[17] The movement 'counterculture' included many elements clearly derived from the national tradition, as well as the traditions of the intelligentsia (and nobility).

Attempts to link the overall political vector and outcomes of the movement with any consistent model of 'class interests' would pose even greater problems. How could a 'working-class' movement embrace liberal democracy and a market economy? What 'class' of Polish society would benefit from the libertarian-democratic reforms, such as those advocated by movement leaders? As the obvious difficulties in answering these questions indicate, class interpretations of the Solidarity movement – and the movement-propelled East European revolutions of 1989 – pose serious interpretive difficulties.

A better fit is provided by Dahrendorf's (1959) concept of class as a social category distinguished in terms of general authority (rather than property) relations. Such a notion of a 'class of subordinates' versus the 'class of controllers' has been quite popular among Polish sociologists.[18] These two divisions, it has been claimed, form a basis for shared interests among 'subordinates', which are opposed to the interests of the 'controllers'. Such class schemes, although more adequate for the analyses of East European mass movements than the more orthodox Marxist model, are, nevertheless, vague and weak. They ignore the strikingly young age of Solidarity supporters (between 25 and 35), their political peripheralization, particular location and considerable occupational autonomy.[19]

Western eco-pax movements, the (new) middle class and the 'new class'

Most class accounts of the Western eco-pax movements link them with either the 'new middle class(es)' or an altogether 'new class'. The former follow Parkin's (1968) study of the Campaign for Nuclear Disarmament (CND) in Britain and the more recent analyses of Eder (1993), while the latter draw heavily on Gouldner's (1979) and Inglehart's (1977, 1990) arguments.

Parkin's study showed that the CND supporters were drawn disproportionately from the ranks of the young professionals employed in the public sector, mainly in the areas of education and welfare. The link between their occupational position and movement involvement was not straightforward: individuals who had been radical prior to entering occupational careers tended to enter those types of employment which facilitated the maintenance of critical and radical orientations. Involvement in the movement was also linked with value commitments and idealism inculcated by a 'middle-class' pattern of socialization.

Such an indirect movement–class link raises important questions. For a start, the notion of 'middle class' gains a clear sociocultural (rather than socioeconomic) reference. If the process of 'embourgeoisement' leads, as some observers argue, to the blurring and/or decoupling of sociocultural divisions, class as a socioeconomic category loses its explanatory potential. Moreover, if styles, norms and ethoses reflected in movement activism are the product of specific socialization patterns and lifestyles, the concept of status group, rather than class, appears to be more appropriate for explaining movements' origins and persistence. As we will see, such an interpretation has been suggested by Turner (1988).

In more recent new middle-class analyses, the link between class and movement concerns is almost completely severed. Offe (1985), for example, sees Western eco-pax movements as an expression of a 'new-middle-class politics' which, unlike politics of other classes, is conducted by class members but not in their class interest. High levels of education, relatively high economic security and specific experiences, combined with the exposure to bureaucratic control due to employment in the service sector, make the 'new middle class' receptive to the expressive style and universalistic concerns of new movements. Given their strategic occupational position, they see more clearly the contradictions of capitalist state-administrative systems, and are therefore in the forefront of such (anti-statist) protest movements. They also have knowledge and skills which increase the effectiveness of their political actions and enjoy considerable autonomy and freedom from conformist pressures.

By separating the concept of class from structurally derived socioeconomic interests, Offe's analysis gains descriptive accuracy but loses much of the explanatory power which the classical concept of class gives. What he accounts for is not, strictly speaking, 'class action' articulating some objective class interests, but the 'social reaction' of certain social categories. He characterizes these categories in class terms, rather than as heterogeneous groupings which include such ('decommodified') categories as students and the unemployed.

Partly in response to the problems experienced in linking the new movements with the major classes, many students of Western eco-pax movements have turned to the concept of a 'new class' – allegedly a product of new social developments in advanced Western societies. Out of all the modified class accounts mentioned above, these 'new class' arguments deserve most attention, because of their popularity and their highly problematic nature.[20]

As a tool in movement analysis, the 'new class' turns out to be at least as problematic as the 'new middle class'. For a start, it is 'a linguistic and sociological muddle' (Bell, 1979:169); at best, it describes an adversarial intellectual style typical of Western intellectuals and a cultural mentality typical of the post-war period. Arguments linking intellectual roles and positions ('intellectual class', 'humanistic intelligentsia') with any consistent 'emancipatory interests', cosmopolitan orientation and universalism are open to serious challenge. After all, conservative, non-critical discourse has been at least as widespread as critical discourse among Western intellectuals. Adversarial moods seem to follow historical changes, rather than being structurally rooted. Waves of critical orientations seem to be followed by apologetic and/or complacent ones; and these waves have been reflected in changing political moods among the intellectuals and among general populations.[21]

The statist versions of 'new class', seeing it as consisting of state employees and welfare-dependent categories, do not fare any better.[22] If the 'new class' is the product of increasing state power and growing state intervention ('state class'), its interests and its styles of political action should be pro-statist, that is, supportive of the state and state interventions. In fact, many aspects of new movements are distinctly anti-statist (e.g. eco-anarchists), resisting 'administrative colonisation of the life world' and vindicating 'civil society' (Habermas, 1987).

The concept of 'new class' is not only vague but also contradicts the results of the empirical studies of West European new movements. These studies point to the occupational heterogeneity of movement supporters and stress the importance of generation, education and urban location as the correlates of movement activism. Therefore the concept of a new middle class, Kriesi concludes, is simultaneously too narrow and too broad:

> It turns out to be too narrow because dissent in the sense of readiness to support New Social Movements is not restricted to the educated new middle class . . . [It] is too broad, because only part of the new middle class seems to support oppositional tendencies such as those articulated by the new social movements. More specifically, there is a split in the younger generations of this new middle class. This split, which was found by Brint and Parkin as well, separates the social and cultural specialists from the technocrats made up of the managers (i.e. those controlling organisational assets in general), of the technical specialists, of the craft specialists, and of the protective services. While the young social and cultural specialists form the avant-garde of the new social movements, the technocrats support these movements only to a limited extent. (Kriesi, 1989: 1111)

As pointed out by one researcher, 'the social profile of green voters in Germany is close to the social profile of the under-forty age-group in the population as a whole'.[23] Social profiles of ecological movement activists and supporters in the US, Western Europe and Australia are similar to those of German Greens, as well as peace and feminist activists.[24]

Re-working the class model

Not all class theorists follow the orthodox Marxist/Weberian path. Many Marxist-inspired thinkers in Europe see the general adversarial and anti-systemic orientations, rather than specific socioeconomic claims, as the primary criteria of 'class character'. Touraine (1981, 1985), for example, analyses social movements (Western as well as Polish Solidarity) as collective 'class actors' involved in social conflicts which transcend the system by questioning the very sociocultural and sociopolitical 'rules of the game'. The class character of such movements lies in their social focus, radical and critical orientation, and 'transforming potential' – not in the occupational/economic position and economically relevant sectional interests of the supporters. It is this social focus and these radical anti-systemic orientations that define movements as 'class actors' involved in class conflicts.[25] Such class conflicts, according to Touraine, are the essential components of a healthy social life which involves the continuous 'self-creation' or 'self-reproduction' of society through collective challenges to established norms: institutional and cognitive rules and norms of investment. These challenged norms are seen as impositions of the ruling classes, that is, groups that dominate the processes of socioeconomic reproduction, shape social norms, define cultural orientations and benefit from the outcomes of these processes.

Touraine locates these contemporary 'class struggles' – i.e. radical social-normative challenges to the status quo – within a broader sociohistorical framework. The old form of industrial society in the West is gradually replaced by a new post-industrial 'programmed' society with a fundamentally different pattern of class relations and class conflicts. In a programmed society, investment no longer primarily follows the profit motive, the dominant class is the technocracy, and workers cease to be the main challengers of the status quo and the 'bearers of the future'. The key class conflict is sociocultural rather than socioeconomic; it revolves around the control of knowledge and investment, and it engenders resistance to technocratic domination. Sociological studies of these processes require concepts which are radically different from the concepts of traditional 'systemic' social analysis.

As Touraine et al. (1983) clearly point out in their analysis of the Solidarity movement in Poland, class character has little to do with capitalism, market, property relations and/or the social composition of participants and supporters. Class character lies, rather, in participants' broadly social, adversarial and generally 'anti-systematic' orientation. Moreover, Touraine et al. reverse the causality implied by the orthodox version of the 'class interpretation': it is not classes that are reflected in movements, but movements that generate and articulate class actors.[26] This, however, poses a problem: since all of the activities which Touraine et al. call 'social movements' involve challenges to the sociocultural status quo, these authors' version of class cannot be refuted; it forms a presupposition plus semantic convention rather than a verifiable theoretical proposition.

Eder's interpretation follows a similar line. As he argues in Chapter 1 of the present book, classes are 'collective actors creating arenas for social struggles'. The industrial class conflict is no longer a dominant social struggle in advanced post-industrial societies. This, however, does not mean the absence of class conflict, the latter being identified with the social articulation by a collective actor of 'incommensurable interests, norms and values at stake' (ibid.). Since the new social movements appear as collective actors and reveal incommensurable interests, norms and values, they should be seen as articulating a new class conflict, different from industrial class conflict, marking a new class cleavage and involving a new challenging class. The new class conflict reflects 'the two basic problems confronting post-industrial societies: the inclusion of cultural differences into a universalistic political and social order (in a democratically organized civil society) and the fundamental conflict between economy and ecology' (ibid.). The conflict over the means of creating an identity is at the centre of this new class conflict: 'it has a class character because there is no other solution to this antagonism than by structural changes in the distribution of power' (ibid.) and because it involves the 'new middle classes'.

Eder suggests that while analysing the forms of collective action which comprise new social movements, one should remember that collective action is always mediated by culture and that it, in turn, redefines the class structure, thus making the relationship a 'dynamic' one. In this sense, the collective action engendered in new social movements both reflects and creates the new class conflict.

For Eder, the 'new middle classes' which form the social bases of new social movements 'have become the most dynamic element in the reorganization of modern society; they turned out to be an important carrier of collective mobilization, thereby fulfilling a social role ascribed to the lower classes by traditional theory' (ibid.). They include those 'engaged in qualified production and service occupations', who focus on the 'problem of identity as a central concern', and for whom 'a traditional notion of good life and of consensual social relations' plays a prominent role (ibid.).

Like Touraine's theory, Eder's scheme departs from orthodox Marxist theory and traditional terminological conventions; it has to be confronted on its own terms. It provokes a number of questions. Since the centrality of 'class' is assumed, does the scheme admit at all the possibility of questioning the 'class nature' of important social conflicts? How does Eder distinguish class and movement, when both are seen as 'actors', and both are characterized in sociocultural terms? The notion of 'social actor' when applied to 'new social movements' seems to imply much more consistency and unity of purpose than most empirical studies reveal.

The key propositions about the allegedly 'incommensurable interests, norms and values' articulated by the new movements and the contradictory (insoluble) character of conflict over identity creation, raise serious doubts in light of both the relatively successful absorption of principles of ecological prudence in the capitalist productive practices (e.g. Papadakis, 1993) and the proliferation of collective identitites within the framework of liberal democratic societies. One may question, in other words, the degree to which the new movements radically challenge and transcend the social order of advanced liberal democracies (*ergo*, reflect 'class conflicts').

Finally, the claim that the social and cultural features identified with the new social movements correspond to the sociocultural characteristics attributed to the 'new middle classes' (via the allegedly 'central concerns' and normative orientations) is highly questionable. Concerns with the 'good life' and 'identity' can hardly be confined to any class, or any specific category of people. Many analysts argue that materialistic concerns (one meaning of the term 'good life') are typical among the opponents of the new movements.

Eder's interpretive scheme seems to gloss over too many conspicuous features of new movements, such as their cyclical pattern (hard to square with any class account), enormous diversity of concerns (making it difficult to identify the allegedly 'central' ones) and generation-specific bases of support (ignored by the scheme). As argued below, some alternative interpretive paradigms have the advantages of parsimony, sensitivity to these striking features and a good empirical fit.

Beyond the class paradigm

Four such alternative accounts of mass social movements are outlined here. They revolve around the concepts of generation, 'status politics', civil society and action systems. Some movement analyses mix these different accounts and conflate them with versions of (modified) class accounts.[27]

Mass movements and generations
Students of Fascist movements, civil rights campaigns in the USA, Polish Solidarity and the Western 'new movements' agree that both support for movement causes and participation in movement activities have been strongly correlated with age: all these movements have attracted disproportionate numbers of young people.[28] One explanation for this regularity was 'youth radicalism': young people are less integrated into the dominant social order, and youth subcultures tend to be critical and adversarial, thus forming the natural habitat for protest movements. More sophisticated versions utilize the concept of generation, which is more firmly grounded in classical social theory (for example, Mannheim, 1952).

Generations have to be distinguished from mere cohorts and age groups; they include people sharing certain formative experiences and, consequently, certain orientations, value preferences and attitudes, which set them apart from other generations and are carried with them to an older age. Divisions between generations reflect sociohistorical watersheds. Some of these watersheds have been shared by many societies, thus producing common generational categories cutting across societal boundaries. One can distinguish, for example, the 'post-Second-World-War generation' in most advanced Western societies as comprising those people whose 'formative experiences' came at a time of the post-Second-World-War 'long boom', and who, as a result of these experiences, developed specific orientations and value preferences. In Eastern Europe one may identify similar cross-national categories: the 'Stalinist generation', including those who were brought up under the shadow of war and the post-war Stalinist terror, and the 'post-Stalinist' generation formed during political 'thaws' and reforms.[29]

Generational accounts highlight the fact that support for Fascist movements came principally from young men radicalized by the experience of war, economic depression and the political instability of the 1920s. Similarly, the anti-partocratic movements in Eastern Europe mobilized the post-Stalinist generations of people born after the Second World War and brought up in an atmosphere of increasing security, prosperity and optimism.[30] Support for Western eco-pax movements and 'new politics' has been strongly correlated with generational divisions. Perhaps the best-known version of this account is Ingelhart's 'post-materialist' interpretation, supported by a comparative analysis of the orientations of movement supporters and sympathizers in more than a dozen advanced societies.[31]

Explanations in terms of generational orientations shift the emphasis from socioeconomic to sociocultural factors, from structural configurations to sociohistorical sequences. Some critics go one step further and claim that in explaining political behaviour in general, 'the declining importance of class appears to be the major factor in accounting for the decline in the explanatory power of social characteristics as a whole' (Baker et al., 1981: 192).

New social movements and status politics
As suggested earlier, many accounts which are regarded here as 'status interpretations' have been conflated with class interpretations. For example, central elements of Parkin's (1968) arguments, derivations from Gouldner's (1979) 'new class' theories, and some aspects of Eder's class-culturalist interpretations are akin to status accounts.

The latter have been most clearly and self-consciously presented by Turner (1988), who combines the theoretical insights of Weber and T.H. Marshall with contemporary work on lifestyles and consumption patterns. Turner sees status theories as particularly relevant for explaining some of the new Western movements: 'To understand contemporary social movements (such as feminism, gay politics, animal liberation, the politics of aging, or movements related to children's rights) we need a theory of status groups and status politics, because the conventional Marxist emphasis on economic power and economic classes is inadequate' (1988: 44). Such movements, often merging with the dominant eco-pax stream, represent the struggle of 'status columns' and 'status groups' for political recognition of their distinctiveness, needs and interests using the idiom of citizenship and political rights. The mobilization of this idiom, and the consequent formation of 'lifestyle', identity-oriented and civil-rights-oriented 'status politics', is causally linked with the historical development of liberal democratic systems with their specific ideology and powerful welfare state machinery. As a result of this historic change, the old conflict between the working class and the bourgeoisie has been replaced by a more complex pattern of conflicts and struggles of status communities and blocs for identity, political recognition and welfare provision.

While the civil rights movements and minority rights campaigns represent the 'political status politics' which uses the idiom of citizenship and aims at legitimizing political entitlements, 'cultural status politics' aims at defending specific lifestyles, that is, 'the totality of cultural practices such as dress, speech, outlook and bodily dispositions' (Turner, 1988: 66). Although Turner does not explicitly link this aspect of status with new social movements, he clearly opens the way for such an interpretation. Most new movements (e.g. feminism) involve claims for the recognition and legitimization of cultural distinctiveness.

The concept of 'status politics' forms an important part of interpretations that see the rise of new social movements as a symptom of postmodern processes of 'hyper-differentiation', class decomposition and class/partisan de-alignment. Proponents of the 'decomposition thesis' follow Turner's line of argument in questioning the link between socioeconomic classes and contemporary sociopolitical cleavages. For them, class divisions in the industrialized West are waning as a consequence of the fragmentation of the major industrial classes, increasing reflexivity, and the autonomization of the sociopolitical and sociocultural spheres. This weakening of connections between social conflicts and the socioeconomic structure is an aspect of a normal process of social change.[32] One consequence of this change is the end of the polarization of the old class/party blocs; another is the erosion of party-dominated 'power politics' and its gradual supplementation by increasingly prominent 'status politics' and 'life politics' (e.g. Giddens, 1991).

'Status politics' interpretations have two weak spots. First, by assuming that movements focus on the sectional interests of status categories, they cannot adequately explain the clearly universalistic concerns articulated by most new (especially eco-pax) movements. Such concerns cannot easily be linked to any sectional interests or specific status group claims. It is also hard to see all the Green mobilizations as strongly linked with status-lifestyle issues, although some element of lifestyle politics is undoubtedly present in eco-pax mobilizations.[33] Secondly, in its current version at least, the status politics accounts cannot be extended to non-Western mass movements, such as the East European or Islamic mobilizations. They need to be supplemented by more general accounts.

New social movements and civil society
The concept of 'civil society' has been applied by some students of the American feminist and civil rights movements, dissident movements in Soviet-dominated Eastern Europe, and the 'people power' (anti-Marcos) mobilizations in the Philippines.[34] This concept marks a predominantly West European perspective evolving out of critical re-evaluation of Marxist class analysis. The most vigorously challenged aspects of Marxism are its economism, class reductionism, and the anti-capitalist stance critical of all bourgeois institutions, including legal-constitutional and parliamentary ones. The accounts erected on these critical foundations are often branded 'post-Marxist', because of their rejection of both the orthodox class theory and the anti-bourgeois stance. The 'post-Marxist' theorists stress the novelty of the 'new social movements' and contrast them with the 'old' movements, mainly of the class-socialist type. More importantly, they locate the new movements within the broader realm of 'civil society' rather than within class relations and class conflicts.

The 'new social movements' differ from the old (class-based) anti-capitalist labour, racial and agrarian movements by showing

> a self-understanding that abandons revolutionary dreams in favour of the idea of structural reform, along with a defence of civil society that does not seek to abolish the autonomous functioning of political and economic systems – in a phrase, self-limiting radicalism . . . [C]lass background does not determine the collective identities of the actors or the stakes of their action. Contemporary actors abandon what they see as the 'productivist' cultural model of the Old Left, as well as its modes of organization. Instead of forming unions or political parties . . . they focus on grass-roots politics and create horizontal, directly democratic associations that are loosely federated on a national level. Moreover, they target the social domain of 'civil society' rather than the economy or state, raising issues concerned with the democratization of structures

of everyday life and focusing on forms of communication and collective identity. (Cohen, 1985: 664–7)

As far as their social bases and constituencies are concerned, the new movements are transfunctional, and they attract diffuse social categories formed along locality, gender, ethnic and lifestyle lines. Their membership is transient and fluid, with a decentralized, informal and polymorphous organizational structure.[35]

These characteristics reflect a tension between the expanding spheres of human autonomy and growing administrative regulation inherent in the logic of post-industrial (late capitalist) development. This tension cannot be reduced to economically based class conflicts; it is generated at the junction of the economic, political-administrative and normative subsystems. Movements articulate the expanding spheres of 'civil society' in opposition to the administrative domain of the state and its 'colonisation of the life-world' (Habermas, 1987; Offe, 1985).[36]

The concept of 'civil society' lies at the centre of 'post-Marxist' theorizing. It refers to social practices which are located outside the sphere of the political society and the state.[37] Civil society encompasses social relations which develop in the processes of self-identification and self-organization of spontaneously formed social subjects: informal groups, gender categories, local associations and so on. It involves five major dimensions: spatial/territorial (national, regional, neighbourhood communities); sexual (feminist and women's rights groups); religious/ethnic/racial; occupational associations (unions, professional associations); and generational categories (Urry, 1981: 70–3; Keane, 1988: 13–29).

Offe (1985) links the new movements with 'decommodified' social categories. The logic of late capitalist development includes growing étatization and increasing political-administrative penetration of the economy by the state apparatuses. This, in turn, alters the pattern of power distribution by making inequalities more politicized and more state dependent. The distribution of social inequalities and the identities of social actors emerging in the process of stratification include the new essential component: a relation to state power. The process of democratization widens this access, but does not alter the principal market- and property-based matrix of power. Consequently, the socioeconomic classes generated by the market and property relations coexist with increasingly salient 'decommodified categories', such as students and welfare recipients, who lack economic power and political influence. The role of these politically generated groups and peripheral categories – most important for understanding the new social movements – cannot be deduced from, or reduced to, the formulas of orthodox class analysis. New social movements thus reflect new social forces. They seek 'to politicize the institutions of civil society in ways that are not constrained by the channels of representative-bureaucratic political institutions, and thereby to reconstitute a civil society that is no longer dependent upon ever more regulation, control and intervention' (Offe, 1985: 820). They do so in a way which extends the boundaries of conventional politics, broadens the political agendas and mobilizes new social categories. These categories, and the new political idiom they adopt, reflect the contradictions inherent in modern society and offer a promise of their progressive resolution.

Cohen and Arato (1992) offer a more radical critique of the class interpretation. They replace the Marxist class theory with a theory of the historical formation and expansion in Western societies of 'civil society' – social initiatives independent of the state and aiming at self-determination. The key aspects of this 'civil society' – legality, pluralism and public debate – developed during the bourgeois-democratic revolutions and nineteenth-century social movements. The origins of political rights, pluralism and the formation of the public sphere coincided with the development of bourgeois society. They were subsequently institutionalized in parliamentary procedures, democratic constitutions, citizenship rights, and legal norms of due process, and were further enhanced by the development of free associations and media-related public opinion.

Cohen and Arato (1992) see the new social movements as the articulation and progressive institutionalization of civil society through ongoing challenges to power inequalities and the extension of the principles of democratic dialogue, legality, plurality and publicity to all areas of social life, including the economy. The new movements 'construe the cultural models, norms and institutions of civil society as the main stakes of social conflict' (1992: 523) but they also target the institutions and actors in political society. They thus develop a 'dual character' by operating on both sides of the system/lifeworld division.

The civil society accounts face some serious problems. First, the very concept of 'civil society' is vague. It serves more as an identity tag for the 'post-Marxist' camp than as a genuine analytical tool. Accounts of mass movements in terms of 'articulation and targeting of civil society' look more like *ad hoc* descriptions than theoretical explanations. Secondly, the civil society theorists exaggerate the differences between the 'old' and 'new' movements. In their eagerness to present social movements as 'positive', democratizing and emancipatory forces, they ignore those movements (e.g.

Fascist) and forms of contemporary social activism (e.g. nationalist, fundamentalist) which do not fit the liberal-democratic sentiments underlying the civil society schemes. This ideological preference appears as a selective blindness which limits the analytical and theoretical sharpness of the civil society studies. Despite their aspirations to produce a general theory of civil society, 'post-Marxist' studies seldom look outside libertarian activism in Western Europe.

Social movements or action systems?
According to Melucci, environmental, anti-nuclear and feminist activism reflects a new field of conflicts in post-industrial, complex, advanced capitalist societies. It is a cultural and symbolic field where the stakes include identities and autonomy, and it marks a shift from the old political-economic conflicts – represented by actor-like entities (classes) struggling against their class opponents and for the extension of citizenship – to current cultural/symbolic conflicts, where 'highly differentiated systems increasingly produce and distribute resources for individualization, for self-realization, for an autonomous building of personal and collective identities . . . for becoming effective terminals of complex information networks' (Melucci, 1984: 827). While the 'old' movements were primarily concerned with citizenship, political rights and economic interests, the new 'movements' – or rather diffuse systems of action analysed under this label – represent a shift of focus; they mark conflicts about 'frameworks of sense' and general normative and linguistic codes. Such conflicts concern

> codes, formal regulators of knowledge, and the languages which organize our learning processes and our social relations . . . [and] take place principally on symbolic ground, by means of the challenging and upsetting of the dominant codes upon which social relations are founded in high density informational systems. The mere existence of a symbolic challenge is in itself a method of unmasking the dominant codes, a different way of perceiving and naming the world. (Melucci, 1988: 248)

Actors in such conflicts lack permanence and organizational identity. They form loose and ephemeral 'networks submerged in everyday life'. The networks act as both media and message, since their very form carries 'alternative frameworks of sense', alternative experiences and the messages of symbolic defiance. Because of their cultural/symbolic focus, the success or failure of such actions cannot be assessed in terms of their political efficacy (impact on decision-making). Instead, one should focus on their sociocultural efficacy; promoting institutional modernization through changing social practices; cultural innovation in the area of the norms guiding 'language, sexual customs, affective relationships, dress and eating habits', and spawning new elites (Melucci, 1988: 249).

There is an important difference in interpretation, however, which sets Melucci apart from other 'new social movement' and 'civil society' theorists. In his analysis, the differentiation and fragmentation of both the state and private interests make the notions of a 'movement' and a 'civil society' lose their substance. In a complex society, the former need to be analysed as diffuse systems of action; the latter as general symbolic orientations detached from social groups and organizational entities (parties, interest groups, etc.). As Melucci argues in Chapter 4 of this volume, '[s]ocial movements, therefore, should not be viewed as *personnages*, as living characters acting on the stage of history, but as socially constructed collective realities' (p. 110). They are social accomplishments, and the key task of social analysts is to identify the processes through which the unity of action – for both the participants and observers – is accomplished. Sociological analysis of these processes of social de- and re-composition leads Melucci to conclude that we may be facing the end of (old) politics, as well as the end of (actor-type) social movements. This is a most radical breach not only with class interpretation, but also with traditional sociology which views action as socially embedded and structurally rooted (and therefore moulded and constrained). Authentic action, Melucci suggests, is free action, that is, open-ended and creative; attempts to derive it from 'structural class condition', as a reflection of a class actor, result in constructing 'an actor without an action' (see p. 107 in this volume). Melucci's suggestion is a welcome corrective and supplement to the mainstream sociological studies; however, as a sole preoccupation, as 'the task of sociological analysis',[38] it would unnecessarily constrain and impoverish movement studies.

Conclusions

The arguments presented here go one step further than standard critiques of the Marxist class theory which question the relevance of only the old class divisions for understanding contemporary conflicts and mass social movements. They question the utility of class analysis in general by addressing a seemingly obvious but often ignored question: why should mass social movements have a class basis? The key assumption of class analysis – that all important social conflicts have a class basis and class character because class represents the key social dimension of modern (capitalist) society – does not withstand critical scrutiny. In contemporary advanced society class divisions are waning and the political relevance of class in general is declining.[39] Contemporary mass movements are a symptom of this process: they show few links with what are traditionally identified as class issues, interests and occupational bases. They are more diverse, fragmented and more detached from socioeconomic bases than the class interpretations suggest.

Despite the decline in the political importance of class, attempts to identify class bases of mass social movements persist. Behind these attempts lie not only heavy intellectual and career investments and strong attachments to the long-standing European tradition, but also a notion that identification of the class bases would somehow fortify the political importance of social movements. This is a misconception. Social conflicts do not need to have a class basis in order to be widespread, persistent and historically important. The contemporary movements in Europe (as well as the recent mobilizations in Africa, the Middle East, India, Pakistan and throughout East Asia) have been important, and sometimes revolutionary (as in Eastern Europe), without being obviously or directly class based. In fact, as the students of 'postmodern' change suggest, their importance may lie precisely in their being non-class-based, that is, separated from socioeconomic divisions.

Out of the four alternatives to class explanations discussed above, the generational one (supplemented by situs and mobility) seems to be the most persuasive. It is supported by both a good empirical 'fit' with the data on the social composition of movement supporters, and a convincing theoretical argument about the relationship between movement orientations and the formative experiences. Movements, as argued here, are driven primarily by moral impetus, not by sectional interests. They mobilize intense value concerns, that is, concerns about the violation, corruption or neglect of the general principles and ideals that underlie the cherished visions of good society and dignified life. Unlike modern conventional power politics, which is highly bureaucratized and routinely translates value concerns into questions of influence and proper administrative procedures, movement politics activates concerns about the threatened values and mobilizes the value idiom of protest. The content of thus activated values, and with it the orientations of the dominant movements, may vary. What is constant and found among all mass movements is the intense value-focus, a strikingly *Wert*-rational character which is clearly articulated in movement actions. Such intense value-focus, as Mannheim and Inglehart suggest, tends to appear at the generational junctions; it reflects historical watersheds and changing formative experiences. It is carried by cultural-historical, rather than structural-economic, segments of society.

This is, obviously, not an attempt to replace one deterministic formula (class) by another (generation). Rather, it is argued that, in relative terms and as far as mass social movements are concerned, the generational explanation fares much better than other general explanations. There are, of course, also some other important determinants of movement support, some of which may be specific to certain types of movement. Elsewhere I claim, for example, that the capacity to express value commitments in action also depends on autonomy and freedom from communal and traditional constraints, which is associated with certain occupational-sectoral locations (social 'situs') and mobilities (for details see Pakulski, 1991).

Generational accounts seem to fare better than class interpretations, as well as the popular 'status' accounts that point to the importance of (high) education and professional status (e.g. Rootes, Chapter 9 in this volume). The latter face the major problem of explanatory efficacy – the characteristics used by their advocates in explaining movement support are not distinctive to movement supporters; they are also found, with similar intensity, outside movements, for example among activists of 'conventional' political parties. The error of such accounts is not in attributing high educational and certain types of professional status to movement supporters, but in attributing a distinctiveness – and therefore an explanatory potential – to this fact. To put it bluntly, all political activism – new and old, Left and Right – attracts a disproportionately high proportion of educated people with professional status (including the teachers and the 'caring professions'). This is as true of Green movement activists as it is of Labour Party activists.

The generational account is one example of a broader family of post-Marxist explanations which mark a paradigmatic shift away from class analysis. This shift follows the process not only of a broadening of the research horizon, but also of social change. This is particularly clear in Western Europe where the processes of postmodernization erode bureaucratic-corporatist politics, trigger value-concerns, generate new identities, and spawn new political actors. Contemporary Western social movements are seldom numerically strong, but they seem to be particularly diverse and more separated from socioeconomic divisions than their early-industrial predecessors. This diversity and autonomy limits the heuristic value and theoretical utility of the Marxist paradigm. The class paradigm must either be supplemented or altogether discarded.

Notes

1. Nisbet (1966: 179–82) and Luhman (1993: 135) point to the early nineteenth-century formation of both concepts. Sombart's *Socialism and the Social Movement* was first published in 1896. In the Leninist and Maoist versions of Marxism, the challenge to the bourgeois status quo comes from the alliance of workers and (poor) peasants.

2. See, for example, Arendt (1966) and Kornhauser (1959). For a more detailed and critical discussion of the mass society interpretation of Fascism see Hagtvet and Kuhnl (1980).

3. The orthodox Marxists saw Fascism either as the 'power of finance capital' or as a version of Bonapartism (i.e. a dictatorship defending dominant class interests against the radical challenge). The middle-class interpretations discussed here depict Fascism as a petit-bourgeois response to the increasing precariousness of their social position caused by the concentration of capital, proletarianization of small businessmen, and the trade union challenge (see Hagtvet and Kuhnl, 1980).

4. It reverberates in Parkin's (1968) study of 'middle-class radicalism', Gouldner's (1979) version of the intellectual 'new class', and Offe's (1985) account of new social movements.

5. For a discussion of 'conceptual stretch', see Sartori (1970). Problems with definitions of social movement are discussed in Wilkinson (1971: ch.1), Tilly (1978: ch.1) and Pakulski (1991: chs 1–2). The sarcastic comment was made by Alberto Melucci.

6. Polymorphy means many diverse forms, the absence of a single organizational structure. Value-charged refers to 'substantive' (in Weberian parlance) orientations in movement actions as distinct from formal and instrumental orientations.

7. The former position is represented by Miliband (1989); the latter by Touraine. According to Touraine (1981: 68), 'There can be no class without class consciousness.'

8. See Salvatorelli (1923) quoted in Lipset (1959: 135) and Hagtvet and Kuhnl (1980: 28). A similar diagnosis was offered by Geiger in 1932.

9. According to Lipset (1959: 131), 'a study of the social bases of different modern mass movements suggests that each major social stratum has both democratic and extremist political expressions. The extremist movements of the left, right, and centre (communism and Peronism, traditional authoritarianism, and fascism) are based primarily on the working, upper, and middle classes, respectively.'

10. Some Marxists link Fascism with the interests of the dominant propertied classes, as a 'Bonapartist' coup pre-empting a revolution and destroying the political influence of the Left.

11. The argument linking liberal democracy with the middle class is presented by Barrington Moore (1966) and Huntington (1984). Attempts to explain Fascism in terms of 'middle-class action' are even less convincing. Both the immediate effects of Fascist mobilizations (the chaotic 'politics of the street') and their ultimate consequences (the aggressive and illiberal Fascist regimes in Germany and Italy) are difficult to link with any consistent notion of class interests.

12. As Merkl (1980c: 767) pointed out, the social composition of the NSDAP became very similar to that of other bourgeois parties and even the Catholic Centre Party. (The German Communist Party, though, had a bigger proportion of manual workers than did other parties.)

13. See, for example, Kele (1972), Merkl (1980a, 1980c), Felice (1977: 179), Hamilton (1971) and Winkler (1979).

14. About 24 per cent of the PNF members in 1921 were under 21 years old. Compared with the Italian population at that time, students were over-represented by nearly 10: 1. Males were 14 times as numerous as females. Of the male members of military age 80 per cent were war veterans. Most of the members came from urban areas. The pre-1933 composition of the NSDAP shows a similar profile. In 1923 half of the party members were under 23 years of age. In 1930 it was still a remarkably youthful organization, with 37–40 per cent aged under 26 years. Students, white-collar employees, professionals and businessmen were two to three times as numerous as in the general population. See, for example, Merkl (1980a: 259–62; 1980c: 764–70), Felice (1980: 314), Baglieri (1980: 324–30) and Roberts (1980: 341). Social profiles of Fascist activists are discussed by Merkl (1980b: 271–2) and Baglieri (1980: 333).

15. See Childers (1979), Merkl (1980a, 1980c) and Noakes and Pridham (1983: 78–9). On the issue of takeovers and transformation of mass movements into mass parties see Pakulski (1991). On the changing social composition of the movement see Winkler (1979: 163–76) and Merkl (1980b, 1980c).

16. See, for example, Kennedy (1991) and Pakulski (1986, 1991: ch.5).

17. It is true that some movement activists, and some commentators, referred to the 'working class' and, more frequently, the 'working people' as the principal constitutency (e.g. Starski, 1982). However, these terms had a rather specific meaning. 'Workers', in these contexts, meant 'all those who work' as opposed to 'those who rule'. The division was political-organizational rather than socioeconomic. It separated rank-and-file employees in non-managerial positions from party activists and company executives (who usually are also party officials). Moreover, the term was deployed in a highly critical context where references to 'working class' rebellion were exceptionally embarrassing to the nominally 'working-class' regime. For Solidarity supporters this label served as a shield. This critical and defensive potential of the term, rather than its accuracy in depicting the movement constituency, caused its popularity. See Adamski (1982a, 1982b), Jasiewicz and Rychard (1986) and Adamski et al. (1989).

18. For example, Starski (1982), Kurczewski (1982), Pankow (1987) saw the movement as rooted in subordinate positions in both the division of labour (producers) and power (subordinates).

19. The vanguard of the movement was located in 'key' industries with a long tradition of worker organization, high wages, and dense networks of social contacts. It was in these centres that social protests erupted in 1956, 1970 and 1976, and the first underground trade unions were formed in the 1970s. Such strategic locations, combined with communication links, social cohesion and a tradition of dissent, formed a good medium for mobilization. See Johnson (1981), Adamski (1982a), Pakulski (1986) and Pankow (1987).

20. 'New class' theories have diverse sources: an anarchist stream, which points to the dangers of a state-based 'intellectual class'; a technocratic-bureaucratic stream, popularized in the 1930–1950s and diagnosing the rise of the new 'managerial class' (e.g. Burnham, 1941); and a 'knowledge class'/'critical intellectuals' stream of the 1970s and 1980s, professing the rise of the new radical and critical social forces (e.g. Gouldner, 1979; Bell, 1973). For a review of the new class streams see Brint (1984), and Szelenyi and Martin (1988–9). Applicability to the analysis of the Western Green movements is discussed by Rootes (1990). East European new class theorists are divided between the views expressed by Konrad and Szelenyi (1979), who see the new class as the social basis of the communist authorities, and their

critics (e.g. Frentzel-Zagorska and Zagorski, 1989) who claim that the intelligentsia formed the major oppositional force to state-socialist regimes. Some Western commentators, like Kristol (1979), treat the new class as dangerous rebels against liberal-conservative values. Others, like Gouldner (1979), see them as a counter-class challenging the old class of technocrats, owners and business executives. Following Inglehart's (1977) arguments, Cotgrove and Duff (1981) define the 'new class' as the collective carrier of new values and orientations, and a similar perspective has been adopted by many European and Australian students of new politics (e.g. Eckersley, 1989).

21. See Brandt (1990) for a good account of cycles of cultural criticism and Brym (1980) on the role of intellectuals in politics. Movements of the 'New Right' also attract predominantly urban, educated and white-collar supporters.

22. They are based on Dahrendorf's (1959, 1988) interpretations, and have been used by Kriesi (1989) and Mattausch (1989). Kriesi (1989) analysed supporters of peace, anti-nuclear, ecology, women's and squatter movements in the Netherlands. Mattausch (1989) suggests that the label 'state class' could be useful in describing the principal constituency of the peace movement (CND) in Britain.

23. The German Green supporters and activists are markedly over-represented in the under-35 age group; they are frequently academics, students and generally public employees; the single most numerous category among them is that of students (22 per cent; compared with 3–4 per cent among supporters of other parties). Highly educated people are almost three times more frequently found among them than among the general public; professionals and other white-collar workers are almost twice as numerous as in the population at large. The most striking disproportion, however, is in age composition. See Baker et al. (1981: chs 2, 6), Papadakis (1984: 120–2, 139–41; 1993), Hulsberg (1988: 70–85) and Von Oertzen quoted in Hulsberg (1988: 115). It is also noted, however, that they are predominantly urban, better educated and more likely to be public sector employed than are typical members of the 'young generation'. For a comprehensive review of the results see Hulsberg (1988: ch. 7).

24. For a review of results, see Cotgrove (1982), Morrison and Dunlap (1986), Eckersley (1989), Kriesi (1989), Pakulski (1991) and Rucht (1991). The most frequent occupational categories among them were professionals (mainly teachers) and students, and they showed high territorial mobility, high autonomy (in the workplace) and weak religious affiliations. The social composition of peace, feminist, minority rights and pro-Third World movements' constituencies is analysed in Muller-Rommel (1985), Hulsberg (1988) and Kriesi (1989).

25. A movement is, in Touraine's (1981: 77) words, 'the organized collective behaviour of a class actor struggling against its class adversary for the social control of his historicity'. Historicity (*l'historicité*) is one of the basic categories in Touraine's analysis. It refers to the ability of a society, class or group to produce a model of its own functioning that embraces knowledge, investment and social norms.

26. In fact, as argued below, Touraine belongs to the stream of theorizing which poses the most radical challenge to the orthodox (that is structural and socioeconomic) class interpretation.

27. These four 'alternative' interpretations do not exhaust the list of interpretive paradigms. One may also mention socio-demographic or age-group interpretations ('youth movements') favoured by social psychologists (reviewed in Van Liere and Dunlap, 1980); 'mass society' or 'marginalization' accounts, largely discredited by contemporary students of social movements but applied to 'Islamic' movements and

contemporary nationalistic movements; and somewhat vague 'frustration/deprivation' accounts (e.g. Gurr, 1970).

28. See, for example, Merkl (1980b), Adamski (1982a), Van Liere and Dunlap (1980), McAdam (1982), Baker et al. (1981), Dalton (1988), Papadakis (1993).

29. The concept of generation was utilized in the 1920s and 1930s by students of Fascist movements. More recently, it was deployed by Baker et al. (1981), Inglehart (1977, 1989, 1990), and Abramson and Inglehart (1992) in the analysis of new social movements in the West. Generational watersheds vary among the East European societies, depending on the pattern of de-Stalinization (see Higley and Pakulski, 1992).

30. People belonging to this generation show assertiveness, high aspiration and a low level of deference and fear. It must be kept in mind that generational watersheds may vary among East European societies, because of differences in times and depths of political 'thaws'.

31. See Baker et al. (1981), Dalton (1988), Papadakis (1993), Inglehart (1989, 1990), Abramson and Inglehart (1992). There is no agreement among the students of the 'new' Western movements as to the permanence of the generational effects. While most students agree with Inglehart that the post-materialist value shift is more or less permanent, some critics point to the declining support for the new movements among the youngest cohorts (the 'post-post-war generation').

32. Its symptoms include political/class de-alignment, decline in class voting and erosion of identification with, allegiance to, and support for the major class-based 'milieu parties'. The decomposition thesis was most clearly formulated by Dahrendorf (1959) and subsequently elaborated by students of 'new (citizen) politics' (e.g. Dalton et al., 1984; Crook et al., 1992: chs 4–6). Milieu parties, also called 'people's parties' and 'parties of democratic integration', are mass parties representing the interests of large-scale structurally based segments of society.

33. Especially those concerned with urban developments (e.g. mass mobilizations in Germany against urban redevelopments, airport construction, nuclear power, etc.); see Hulsberg (1988) and Papadakis (1984).

34. Keane (1988: 2–13) links the revival of interests in civil society vs. the state distinction in the 1970s and 1980s with (1) the difficulties in economic restructuring experienced by West European societies; (2) political controversies surrounding the failures of Keynesian economics and welfare state policies; (3) the sudden growth of civil rights, feminist and eco-pax movements; and (4) the reinvigoration of dissident movements in Eastern Europe, especially in Poland. For application of the concept in the analysis of East European movements see the contributions to Keane's (1988) and Misztal's (1985) volumes. The Philippines movement is analysed in Misztal and Misztal (1986).

35. See, for example, Feher and Heller (1983), Cohen (1985), Offe (1985) and Scott (1990: ch. 1).

36. The epistemological and normative foundations of the 'post-Marxist' perspective were laid by Habermas. Although he did not develop a fully-fledged theory of new social movements, his critique of instrumental rationality and his normative theory of discursive rationality and communicative ethics provided the background for the theoretical reflections of Offe, Arato and Cohen. Habermas devoted to this subject only a few pages of his *magnum opus, The Theory of Communicative Action*, Vol. 2, pp. 391–7 (1987). These remarks were translated and published separately in *Telos* (Habermas, 1981). The new social movements, according to Habermas, appear at the 'seam between the system and life world' and are symptomatic of the

waning self-evidence of the old value standards reflected in the concepts of natural law, economic laws, rational man, etc. They mark new conflicts which 'no longer arise in the areas of material reproduction; they are no longer channelled through parties and organizations; and they can no longer be alleviated by compensations that conform to the system. Rather, the new conflicts arise in areas of cultural reproduction, social integration and socialization. They are manifested in sub-institutional, extra-parliamentary forms of protest . . . . In short, the new conflicts are not sparked by problems of distribution, but concern the grammar of forms of life' (1981: 34). The new movements also contain utopian elements, instrumental orientations and articulate anti-modernist romanticism.

37. The concept has a long history dating from at least the mid-eighteenth century (Keane, 1988: 43). Current usage among the 'post-Marxist' theorists follow its rather loose Gramscian incarnation in which (unlike in Hegel's version) civil society is contrasted with the state. It refers to 'the ensemble of organisms commonly called "private" . . . the sum of social institutions which are not directly part of the government, the judiciary or the repressive bodies (police, armed forces) . . . the sphere in which a dominant social group organizes consent and hegemony, as opposed to political society where it rules by coercion and direct domination. It is also a sphere where the dominated social groups may organize their opposition and where an alternative hegemony may be constructed' (Forgacs, 1988: 420).

38. And this is what Melucci, in Chapter 4 of the present volume, seems to suggest: 'The task of sociological analysis should be to question the datum [i.e. the notion of unified 'movement-actor'] in order to ascertain how it is produced and dissect the empirical unity to discover the plurality of analytical elements – orientations, meanings and relationships – which converge in the same phenomenon.'

39. See, for example, Clark and Lipset (1991) and Clark et al. (1993).

References

Abramson, P.R. and Inglehart, R. (1992) 'Generational replacement and value change in eight West European societies', *British Journal of Political Science*, 22(2): 183–228.

Adamski, W.W. (1982a) 'Structural and generational aspects of a social conflict', *Sisyphus*, 3 (IFiS, Polish Academy of Sciences, Warsaw): 49–57.

Adamski, W.W. (1982b) 'In the face of political crisis', *Sisyphus*, 4 (IFiS, Polish Academy of Sciences, Warsaw): 174–81.

Adamski, W.W., Bialecki, I., Jasiewicz, K., Kolarska-Bobinska, L. and Rychard, A. (1989) 'Poles 1980–84: dynamics of social conflict and consensus', *Sisyphus*, 5 (IFiS, Polish Academy of Sciences, Warsaw): 241–60.

Arendt, H. (1966) *The Origins of Totalitarianism*. Glencoe, IL: Free Press.

Baglieri, J. (1980) 'Italian Fascism and the crisis of liberal hegemony: 1901–22', in S.U. Larsen, B. Hagtvet and J.P. Myklebust (eds), *Who Were the Fascists? Social Roots of European Fascism*. Bergen: Universitetsforlaget. pp. 318–36.

Baker, K.L., Dalton, R.J. and Hildebrandt, K. (1981) *Germany Transformed; Political Culture and the New Politics*. Cambridge, MA: Harvard University Press.

Bell, D. (1973) *The Coming of Post Industrial Society*. New York: Basic Books.

Bell, D. (1979) 'The new class: a muddled concept', *Society*, January/February: 15–23.

Brandt, K-W. (1990) 'Cyclical aspects of new social movements', in R.J. Dalton and M. Kuechler (eds), *Challenging the Political Order*. Cambridge: Polity Press. pp. 23–42.

Brint, S. (1984) '"New class" and cumulative trend explanations of the liberal political attitudes of professionals', *American Journal of Sociology*, 90: 30–71.

Brym, R.J. (1980) *Intellectuals and Politics*. London: Allen & Unwin.

Burnham, J. (1941) *The Managerial Revolution*. New York: John Day.

Childers, T. (1979) 'The social bases of the National Socialist vote', in G.L. Mosse (ed.), *International Fascism: New Thoughts and New Approaches*. London: Sage. pp. 161–88.

Clark, T.N. and Lipset, S.M. (1991) 'Are social classes dying?', *International Sociology*, 6(4): 397–410.

Clark, T.N., Lipset, S.M. and Rempel, M. (1993) 'The declining political significance of social class', *International Sociology*, 8(3): 293–316.

Cohen, J.L. (1985) 'Strategy or identity: new theoretical paradigms and contemporary social movements', *Social Research*, 52(4): 663–716.

Cohen, J.L. and Arato, A. (1992) *Civil Society and Political Theory*. Cambridge, MA: MIT Press.

Cotgrove, S. (1982) *Catastrophe or Cornucopia*. Chichester: John Wiley.

Cotgrove, S. and Duff, A. (1981) 'Environmentalism, values and social change', *British Journal of Sociology*, 32(1): 92–110.

Crook, S., Pakulski, J. and Waters, M. (1992) *Postmodernization*. London: Sage.

Dahrendorf, R. (1959) *Class and Class Conflict in Industrial Societies*. London: Routledge.

Dahrendorf, R. (1988) *The Modern Social Conflict*. London: Weidenfeld & Nicholson.

Dalton, R.J. (1988) *Citizen Politics in Western Democracies*. Chatham, NJ: Chatham Publishers.

Dalton, R.J. et al. (eds) (1984) *Electoral Change in Advanced Industrial Democracies*. Princeton, NJ: Princeton University Press.

Eckersley, R. (1989) 'Green politics and the new class', *Political Studies*, 37(2): 205–23.

Eder, K. (1993) *The New Politics of Class. Social Movements and Cultural Dynamics in Advanced Societies*. London: Sage.

Feher, F. and Heller, A. (1983) 'From red to green', *Telos*, 4 (September): 35–45.

Felice, R. de (1977) *Interpretations of Fascism*. Cambridge: Harvard University Press.

Felice, R. de (1980) 'Italian fascism and the middle class', in S.U. Larsen, B. Hagtvet and J.P. Myklebust (eds), *Who Were the Fascists? Social Roots of European Fascism*. Bergen: Universitetsforlaget. pp. 312–17

Forgacs, D. (ed.) (1988) *A Gramsci Reader: Selected Writings 1916–35*. London: Lawrence & Wishart.

Frentzel-Zagorska, J. and Zagorski, K. (1989) 'East European intellectuals on the road of dissent: the old prophecy of a new class re-examined', *Politics and Society*, 17(1): 89–113.

Geiger, T.J. (1932) *Die soziale Schichtung des deutschen Volkes: soziographischer Versuch auf statistischer Grundlage*. Stuttgart: F. Enke.

Giddens, A. (1991) *Modernity and Self-Identity*. London: Polity.

84   *Foundations for Collective Action*

Gouldner, A. (1979) *The Future of Intellectuals and the Rise of the New Class*. New York: Seabury.

Gurr, T. (1970) *Why Men Rebel*. Princeton, NJ: Princeton University Press.

Habermas, J. (1981) 'New social movements', *Telos*, 49(Fall): 33–7.

Habermas, J. (1987) *The Theory of Communicative Action*, Vol. 2 (translated by T. McCarthy). London: Polity Press.

Hagtvet, B., and Kuhnl, R. (1980) 'Contemporary approaches to fascism: a survey of paradigms', in S.U. Larsen, B. Hagtvet, and J.P. Myklebust (eds), *Who Were the Fascists? Social Roots of European Fascism*. Bergen: Universitetsforlaget. pp. 26–51.

Hamilton, R.F. (1971) *The Appeal of Fascism*. New York: Avon Books.

Higley, J. and Pakulski, J. (1992) 'Revolution and elite transformation in Eastern Europe', *Australian Journal of Political Science*, 27(1): 104–19.

Hulsberg, W. (1988) *The German Greens: A Social and Political Profile*. London: Verso.

Huntington, S. (1984) 'Will more countries become democratic?', *Political Science Quarterly*, 99(2): 174–95

Inglehart, R. (1977) *The Silent Revolution: Changing Values and Political Styles among Western Publics*. Princeton, NJ: Princeton University Press.

Inglehart, R. (1989) 'Observations on cultural change and postmodernism', in J. R. Gibbins (ed.), *Contemporary Political Culture: Politics in a Postmodern Age*. London: Sage. pp. 251–6.

Inglehart, R. (1990) 'Values, ideology and cognitive mobilization in new social movements', in R.J. Dalton and M. Kuechler (eds), *Challenging the Political Order*. Cambridge: Polity Press. pp. 43–67.

Jasiewicz, K. and Rychard, A. (1986) 'Sociological studies of political attitudes', mimeo, Warsaw: IFiS, Polish Academy of Sciences.

Johnson, P.M. (1981) 'Changing social structure and the political role of manual workers', in J.F. Triska and C. Gatti (eds), *Blue Collar Workers in Eastern Europe*. London: Allen & Unwin. pp. 29–43.

Keane, J. (ed.) (1988) *Civil Society and the State*. London: Verso.

Kele, M. (1972) *Nazis and Workers 1919–33*. Chapel Hill: University of North Carolina Press.

Kennedy, M.D. (1991) *Professionals, Power and Solidarity in Poland*. Cambridge: Cambridge University Press.

Konrad, G. and Szelenyi, I. (1979) *The Intellectuals on the Road to Class Power*. New York: Harcourt Brace Jovanovich.

Kornhauser, W. (1959) *The Politics of Mass Society*. Glencoe, IL: Free Press.

Kriesi, H.P. (1989) 'New social movements and the new class in the Netherlands', *American Journal of Sociology*, 94(5): 1078–116.

Kristol, I. (1979) *Two Cheers for Capitalism*. New York: Basic Books.

Kurczewski, J. (1982) 'The old system and the revolution', *Sisyphus*, 3 (IFiS, Polish Academy of Sciences, Warsaw): 21–32.

Lipset, S.M. (1959) *Political Man*. Garden City, NY: Doubleday.

Lipset, S.M. (1981) *Political Man*, revised edn. London: Heinemann. First published 1959.

Luhman, N. (1993) *Risk: A Sociological Theory*. Berlin and New York: Walter de Gruyter.

McAdam, D. (1982) *Political Process and the Development of Black Insurgency 1930–1970*. Chicago and London: University of Chicago Press.

Mannheim, K. (1952) 'The problem of generations', in P. Kecskemeti (ed.), *Essays on the Sociology of Knowledge*. Oxford: Oxford University Press. pp. 276–422.

Mattausch, J. (1989) 'The peace movement: some answers concerning its social nature and structure', *International Sociology*, 4(2): 217–26.

Melucci, A. (1984) 'An end to social movements?', *Social Science Information*, 23: 819–34.

Melucci, A. (1988) 'Social movements and the democratization of everyday life', in J. Keane (ed.), *Civil Society and the State*. London: Verso. pp. 245–60.

Merkl, P.H. (1980a) 'Introduction', in S.U. Larsen, B. Hagtvet and J.P. Myklebust (eds), *Who Were the Fascists? Social Roots of European Fascism*. Bergen: Universitetsforlaget. pp. 258–67.

Merkl, P.H. (1980b) 'The Nazis of the Abel Collection: why they joined the NSDAP', in S.U. Larsen, B. Hagtvet and J.P. Myklebust (eds), *Who Were the Fascists? Social Roots of European Fascism*. Bergen: Universitetsforlaget. pp. 268–82.

Merkl, P.H. (1980c) 'Comparing Fascist movements', in S.U. Larsen, B. Hagtvet and J.P. Myklebust (eds), *Who Were the Fascists? Social Roots of European Fascism*. Bergen: Universitetsforlaget. pp. 752–83.

Miliband, R. (1989) *Divided Societies: Class Struggle in Contemporary Capitalism*. Oxford: Clarendon Press.

Misztal, B. (1985) 'Social movement against the state', in B. Misztal (ed.), *Poland after Solidarity*. London: Transaction Books. pp. 143–64.

Misztal, B.A. and Misztal, B. (1986) 'The state's capacity to change: the case of Poland and the Philippines', mimeo, School of Humanities, Griffith University, Brisbane.

Moore, B., Jr. (1966) *Social Origins of Dictatorship and Democracy*. Boston: Beacon Press.

Morrison, D.E. and Dunlap, R.E. (1986) 'Environmentalism and elitism: a conceptual and empirical analysis', *Environment Management*, 10(5): 581–9.

Muller-Rommel, F. (1985) 'Social movements and the Greens', *European Journal of Political Research*, 13: 53–67.

Nisbet, R.A. (1966) *The Sociological Tradition*. London: Heinemann.

Noakes, J. and Pridham, G. (1983) *Nazism 1919–45: A Documentary Reader* (Exeter Studies in History No. 6), Vols 1 and 2. Exeter: University of Exeter.

Offe, C. (1985) 'New social movements: challenging the boundaries of institutional politics', *Social Research*, 52(4): 817–67.

Pakulski, J. (1986) 'Leaders of the Solidarity Movement', *Sociology*, 20(1): 64–81.

Pakulski, J. (1991) *Social Movements: The Politics of Moral Protest*. Melbourne: Longman Cheshire.

Pankow, W. (1987) 'U zrodel konfliktu przemyslowego w powojennej Polsce', in M. Marody and A. Sulek (eds), *Rzeczywistosc polska i sposoby radzenia sobie z nia*. Warsaw: Institute of Sociology, University of Warsaw. pp. 65–88.

Papadakis, E. (1984) *The Green Movement in West Germany*. London: Croom Helm.

Papadakis, E. (1993) *Politics and Environment: The Australian Experience*. Sydney: Allen & Unwin.

Parkin, F. (1968) *Middle-class Radicalism*. Manchester: Manchester University Press.

Roberts, D.D. (1980) 'Petty bourgeois fascism in Italy: form and content', in S.U. Larsen, B. Hagtvet, and J.P. Myklebust (eds), *Who Were the Fascists? Social Roots of European Fascism*. Bergen: Universitetsforlaget. pp. 336–49.

Rootes, C.A. (1990) 'A new class? The higher educated and the new politics', paper prepared for the session on 'Intellectuals as New Class', XIIth World Congress of Sociology, Madrid, 9–13 July. (Vol. 2).

86 The Decline of the Marxist Paradigm

Rucht, D. (ed.) (1991) *Research on Social Movements: The State of the Art in Western Europe and the USA*. Frankfurt: Campus Verlag; Boulder, CO: Westview Press.

Salvatorelli, L. (1923) *Nazionalfascismo*. Turin: Piero Gobetti.

Sartori, G. (1970) 'Concept misformation in comparative politics', *American Political Science Review*, 64(4): 1033–53.

Scott, A. (1990) *Ideology and New Social Movements*. London: Unwin Hyman.

Sombart, W. (1909) *Socialism and the Social Movement*. London: Dent.

Starski, S. (1982) *Class Struggle in Classless Poland*. Boston: South End Press.

Szelenyi, I. and Martin, B. (1988–9) 'The three waves of new class theories', *Theory and Society*, 17(5): 645–67.

Tilly, C. (1978) *From Mobilization to Revolution*. Reading, MA: Addison-Wesley.

Touraine, A. (1981) *The Voice and the Eye: An Analysis of Social Movements*. Cambridge and New York: Cambridge University Press.

Touraine, A. (1985) 'An introduction to the study of social movements', *Social Research*, 52(4): 749–88.

Touraine, A., Dubet, F., Wieviorka, M. and Strzelecki, J. (1983) *Solidarity: Poland, 1980–1981*. Cambridge: Cambridge University Press.

Turner, B.S. (1988) *Status*. Milton Keynes: Open University Press.

Urry, J. (1981) *The Anatomy of Capitalist Societies. The Economy, Civil Society and the State*. Cambridge: Polity Press.

Van Liere, K.D. and Dunlap, R.E. (1980) 'The social bases of environmental concern: a review of hypotheses, explanations, and empirical evidence', *Public Opinion Quarterly*, 44: 181–97.

Wilkinson, P. (1971) *Social Movement*. London: Pall Mall.

Winkler, H.A. (1979) 'German society, Hitler and the illusion of restoration 1930–33', in G.L. Mosse (ed.), *International Fascism: New Thoughts and New Approaches*. London: Sage. pp. 143–60.

3

Racism and Social Movements

Michel Wieviorka

An analytic category: social movements

In the study of social movements, racism has never been a central analytic category. Two quite different approaches have been used to address this problem.

First, from a historical perspective, studies have tried to explain why racist ideas have penetrated the labour movement and why the working class, or fractions of it, have adopted racist behaviours. These manifestations of racism have ranged from acts of unorganized violence to situations where a racist ideology was prevalent. The labour movement has sometimes even sustained and institutionalized racist practices. For example, Pierre Milza (1981) has described the violence against Italian farm hands and labourers accused of taking locals' jobs in southern France during the late nineteenth century. This almost riotous violence culminated in eight deaths (according to authorities) at Aigues-Mortes in 1893.[1] For this same period, Michel Winock (1982) has shown how far anti-Semitism permeated French labour organizations. Winock has also demonstrated how, more often than is generally admitted, it turned them against Dreyfus, the French army officer of Jewish descent who had been unjustly convicted of treason but would, thanks to massive protest, be acquitted 12 years later. Studies abound on the American labour movement's longtime colour bar (Hill, 1967; Harris and Spero, 1974) and its discrimination against Asians in California at the turn of the century.

Secondly, from a sociological, political or psycho-sociological perspective, studies have seen collective behaviours marked or motivated by racism as being part of, or related to, a social movement. For example, Hadley Cantril's (1941) psychological theory of social movements focused on lynchings and Nazism. More recently, Birgitta Orfali (1990), while frequently referring to Cantril's research, has sought to show how the far-right French National Front has grown from an activist minority into a movement. If we define 'social movement' in terms similar to Alain Touraine's (1974), then the behaviours studied by Cantril or Orfali turn out to be something else. Nonetheless, this concept can still be helpful when analysing them.

Herein, the phrase 'social movement' will not be used, as is often done in the sociology of collective behaviour, to refer to group reactions to a definite situation. Nor will it serve, as in the sociology of resource mobilization, to refer to behaviours with the aim or strategy of penetrating an institutional system. Instead, the concept 'social movement' will refer to collective actions with a special significance, perhaps deeply hidden under other meanings. These actions are significant because the movement represents the highest level of social action, a protest about very general issues related to what Touraine has called 'historicity'. The actors in a social movement have to be capable of defining their social identities. They have to recognize that they are struggling as subordinates against a dominant social opponent. And they have to see their cause in terms of historicity. Furthermore, these three principles of action should be tightly bound up with each other.

This is a purely analytic definition, not to be confused with any images, or representations, of a social struggle or set of struggles. When talking about the working-class movement, for example, we are designating a historical 'set of facts' of considerable density. This 'whole' teems with meanings; but it does not, at least not always and everywhere, correspond to a movement. In its struggle, the working class may voice limited economic demands, may react to threats against jobs, or may adopt a pressure-group strategy in politics. These multiple meanings of action may (but this does not always happen) form a whole that includes something related to the concept of a social movement as intended here. When this something is so decisive that it shapes other levels and meanings of collective action, we can shift from a sociological definition to a historical proposition. When a set of concrete actions bears on a society's most general orientations, when it polarizes political and intellectual debates, when it serves as a reference mark for other actors' struggles, we can conclude that it is organizing society around the central principle, or cause, it conveys. In this respect, the working-class movement played a leading role in industrial societies (Touraine et al., 1984).

Race and class

Racism has frequently been studied in terms of a society riven with social conflict, shaped by relations of domination and, therefore, animated by the class struggle if not by a social movement. Marxism, in particular, has done this. Its classic is Oliver Cox's *Castes, Class and Race*, which academic sociology ignored or repudiated when it came out in 1948.[2] This Marxist stance was increasingly advocated during the 1960s and 1970s in the United States and United Kingdom, where it is still strong.

Breaking with the ideas prevailing in the United States during the 1930s and 1940s, Cox refused to see race relations as a caste system (i.e. as a relationship forbidding conflict), a concept he thought inappropriate to societies other than India's. Grounding his arguments in the sociology of castes as formulated by Célestin Bouglé (1989) in particular, Cox blamed other authors for ignoring the class conflict between the American oligarchy in the South and workers, white as well as black. For this reason, too much importance had been given to poor whites' role in oppressing blacks. Cox also attacked W.L. Warner's (1936) hypothesis of a 'caste line' cross-cutting class relations so as to assign most whites to the upper strata and most blacks to the lower, even though this hypothesis did not preclude the existence of a white proletariat, nor of a black bourgeoisie. For Cox, racism stemmed from capitalism; the dominant class nurtured it in order to justify and maintain its exploitation of workers.

Later, several scholars, criticizing Cox for his cursory Marxism, broadened the scope of debate about the class struggle. Some of them have placed this problem in a worldwide context by associating racism with the global economy, as capitalism spreads over the planet. In line with Cox, Immanuel Wallerstein (Balibar and Wallerstein, 1988: 48) has affirmed that racism is 'the magic formula' for maximizing capital accumulation and thereby minimizing costs (with, as consequences, political turmoil and labour strife). Other scholars have preferred carrying out less ambitious studies, often based on empirical data about a single country or even area, city or neighbourhood. Questions have thus been raised in clearer terms. Do socially dominated groups characterized by race form the working class's lower stratum? Or are they separate, distinct from white workers? Does racism work like an ideology that, though autonomous from inter-class relations, legitimizes the reproduction of social classes? Or do these relations produce it? Major scholars (Mason and Rex, 1986; Miles, 1984) have taken part in these debates, which cannot be reduced to 'race and class'.

Besides this perspective, which, like Cox's pioneering research, centred around racial prejudice against black people, another viewpoint has been used to look at the race–class relationship. It has focused on the rise of Nazism in Germany, on the parts played by various classes in an anti-Semitism that ended in the 'final solution' – exterminating Jews. Historical studies on this topic, intelligently reviewed by Pierre Aycoberry (1979), have proposed all sorts of arguments about big capital, the working class or, especially, the middle classes. Nicos Poulantzas (1970) has tried to work out an analysis encompassing all these social groups.

Whether about black people or Jews, a vast corpus of interpretations has posited a link between racism and society's division into social classes. But these studies are of little help for dealing with the topic treated here. I do not aim to settle the question of whether capitalism produces racism, nor whether the working class is a homogeneous whole or a heterogeneous mixture wherein certain fractions, because of racism, are shoved farther down in the hierarchy of exploitation and shoved into 'underclass ghettos'. I do not intend to arrange social groups according to their positions on racism, nor to examine how racism works like an ideology legitimizing the reproduction of a social order. I intend to focus on the links between two types of social action, or behaviour: those having to do with a social movement in the previously defined sense and those having to do with racism.

This approach has several advantages over the attempts to formulate problems in terms of 'race and class'. Instead of reducing class to race or trying to 'articulate' them, it leads us to examine the conditions abetting or restraining the assertion of racism within social movements or, more broadly, in society. In other words, it helps us see how racism emerges out of the situation, or state, of social actors. This keeps us out of the dead end that race-and-class studies have reached. The latter, if they do not absolutely reduce race to social class, are nearly always forced to bring other categories (such as 'nation' or 'ethnic group') into the picture. Authors as different as Etienne Balibar and Floya Anthias have pointed this out. Noting that the question of the class basis of racism has been poorly formulated, Balibar (Balibar and Wallerstein, 1988: 273) has advocated turning attention to the relation between racism, as a supplement to nationalism, and the irreducibility of class conflict in society. Accordingly, we should inquire into the ways racism, as it develops, transforms class conflict. After scrutinizing the race-and-class question, Anthias (1990) has concluded that nationality and ethnicity serve as the major organizing principles of social relations in the modern era.

Elsewhere, I have dwelt on the relations between nationalism and racism (Wieviorka, 1991), and also on the intricate interplay of social or community-based (including nationalist) movements and racism. The approach presented here makes it possible, more so than the race-and-class one, to analyse the relation between racism and society without introducing factors extraneous to sociological debate.

Racism and the breakdown of a social movement

A social movement has two sides. On the one hand, it launches a counter-offensive, based on its capacity for drawing up plans or objectives and advocating a positive principle, skill or know-how: based, in other words, on its capacity for constituting a cause. On the other hand, a social movement is on the defensive as it speaks on behalf of the underprivileged, the victims of discrimination or exploitation, who have no cause, or positive principle, to advance.

In this respect, the labour movement is exemplary (see Touraine et al., 1984). Owing to skills and qualifications, some workers can give a turn to disputes so that the ultimate demand challenges the control over industrial production and progress exercised by employers, who are held to be parasitic and redundant. Motivated by the fight against poverty, low wages and insecurity in the labour market, unskilled workers have taken part in actions for which they are less well equipped than their colleagues. The working-class movement has never been as powerful and as capable of making a stand at the level of the most general issues of concern to society as when it manages to unite both skilled workers threatened by a loss of qualifications and proletarian workers with few or no skills. This need for unity, which is specific to a social movement, has encountered obstacles: employers' ability to divide and rule the labour force, highly qualified wage-earners' opposition to associating with pure proletarians, labour organizations' political and ideological differences – and even racism. When present, the last gravely hurts the labour movement, as can be inferred from the history of American unions.

Early in the labour history of the United States, the question of whether or not to admit coloured workers to trade unions arose. Besides motives based on the tactical utility of not practising segregation, beyond any moral or humanistic considerations, integrating black workers was often said to be necessary for building a broad social movement. Listen to Robert Baker (quoted by Foner, 1984: x), as he addressed the Central Labor Union of Brooklyn in 1902:

> The more organized labor champions the cause of all labor, unorganized as well as organized, black as well as white, the greater will be the victories; the more lasting, the more permanent, the more beneficial and the more far-reaching will be its successes. If it would extend and broaden its influence, aye, if it would accomplish most for itself it must

persistently and vigorously attack special privilege in every form; it must make the cause of humanity, regardless of race, color, or sex, its cause.

Although this was advocated from the start, trade unions were built on a quite different foundation for a long time. Until the mid-1930s, American workers were mainly organized on a segregated basis. When they set up the American Federation of Labor (AFL) in 1881, the white craft unions paid lip-service to anti-discriminatory principles in an appeal to reason and morals. After all, was it not better to have coloured people with you than against you during a strike? Nonetheless, a colour line was soon drawn, as the humanistic declarations of the AFL's principal leader, Samuel Gompers, yielded to discriminatory policies, which even Gompers approved. The AFL's arguments ever more tendentiously insisted on coloured people's responsibility for unions' attitudes. Accordingly, the craft unions were not organizing black workers because the latter were class traitors and strike-breakers, because they worked for starvation wages, because they were not ready to be part of urban society (or to take part in union activities), ultimately because they had excluded themselves from the movement. In his well-known analysis of self-fulfilling prophecies, Robert Merton (1965) has shown how this perverse reasoning reversed the order of events and brought forth what it was attacking. Indeed, because blacks were kept out of most major trade unions till 1935, they had no other recourse in their struggle for survival than to break strikes or work for less, thus forcing wages down.

During a social movement's formative phase, racism impedes the pursuit of a cause capable of speaking in the name of all workers, of calling for a more humane and just society. In turn, when a movement is in crisis or on the decline, room may open for racist discourses and behaviours, as in Poland's Solidarnosc (see Wieviorka, 1984).

In August 1980, Solidarnosc was formed out of the historical conjuncture of three distinct forces. This total social movement comprised working-class (labour) actions, national aspirations and political demands for democratic rights and freedoms (see Touraine et al., 1982). When they came together, these three forces left no room for anti-Semitism, which has been pronounced in national as well as religious aspirations in Poland. True, no more than a few thousand Jews were living in the country, as compared with about 3 million before the Second World War. But this explanation does not suffice, since an anti-Semitism without Jews existed before 1980 and has cropped up again since then.

In 1980, everything lessened the probability of the new union giving in to anti-Semitism, even though popular culture was hostile to Jews, the people 'who killed God'. Although the latter were often accused of having helped to set up and run the communist state, they had been eliminated from nearly all positions of power since the 1968 purges. The new union's opponent was not a mythical Jew but a clearly identified Party. Owing much to the involvement of intellectuals, Solidarnosc's democratic platform did not have anything to do with racial hate-mongering. Inseparable from a powerful, pervasive Catholicism, the national aspirations borne by this movement seemed a far cry from anti-Semitism. Since Vatican II and especially Cardinal Wojtyla's election as Pope, the Polish Church had turned away from anti-Semitism. Over the past 20 years, it had ever more strongly objected to anti-Jewish themes. The anti-Semitism existent in the Poland of 1980 was located in certain spheres of power and in very marginal Catholic circles with no influence in the emerging movement.

Within a year, the picture had changed. The first signs of change appeared during Solidarnosc's congress in September 1981. They became clearer in the following months, especially in November when Jurczyk, who had played a historic role in 1970 at Szczecinek, publicly demanded that the communists and Jews who were governing the country be hanged.

This affair signalled the beginning of the end. The movement would continue to break down when Solidarnosc went underground; and the process accelerated after 1989, when th_ union was re-legalized and Poland could assert its political independence. By autumn 1981, tensions had increased, fuelled by the economic recession and political deadlock. The forces most on the defensive within this movement began calling for radical action. Overwrought because of the scarcity of food and the near impossibility of keeping factories running, more and more people were criticizing Lech Walesa's bargaining-table unionism. Nationalistic tendencies hardened, making stronger appeals to the community, to the fact of being Polish and constituting a homogeneous nation. Calls were heard for restoring law and order. The labour forces calling for radical action and these nationalistic tendencies combined into a dismal populism, which turned on intellectuals and the Solidarnosc leaders most closely associated with the cause of democracy. As Solidarnosc broke down, room was made for anti-Semitism to spread through an exasperated rank and file. Hypernationalistic ideologists, the 'true Poles', fed on this anti-Semitism, which waxed as the 1980s advanced. These populists turned back to a conservative Catholicism, symbolized by Glemp, Poland's prelate, whose anti-Semitic declarations about the Auschwitz camp hit international headlines in 1989.

Ten years after the formation of a total social movement in Poland, a split has taken place. Once again, the 'Jewish question' is on people's minds. In the post-Solidarnosc period, anti-Semitism is, more than ever, a means of pointing out a mythical enemy. This enemy is not the handful of Jews who exercise influence as intellectuals or hold positions in politics or the unions. These are not targeted as there are so few of them. No, the enemy is the cosmopolitan Jews omnipresent throughout the Western world. They are the ones said to have money, wield power and run the mass media.

As Solidarnosc waxed, it did not yield to the temptation of anti-Semitism. But as it wanes, it is being enticed: anti-Semitism, though seldom forthright, has become so diffusely present that all observers have noticed it. It has taken the place left vacant by the social movement.

We thus have two examples of a single phenomenon: a social movement breaking down because of behaviours and discourses denying its principles of action. Like white American workers' racism, the anti-Semitism arising out of Solidarnosc's decline negates the social movement. This negation is all the stronger in so far as the movement is weak, or weakened, either because it is going through a difficult formative phase or because it is in a crisis or on the decline. In extreme cases this negation produces an image opposite to the movement's, and it becomes a wellspring of action. If this happens, the process can be explained with a theoretical concept accounting for this inversion: the social anti-movement.

Racism as a social anti-movement

When, in order to protect their jobs and wages, white workers keep blacks out of unions, or when Solidarnosc members allow voices from their ranks to advocate an anti-Semitism directed against an imaginary enemy, they are defending their own personal or group interests. But at the same time they are keeping themselves from developing a grand cause. They thus tend to deal in a racist way with problems that, in other circumstances, might lead to the formation of a social movement. Instead of joining with the black proletariat and, together, attacking those who control the economy, white workers often force those whom they have rejected, whom they see as rivals in the labour market, to resort to violence. Instead of launching an attack against an opponent who has organized production in a hopeless way, some Polish workers have become polarized around the mythical 'Jew', the imaginary source of their misfortune. In both cases, there is an action that might become collective. The lack of a movement in this sort of situation does not imply a social vacuum wherein behaviours are purely individualistic. It implies the presence of negative elements, the opposite of a social movement's. It leaves room for the imagination to work out meanings by defining obstacles or enemies in more or less racist terms and appealing to an identity constituted on this basis. The opposite of an impossible social movement is not atomistic individual behaviours in defence of personal interests. The opposite is a social anti-movement, which may be more or less organized.

The formation of a social anti-movement

In contrast to a social movement, defined by the actor's capacity for combining three principles of action (identity, opposition and historicity) into a general cause, a social anti-movement's action alters these three principles, even though it may also advocate them, and turns out to be incapable of bringing them together into a coherent whole.

In an anti-movement, references to a being, an essence or a nature replace the actor's social identity. The actor identifies with a moral or religious category (such as the forces of Good or Justice) or with a mythical figure (like the nonexistent classical worker in whom the working class cannot recognize itself). The latter happened to far-left terrorism when it spuriously and voluntaristically spoke out for the working class (see Wieviorka, 1988). In contrast, racist actors do not speak in the name of workers, of parents with children in school, or of any other social category. They become the very expression of a race and deny the humanity of other races. In less extreme cases, when Self and Other are not defined in purely biological terms, actors see themselves as representatives of an ethnic, cultural or religious community.

In an anti-movement, the image of the opponent splits in two. The actor opposes either an enemy against whom he must implacably wage war or an abstract, relatively indeterminate, imaginary system. The Other is not a real actor. It is either an objectified 'natural' enemy or else a meta-social principle (such as Evil, Satan or Decadence). Far away and incomprehensible, the Other is constantly plotting against the Self, secretly manipulating, even wielding, power as it attacks the Self with mysterious, evil means. Or, close at hand and nearly tangible, the Other is reduced to a non- or sub-human category to be kept at bay. It can thus be identified with beasts, and deadly violence can be used against it. Racism, the 'biologizing' of the Other, leads to seeing the Other as either an evildoer to be unsparingly fought or an inferior to be treated as such.

The stakes, or issues, in a social anti-movement are not something both parties – actor and opponent – share. The sense of history is no longer the same. The language describing conflict has changed. There is no awareness that actions are intended for gaining (some) control over the same resources as the adversary controls. For instance, there is no longer the idea, shared by labour and employers, that progress and industry go together and have to be managed. There is no consciousness that both parties are acting towards a common end. The actor no longer thinks history has a direction or meaning; there is no positive historicity save his own. He defines himself by a rupture, by his distance. Instead of situating himself on the same field as his opponent, he is centred on himself. He becomes sectarian or warlike, denying his involvement in a structural conflict or a social relation: he is the force of historical change. He shuts himself off from communication with the outside. His plans are not intended for the society wherein he lives, since he intends to 'deliver' this society so as to make it a purified whole. In more or less pronounced ways, racism implies subjecting, avoiding or eliminating those who define their historicity in economic or cultural terms rather than seeing themselves as belonging to the superior race.

Fission and fusion

As pointed out, a social movement is characterized by its capacity for combining into a single action three principles: to speak in the name of a social category and for the sake of a general conception of society; to recognize issues common to itself and its opponent; and to manage the means of protest and political pressure so as to accept internal tension and debate and so as not to reduce the end to the means. On the contrary, an anti-movement cannot tolerate internal tension and debate. These can only end in scission (or excommunication), whence two opposite possibilities: fission or fusion.

In the case of fission, the social anti-movement is weak, apparently dispersed among many seemingly unrelated actors and problems. Behaviours seem to be incoherent or, at least, to provide evidence of non-communication. Taken separately, each of these behaviours is but a limited inversion of the negated social movement. Taken together, they are evidence of the breakdown of a social movement. The movement's cause is not entirely lost, since it is easy to imagine reconstituting it. For example, white workers could change their attitudes towards blacks; or anti-Semitic union members, towards Jews.

In the case of fusion, the social anti-movement looks as though it is united, as though no tension can exist within it. The actor does not tolerate differences, and cannot stand back from himself. His identity is mixed up with his plans. He is carried away, proclaiming that he bears a community's aspirations and is preparing the way for the future. Being and becoming are the same; his nature and culture are merged into a single entity. Fusion does not happen spontaneously following fission, as the splinters of an anti-movement come back together. It requires political and ideological structures. It necessitates interventions by intellectuals, clericals or politicians. In extreme forms, it confuses ends and means through recourse to a violence with no limits. What is not like the self-defined actor is frantically purged, even within his ranks. Racism, especially when a key part in a totalitarian process, may become an anti-movement undergoing fusion. This is, indeed, a crucial point to keep in mind when analysing contemporary societies where populist political organizations, more or less pervious to racist themes, seem capable of institutionalizing very diffusive but tenuous sorts of behaviour, giving them a political or ideological status and thus setting off the process of fusion.

As a social anti-movement, racism seems to undergo fission more often than fusion. Often, it is so much a part of social behaviour that it can hardly be sorted out. In this case, it is so bound up with social problems that we always have doubts about what we are observing. Professing a clear conscience, actors can successfully object to accusations of racism. A process of fusion causes the shift towards exacerbated discourses and practices, which are disconnected from the actual experiences of the actor and of those whose identities are cast in racial terms. A spiralling loss of meaning then occurs, and racial hate is voiced without restraint. Alternatively, in the case of fission, racism assumes forms that are not completely disconnected from the reality on which racist thought feeds.

Racism and social structures

The reader should not conclude from the preceding lines that the single cause of the expansion of racism is the inversion of a social movement, as it breaks up and becomes an anti-movement undergoing fission or fusion. This happens often enough, but it does not directly explain the racism's major manifestations. A social movement, whether unsuccessful or powerful, does not account for racist thought and actions. Let us look deeper into the relation between social movements and racism.

A powerful movement representing a cause does not simply mobilize people who recognize it as their own because they have been oppressed and are now rebelling. It moves not just its supporters but all of society. It guides political action. It inspires the debate of ideas. It bestows meaning on behaviours lying beyond the movement's range of action. For example, the working-class movement, wherever it has played a leading role, has served as the reference mark for all sorts of actors: actors who have become activists in neighbourhoods, universities, cultural organizations or sports; who have spoken out in the name of women, consumers, users; or who have advocated revolutionary or reformist politics or even grand principles (such as justice or democracy) – *but* who have not necessarily recognized the working-class movement as their own, nor identified themselves with workers. When this reference mark loses its pull, when what it represents becomes ever more artificial or ideological, the actors to whom it offered meaning are left orphans. They can no longer place their actions in a more general struggle. Furthermore, they lose a political force that provided them with the chance of living as a fully-fledged party to the basic relationship that organizes the whole society. For this reason, the weakness, breakdown or absence of a social movement has considerable, though indirect, effects on racism, especially among the common people.

Racism and social exclusion
To illustrate this, let us review the recent debate on the enormous pockets of poverty in most big American cities. This debate starts from an undeniable fact: the existence of, to use William Wilson or Loic Wacquant's (1989) term, a hyperghetto characterized by utter poverty, rundown housing, poor schools, broken families, massive unemployment and economic segregation. Contrary to the more positive descriptions of traditional ghettos made, a long time ago now, by the first sociologists of the Chicago School, the hyperghetto provides its inhabitants with no resources. It cuts them off from the labour market and shuts them inside a jungle where gang violence reigns and drugs abound. Should we agree with Kenneth Clark (1980), who sees the hyperghetto as related to anti-black racism and segregation, which also affect the black lower-middle class, whose status, still precarious, has not improved as much as we might expect? Or should we adopt William Wilson's (1977, 1987) point of view? Without denying the key part played by racism, Wilson insists on socioeconomic processes in the formation of a black 'underclass', whose problems have little in common with those of the black lower-middle class. During the 1960s and 1970s, according to Wilson, civil rights mainly helped the black middle classes. The latter were sufficiently integrated in American society to benefit from anti-racist measures, such as the quotas set in the Civil Service or colleges. The important point is that all sides in this debate recognize that people have been left out of social and economic development, people suffering from both racism and poverty,

people primarily defined by their 'social non-relations'. Blacks in the hyperghetto are unable to mobilize the resources necessary to group action. Even an exemplary action like Black Power, with its violent tendencies, is impossible for them.

When, from 1915 onwards, they were attracted from the South towards Northern cities and industries, black people, though kept out of white craft unions, could nonetheless think of themselves as a proletariat, as a full part of the working class. They could hope to bring pressure to bear on society, to make themselves heard by the unions as they called for a labour movement in which their fate would not be separated from that of other workers. Though poor, these black immigrants were not condemned to live for ever on society's fringes. They could imagine giving a social meaning to their demands. Nowadays, the hyperghetto is a universe separate from the rest of society and, as Wilson states, from the black lower-middle class. Its inhabitants can kill each other, as they turn on themselves with drugs and acts of delinquency, which are mainly restricted to their universe. They can sink in poverty. They no longer have any organized means, whether symbolic or political (regardless of how insufficient these used to be) for reaching out towards a labour movement, even if the latter has been mythologized. Nor do they even want to participate in such an action.

For this reason, the combination of racism and socioeconomic exclusion makes things worse than ever. It enables some lower-class whites to escape from the awesome process that is ever more massively marginalizing the poor, in particular blacks, who are segregated and left to themselves or, at best, to welfare services. Paradoxically, the problem of racism may seem secondary since social and economic hardships obviate all else. In other words, whenever the idea is spent of a general social cause uniting all workers, regardless of race, then millions of black people are left in poverty, in un- and underemployment. Totally segregated and excluded, they cannot participate in social debate and conflict in their land. They fall victim to urban or industrial changes, which undeniably proceed on a racist basis. For a few decades, the labour movement gave these people the hope (and sometimes more) that forces of socioeconomic integration would prevail over racism. With the decline of the working-class movement, such goals have vanished for many who now face total racial and social segregation.

Middle-class racism

Let us now turn to the middle classes. An especially enlightening example comes from what has happened in France during the past 30 years.

As elsewhere in the West, the French middle classes are now an immense, heterogeneous agglomeration with considerable cultural and political clout. When, until some time in the 1970s, the central conflict in society was still between the working class and employers, the middle classes were forced to take a position with respect to these two opponents, whose struggle organized society. An abundant literature, usually of Marxist inspiration, has tried to account for this (e.g. Poulantzas, 1974). However there is no reason to think that the middle classes were more, or less, racist then than today. The idea of a fundamental social division underlay debates and largely determined commitments, including those of the middle classes. As Hirschman (1983) has pointed out, these politically and culturally active classes took part in the pursuit of happiness in the public sense. They were certainly not obsessed with an already massive immigration. At the time, immigration was discussed in economic rather than demographic terms, as a matter of jobs and not of an 'invasion' or 'peopling' of the country.

Owing to the crisis of industrial society, in particular the waning of the working-class movement, the middle classes have been demobilized. Staring at this vast agglomeration of social categories and looking at nothing else, many observers (such as Lipovetsky, 1983) have explained this determination in terms of a social vacuum, widespread narcissism and individualism. Within a few years, these classes have, it seems, definitively lost interest in any collective cause with a general scope. They seem to have turned to the pursuit of private happiness. Because the cause that had shaped society has broken down, these classes have been launched into a new world, where the problem is no longer what position to adopt about a general principle of social organization but, instead, how to position oneself on the social ladder. As far from the centres of power as from the fringes where the excluded dwell, the middle classes now seem to belong to a mobile society with opportunities for rising on the social ladder and risks of falling.

In France, the transition from a society organized around a general cause to a society of exclusion has affected the middle classes in several ways, all more or less related to people's relative positions on the social ladder. For the present purpose, suffice it to point out that room has been made for attitudes and behaviours prone to racism.

For one thing, the middle classes (and even the less poor lower classes) have sought to distinguish themselves not so much from poverty or the working class as from immigrants, increasingly seen as an ethnic and religious threat. Deserting certain neighbourhoods, they have moved to homogeneous suburbs. They have sent their children to private schools or obtained permission to take them out of establishments where immigrant children are concentrated. Ethnic and social segregation is under way, and it bears the marks of racism.

Furthermore, in the political crisis set off by the decline of industrial society and of the political forces representing it, the middle classes have abetted a populism incarnated by the National Front, a party wherein racism (including anti-Semitism) has a place.

It would be erroneous to affirm that the French middle classes are turning away from the ideal of democracy. It would be just as mistaken to label them as racist, since racism, in this country, is but one factor in a rising populism that basically criticizes political parties and appeals to order and the Nation. But we would be blind if we failed to notice that these middle classes now tend to voice more than they used to racist fears about immigration. In this respect, the decline of a social movement bearing an organizing principle and a meaning has, indeed, made room for racism, even though the movement itself did not directly cause this to happen. Hopefully, new meanings, causes and issues will be worked out so that the middle classes will position themselves in a space structured by a social movement rather than give full play to individual strategies and populist attitudes, which lead to *de facto* segregation, calls for institutional discrimination and, here and there, racist acts of violence.

Whether we are talking about the inversion of a social movement into an anti-movement, about segregation and exclusion, or about the middle classes, comportment, the aforementioned examples lead towards a single conclusion: the room for racism depends on the existence of a movement that, with lofty aspirations, bears a principle for organizing meaning and behaviours in society. The more a social movement takes shape, the less racism has room for developing. The weaker a social movement (and all the more so if none exists), the greater the risk that racism will become manifest in rigidly contracted forms, which subsist as the inverse of a former movement in various sectors of society. This is not a general explanation, even less a theory, of the rise of racism. But for the analysis of this specific social evil, it does enable us to introduce factors that are too often neglected or reduced to superficial, global and hasty references to the recession and its consequences, or that are too often formulated in categories inadequate for criticizing capitalism.

The hypothesis of an ethnic social movement

The concept of social movement encompasses the idea of the dominated actor enlarging his struggle to embrace not only his own interests but also broader issues having to do with the values of freedom, dignity and justice. These values may be denied to groups that are defined, or define themselves, not in social but in cultural terms, which may be more or less 'naturalized' through ethnic (or racial) categories. Can we coin the phrase 'ethnic social movement' to refer either to a classical social movement (such as the working-class movement) that incorporates ethnic-based demands or to a directly ethnic action with elements other than purely cultural or racial ones?[3]

In various cases, the question of linking the cause of the working class to the assertion of national or ethnic identities has cropped up in the labour movement and its union and political organizations. This happened in central Europe, in particular before the First World War, as evidenced by 'Austro-Marxism', whose efforts were intellectual rather than practical (Haupt et al., 1974). Above all, the Jewish workers' movement, the Bund, deserves attention.

At the time when Theodor Herzl was forming the nationalist Jewish movement of Zionism, other persons, mainly in Russia and then independent Poland, were trying to socially and politically mobilize Jewish workers for actions wherein full recognition would be given to the Yiddish culture and language. The Bund was a leading actor in the social democratic movement prior to the Bolshevik Revolution, and it continued to play an important role until the Second World War (Weinstock, 1984). This provides evidence that industrial societies have room for movements with an ethnic dimension.

On the whole, however, industrial societies in Europe have been shaped by a central social conflict with, at most, marginal room for an ethnic sort of action. Claims to national, religious or ethnic identities could only weaken the working-class movement. They introduced a principle of division whenever unity had to be forged around the highest cause: worker control over progress and industry. The working-class movement could incorporate ethnic groups only in so far as the principal meaning of their actions was not ethnic but social and political, in so far as a particularism, as in the Bund, remained subordinate to the social emancipation of the proletariat.

But the industrial age is over; our societies are post-industrial. The major issues we now observe are cultural, and no longer have to do with control over industrial progress alone. They appeal to the subjectivity of individuals and groups. They value communication, exchange and creativity beyond the mere production of material goods. They do not criticize exploitation so much as contempt or scorn for the underprivileged, and they denounce the manipulation of needs by cultural industries and techno-bureaucracies. In this new 'society-scape', actions have, in the past 20 years, been initiated by the feminist and ecological movements, by students, and by groups interested in education or demanding that the health care system have more concern for patients instead of merely in technically, economically and bureaucratically managing illness. Could ethnicity not find a place here?

For ethnicity to have a place in this nebula of new social movements, ethnic-based groups must meet a fundamental condition that depends on their ability and willingness to refuse to separate their definition of a sense of identity from claims formulated in terms of equal rights and opportunities for individuals. This condition applies to all the new social movements. They must avoid being purely 'differentialist'. By this term, I am referring to the tendency to assert a particularism or difference rather than to seek involvement in social relations with others. Feminism, for example, still risks being torn apart. On the one hand, differentialist tendencies, if left to themselves, will end in sectarianism – splintered groups cut off from all else. On the other hand, feminist claims to equality imply that any specifically feminist identity will eventually fade away; and so gender relations cannot easily serve as a ground for thought and action. Yet another example is the extremely dangerous 'eco-fascism' that denies human values for the sake of the biological rights of all living species. But ecology also has more democratic and political tendencies, which criticize the technocracy's way of thinking and making decisions about the environment, urbanization or development.

Is the aforementioned condition fulfilled when ethnicity is institutionalized; when, pursuing a 'situationalist' rationale, it acts like a pressure group and, for example, lobbies? We might think so. Owing to this institutionalization, demands from these groups will, we might suppose, be handled politically. But this supposition does not stand up to the facts, as can be seen in Great Britain in particular. Ethnic minorities there are well represented at the local level.[4] In such situations, political and intellectual elites form or organize so as to take advantage of the institutional possibilities offered. But separating themselves ever farther from the population in whose name they are speaking, they tend to build up networks of clients and draw up strategies in line with their own economic and political interests. Besides, the institutionalization of minorities does not place all of them on the same level. It does nothing to solve the social and economic problems of the weakest minority groups, who are, very often, most exposed to racism. It strengthens the ability of the most powerful, best organized communities to undertake actions, but it does nothing to help the underprivileged.

In the United States, where a pluralist ethnic society has existed for a long time, African-Americans have been visibly absent. In addition, the institutionalization of minorities may refer to processes of political mobilization that are not at all, properly speaking, ethnic. According to Bell (1975), the rise of ethnicity during the 1960s in the United States can be explained, for certain groups, by political and economic opportunities even as these groups were being culturally assimilated.

There are sound reasons to reject the hypothesis that ethnicity can serve as the basis for a social movement. The most strongly made ethnic claims protest against racist exclusion or discrimination. But for us to talk about a social movement, these claims must be made in a context of domination, which serves as the ground for a conflict and for taking sides. However, ethnic actors are not defined by a social relation. They do not contend with an opponent but with a system that rejects them like outcasts. Their rage, or riots, reflect their inability to transform their revolt into a genuine social conflict, though they may want to form a social movement. They may realize that something is missing, that no collective action is possible apart from outbreaks of what will soon become self-destructive violence. They bear, we might say, a social movement in intaglio. It is hard to see how they can switch to positive protest, to actions that can develop, back up negotiations, and question the general orientations of the culture and economy. For this reason, we can, at best, see ethnic-based actions as the sign of a disjointed movement that is breaking up under the weight of segregation, discrimination and exclusion and that can break up still further into countercultural practices, into gesticulations rejecting an out-of-reach consumer society, or into self-destructive behaviours.

Despite all the evidence about the formation of ethnic-based identities, there is no sign that, in our societies, ethnic social movements will become capable of managing the internal tensions between the universal and the particular. In any case, racism and xenophobia are not likely to recede very quickly. If ethnic-based social movements do not form, we can foresee increasing tensions in which differentialist racism will play an ever larger part.

(Translated from French by Noal Mellott, CNRS, Paris.)

Notes

1. For an overview of this violence in France, see Gérard Noiriel (1986: 257–62).

2. See also Cox's major articles compiled by Abraham and Hunter (1948).

3. This section borrows from my book, *La démocratie à l'épreuve. Nationalisme, populisme, ethnicité* (Paris: La Découverte, 1993), pp. 139–44.

4. According to Rex (1991), more than 700 ethnic associations are registered in the city of Birmingham alone.

References

Abraham, Sameer and Hunter, Herbert (eds) (1948) *Race, Class and the World System: The Sociology of Oliver C. Cox*. New York: Monthly Review Press.

Anthias, Floya (1990) 'Race and class revisited: conceptualizing race and racism', *Sociological Review*, 38(1): 19–42.

Aycoberry, Pierre (1979) *La question nazi*. Paris: Seuil.

Balibar, E. and Wallerstein, I. (1988) *Race, nation, classe. Les identités ambiguës*. Paris: La Découverte.

Bell, Daniel (1975) 'Ethnicity and social change', in N. Glazer and D. Moynihan (eds), *Ethnicity, Theory and Experience*. Cambridge, MA: Harvard University Press. pp. 141–74.

Bouglé, Célestin (1989) *Essai sur le régime des castes*. Paris: Presses Universitaires de France. First published 1908.

Cantril, Hadley (1941) *The Psychology of Social Movements*. New York: John Wiley.

Clark, Kenneth (1980) 'The role of race', *New York Times Magazine*, 5 October.

Cox, Oliver (1948) *Castes, Class and Race*. New York: Doubleday.

Foner, Philip (1974) *Organized Labor and the Black Worker, 1619–1973*. New York: International Publishers.

Harris, A.L. and Spero, S.D. (1974) *The Black Worker*. New York: Atheneum.

Haupt, Georges, Lowy, Michael and Weill, Claudie (1974) *Les Marxistes et la question nationale, 1848–1914*. Paris: Maspéro.

Hill, H. (1967) 'The racial practices of organized labor', in A. Ross and H. Hill (eds), *Employment, Race and Poverty*. New York: Harcourt, Brace and World.

Hirschman, Albert (1983) *Bonheur privé, action publique*. Paris: Fayard.

Lipovetsky, Gilles (1983) *L'ère du vide. Essais sur l'individualisme contemporain*. Paris: Gallimard.

Mason, David and Rex, John (eds) (1986) *Theories of Race and Ethnic Relations*. Cambridge: Cambridge University Press.

Merton, Robert (1965) *Eléments de théorie et de méthode sociologique*. Paris: Plon.

Miles, Robert (1984) 'Marxism versus the sociology of race relations', *Ethnic and Racial Studies*, 7(2): 217–37.

Milza, Pierre (1981) *Français et Italiens à la fin du XIXème siècle*. Rome: Ecole Française de Rome.

Noiriel, Gérard (1986) *Le creuset français*. Paris: Seuil.

Orfali, Birgitta (1990) *L'adhésion au Front National. De la minorité active au mouvement social*. Paris: Kimé.

Poulantzas, Nicos (1970) *Fascisme et dictature. La IIIème Internationale face au fascisme*. Paris: Maspéro.

Poulantzas, Nicos (1974) *Les classes sociales dans le capitalisme aujourd'hui*. Paris: Seuil.

Rex, John (1991) *Ethnic Identity and Ethnic Mobilization in Britain*. Coventry: Centre for Research in Ethnic Relations.

Touraine, Alain (1974) *Production de la société*. Paris: Seuil.

Touraine, Alain, Strzelecki, Jan, Dubet, François and Wieviorka, Michel (1982) *Solidarité*. Paris: Fayard.

Touraine, Alain, Wieviorka, Michel and Dubet, François (1984) *Le mouvement ouvrier*. Paris: Fayard.

Wacquant, Loic and Wilson, William (1989) 'The cost of racial and class exclusion within the inner city', *Annals of the American Academy of Political and Social Science*, January: 8–25.

Warner, W.L. (1936) 'American caste and class', *American Journal of Sociology*, 42 (September): 234–7.

Weinstock, Nathan (1984) *Le pain de misère*, Vol. 3. Paris: La Découverte.

Wieviorka, Michel (1984) *Les Juifs, la Pologne et Solidarnosc*. Paris: Denoël.

Wieviorka, Michel (1988) *Sociétés et terrorisme*. Paris: Fayard.

Wieviorka, Michel (1991) *L'espace du racisme*. Paris: Seuil.

Wilson, William (1977) *The Declining Significance of Race*. Chicago: University of Chicago Press.

Wilson, William (1987) *The Truly Disadvantaged: The Inner City, the Underclass and Public Policy*. Chicago: University of Chicago Press.

Winock, Michel (1982) *Edouard Drumont et Compagnie. Antisémitisme et fascisme en France*. Paris: Seuil.

4
The New Social Movements Revisited: Reflections on a Sociological Misunderstanding

Alberto Melucci

The rise and fall of the dualistic epic

When in the early 1970s I started working on collective action and social movements, the various empirical phenomena associated with the field (from panic to political violence, from fashion to revolution) were traditionally explained in two parallel ways. On the one hand, in the functionalist tradition (see Turner and Killian, 1987), these phenomena were considered to be the sum of atomized events, which due to one circumstance or another come together to form a collective reality: for example, in the tradition of crowd psychology, influential from the late nineteenth century up to the theories of mass society of the 1950s (Kornhauser, 1959), empirical phenomena were attributed to an imbalance in the social order and their collective character depended on the spatial and temporal coincidence of individual behaviours (see Moscovici, 1981; Alberoni, 1977). One could speak in this case of *an action without an actor*.

On the other hand, the Marxist tradition saw collective action as the expression of a structural class condition from which behaviour sprang: it expressed the structural contradictions to which the actor was subjected. The true interests of the actors depended upon these contradictions, even if they were not conscious of their motivations. Here we meet *an actor without an action*. The structural condition objectively selects the actor, without however being able to bridge the gap between objective potential and the action effectively observed. Concrete action always differs from the objective interests and cannot be deduced from the actor's condition. This is the old Marxist problem, that of the passage from a class in itself to a class for itself, from the material roots of class interests in capitalist relationships to revolutionary action (or, more often, to the lack of such action). This immense chasm was inevitably filled up by a kind of *deus ex machina* (the party, the intellectuals) that served as the external supplier of that consciousness which the actor lacked. Leninism as a theoretical construct, before it was political practice, was an inevitable consequence of this dualism.

This historical legacy was based mainly on an observation of the popular and working-class movements in the process of capitalist industrialization. It was around this historical reference point that both the idea of the actor as a revolutionary embodiment of the destiny of the social structure, and that of the manipulated mob, under the influence of the suggestive power of a few agitators, were given form: movements as interpreters of History or as expression of social pathology.

Today, historical and sociological research helps us to understand that the popular movements of the industrialization period combined two different processes, analytically distinct from one another, although empirically linked. One was the actual industrial conflict, tied to the capitalist mode of production and to the factory system: a social conflict, opposing the working class (the new producers) against the capitalists, in a struggle for controlling the ends, means and organization of industrial production. The second process, also marked by conflicts, was the progressive integration into citizenship of social categories which had been excluded from the construction of the modern nation-state (Bendix, 1964, 1978). This was a political process which widened the base of legitimacy of the state and extended political democracy.

In the working-class action of the nineteenth century, these two processes – a class struggle and a fight for citizenship and the extension of political rights – combined and complemented one another (Tilly, 1986). But they seem to have drawn further apart as the systems became more complex and differentiated. The struggle for democracy and citizenship and the conflict that affects the central resources of the system no longer follow the same path nor involve the same actors. Moreover, here begins the separation of theoretical approaches dealing with one or the other of these processes. Concern about citizenship and the extension of democratic rights has not ceased to be important, nor are the claims to civil spaces in modern democracies exhausted. This is, however, a different point of view from that concerned with the forms of conflict which regard the crucial resources of contemporary systems.

I began studying social movements in the early 1970s. My approach to collective phenomena was affected both by the changing historical conditions and by a considerable evolution in the social sciences (Melucci, 1984, 1989). Social scientists have developed macro-theories which seek to link contemporary collective action to a systems analysis of post-industrial or post-material society (Touraine, 1974, 1978, 1984; Habermas, 1984; Giddens, 1984). Organizational theory and research have come a long way from Weber and the functionalist model (Crozier and Friedberg, 1977): organization is now conceived of as a field of resources and limits with an autonomous capacity of mediating between objective constraints and the actual organizational output. This constructivist view on organizations has been significantly paralleled by the development of cognitive theories which closely connect action to the actors' capacity to construct their scripts of reality, to influence each other, and to negotiate the meanings of their experience (Abelson, 1981; Bateson, 1972, 1979; Eiser, 1980; Neisser, 1976).

In two articles published in 1977 (later translated into English: Melucci, 1981) and 1980 (Melucci, 1980), I introduced and discussed the notion of 'new social movements'. Since then, this notion has become a common reference in current sociological debates (Cohen, 1985; Gamson, 1990; Tarrow, 1989, 1994; Klandermans et al., 1988). The problem of the 'novelty' of the 'new movements' has been extensively discussed and criticized in this literature. The debates are focused, however, on a false problem. The concept of 'novelty' is, by definition, a relative notion, whose temporary function is that of emphasizing the differences between the traditional working-class action in the framework of industrial capitalism and the emerging forms of collective action in a highly differentiated social system. The notion of 'novelty' was first used to indicate the weaknesses of the existing theories of collective action, if applied to the emerging phenomena, and to stress the need for a more comprehensive framework. It was also a temporary critical tool for addressing the shortcomings of resource mobilization theory (McCarthy and Zald, 1977, 1981; Jenkins, 1983), whose influence was beginning to spread at the time of my first articles and whose importance for the analysis of social movements I recognized from the beginning. But apart from these 'conjunctural' functions of the notion of the 'new movements' within the scientific community, if sociological theory is incapable of transcending this provisional label and cannot provide an appropriate analysis of the specific and distinctive features of what is defined as 'new', the concept of 'novelty' is only a weak substitute for the lack of theoretical explanation.

Both the supporters and the critics of the 'new social movements' seem to ignore the relative and transitory nature of this notion and are unaware of the underlying epistemological misunderstanding. The supporters seek to qualify the 'novelty' of the 'new movements', while the critics question or deny it, basing their argument on the similarities between contemporary and past forms of action (for a recent example of this second argument, see Pickvance, Chapter 5 in this volume). The former try to identify historical differences, while the latter stress the continuity of social movements from earlier periods to the present. Both sides treat contemporary movements as a unified empirical object, and by assuming this ontological unity they fail to recognize that collective action always consists of various components (analytical levels, types of relationship, orientations and meanings).

The recognition of this plurality helps to break down empirical generalizations and allows us to compare analytical components instead of global historical unities. Social movements, therefore, should not be viewed as *personnages*, as living characters acting on the stage of history, but as socially constructed collective realities.

The metaphysics of the actor

One of the most resistant legacies of the nineteenth century is the tendency to attribute a kind of substantial unity to the observed actor. The essentialist and teleological idea of social movements as unified subjects acting on the stage of history, oriented towards luminous destinies or pledged to an inevitable collapse, is the last expression of a philosophy of history and metaphysical assumptions. That which one observes as unity, as a given reality, is actually the result of multiple processes, of different orientations, of a constructive dynamic which the actors bring about (or fail to bring about): in any case it is thanks to this dynamic that an action develops or fails to develop, evolves or is arrested, reaches its objectives or falls apart.

A collective actor is a composite, constructed reality, which nevertheless presents itself empirically as a unity. And it does so in a dual sense. On one hand, the actors tend to give themselves a unified definition which reinforces, at least in terms of ideology, their capacity for action and their relationship to their opponents, allies and potential supporters. On the other hand observers tend to attribute this unity to an empirical collective phenomenon, simplifying it and transforming it in a homogeneous subject according to the logic of common sense. Thus the unity of collective action is currently seen as a given.

This unity, however, must be seen merely as an empirical starting point. There is no doubt that we can observe a group of individuals who, acting together, define themselves as 'we', and to whom we tend to attribute unity. But everyday common sense becomes naïve realism when it assumes the metaphysical existence of the actor. From the analytical point of view, it is precisely this datum which needs to be questioned. The unity is a result of exchanges, negotiations, decisions and conflicts that the actors continually bring about, but which are never in the foreground. Such processes are not immediately visible, as the actors tend to hide their fragmentation. But when unification is realized, this in itself is already a product. The commonsense understanding of social movements sees them as unified empirical actors, whose values, intentions and goals are taken for granted; so that the ideology of the leaders or the attributions made by the observers become the true reality of the movement. The task of sociological analysis should be to question the data in order to ascertain how it is produced, and to dissect the empirical unity to discover the plurality of analytical elements – orientations, meanings and relationships – which converge in the same phenomenon.

Any investigation into the formation of a collective actor should acknowledge the complex and diverse nature of collective action as a fundamental criterion. What is empirically referred to as a movement, and for convenience of observation and description is treated as an essential unity, in reality embodies a whole range of social processes, actors and forms of action. The problem, for politics as well as theory, is to understand how and why these different processes hold together. This statement of the problem is crucial for the outcome of the investigation. To know what lies behind an empirical movement means to identify the range of components and meanings within it, and inquire as to the changes these components, with their diverse positions and orientations, may give rise to.

Collective action should thus be considered as the result of purposes, resources and limits: as a purposive orientation con- structed by means of social relationships within a system of opportunities and constraints. It therefore cannot be viewed as the simple effect of structural preconditions or the expression of values and beliefs. Individuals acting together construct their action by means of organized investments: that is, they define in cognitive, affective and relational terms the field of possibilities and limits which they perceive, while at the same time activating their relationships so as to give sense to their being together and to the goals they pursue. Each time we observe a number of individuals acting collectively we confront what I call a multi-polar action system.

Collective action is not a unitary empirical phenomenon, and the unity, if it exists, should be considered as a result rather than a starting point, as a fact to be explained rather than as evidence. The events in which individuals act collectively combine different orientations, involve multiple actors, and implicate a system of opportunities and constraints that shape their relationships.

The actors produce the collective action because they are able to define themselves and the field of their action (relationships with other actors, available resources, opportunities and constraints). The definition that the actors construct is not linear, but is produced by interactions and negotiations and sometimes by the opposition of different orientations. Individuals create a collective 'we' (more or less stable and integrated according to the type of action) by sharing and laboriously adjusting at least three kinds of orientation: those relating to the ends of the actions (i.e. the sense the action has for the actor); those relating to the means (i.e. the possibilities and the limits of the action); and finally those relating to relationships with the environment (i.e. the field in which the action takes place).

The plurality of meanings and forms of action which constitute an empirical collective actor prompts us to recognize that contemporary movements are multi-dimensional realities that affect different levels of the social system, pursue diverse goals, and belong to different phases of development of a system or even to different historical systems. The analysis of a social movement should explain how these diverse elements are combined in a unified empirical actor.

At this point, the question concerning the emergence of a new paradigm of collective action can legitimately be raised: it is now analytically grounded and it addresses not empirical global phenomena, but specific levels, elements and meanings of the 'new movements'. Are there dimensions of contemporary movements which cannot be explained within the traditional conceptual framework and which are qualitatively different from those of industrial capitalism?

Critics of the 'new social movements' simply eliminate this question from the scene and fall into the trap of political reductionism. The only basis of comparison among different historical forms of action inevitably becomes their impact on the political system (Tilly, 1978; Tarrow, 1994). Movements are considered only as political actors. The contribution of Pickvance in this book (see Chapter 5) is a good example of such reductionism. But in this case it seems increasingly difficult to differentiate movements from other political actors only by referring to some specific empirical feature.

Actually, any empirical characteristic that should represent a distinctive dimension of social movements (like, for example, the exclusion from a prevailing political agenda) can easily be associated with other political actors, such as parties and pressure groups. In order to find a significant difference, the reductionist approach then examines those forms of action that involve a direct confrontation with authorities (for an excellent analysis of such encounters see Gamson et al., 1982). This tends to eliminate from consideration those levels of collective action which are outside the political domain. Such an unjustified and unassumed selection (which would of course be legitimate if explicitly and analytically founded) is the basis for the confusion of languages in the realm of social movements studies. It confirms once again the necessity of a shift from empirical generalizations to analytical definitions of the plurality of elements and levels that are always comprised within an empirical phenomenon called a 'social movement'. The political level is just one of the possible fields for collective action, more or less important according to the specific 'compound' that a given empirical actor and a given environment represent. The task of sociological analysis is precisely that of separating what is empirically mixed up, using distinctive analytical tools.

If directed at contemporary movements, the reductionist attitude that focuses only on the political dimensions of collective action ignores the creation of cultural models and symbolic challenges that are inherent in certain levels of the 'new' movements. I emphasize 'certain levels'. I am not speaking of global actors, taken in their empirical unity, but of specific analytical elements that can be detected within the magma of what is now empirically called a 'new social movement'. These less visible elements cannot be perceived if one focuses exclusively on the political domain. Let us try now to give a short outline of these elements which are present in contemporary forms of collective action, together with many other aspects that can be explained using the more traditional tools of political or organizational analysis.

Is there anything new?

Information resources are at the centre of collective conflicts emerging in highly differentiated societies. Conflicts shift to the formal frameworks of knowledge: the codes. This shift is made possible by the increasing self-reflective capacity of information-based social systems.

Unlike their nineteenth-century counterparts, contemporary forms of collective action are not preoccupied with struggles over the production and distribution of material goods. They challenge the administrative rationality of systems based on information primarily on symbolic grounds: the ways in which an information-based society generates meaning and communication for its members.

The *self-reflective form of action* is another specific feature of the emerging collective phenomena. Action is a message sent to the rest of society, which speaks through its own forms and with a high degree of self-reflexivity. Organizational forms, patterns of interpersonal relationships and decision-making processes are themselves meaningful signs addressed to the society as a whole. But they are also a goal in themselves: actors consciously practise in the present the objective they pursue.

The *planetary dimension* of action is the expression of the global interdependence of our world. Even when the action is located at a specific and particularistic level, actors display a high degree of awareness of planetary interdependence. Movements acquire a transnational dimension.

They also rely on a *specific relation between latency and visibility*. Submerged networks in everyday life create and practise new meanings. The production of new codes challenges the dominant logic of technological rationality. These networks are the laboratories in which other views of reality are created. They emerge only on specific grounds to confront a public authority on a given issue. Submerged networks nourish and give meanings to public mobilizations by providing names and codes for issues raised. Cycles of mobilization feed the submerged networks with new members and new experiences.

The effectiveness of such forms of action should not be measured only at the political level. Movements produce both measurable and non-measurable effects. *Institutional change, new elites* and *cultural innovation* can be measured and are the most visible effects of collective action. But there are also less visible outcomes of collective action which can be detected only at the cultural level. The reversal of cultural codes is a challenge which addresses forms of power hidden in the allegedly neutral rationality of administrative apparatuses. The very existence of collective action is the message sent to the society: power becomes visible because it is challenged by the production of different meanings. Power hides behind the rationality of organizational and technological procedures and behind the construction of names and meanings. Making power visible is possible when other names, other meanings are offered to the society by the practice of collective action.

The ambivalence of representation processes

A necessary condition for the survival of such forms of action is the existence of public spaces (Keane, 1988) independent of the institutions of government, the party system and state structures. These spaces assume the form of an articulated system of decision-making, negotiation and representation, in which the signifying practices developed in everyday life can be expressed and heard independently of formal political institutions. Public spaces of this kind should include some guarantees that individual and collective identities can exist, soft institutionalized systems favouring the appropriation of knowledge and the production of symbolic resources, and open systems in which information can be circulated and controlled. Public spaces are highly fluid, and their size may increase or diminish according to the autonomy they are accorded: they are by definition a mobile system of instances kept open only by creative confrontation between collective actors and institutions.

Inasmuch as public spaces form an intermediate level between the levels of political power and decision-making and networks of everyday life, they are structurally ambivalent: they express the double meaning of the terms *representation* and *participation*. Representation means the possibility of presenting interests and demands; but it also means remaining different and never being heard entirely through the political channels that give voice to social demands. Participation also has a double meaning. It means both taking part, that is, acting so as to promote the interests and the needs of an actor, and also belonging to a system, identifying with the general interests of the community.

The ambivalence of public spaces is always part of the political game and it is regulated, to a certain extent, by the state, according to its more or less dominant role, its degree of centralization and the autonomy it allows representative institutions. The choice between freedom of expression and external regulation, as well as between particularism and general interests, is not made once and for all. On the contrary, substantial democracy in complex societies will increasingly be measured by the capacity of political systems to keep these polarities as open as possible. The transparency of the rules, the flexibility of the gatekeepers and agendas, and sensitivity to institutional change are all tentative ways of improving the quality of democratic life. Social movements can contribute to this game by their capacity to reveal the loci and languages of power.

The main function of public spaces, then, is to make the questions raised by the movements visible and collective. They enable the movements to avoid being institutionalized as such and, conversely, ensure that society as a whole is able to assume responsibility for (that is, institutionally process) the issues, demands and conflicts concerning the goals and meaning of social action raised by the movements. In this sense, the consolidation of independent public spaces is a vital condition of retaining – without seeking to falsely resolve – the paradoxical dimension of post-industrial democracy. For when society assumes responsibility for its own issues, demands and conflicts, it subjects them openly to negotiation and to decisions, and transforms them into possibilities of change. It thereby makes possible a democracy of everyday life, without either annulling the specificity and the independence of the movements or concealing the use of power behind allegedly neutral decision-making procedures.

Some theoretical conclusions

Conflicts of a systematic nature, which used to be referred to as 'class conflicts', are therefore carried forward by temporary actors who bring to light the crucial dilemmas of the planetary society. The conflicts I describe here (which do not exhaust the range of social conflicts that can affect specific national societies or areas of the world system) concern the production and the appropriation of resources which are crucial for a global information-based society. These same processes generate both new forms of power and new forms of opposition: conflict emerges only in so far as actors fight for control and allocation of socially produced potential for action. This potential is no longer based exclusively on material resources or on forms of social organization, but to an increasing extent on the ability to produce information.

Conflicts do not chiefly express themselves through action designed to achieve outcomes in the political system. Rather, they raise a challenge which recasts the language and cultural codes that organize information. The ceaseless flow of messages acquires meaning only through the codes that order the flux and allow its meanings to be read. The forms of power now emerging in contemporary societies are grounded in an ability to inform (give form). Collective action occupies the same terrain and is in itself a message broadcast to society conveying symbolic forms and relational patterns which cast light on the dark side of the moon – a system of meanings which runs counter to the sense that the apparatuses seek to impose on individual and collective events. This type of action affects institutions because it selects new elites, modernizes organizational forms, and creates new goals and new languages. At the same time, however, it challenges the apparatuses that govern the production of information, and prevents the channels of representation and decision-making in pluralist societies from adopting instrumental rationality as the only logic with which to govern complexity. Such rationality applies solely to procedures and imposes the criterion of efficiency and effectiveness as the only measure of sense. The action of movements reveals that the neutral rationality of means masks interests and forms of power; that it is impossible to confront the massive challenge of living together on a planet, by now become a global society, without openly discussing the ends and values that make such cohabitation possible. It highlights the insuperable dilemmas facing complex societies, and by doing so forces them openly to assume responsibility for their choices, their conflicts and their limitations.

By drawing on forms of action that relate to daily life and individual identity, some forms of contemporary collective action detach themselves from the traditional model of political organization and increasingly distance themselves from political systems. They move in to occupy an intermediate space of social life where individual needs and the pressures of political innovation come together. Because of the particular features of movements, social conflicts can only become effective through the mediation of political actors, even though they will never restrict themselves to politics. The innovative thrust of movements, therefore, does not exhaust itself in changes to the political system brought about by institutional actors. Nevertheless, the ability of collective demands to expand and to find expression depends on the way in which political actors are able to translate them into democratic guarantees.

As my thinking in this area has developed, I have gradually abandoned the concept of class relationships to address the question of systemic conflicts. This concept seems to me inseparably linked with capitalist industrial society, but I used it as an analytical tool to define a system of conflicting relationships within which social resources are produced and appropriated (Melucci, 1980). The notion of class relationships has been for me a temporary tool with which to analyse systemic conflicts and forms of domination in complex societies. I have therefore used a traditional category to focus on the relational and conflicting dimension of the production of a society's basic orientations. But in contemporary systems, where classes as real social groups are withering away, more appropriate concepts are required – without, however, ignoring the theoretical problem that the category of class relationships has left behind as its legacy: the problem of knowing what relations and what conflicts are involved in the production of the crucial resources of a particular system.

Addressing this question (as Eder does in Chapter 1 in this volume) is essential to understanding the dual articulation of autonomy and dependence that characterizes the political system and the relationship between movements and processes of representation and decision-making. And the concept of class relationships can still matter for the analysis of a specific historical society. But, as Marx has taught us, when we deal with a historical 'social formation' (say Italy, or Germany, Peru or the US in 1993, or in 1963) we are always confronted with a compound made up of many historical layers. Class relationships can certainly affect the understanding of the quality of a particular compound. But I do not think that this concept is useful to understand the quality and the direction of systemic conflicts at the planetary scale today. These conflicts are the expression of new social relationships that inform, in any case, every single part of the world system, therefore transforming the role and the meaning of previous forms of domination and conflict.

So the theoretical problem is whether there are forms of conflict which engage the constitutive logic of a global system. The notion of the mode of production is too closely associated with economicist reductionism. Production cannot be restricted to the economic-material sphere; it embraces the entirety of social relationships and cultural orientations. The problem is whether one can still talk of antagonistic conflicts; that is, conflicts which involve the social relationships that produce the constitutive resource of complex systems, i.e. information. Analysis of exchanges internal to the political market, or the knowledge we have acquired concerning strategic behaviour in organizations and political systems, shows that many contemporary conflicts, sometimes even violent ones, are the expression of social categories or groups claiming access to representation. A demand for inclusion in an institutional system of benefits may even be radical, but it implies not so much antagonism towards the logic of the system as pressure for redistribution.

However, if no analytical space is left open for asking the question about antagonistic conflicts, then one has not only erased such a question and failed to resolve the problem it raises but also failed to demonstrate its futility. The European Left now seems to be replacing the Marxist model with a model of exchange or of the rationality of decision-making choices. For my part, when in the past I have analysed class conflicts I have done so from within a constructivist and systemic framework already very far from the Marxist model, but explanation of contemporary conflicts solely in terms of exchange strikes me as inadequate. I believe that the question of the systemic nature of conflicts should be kept open: what does the term system logic mean in highly differentiated systems? Is it possible to identify antagonistic conflicts without their actors being characterized by a stable social condition? Can the arenas of conflict change? These questions become stimulating working hypotheses if the analytic space for their formulation is kept open. These questions may serve to guide the analysis of contemporary movements.

References

Abelson, R.A. (1981) 'Psychological status of the script concept', *American Psychologist*, 36 (July): 715–29.

Alberoni, F. (1977) *Movimento e instituzione*. Bologna: Il Mulino.

Bateson, G. (1972) *Steps to an Ecology of Mind*. New York: Ballantine.

Bateson, G. (1979) *Mind and Nature*. New York: Dutton.

Bendix, R. (1964) *Nation-Building and Citizenship*. New York: John Wiley.

Bendix, R. (1978) *Kings or People*. Berkeley: University of California Press.

Cohen, J.L. (1985) 'Strategy or identity: new theoretical paradigms and contemporary social movements', *Social Research*, 52(4): 663–716.

Crozier, M. and Friedberg, E. (1977) *L'acteur et le système*. Paris: Seuil.

Eiser, J.R. (1980) *Cognitive Social Psychology*. London: McGraw-Hill.

Gamson, W.A. (1990) *The Strategy of Social Protest*, 2nd edn. Belmont, CA: Wadsworth.

Gamson, W.A., Fireman, B. and Rytina, S. (1982) *Encounters with Unjust Authorities*. Homewood, IL: Dorsey Press.

Giddens, A. (1984) *The Constitution of Society*. Berkeley: University of California Press.

Habermas, J. (1984) *Theory of Communicative Action*. Boston: Beacon Press.

Jenkins, J.C. (1983) 'Resource mobilization theory and the study of social movements', *Annual Review of Sociology*, 9: 527–53.

Keane, J. (ed.) (1988) *Civil Society and the State*. London: Verso.

Klandermans, B., Kriesi, H. and Tarrow, S. (eds) (1988) *From Structure to Action*. Greenwich, CT: JAI Press.

Kornhauser, W. (1959) *The Politics of Mass Society*. Glencoe, IL: Free Press.

McCarthy, J.D. and Zald, M.N. (1977) 'Resource mobilization and social movements: a partial theory', *American Journal of Sociology*, 82(6): 1212–41.

McCarthy, J.D. and Zald, M.N. (1981) *Social Movements in Organizational Society*. New Brunswick: Transaction Books.

Melucci, A. (1980) 'The new social movements: a theoretical approach', *Social Science Information*, 19(2): 199–226.

Melucci, A. (1981) 'Ten hypotheses for the analysis of new movements', in D. Pinto (ed.), *Contemporary Italian Sociology*. New York: Cambridge University Press.

Melucci, A. (1984) *Altri Codici*. Bologna: Il Mulino.

Melucci, A. (1989) *Nomads of the Present*. London: Hutchinson; Philadelphia: Temple University Press.

Moscovici, S. (1981) *L'âge des foules*. Paris: Fayard.

Neisser, U. (1976) *Cognition and Reality*. San Francisco: Freeman.

Tarrow, S. (1989) *Democracy and Disorder*. Oxford: Clarendon.

Tarrow, S. (1994) *Power in Movement*. New York: Cambridge University Press.

Tilly, C. (1978) *From Mobilization to Revolution*. Chicago: Addison-Wesley.

Tilly, C. (1986) *The Contentious French*. Cambridge, MA: Harvard University Press.

Touraine, A. (1974) *La Production de la société*. Paris: Seuil.

Touraine, A. (1978) *La Voix et le regard*. Paris: Seuil.

Touraine, A. (1984) *Le Retour de l'acteur*. Paris: Fayard.

Turner, R.H. and Killian, L.M. (1987) *Collective Behavior*, 3rd edn. Englewood Cliffs, NJ: Prentice-Hall.

PART II
SPACE, POWER AND
COLLECTIVE ACTION

Introduction

Collective action is the end result of a delicate and nuanced combination of conflicts and actors. Within its parameters we can locate the roots of deep historical grievances, structural strain and mobilized collective actors. Social movements have their own relationship to memory chains, linking one type of action to another in time and space. This has both positive and negative aspects, the latter visibly evident in the rise of chauvinistic nationalism in the republics of Eastern Europe. Most importantly, these phenomena cannot be understood in an *a priori* manner. They are socially constructed events exposing the complexity of conflict-laden relationships with historical and present Others.

The social movement literature is rife with analyses which examine the dense articulation between structural conflicts and collective actors. It is not surprising that this theme places considerable attention on social mechanisms that are integral to the construction of action; on strategies and the means through which an actor defines his or her insertion into any given field of conflict.

The key concepts here are well known to practitioners and scholars in the field of social movements. Most are of an organizational and resource-based nature. The array of cultural, media, community and institutional resources, and their effects on mobilization, are usually closely examined. It is also common to refer to the construction of 'master frames of meaning' around the very notion of action and to the ensemble of opportunity structures which mediate it.

Chris Pickvance, John Urry, Henri Lustiger-Thaler and Louis Maheu, the authors of this part of our book, do not ignore these critical dimensions of collective action. Pickvance, for example, deplores the shortcomings of macro-theories of collective action. He insists that we explore the many diversified patterns of social movements: trends they build over time and space, not forgetting the social backgrounds of participants.

For Urry, collective action remains central to an understanding of class. But, he argues, to fully grasp this we must disabuse ourselves of conventional class models of analysis. New avenues of theorization should accord particular attention to resources and political opportunity structures. It is these assets and opportunities which structure the collective practices of social classes.

Lustiger-Thaler and Maheu look at urban social movements from the standpoint of the multi-dimensional construction of collective action. This underscores the interface between the social and political. An analytical position that puts too much emphasis on this point however may be costly, erasing the distinction between social movements and interest groups. And in no sense does it exhaust the way one might view social movements, particularly urban movements, which are amply treated by several authors in Part II.

However important it is to examine the construction of social action, one must not forget its conflict-laden and structural dimensions. These must in turn be understood through the details of everyday grievances and power strategies. On this point, the chapters in this volume are unequivocal. Pickvance takes a critical stance regarding the many theories of social movements. He argues, for example, that almost all of these perspectives do not take seriously enough the state and its relation to social movements. This is a dimension too often lost in the discussion of political opportunity structures. It does not only concern the functioning of a political system through parties and/or other agents of mediation. It also has to do with the relationship between old and new ruling elites, between social forces that are active in the construction of local structures of power.

Pickvance demonstrates the importance of local space in the consideration of collective action. He views the construction of local space through struggles, conflicts and social forces that compose local power structures and civil society. This allows him to look at the divergences and convergences between social movements of East European societies and those of the West. The same type of analytical highlighting also allows him to link patterns and forms, necessary for the emergence of social movements, by examining very precise social processes. Some of these are: the transition of regimes; weak levels of economic growth; diminishing or newly opened political and public spaces; and the relationships between dominant elites, private and public enterprises as well as political actors.

Urry is interested in the collective action of classes within capitalist society. He draws our attention to a third class force, the American service class. Collective action has become their strategic vehicle as competing actors. He examines class formations through particular social characteristics embedded within enabling as well as constraining structures. But structures are *not* enabling solely in the sense of providing resources to putative collective agents. Social structures are enabling through the causal powers of institutions and social groupings.

Social relations, particularly relations of exploitation, inhere within structures as well as places and spaces. As a result of these strategic sites and conducts, classes as social forces have transformative consequences. They manifest structurally defined powers. Social structures create the objective conditions for the collective action of classes. The latter in turn marks these structures in the same manner as it affects space and place.

Lustiger-Thaler and Maheu also begin their analysis with questions of place, local social structures and civil society. They do this to draw ample attention to the structural grievances that urban social movements inscribe within the political and the social. They argue that political regulation, and the construction of the local state and civil society through social struggle, animate the collective actions of movements. This logic of collective action is distinct from the dynamic behind the process of institutionalization of collective actors *as* social movements. This is a notion of institutionalization that is different from the functionalist model according to which social movements essentially complete the functions of political parties or pressure groups, or formulate questions in ways that are later taken aboard by political parties.

As Lustiger-Thaler and Maheu argue, institutionalization is a conflict-laden field in which agents introduce and develop frameworks and spaces for experiencing autonomy. Through this dynamic they confront the politico-institutional network directly rather than through public opinion networks, as many writers suggest. These spaces of experiencing are beyond strictly 'identity' issues: they are attached to structural, economic and cultural facets of a late and radical modernity. Collective action, in this sense, when inscribed within the spatial confines of a locality, a place, manifests itself on more than the political register of the social. Through this process of institutionalization, urban social movements are inscribed in a field of social conflicts around issues of autonomy, cultural authenticity and multi-dimensional risks. Such social conflicts characterize their relations to regulating institutions and raise important questions of democracy and regulation. The linkages which bind these various dimensions of collective action and political life is a theme we shall return to in Part III.

5

Social Movements in the Transition from State Socialism: Convergence or Divergence?

Chris Pickvance

The aim of this chapter is to take some first steps towards an examination of the degree of convergence and divergence between social movements in the former state socialist bloc and in Western capitalist societies.[1] The chapter is divided into four sections. In section I, we comment briefly on aspects of social movement theory. In section II, we discuss local power structure under state socialism and in the current transition. In sections III and IV, we explore the question of convergence between social movements in East and West. We do this by making a critical assessment of the literature on social movements in the 'West', and by making a provisional assessment of relevant features of 'Eastern' social movements. Section V is the conclusion. The focus throughout is mainly on Hungary and Russia. No attempt has been made to cover a wider range of countries.

I The concept of social movement and social movement theory

The concept of social movement
Social movements can be understood at different levels of abstraction. At the most abstract level, they are movements of opinion or social forces which challenge prevailing views. The challenge may come from any political standpoint: racist, feminist, anti-abortion, anti-tax, anti-war or anti-nuclear power. (We do not follow Eder's [1993] view that the term applies only to movements which contribute to the 'modernization' of society.) At a more concrete level, social movements are made up of organizations existing on a neighbourhood, city, regional, national or even international basis to advance the declared aims of the movement. However, we use

the term social movement even when organizationally, the local movement organizations are not linked into a wider federation or unitary organization.[2]

Social movement organizations (referred to below as social movements) are mobilized groups with three features. First, they advance claims which range from cultural critique to demands for a change in resource allocation within the existing socioeconomic framework. Secondly, because social movements have an 'outsider' status vis-à-vis the political system, they are often deprived of the behind-the-scenes channels of influence available to established pressure groups and interest groups, and therefore engage in public and non-institutionalized forms of action such as demonstrations. However, movements use a variety of methods of action, and more long-lived movements may develop behind-the-scenes forms of influence. Thirdly, social movements are defined in contrast to political parties. This opposition is clearest between social movements and parties with wide support, since the latter's programmes will be drawn from the widely shared political agenda from which social movement demands are excluded. The contrast is less clear in the case of small parties which are formed by movements to advance their cause in the formal political sphere. For example, a Green party clearly has attributes both of a movement organization and of a party. If such parties succeed in winning seats, they are subject to pressures pulling them towards both the broader movement of which they are a part and towards the political system into which they have made an entry.[3]

Finally, it should be noted that the above definition does not refer to the degree of success of a social movement. The concept of success is problematic. For example, success may be measured by political impact or (as Melucci notes in Chapter 4 in this book) cultural impact, short-term effects may be different from medium-term effects, and success may occur despite the disintegration of social movement organizations. It follows that we shall not restrict the term social movement to cases where there are large-scale political effects.

Social movement theory
Having clarified what we understand by social movements, we now consider briefly their status within sociological theory. For reasons of brevity we shall not discuss the various middle-range theories of social movement participation which are covered elsewhere in this book (see, for example, Chapter 10, by Hamel). We restrict our discussion to (a) two macro-theories of social movements; and (b) theories of the interaction of social movements and the state.

Macro-theories   Some writers give social movements a special importance in their theories of society and social change. My own view is to the contrary: if defined as above, social movements are of quite variable importance in social change. Hence it is useful to examine the arguments of macro-theorists. We consider in turn structural-functionalist theories and Touraine's theory of social action.

Structural-functionalists see social movements as recurrent features of society, but regard any particular movement as transitory. The reasoning here is that political parties are the 'normal' means of interest aggregation, but they are imperfectly adapted to responding to new movements of opinion. Social movements are seen as having the role of drawing the attention of parties to new bodies of opinion which are currently excluded from representation. They are 'functional' in this sense to the stability of the political system, but individually they are short-lived because it is assumed that the political system is responsive to new currents of opinion.

The advantage of this model is that it points to the role of parties in taking on board movement demands, and hence reducing the reasons for such movements to persist. It means that every study of social movements must focus on the degree of openness of the political system to new demands, and on the interaction of social movements and political parties.

The defect in the model is its assumption that the political system is fundamentally open and that *all* new demands advanced by a social movement will eventually be taken up by a party. It does not allow for the possibility that some demands will be unwelcome by any party and will therefore remain excluded from the political agenda; in this case the *raison d'être* of movements will remain. Secondly, it does not recognize that the expression of demands uncongenial to the state or to established parties may be obstructed or that movements making such demands may be subjected to repression or co-optation by state institutions. So it seems unwise to accept the claim that social movements act as early warning signals of new currents of opinion prior to their absorption into the political system.

A second macro-theory in which social movements play a special role is *Touraine's sociology of action*. Whereas in structural-functionalism, social movements are not a central phenomenon (they help societal 'equilibrium' to be reached but are not fundamental to it), for Touraine the opposite is true. Touraine (1981, 1988) sees social movements as the main forces in the development of societies. He denies the need for a 'structural' level of analysis, so does not talk about structural elements such as classes with conflicting latent interests. In contrast, he argues that classes are significant only through their action, and this means through social movements. Touraine goes on to argue that each type of society has a particular type of social movement: 'merchant' societies have movements for civil liberties and political rights; industrial societies (whether capitalist or state socialist) have movements over the distribution of the material product and economic justice; and post-industrial societies have new social movements for self-management and identity.

Touraine's approach to social movements is distinctive in two ways. First, he distinguishes between three types of conflict: 'collective behaviour' which seeks to defend, reconstruct or adapt a 'sick element of the social system'; 'struggles' – the broadest category of 'factors of change or political forces'; and 'social movements' – 'conflictual actions [which] seek to transform the relations of social domination that are applied to the principal cultural resources (production, knowledge, ethical rules)' (Touraine, 1988: 63–4). From the idea that every society has one type of social movement it follows that most struggles will *not* involve social movements as he defines them. For example, he notes that many urban attempts to defend a threatened environment are akin to collective behaviour. On the other hand he sees the anti-nuclear struggle as a social movement, since it combines the protection of nature with 'the struggle to overthrow technocracy and the fight to establish a different, more modern, type of development' (Touraine et al., 1983). The second distinctive feature of Touraine's approach is his method, which involves creating groups of activists drawn from a variety of movement organizations and trying to raise their understanding of the issues involved until a 'conversion' is achieved, when the activists accept Touraine's interpretation. (This was said to have happened in the anti-nuclear research study; see Touraine et al.,1983: 171, 179.)

The theory has a number of virtues. It draws attention to the substance of the demands of different social movements, and hence seeks to understand why dominant ideas in society change; and it focuses on how social movements help groups to create their identities and does not reduce success to political acceptance of their demands. Moreover, like writers such as Hindess (1987), it adopts a constructionist rather than a structuralist picture of social action and is a useful counterweight to deterministic accounts which have no space for social action.

On the other hand, the theory has severe defects. (For a more general assessment see Cohen, 1983; Scott, 1990, 1991.)[4] Touraine's attribution of particular types of movement to particular types of society is arbitrary and prematurely judges the significance of different types of movement; there is an inconsistency between his rejection of structuralism and his *de facto* evolutionism and restrictive view of appropriate social movements for each societal type; and his analysis of the interaction of movements, parties and state institutions is underdeveloped – he considers state institutions to have a role in diachronic analysis, whereas social movements belong to the synchronic sphere. His exclusive interest in movements bearing new cultural models means that he is forced to classify groups as social movements or collective behaviour when in fact many have both defensive and innovative aspects. This means that only a handful of what other researchers consider to be social movements fall into Touraine's category of social movement. (In practice in both his work and that of Castells [1983], who developed Touraine's ideas in the urban field, the term social movement fluctuates continuously between the strict definition given above and a looser, all-embracing meaning.) Finally, his research method – described as 'sociological Leninism' by one critic (Cohen, 1983) – focuses on the ideas of an artificially created group of activists rather than on the development, experience and success or failure of *actual* groups. It tends to emphasize 'incorrect' *ideas* as the cause of success or failure (and in particular the gap between activists' understandings and Touraine's understanding), rather than the movement's actions and the state's responses.

As in the case of structural-functionalism, the theoretical weight given by Touraine to social movements appears to be predetermined. We do not see the need to make any such prejudgement.

Social movements and the state   Studies of social movements frequently ignore the state. This is partly because those who study social movements are often sympathetic to them and tend to exaggerate their importance. This leads them to underestimate the importance of the state authorities against which they are often making demands (for a critique of 'movement-centred' analyses in the case of urban movements, see Pickvance, 1975). It is also because 'social movements' and 'state theory' have developed as relatively independent branches of sociology, and specialists in the former have treated the state as a context rather than as a central theme.

One effect of this is that studies of social movements often use the 'umbrella' concept of 'political opportunity structure' to designate everything in the political context which they treat as a given. This practice has been criticized by writers such as Kriesi (1991), who note that the term covers such diverse topics as rules of parliamentary representation, openness of state institutions to external pressure, centralization of state structure, state policy capacity and state strategies towards social movements. Rootes (1992a) goes further and denies that all of these are structural features since some depend on which party is in power.

The importance of disentangling the elements of 'political opportunity structure' and giving proper weight to the effects of the state can be seen from a number of considerations:

- Demands made by movements are conditioned by political reality, which includes the likely responses of the state. They are not formulated in a vacuum, and may well be adjusted in the light of state responses.
- State authorities vary in their strength or weakness in response to demands, and in their capacity for policy implementation (Kitschelt, 1986).
- State authorities may be more or less internally divided and more or less open to external influence. To the extent that they are fragmented rather than monolithic, the chances of some departments supporting movement demands is greater. For example, it is often found that one department welcomes the existence of external pressure, since it enables that department to claim external support (and hence legitimacy) for its positions in internal conflicts over budget shares.
- Last but not least, state authorities are rarely passive, but normally pursue strategies (within their capacity to do so) to deal with external pressures. These range from the positive to the negative. Positive strategies may involve the provision of information, of funding and of other support. State bodies may even have a policy of supporting the creation of 'grassroots' bodies. Negative strategies range from non-cooperation (restriction of information, refusal to meet representatives), to co-optation (when the state succeeds in persuading movements to alter their demands in line with state preferences), to deliberate weakening (for example by ending cooperation, or by setting up rival associations), and to repression of action by movements (prohibition of demonstrations, arrest of participants, etc.)

These ideas will be drawn upon below.

II Local power structures

In discussing social movements in Eastern Europe and the former Soviet Union it is obviously crucial to understand the configuration of state power, especially at the local level. We consider in turn the period of state socialism, and the transition from state socialism.

Local power under state socialism

Under state socialism, the configuration of local power relations was very different from that in capitalist societies. Firstly, the scope of local authorities and of central state responsibility was narrower, since many infrastructural and welfare state functions were undertaken, at least in part, by enterprises – for example the provision of housing, access to health care, leisure and holiday facilities and even the supply of food.

There are two reasons for this, one structural and one contingent. The state socialist economic system worked through large enterprises reporting to central ministries (Kornai, 1992), so large enterprises had huge influence at the central level of resource allocation. In a real sense they *were* the economy, so the central authorities could not seriously consider acting against their interests. Likewise, central planning, to the extent it existed, involved the reconciliation of demands from the major centres of power represented by large enterprises, as much as an attempt to impose centrally decided plans. Recognition of the power of major enterprises is evident from Kornai's analysis of the 'soft budget constraint' applying to state socialist enterprises. The softness of budget constraints is a direct reflection of the leverage exerted by state enterprises over central ministries. In Hungary, the 1968 economic reform sought to weaken the power of major enterprises, and this is one of the reasons for the 1972 recentralization and the subsequent difficulties in moving away from a centralized system (see Szalai, 1989, 1991).

The contingent reason for the power of state enterprises is the priority given to rapid industrialization. This meant that public resources were concentrated spatially in those areas most involved in the industrialization drive. In particular, state housing was built (though on an insufficient scale) in support of industrial growth – so it was concentrated in cities (existing or new) at the expense of rural areas. As this rapid industrialization phase ended, and the satisfaction of consumer needs rose in importance, so the contingent power of state enterprises declined – though their structural power within the system remained.

One effect of the power of the state enterprises at the local level is that the local authority has fewer resources and hence less power. Shomina (1992) has distinguished four relations of enterprises to local authorities in the Soviet Union: landlord, neighbour, sponger and (rarely) partner. Interestingly, all of these imply at least equal status for enterprises. Yanitsky (1991a) refers to enterprises as 'feeding' the community. There is certainly no sense in which local authorities 'plan' the spatial development of their area. Rather, they 'pick up the pieces' of decisions made by enterprises independently of their local repercussions (Urban, 1990). The role of local authorities under state socialism is therefore a very distinctive one.[5]

The second major feature of state socialism at a local level is the interdependence of economic, administrative and party structures. The party had a structure which paralleled and intertwined with that of enterprises and state authorities. The effect of this was to allow party intervention in economic and administrative decisions. The underlying rationale was that the legitimacy of the regime depended on the functioning of local enterprises (which were responsible for full employment) and on the performance of the local authority (which provided schools and those other facilities not provided by enterprises).

In fact, however, the failure of central economic planning meant that a major role devolved on the party in helping the 'system' to operate at even a modest level of performance. Party officials became important in securing inputs for enterprises, and local authorities – deprived of resources within an allocation system that favoured large enterprises – turned to party officials to help out. The best model is probably that of a network in which party officials influence resource allocation in order to maintain a minimum level of performance which would not otherwise occur.

Clearly, the Soviet Union and Hungary were at very different positions in terms of the configuration of local power. The Hungarian economic reforms, which were a delayed response to the 1956 uprising, had no parallel in the Soviet Union, which was burdened with a highly centralized system. On the other hand, the Hungarian system 'delivered' more because of the extensive 'second economy' which was allowed to flourish outside – but not always independently of – the state sector. In the mid-1980s about one-third of all personal incomes were derived from the second economy.

Secondly, the position of the party in the two countries in the 1980s was very different. In the USSR the party was still the crucial structure in both national economic and political management and in local-level industrial management. In Hungary, the party's economic role at the firm level had been reduced under the economic reforms, but it maintained its overall economic and political role. Hence at the local level there was a sharp difference in party power.

Local power in the transition from state socialism[6]

The two former state socialist countries of interest here, Russia and Hungary, are at very different stages on the road to having capitalist economies and multi-party democratic systems.

Measures of transition are highly problematic. Measures of economic transition based on the proportion of firms or employees in the private sector are open to the objection that a change in ownership may be formal and may not mean a change in management practice, or in financing (for example if state banks take over the reins from ministries).[7] In Hungary it has even been shown that managers of a large firm may turn the divisions into private companies in order to avert change (Stark, 1993). Nevertheless, based on the previous scale of the second economy and the extent of foreign investment (larger in Hungary than in the rest of Eastern Europe as a whole), it is certain that the private economic sector in Hungary is further advanced than in Russia.

In terms of political transition, Hungary has a degree of institutional stability, public confidence in the legal order, and adoption of democratic institutions, including stable political parties, which give it a very 'Western' image. In Russia, by contrast, the break-up of the Soviet Union, the clashes between President and Parliament, the conflict between centre and periphery, and the contradictions between the Soviet constitution and new laws or decrees mean that the institutional framework is highly unstable. Likewise, stable political parties and stable working arrangements within elected bodies have failed to emerge.

We will now consider the impact of economic and political change on local power structures in Russia and Hungary.

Russia   The obstacles to economic transition in Russia have been the entrenched power position of managers of state enterprises and the fear of political repercussions if mass unemployment were to follow economic restructuring. The advancement and retraction of successive plans for economic reform and subsequent hesitation about their implementation are thus entirely understandable.

At the local level, most state enterprises still exist. They have secured funding by their *de facto* influence on banking institutions, one effect of which is the high level of inflation. As International Monetary Fund (IMF) pressure for banking discipline grows, state enterprises will experience a reduction of funding and increased exposure to market forces. On the other hand, private enterprise, especially in commerce, has started to develop, and officials have converted the privileges of their existing power positions either legally or illegally into new economic forms (Levitas and Strzal-kowski, 1990).

The political changes in Russia have been greater than the economic changes but they are still a long way behind those in Hungary. The ending of the Communist Party (CPSU) monopoly on political positions and the holding of elections open to non-CPSU candidates have led to a mushrooming of political groups. However, as Tyomkina (1991) points out, these are based on the personal appeal of the leader rather than on an ideological message; they are far from being highly organized parties with elaborate manifestos, and do not compete for socially distinctive constituencies.

The position of local government institutions is changing rapidly. In some ways there are important links with the past: they remain very dependent for fiscal and other income upon enterprises in their area, their permanent officials have changed relatively little and, given the uneven development of market mechanisms for obtaining resources, they remain dependent on networks of exchange with state enterprises, collective farms and private firms in which previous party links are important. In other ways there is a break with the past: the replacement of unified CPSU control of political institutions by reform politicians of different hues has led to new conflicts. For example, there are conflicts between (a) 'radical' city mayors and more conservative republican leaders; (b) elected politicians at city and district council levels; (c) local politicians and conservative council officials; (d) different factions of radical politicians; and (e) ordinary council members and the mayor's clique (see Pickvance, 1993a). The abolition of district councils in Moscow by Moscow City Council in 1991 is an index of this conflict.

Local authorities have real bases of power through their provision of employment, purchasing of goods and services, undertaking of building and capital projects, provision of subsidies to local firms, power to tax, power to sell assets, provision of services and operation of planning and other regulatory powers. But at the same time, as mentioned above, they are subject to real constraints, so are obliged to enter bargaining relationships with economic and other actors of varying degrees of legality (Pickvance, 1993a).

Hungary   In Hungary the situation is very different. Economic reform started in 1968 and led to greater freedom for industrial managers and the development of the second economy.[8] This created greater inequalities of income, and was associated with some tolerance of dissent. Since 1990 there has been a more consistent approval of small business and a successful policy of attracting foreign capital. Official policy towards state enterprises has been to allow bankruptcies to take place and to allow unemployment. In the past, this policy has been announced in Hungary but never implemented. In fact, the government has shown hesitation about allowing those state enterprises which did not attract foreign investment to fold, and has been as concerned about the political repercussions of unemployment as the Russian government. Nevertheless unemployment has risen to 10 per cent.

On the political side, Hungary has held multi-party elections and the parties have proved much more durable than the political groups in Russia. Both the coalition in national power and the 'opposition' parties running local government in Budapest have seen their support fall away, but these swings in opinion have been expressed within the party system rather than outside it.

At the local government level, in Budapest there has been a high degree of decentralization of authority to district town halls. At present the popularity of housing privatization (35 per cent of all tenants in Budapest had bought their flats by mid-1993: Pickvance, 1994) means that councils have an assured source of income and can avoid levying new taxes. But there is a reluctance to adopt policies that would imply new tax burdens at a time of rapid inflation.

Again, the question of the degree of change in the real functioning of the state in response to social movements needs to be posed. Many personnel, especially at the middle level, remain unchanged, and economic constraints are still severe. Has local authority responsiveness to protest increased, or are political parties considered the main legitimate form of expression of public opinion? Are Free Democrat councillors with a dissident background likely to respond more favourably to new protest groups? We shall return to these questions below.

In sum, the new configuration of local power with which social movements are confronted remains a matter of great speculation, and is one of our research foci.

There are reasons for thinking change has been superficial: economic constraints on the state remain severe; state personnel are little changed; in Russia state enterprises retain considerable power; in both countries party-based networks persist (Czabo and Sik, 1993); and those in official positions will often have successfully converted their privileges into legal or illegal forms of power.

Yet there are reasons for thinking that changes have been real: single-party control has been replaced, stable political parties have emerged in Hungary, the economic influence of state enterprises is declining in Hungary, and small business is either starting (Russia) or developing further (Hungary).

We would want to argue against those writers who refer to a 'system change' in which the forces deriving from the previous socioeconomic system have collapsed. Rather, we suggest that the conflict between the forces deriving from the past and those deriving from the present is central to an understanding of the current transition.

III Social movements in capitalist democracies

In order to approach the question of whether the social movement experience of state socialist and former state socialist countries is distinctive from that of capitalist countries, we start by asking whether there is a model of social movement activity in capitalist democracies which can be taken as a yardstick.

The first point to make is that in terms of *level of social movement activity*, capitalist democracies have experienced great variations. In the post-war period, the 1960s witnessed a peak of social movement activity in many countries; since then there has been a decline (Ceccarelli, 1982; Pickvance, 1985, 1993b). In other words, there is no 'normal' level of social movement activity. The main explanations of changes in overall level are related not so much to changes in levels of grievances as to the rise and fall of a more generalized challenge to authorities which is expressed in a diversity of social movements. In the 1960s this challenge was focused on the student movement but spread outwards to civil rights and urban protest. This in turn was due to the development of the critique that affluence had left many civil rights unmet and many issues untackled.

A second point is that the upsurge of social movement activity has been characteristic of the period of *collapse of authoritarian regimes*, and prior to the establishment of political parties. This can be seen in Spain at the end of the Franco regime in the mid-1970s, in Brazil at the end of the military regime and before the re-establishment of democracy in 1985, and today in Hong Kong as a partial opening occurs within the colonial regime. In each case, *regime transition* creates a flourishing of political activity which takes the form of social movements initially, before 'settling down' to a lower level once political parties emerge.

A third point concerns the *degree of variation in social movement activity* between capitalist democracies. This is usually understood in terms of differences in the permeability of parties to new ideas (the more permeable, the more social movement activity), in the ease of group formation (some democracies are more restrictive than others), in the resistance capacity of the state (decentralized state systems have less resistance capacity than centralized systems), and in the tolerance of unconventional tactics (Kitschelt, 1986; Wilson, 1990; Rootes, 1992b).

A final point concerns the character of *social movement demands*. In recent years, much has been written about the 'new social movements' (NSMs) which are said to be distinctive in their demands (advocating the right to participate and to choose one's own lifestyle, rather than demanding more economic and political power within the existing system), their social base (which is described as either diverse and 'non-class' or 'educated middle-class', depending on the writer), their members' motivation (expressive rather than economically self-interested), their form of organization (decentralized and fluid rather than centralized and hierarchical) and their mode of political action (preference for unconventional methods) (Dalton et al., 1990).

The main examples usually given of new social movements are the student, women's, environmental, peace and anti-nuclear movements. The implicit contrast is with the labour movement.

In our view there are two major weaknesses in this theory. First it is ahistorical. If, as Dalton et al. (1990) argue, it is the ideological orientation of NSMs which 'determines what might be truly new about these movements' (1990: 11), it is immediately obvious that most of the demands they refer to have remarkably long histories. As Brand (1990) points out, environmentalism, pacifism and feminism were all significant movements in the 1890–1910 period and in many cases before that (see also d'Anieri et al., 1990). In other words, 'new social movement' theorists appear to have created a myth according to which until the 1960s the only agent of conflict in capitalist societies was the labour movement and no tradition of cultural critique existed. A corollary of this rewriting of history is the marginalization of those groups who made concrete economic and political demands after 1960 rather than the cultural critique privileged by new social movement theorists, for example urban movements.

The second weakness of NSM theory is that it exaggerates the sharpness of the distinctions between the types of demand, social base, motivation, organizational form, and mode of action of NSMs and other movements. First, NSM demands are not purely culturally critical[9] any more than the demands of 'old' social movements were purely economically and politically instrumental; secondly, the social base of the labour movement is untypical of social movements generally – the social base of most types of social movement is more middle class than working class; thirdly, expressive motivation did not start in 1960 (it is also to be found among pacifists and environmentalists of the past); fourthly, loose organizational forms are not something new (see Piven and Cloward, 1977); and finally, Tilly's (1978) historical work shows the great continuities in the repertoires of forms of protest action over time.

In brief, in our view, the attempt to demarcate a category of 'new social movement' (which is presumably more deserving of our attention) as characteristic of advanced capitalist societies today fails totally. (The term 'new social movement' may, however, be more important in acting as a unifying slogan for a rising school of social researchers.) The question of convergence between Eastern and Western experience of social movements should not start from the assumption that NSMs are either new or the only type of Western social movement.

Melucci, in Chapter 4 in this book, adopts an ambivalent approach to the term 'new social movement'. On the one hand, despite being its originator, he adopts a self-critical position, noting that it was intended to refer to the *relative* novelty of contemporary social movements in contrast to the labour movement in industrial capitalism, and as a 'temporary critical tool' directed against resource mobilization theory. He criticizes it as a temporary concept which is justified only if sociological theory can give it analytical substance. In a similarly critical vein, he denies that it refers to a 'unified empirical object' and criticizes those who do not look beneath the surface. On the other hand, Melucci takes a more defensive position and makes sweeping statements such as that 'contemporary forms of collective action are not preoccupied with struggles over the production and distribution of material goods' but centre on information resources, are self-reflextive, planetary in their interdependency, and so on.

We agree with most of Melucci's self-critical view, but not with his defensive view. As indicated above, we do not think that attempts to give new social movements a coherent analytical definition have succeeded. In addition, as we shall see, in Hungary and Russia protests about material goods are far from having disappeared. Nor would we accept the view that such differences can be dismissed as beneath-the-surface complexity.

IV Social movements under state socialism and in the transition from state socialism

Having outlined a picture of social movements in capitalist democracies, we now examine how far societies undergoing the transition from state socialism show similarities.

Initially we would reiterate that our interest in social movements is not restricted to those with a major role in the ending of state socialism. Writers on this subject distinguish between countries where internal reform forces were more elite-led (Russia, Hungary) and those where citizen organizations were more important (Poland) (Bozoki, 1992; Szabo, 1992; Tarrow, 1992). In Hungary it is argued that the 'mode of extrication' from state socialism (Stark, 1992) was relatively strongly controlled, with only a minor role for citizen organizations. In Russia, on the other hand, reform elites lost control, and citizen mobilization was stronger but its fragmentation weakened its potential power. As a result, apart from Solidarity, the social movements referred to below are mostly localized and do not have a major macro-political role.

We examine in turn: trends over time in social movement activity; the diversity of types of social movement; movement support; and relations between the state and social movements.

Trends over time

Existing theories of the possibility of social movements under state socialism suggest either that they will be repressed as part of the general clamp-down on popular expression (Zald, 1988), or that if they do take hold they will be broad-scale and involve a challenge to the regime (Crighton, 1985). These propositions are clearly in contradiction, and the latter represents a rather unsatisfactory '*ad hoc*' explanation of the Solidarity movement in Poland. At the very least, the two possibilities indicate the limited value of a concept like state socialism, which does not take into account the very different balances of class forces and forms of political management among state socialist countries. The strength of the Polish working class and the Catholic Church, and the Hungarian 'bargain' of 'reformed' state socialism in exchange for political quiescence (Bozoki, 1992), have distinctive effects on popular expression. Melucci's argument in Chapter 4 of the present book regarding the need for 'public spaces of civil society' to exist before social movements can develop has a clear relevance for understanding the scarcity of social movements in state socialist societies.

A second general point is that environmental movements have occupied a privileged position under state socialist regimes. In both Hungary and the USSR, environmental movements were tolerated before other types of movement. In 1974 in Hungary there was a conflict over an oil spill which contaminated a river; in 1978 a movement occurred against lead poisoning at a Budapest factory; and in 1980 the pollution of water supplies by dangerous waste was alleged. This was followed by a protest against dust pollution (in Ajka – 1984), and a waste incinerator (in Dorog – 1984) and the well-known Danube Circle movement against the Nagymaros dam (see Waller, 1989; Szirmai, 1993; Galambos, 1992; Fleischer, 1993).

(The conflict over the importation of polluted waste at Mosonmagy-arovar in 1985–7 is described by Persanyi and Lanyi, 1991.)

In the Soviet Union, environmental activism goes back to the student *druzhinas* movement in the 1950s (Schwartz, 1990). Environmental movements existed in the state socialist period – for example the movements against pollution in Lake Baikal and the Aral Sea – and saw a considerable increase from 1986 (Yanitsky, 1993). At the urban level, Yanitsky (1991b) describes the fight against a plan for a new Moscow ring road to pass through the historic Lefortovo area (in the 1986–8 period).

It is as though it was more difficult for state socialist regimes to deny citizen action over environmental issues, either because it involved less of an ideological conflict (Yanitsky, 1991a), because of the demonstrable shortsightedness of central decisions, because of the immediacy and 'non-political' character of environmental issues, or because of the authority of the scientific expertise that was often deployed in support of environmental demands. The Chernobyl catastrophe in 1986 gave renewed legitimacy to environmental activism.

A third general point is that the development of social movements in the transition period seems to have followed the pattern previously observed in Spain, Portugal, Brazil and Hong Kong when regimes were undergoing transition. There is evidence of a *three-stage pattern:* (a) a period of *quiescence* with sporadic and quickly repressed movement activity; followed by (b) the *rapid upsurge* of social movements in the period prior to free elections; followed by (c) a *decline* as political parties form.

Evidence of these stages can be found in Russia, Estonia and Hungary. (On Russia see Igrunov, 1989, also discussed in Andrusz, 1990; Tyomkina, 1991; Alexejev et al., 1991; Yanitsky, 1993; on Hungary, see Szirmai, 1993; Enyedi, 1992.) In Estonia for example, the nationwide Estonian Society of Nature Protection started in 1966 as a non-political body guided by humanitarian and conservationist values.[10] In 1987 a Society for Preserving Historical Monuments was founded which later gave birth to several right-wing political parties. The Estonian Green Movement and Popular Front, founded in 1988, had similar aims of democracy and national liberalization. (The Green movement had support from the Russian population of Estonia.) The peak of movement activity was in 1988–9. From late 1988, social movements fragmented and 30 small parties and political societies emerged. From January 1990, in anticipation of the first free elections in March of that year, there was some consolidation among the parties and the formation of coalitions. In December 1991 the two Green parties united to form the 'Estonian Green' Party.

In Hungary the best-known social movement of the 1980s, the Danube Circle, also illustrated the three-stage pattern. Formed in 1984 in protest against a proposal to build a dam on the Danube on the Slovakia/Hungary border, the movement attracted thousands as signatories for petitions and later as participants in protests. This mobilization was paralleled by a counter-mobilization by party organizations, which meant that official registration was refused to the Danube Circle in 1988 (Fleischer, 1993). Nevertheless the movement continued and cancellation of the dam on the Hungarian side was announced in 1989. Szabo (1992) argues that this decision was due to the common cause made by the environmental movement and the democracy movement, and that when the latter crystallized into parties, activists flowed out of the environmental movement, which lost its impetus and was not represented at the round-table negotiations in 1989. (The Danube Circle still exists, but no longer has a commanding political position.)

It is premature to reach any conclusions about the various processes which account for the three-stage model. They may include some of the processes observed in past transitions from authoritarian to democratic regimes: the more secure 'political economy' of parties compared with social movements in the sense that their resource base is more firmly established; the fact that parties hold out the possibility of access to power from 'inside', whereas social movements seek to influence power from the outside; the incorporation of issues advanced by movements into party programmes – which, unless it is totally cynical, represents some success for the movement;[11] and finally the departure of movement activists for political parties once parties exist (Yanitsky, 1991a). (The subsequent election of some of them to power may or may not represent a success for the movement.)

On the other hand, there may be some novel phenomena. First there may be reasons for the decline in movement activity other than the institutionalization of movement demands. For example, in Russia it is likely that the severe economic situation in 1991 and 1992 (inflation of 93 per cent and 1354 per cent, and a decline in GDP of 11 per cent and 19 per cent) have reduced collective action in favour of individual economic survival strategies. Secondly, political parties (which often do not call themselves that because of the connotation of the word 'party') seem to be made up of cliques of individuals united by cultural values more often than by a clear ideology or programme (Lomax, 1991). In Hungary where parties are more fully formed than in the former Soviet Union, the decline in social movement activity has been more marked. There have been two nationally noted actions: in 1990 the taxi-drivers' protest against increased petrol prices blocked all the bridges in Budapest (Sik, 1991; Szabo, 1992) and the Democratic Charter declaration signed by 100 intellectuals against the erosion of civil rights under the new government (*Eastern European Reporter*, January 1992: 36–7). However, at the local level there are numerous organizations – in 1993 there were estimated to be 120 environmental groups throughout Hungary.

Hence the three-stage pattern of social movement activity does not imply that the era of social movements in the former socialist bloc has ended.

The diversity of types of movement

As in Western countries, the aims of social movements are very diverse and are not all located at one end of a continuum. In Russia there are anti-capitalist movements as well as anti-totalitarian movements (Tyomkina, 1991). Their goals are highly diverse, ranging from political and civil rights to feminist, leisure, arts and environmental. But the range of types of social movement in former state socialist societies looks very different from that in the West. Of the four so-called 'new' social movements, environmental movements exist (but are concerned with immediate goals rather than the 'deep green' goals of political ecology), as do to a very limited extent anti-nuclear movements – but the peace and women's movements are much less prevalent. Movements with more immediate aims seem more typical. The level of movements, however, is far lower than the level of potential grievances. Although housing movements are increasing, housing is the scene of far less movement activity than might be expected, given the long waiting lists for state flats, the numerous concealed households and so on. There are housing movements linked to the grievances of state flat applicants (one Estonian organization is entitled the Union of Hostel Residents and Flat Application Veterans: Raudsepp, 1992), 'housing partnerships' in central Moscow which seek to obtain ownership of the whole block so that residents can benefit from the rents of commercial premises which are part of it, and in Hungary a lobby in favour of the homeless and a Tenants' Association which takes up individual complaints by tenants about maintenance and advises on privatization (all discussed in Pickvance, 1994). In Russia in 1989 there was also a specific type of movement – the sociopolitical discussion club (e.g. Club for Social Initiatives, Perestroika) which seemed to act as a multi-nucleated group capable of developing in a variety of directions according to circumstances (Hosking et al., 1992).

Movement support

In Hungary there is evidence of continuity between current movement supporters and the dissident movement, and of a generational or cohort effect. In Russia, according to Igrunov (1989), the informal groups were not direct successors to dissident traditions, and did not contain dissidents in their ranks. Shlapentokh says that the most prominent liberal intellectuals avoided involvement in informal groups in the initial period 1986–8 (1990: 268) but subsequently took part. Yanitsky (1991b, 1993) and Györi (1989) both emphasize the role of intellectuals in social movements in Russia and Hungary (see also Waller, 1989). Information about the social base of social movements is limited, but there is evidence of the active role of students and scientists in environmental movements (see Waller, 1989; Schwartz, 1990; Amonashvili, 1990; Kulvik and Lotman, 1991; Yanitsky, 1993). Some movements are also referred to as of elite status – the Club of Social Initiatives (formed in 1986) was co-founded by and supported by the Soviet Sociological Association to which it 'owes much of its success', according to Igrunov (1989). There is evidence of the concentration of memberships among a relatively small core of highly active individuals. Finally, it has been argued that the development (and atypicality) of Solidarity was due to the highly developed network of Church and secular groups in Poland – in line with resource mobilization theory predictions (Crighton, 1985; Szjakowski, 1985). There are thus important continuities between the social origins of movement supporters in the former state socialist countries and in the West.

Relations between the state and social movements

Under state socialism, the general image is of a more or less all-controlling party-state discouraging potential protest and repressing the first signs of any actual protest. As hinted above, this is not entirely accurate. In addition to Solidarity, environmental protests – especially in Hungary but also elsewhere – were tolerated in a way in which other movements were not. There is even evidence of local authorities acting together with local protesters and local enterprises. This is provided in Szirmai's (1989) analysis of the protest against the Ajka flue-ash factory in Hungary. Ajka is a centrally created town in which the local authorities are subordinate to the local plant and its superior ministerial authority. Szirmai argues that rather than repressing the protest against the pollution caused by the factory, the local authority joined with the local movement, the local party apparatus, and the managers of the factory to demand resources from the superior ministry to install filtering equipment.

This surprising combination is a reflection of the distinctive institutional structure of state socialism.

There were other successful movements in post-1985 Russia and in the final years of state socialist Hungary. These include the Lefortovo (Moscow) movement which led to a halt in a road plan (Yanitsky, 1991b), the movement against a hydroelectric project in Georgia (Amonashvili, 1990) and the Danube Circle movement in Hungary (Waller, 1989; Galambos, 1992; Fleischer, 1993). The Georgian example demonstrates the importance of the political context – in that case the concurrent strength of the nationalist movement. The Danube dam example shows the importance of scientific expertise and the intertwining of the movement with the movement for political reform. One may conclude that in the presence of favourable political conditions social movements have been successful.

However, it is too early to reach conclusions about the typical reaction of post-state socialist authorities to social movements. One could hypothesize that state socialism provided little basis for a tradition of interaction and compromise between movements and state authorities, and therefore that authorities would react strongly to repress movements – unless it was advantageous to support them (as in the Ajka case mentioned above). If this is so, one would expect that in the transition from state socialism, authorities would lack the cultural experience of knowing how to deal with movements – and that movements would lack the experience of learning how to negotiate and compromise. This implies that social movements would be the source of considerable unmanaged conflict. On the other hand, it may be that learning processes are rapid and that experience elsewhere is transmitted (for example via activists occupying positions of authority, international news, and so on).

It is clear that there exists in Russia and Estonia a system of registration of voluntary associations. According to some reports it entitles a movement organization to have a bank account, rent or own buildings, and publish a newspaper. But there is also evidence that these activities often occur in the absence of registration, and organizations can exist without being registered. There is evidence of the use of 'registration' to favour moderate groups over radical groups (see the failure of the radical Perestroika 88 to obtain registration or premises, while its moderate counterpart, Democratic Perestroika, was able to obtain both: Igrunov, 1989: 5). If registration is effective, it would have parallels with the French 'Law of 1901' which regulates voluntary associations, and would place Russia and Estonia in the category of being potentially restrictive of group formation.

Beyond registration, authorities have adopted a diversity of responses to citizen demands. Our research leads us to make a sharp contrast between Russia and Hungary, at least as evidenced by the much more closed 'political opportunity structure' in Moscow compared with Budapest. At the repressive extreme, Yanitsky (1991a) gives evidence of the prohibition of public demonstrations in Moscow in 1988 (whereas indoor meetings were permitted) and describes confrontation as being the norm in relations between movements and authorities. He also describes the tactic – well known elsewhere – of state sponsorship of 'pseudo-movements' to delegitimize organizations making tough demands. State support for movements in Moscow in the 'leisure, family and education, physical culture and medicare' spheres (Igrunov, 1989: 11) may have something of a 'protest defusing' role, but may also have more immediate managerial purposes. Our own research has revealed cases of 'housing movements' which are created by the authorities for internal bureaucratic reasons, for example to show 'support' for higher levels of house building. Our studies of neighbourhood self-management organizations and housing partnerships in Moscow indicate that they generally make demands which are totally resisted by the authorities.

So far, state authorities (district, city and national) have been portrayed as generally closed to external influence. However, in democratic regimes where parties alternate in power, a more familiar model is one in which state authorities are to some extent open. The election of 'reform' or 'democratic' politicians provides a counterweight to bureaucratic interests which may indeed be repressive in tendency. Likewise, the absorption of movement activists into governmental bodies either as politicians or as administrative officials is likely to make the state more responsive to movement demands. This model fits our evidence on Budapest, where relations between housing and environmental movements and authorities are usually cooperative. In some cases, such as the Tenants' Association, the movement receives state funding and advises on legislation, as well as providing individual help. This cooperation is primarily an effect of the 'maturity' of democracy in Hungary which is linked to the gradual and slow transition (Bozoki, 1992).[12] Although Yanitsky refers to movements in Moscow as having 'an extensively developed informal network that also penetrates state-controlled bodies' (1991b: 531), this conflicts with his view quoted earlier that confrontation is the norm in relations between authorities and movements. There is evidence of a sharp contrast between Hungary and Russia.

V Conclusion

We now return to our point of departure: the question of the convergence or divergence of social movements 'East' and 'West'.

First, we would point to a number of features which are widely found in both types of society. There is some evidence that leadership of social movements, and possibly membership too, is relatively concentrated among the highly educated in former state socialist societies as well as in the 'West'. Leaders of dissident movements in the past are often to be found among social movement activists or politicians today. There is also some evidence of overlapping membership of movements, as in the 'West'. There is evidence too of the importance of the general level of mobilization for the level of activity in particular spheres, again as in the 'West'. Finally, particularly striking is the validity of the three-stage model of regime transition, previously applied to transitions from authoritarian societies. This suggests that repression of movements under an authoritarian regime gives way to an upsurge of social movements as the prospect of a political opening develops, and to a decline as political parties become a legal mode of political expression.

Secondly, there is one major difference in the types of social movement in former state socialist and advanced capitalist societies. Although both types of society share a diversity of types of social movement ('progressive' and 'non-progressive'), 'new' social movements are much less prevalent in the 'East'.

Thirdly, former state socialist societies differ among themselves in a number of features and hence do not form a homogeneous category. The macro-political impact of social movements in the transition from state socialism varies from major (Poland) to minor (Hungary). The policy of the authorities towards social movements ranges from the confrontational (Russia) to the frequently cooperative (Hungary). The use of registration to control movement development also varies.

What has to be explained, then, is the similarities in social movement experience across capitalist and former state socialist societies, the differences between the two categories, and the differences internal to each. To do this we need to separate comparisons between social movement *patterns* (frequency, trends over time, social background of participants) and social movement *processes* (the reasons for high or low frequency, or for particular trends over time, which include resource mobilization and institutionalization) and explore how the two are connected.

With respect to the convergences in social movement patterns across capitalist and former state socialist societies, the obvious explanation is that they are due to similar processes. For example, regime transitions appear to have common effects on social movement incidence wherever they occur; and the development of political parties appears to reduce participation in social movements (though in a far more complex way than the structural-functionalist model implies). But although similar processes may be at work, there is also a possibility that similar patterns come about through different processes.[13]

Regarding differences between social movement patterns in the two sets of societies, there are also two possibilities. The most likely is that differences in pattern are comprehensible within a single process. For example, the lower level of socioeconomic development and the difficulties of creating a space for social movements in former state socialist societies may explain why new social movements are much less common there. The implication is that once these conditions change, new social movements will become stronger. But again, it cannot be ruled out that distinctive processes are at work in each set of societies.

Finally, the difference in social movement patterns among former state socialist societies can also be explained in two ways. They may be due to common processes operating in societies with different 'initial conditions', for example different variants of state socialism or different 'modes of extrication' (Stark, 1992). For example, the stable party system in Hungary has made politics a feasible alternative to social movement participation, and the opposition control of many local governments there has favoured cooperation with social movements. These features in turn reflect the 'mode of extrication' by electoral competition in Hungary. In Russia, the weak development of parties has been a factor encouraging continued social movement participation, though economic conditions have had a contrary effect. Another example is the greater political impact of Solidarity in Poland compared to social movements in Hungary, which is related to the Polish experience of state socialism in which working-class organizations as well as the Catholic Church were much more important. Again, there is a possibility that distinctive processes also exist.

Future research will need to focus as much on the processes affecting social movement development as on their incidence and patterning.

The longer-term prospects of social movement activity in former state socialist societies depend less on the level of grievances than on how responsive authorities are to movement demands. This depends partly on political factors (e.g. the development of 'political cultures' which favour compromise rather than confrontation),

partly on economic factors (e.g. the resources available to authorities) and partly on the extent to which authorities develop close
ties with private (and public) enterprises and place their interests
above those of social movements. In all these respects, the study of
social movements will provide an index of how far old economic
and political structures continue to be influential and how far they
have given way to new ones.

Notes

1. This paper arises from a research project that was undertaken by a team at the
University of Kent at Canterbury on environmental and housing movements in
Hungary, Estonia and Russia. The research team is Chris Pickvance, Nick Manning,
Katy Pickvance and Sveta Klimova. Our collaborators are Peter Györi, Viktoria
Szirmai and Laszlo Kulcsar (Hungary), Yelena Shomina, Lev Perepjolkin and
Ludmilla Khakhulina (Russia) and Toomas Niit and Maaris Raudsepp (Estonia).
   The project was funded for three years from April 1991 and forms part of the
Economic and Social Research Council's 'East-West Initiative'. The project has two
elements: intensive and extensive. In each country five social movement organizations
were studied in depth over an 18–month period. This involves interviews with both
activists and officials in authorities to which the movements are directing their
demands. The extensive part of the research consists of a survey of random samples
of the public who were asked about their housing and environmental conditions and
political attitudes in order to study their responses to these conditions (if any). The
aim of this part of the work is to understand non-participation in collective action.
   I would like to thank all members of the research team and Chris Rootes for their
helpful comments on previous versions which were presented at conferences in Paris,
Prague, Canterbury and Los Angeles between November 1991 and April 1992.
   2. As Melucci shows in Chapter 4 in this book, social movement organizations
can also be analysed at a finer level as the outcome of social construction activity
by their members. This would require a close study of interpersonal relations among
participants – an approach I support (see Pickvance, 1975: 40–6).
   3. Some writers have suggested that social movements are always informal and
network-like in structure (Diani, 1992) but this is certainly not generally true: some
are more informal, some are more formal.
   4. See also Rucht's (1991) assessment and Touraine's reply (1991), which I saw
only after writing this.
   5. It is not totally dissimilar from that in capitalist societies where the resources
of big capitalist firms give them leverage over local authorities.
   6. I use the phrase 'transition from state socialism' with some hesitation. By
emphasizing 'from' the term makes no commitment to the future point of arrival.
Since there are many varieties of capitalism, from welfare to *laissez-faire*, and many
political shells – from democratic to authoritarian – this openness is a virtue.
However, the term 'transition' also implies instability followed by stability, which is
not necessarily accurate.
   7. The scope of illegal economic activity is a further complication.
   8. This leads to the view that the Hungarian transition was gradual and started
long ago. There is some truth in this notion, but it gives an unjustified teleological
interpretation to reforms which at the time were seen as insecure and reversible.

9. Rucht (1990: 169) specifically refers to the contemporary environmental movement as power oriented rather than directed to personal change. And in general it is common to find utopian and practical aims in the same movement.

10. The following paragraph is based on a report by our collaborator in Estonia, Maaris Raudsepp (1992).

11. In Hungary it is suggested by Szirmai (1993) and Enyedi (1992) that in the case of the environmental movement, demands are subsequently incorporated in party-based groups, such as 'Socialist Greens'.

12. Szabo (1992), writing about a different set of protests, describes the Hungarian authorities as showing 'ambivalence', i.e. a combination of permissiveness and rigidity.

13. As an example of this, access to housing in state socialist societies was as stratified as in capitalist societies, while the processes producing this outcome, which relied mainly on administrative allocation rather than market processes, were very different. For a discussion of this type of case, which contradicts the causal assumptions of mainstream comparative analysis, see Pickvance (1986).

References

Alexejev, A., Gelman, V., Kornev, N., Kotjushev, V. and Etkind, A. (1991) 'The social movements and the development of new power in Leningrad 1986–91', unpublished paper, Institute of Sociology, Leningrad.

Amonashvili, P. (1990) 'Perestroika and new pressure groups in Georgia: a successful ecological movement', *International Journal of Urban and Regional Research*, 14: 322–6.

Andrusz, G. (1990) 'Moscow conference report I: the re-emergence of Soviet sociology', *International Journal of Urban and Regional Research*, 14: 302–15.

Bozoki, A. (1992) 'The Hungarian transition in a comparative perspective', in A. Bozoki, A. Korosenyi and G. Schöpflin (eds), *Post-Communist Transition*. London: Pinter.

Brand, K-W. (1990) 'Cyclical aspects of new social movements', in R.J. Dalton and M. Kuechler (eds), *Challenging the Political Order*. Cambridge: Polity Press.

Castells, M. (1983) *The City and the Grassroots*. London: Edward Arnold.

Ceccarelli, P. (1982) 'Politics, parties and urban movements: Western Europe', in N.I. Fainstein and S.S. Fainstein (eds), *Urban Policy under Capitalism*. Beverly Hills: Sage.

Cohen, J.L. (1983) *Class and Civil Society*. Oxford: Martin Robertson.

Crighton, E. (1985) 'Resource mobilisation and Solidarity: comparing social movements across regimes', in B. Misztal (ed.), *Poland after Solidarity*. New Brunswick: Transaction Books.

Czabo, A. and Sik, E. (1993) 'On the role of network capital in economic transactions in post-Communist Hungary', paper presented to the Conference on the Social Embeddedness of the Economic Transformation in Central and Eastern Europe, Berlin.

Dalton, R.J., Kuechler, M. and Burklin, W. (1990) 'The challenge of new movements', in R.J. Dalton and Kuechler (eds), *Challenging the Political Order*. Cambridge: Polity Press.

D'Anieri, P., Ernst, C. and Kier, E. (1990) 'New social movements in historical perspective', *Comparative Politics*, 22: 445–58.

148   *Space, Power and Collective Action*

Diani, M. (1992) 'The concept of social movement', *Sociological Review*, 40: 1–25.

Eder, K. (1993) *The New Politics of Class*. London: Sage.

Enyedi, G. (1992) 'Environmental issues in the urban policy of Budapest local government', paper presented to International Seminar on Urban Planning and Environmental Policy, Prague.

Fleischer, T. (1993) 'Jaws on the Danube: water management, regime change and the movement against the Middle Danube Hydroelectric Dam', *International Journal of Urban and Regional Research*, 17: 429–43.

Galambos, J. (1992) 'Political aspects of an environmental conflict: the case of the Gabcikovo–Nagymaros Dam system', in J. Käkönen (ed.), *Perspectives on Environmental Conflict and International Relations*. London: Pinter.

Györi, P. (1989) 'New social initiatives: conflict and coexistence of the state and society', paper presented at conference on Voluntarism, Non-governmental Organisations and Public Policy, Jerusalem, May.

Hindess, B. (1987) *Politics and Class Analysis*. Oxford: Basil Blackwell.

Hosking, G.A., Aves, J. and Duncan, P.J.S. (1992) *The Road to Post-Communism: Independent Political Movements in the Soviet Union 1985–1991*. London: Pinter.

Igrunov, V.V. (1989) 'Public movement: from protest to political self-consciousness', paper presented to ISA conference, Moscow, October.

Kitschelt, H. (1986) 'Political opportunity structures and political protest: anti-nuclear movements in four democracies', *British Journal of Political Science*, 16: 58–95.

Kornai, J. (1992) *The Socialist Economic System*. Oxford: Oxford University Press.

Kriesi, H. (1991) *The Political Opportunity Structure of New Social Movements: its Impact on their Mobilisation*. Berlin: Wissenschaftszentrum, unpublished paper.

Kulvik, M. and Lotman, A. (1991) 'Public participation in revitalising the environment in Tartu, Estonia', in T. Deelstra and O. Yanitsky (eds), *Cities of Europe: the Public's Role in Shaping the Urban Environment*. Moscow: Mezhdunarodnye Otnoshenia.

Levitas, A. and Strzalkowski, P. (1990) 'What does "uwlaszczenie nomenklatury" [propertization of the nomenklatura] really mean?', *Communist Economies*, 2: 413–16.

Lomax, W. (1991) Intervention at ESRC/CNRS Conference on Elitism in Central Europe, Paris.

Persanyi, M. and Lanyi, G. (1991) 'Waste import at the turn of the epoch: how problems are tackled in Hungary', in T. Deeelstra and O. Yanitsky (eds), *Cities of Europe: the Public's Role in Shaping the Urban Environment*. Moscow: Mezhdunarodnye Otnoshenia.

Pickvance, C.G. (1975) 'On the study of urban social movements', *Sociological Review*, 23: 24–49.

Pickvance, C.G. (1985) 'The rise and fall of urban movements and the role of comparative analysis', *Society and Space*, 3: 31–53.

Pickvance, C.G. (1986) 'Comparative urban analysis and assumptions about causality', *International Journal of Urban and Regional Research*, 10: 162–84.

Pickvance, C.G. (1993a) 'Mediating institutions in the transition from state socialism: the case of local government', paper presented to the Conference on the Social Embeddedness of the Economic Transformation in Central and Eastern Europe, Berlin.

Pickvance, C.G. (1993b) 'Where have urban movements gone?', in C. Hadjimichalis and D. Sadler (eds), *In and Around the Margins of a New Europe*. London: Belhaven.

Pickvance, C.G. (1994) 'Housing privatization and housing protest in the transition from state socialism: a comparative study of Budapest and Moscow', *International Journal of Urban and Regional Research*, 8: 433–50.

Piven, F.F. and Cloward, R. (1977) *Poor People's Movements*. New York: Vintage.

Raudsepp, M. (1992) Unpublished report on social movements in Estonia. Tallinn: Institute of Philosophy, Sociology and Law.

Rootes, C. (1992a) 'Political opportunity structures, political competition and the development of social movements', paper presented to the First European Conference on Social Movements, Berlin.

Rootes, C.A. (1992b) 'The new politics and the new social movements: accounting for British exceptionalism', *European Journal of Political Research*, 22: 171–91.

Rucht, D. (1990) 'The strategies and action repertoires of new movements', in R.J. Dalton and M. Kuechler (eds), *Challenging the Political Order*. Cambridge: Polity Press.

Rucht, D. (1991) 'Sociological theory as a theory of social movements: a critique of Alain Touraine', in D. Rucht (ed.), *Research on Social Movements*. Frankfurt: Campus Verlag.

Schwartz, E.A. (1990) 'Students Druzhinas movement: problems of politicisation', in E. Golovina (ed.), *All Our Life*. Moscow.

Scott, A. (1990) *Ideology and the New Social Movements*. London: Unwin Hyman.

Scott, A. (1991) 'Action, movement and intervention: reflections on the sociology of Alain Touraine', *Canadian Review of Sociology and Anthropology*, 28: 30–45.

Shlapentokh, V. (1990) *Soviet Intellectuals and Political Power*. London: I.B. Tauris.

Shomina, E.S. (1992) 'Enterprises and the urban environment in the USSR', *International Journal of Urban and Regional Research*, 16: 222–33.

Sik, E. (1991) 'The vulture and the calamity, or why were Hungarian taxi drivers able to rebel against increased gasoline prices?', *Research Review*, 91(2): 73–85.

Stark, D. (1992) 'Path dependence and privatisation strategies in East Central Europe', *East European Politics and Societies*, 6: 17–51.

Stark, D. (1993) 'Recombinant property in East European capitalism: organizational innovation in Hungary', paper presented to the Conference on the Social Embeddedness of the Economic Transformation in Central and Eastern Europe, Berlin.

Szabo, M. (1992) 'Political reforms and social movements in Eastern Europe', paper presented to the First European conference on Social Movements, Berlin.

Szalai, E. (1989) 'See-saw: the economic mechanism and large company interests', *Acta Oeconomica*, 41: 101–35.

Szalai, E. (1991) 'Integration of special interests in the Hungarian economy. The struggle between large companies and the party and state bureaucracy', *Journal of Comparative Economics*, 15: 284–303.

Szirmai, V. (1989) 'Social mechanisms of the organisation of local environmental conflicts', paper presented at ISA Conference on Environmental Constraints and Opportunities in the Social Organisation of Space, Udine.

Szirmai, V. (1991) 'The structural mechanisms of the organisation of ecological-social movements in Hungary', in A. Vari and P. Tamas (eds), *Environment and Democratic Transition*. Dordrecht: Kluwer.

Szjakowski, B. (1985) 'The Catholic Church in defense of civil society in Poland', in B. Misztal (ed.), *Poland after Solidarity*. New Brunswick: Transaction Books.

Tarrow, S. (1992) 'Eastern European social movements: globalization, difference and political opportunity', paper presented to the First European Conference on Social Movements, Berlin.

150   *Space, Power and Collective Action*

Tilly, C. (1978) *From Mobilization to Revolution*. Reading, MA: Addison-Wesley.
Touraine, A. (1981) *The Voice and the Eye*. Cambridge: Cambridge University Press. First published 1978.
Touraine, A. (1988) *Return of the Actor*. Minneapolis: University of Minnesota Press. First published 1984.
Touraine, A. (1991) 'Commentary on Dieter Rucht critique', in D. Rucht (ed.), *Research on Social Movements*. Frankfurt: Campus Verlag.
Touraine, A., Hegedus, Z., Dubet, F. and Wieviorka, M. (1983) *Anti-nuclear Protest*. Cambridge: Cambridge University Press. First published 1980.
Tyomkina, A.A. (1991) 'Political movements of Perestroyka'. Unpublished paper, Institute of Sociology, Leningrad.
Urban, M.E. (1990) *More Power to the Soviets*. Aldershot: Edward Elgar.
Waller, M. (1989) 'The ecology issue in Eastern Europe: protest and movements', *Journal of Communist Studies*, 5: 303–28.
Wilson, F.L. (1990) 'Neo-corporatism and the rise of new social movements', in R.J. Dalton and M. Kuechler (eds), *Challenging the Political Order*. Cambridge: Polity Press.
Yanitsky, O. (1991a) 'Environmental movements: some conceptual issues in East–West comparisons', *International Journal of Urban and Regional Research*, 15: 524–41.
Yanitsky, O. (1991b) 'Lefortovo, Moscow: resolving the conflict between urban planners and residents', in T. Deelstra and O. Yanitsky (eds), *Cities of Europe: the Public's Role in Shaping the Urban Environment*. Moscow: Mezhdunarodnye Otnoshenia.
Yanitsky, O. (1993) *Russian Environmentalism: Leading Figures, Facts, Opinions*. Moscow: Mezhdunarodnye Otnoshenia.
Zald, M.N. (1988) 'The trajectory of social movements in America', *Research in Social Movements, Conflict and Change*, 10: 19–41.

6

Social Movements and the Challenge of Urban Politics

Henri Lustiger-Thaler and Louis Maheu

Many contributions to the study of social movements have been deficient in assessing the relationship between collective action and the realm of political power. Two of these deficiencies stand out in the contemporary literature on collective action. In the first instance, theoretical attention has been accorded to strategic social relations, through the musical chairs of interest mediation. We can gauge this empirically in the way social movements avail themselves of political opportunity structures. This, however, does not take into account questions of political domination embedded in state-building and modernization. As Chris Pickvance argues in Chapter 5 of this book, these approaches to social movements lack a very critical component – a theory of the state.

In the second instance, the social movement literature that focuses on the relationship between collective action and the mediation of interests has a tendency to envelop the two within a labyrinthine-like web of formal institutionalization processes. This is particularly evident in the case of urban movements because of their contacts with the everyday operation of municipal decision-making networks. This proximity gives urban movements the appearance of constantly soliciting institutionalized responses from the state, its regulatory environment and/or the institutions of civil society.

This is often more apparent than real, and is part of a complex process of political exchanges. The end result, however, is that collective action as a practice within institutions receives short shrift in the social movement literature. This is especially problematic when considering urban-based movements and their localized forms of action. The limits of this approach can be overcome only through an enriched theory of the institutionalization of local expressions of collective action.

Indeed, the local scene, particularly the growing importance of urban politics in the overall state system, is key to the emergence of social, cultural and political cross-fertilizations that are dramatically reordering public and private space (Lustiger-Thaler, 1992). The contemporary city, as one commentator suggests, exists at the matrix-point of new regimes of cultural signification, political regulation and a 'metaphysics of the street' (Lash, 1990). Why would social movement theorists, searching for a theory of politics want to be elsewhere? Following this insight, our own concern is to examine the loci at which the sphere of social movements and the realm of politics overlap, creating new configurations of social relations and political representations. We will argue that these, in turn, have an effect on the realignment of institutions as experimental fields, inserting new challenges and conflicts into their very core.

The analytical deficiencies mentioned above point to a need to draw upon a more concise literature on social movements and the realm of everyday politics. We can underline at least three distinctive categories here.

The first is a tendency to treat social movements as extended interest groups. Much of this is due to the impact of state regulation. The practices of social movements, from this perspective, come to *resemble* those of interest groups, but they cannot be reduced to them (Kitschelt, 1989; Gamson, 1975). Social movements thus have a clear and quantifiable effect on the functioning of a political system. Their influence is measured through public opinion and policy directives placed at the 'output' side of a political system.

A second means by which social movements have been associated with formal politics is through the 'crisis of the political', or the confrontation of politics with society (Maier, 1987). Emphasis here is on explaining the distance between the practices of movements and political systems. Much of this focus has been on their political style, which has become synonymous with the crisis of representation. Social movements hence avail themselves of strategies of direct action (including street theatre, sit-ins, public protests, boycotts) in order to shed light on issues that have so far been kept off the public ledger. Over and above their many uses of protest against the established political order, social movements from this perspective are actors sited at the matrix of state and civil society. They engage the institutional and non-institutional (Offe, 1987), in a sense completing the functioning of a political system of representation.

A third approach assumes that social movements are vested with contesting identity-based values, presaging a new social paradigm between subordinated Others and dominating Others. This takes many shapes and forms, ranging from what has been referred to as a radical 'life politics' (Giddens, 1990, 1991) to a 'politics of recognition' (Taylor, 1992; see Chapter 11 in this book). Indeed, many authors point to the deep ambivalences of the political sphere, as social practices categorically refuse to be fully bracketed within its confines. Paradoxically, the moment one circumscribes a new political field, one also simultaneously creates a territory and a boundary from which to contest it. Under these polar conditions, the crisis of the political, noted earlier, reconfigures itself as a crisis of democracy. It is therefore illusory to confine collective action to the register of the political (Maheu, 1991, 1992).

Social movements from this angle emerge as extra-institutional conveyors of needs and forms of claims-making that find little solace in the discourses, exchanges and modalities of formal politics. Social movements seek to recreate the political *within* civil society, through celebrating expressions of the self. The notion of identity (Cohen, 1985) has emerged as a prelude to the collapse and fragmentation of the conventional political sphere. Here, a radical realignment of political and sociocultural practices is the only guarantor of fundamental social change. This view has been particularly evident in analyses of Green and environmental movements (Bahro, 1984).

Most of these approaches contain a latent, if productive, tension that cannot be overlooked. On the one hand, there is a recognition of social movements as analytical constructs. As such, social movements emerge as conceptual constructs exemplified by the conflict-laden practices of many different collective actors. They represent practices that raise broad questions of theory, linking collective action to the constitution of society, and the fundamental structures of societal transformation. Quite often, social movements, as analytical constructs, gain their critical import through the simultaneous use of different analytical approaches, highlighting the many facets of collective action.

On the other hand, there is a clear recognition of social movements as constituted and purposeful actors, actors that seek out new grounds for self-representation, collective knowledge and socio-political experiences, including those gained by institutionalizing themselves. In this chapter we will be looking at this process of institutionalization as a relatively new dimension in the articulation between movements and the patterned strictures of late modernity. This will be done by focusing on the relationship between local power structures and collective actions in an urban setting. We will not treat urban social movements as interest groups, but it will become clear that to grasp their impact properly *does* require an understanding of the process that interest groups are engaged in, at least in terms of status attribution. We will moreover be arguing that the construction of the local form of the state, and its apparatuses of domination and regulation, are linked to the nature of concerted conflicts and struggles urban movements bring to the transformative possibilities of the public sphere.

Social movements, in the above sense, are part of the deep structuration of social and political life through politicizing the realm of thought and experience. Treating social movements as analytical constructs in this manner, however, covers but a single dimension of their substantive importance. The study of social movements must be complemented by viewing them as constituted collective actors with the power of agency. We will argue that this is best understood by examining the processes of institutionalization within which movements increasingly find themselves.

The understanding of institutionalization we refer to here does not reduce movements to their structured relationship with, or differentiation from, political parties or other agents of interest mediation, such as pressure groups. As we will explain, institutionalization is actually a multi-dimensional process of recontextualization from which new social relations emerge, even the bases for critical public cultures.

It is in this framework that social movements are constituted as collective actors. They inscribe themselves within cognitive and cultural systems through struggles around autonomy, authenticity and risk. And it is within the flexible institutions of late modernity that these issues are reflexively expressed. Viewing the institutionalization of social movements in this way bridges the analytical construction of collective action and its actualization in everyday life through the practice of agency. We shall return to these issues later. Clearly, social movements, particularly the urban social movements in our case study, have become telling indicators of the many local variants of change, as well as indices of ruptures in more global networks of social and political life.

The politics of economic crisis in Montreal

Interest in local forms of social, economic and cultural development in Montreal can be traced back to the early 1960s as part of the history of struggles for community empowerment. De-industrialization of traditional working-class neighbourhoods, mounting levels of unemployment, the crisis of welfare provision as well as the concomitant building of local networks promoting community control, formed a nexus of issues for many groups, and was the reasoning for their ensuing mobilization in the 1960s and 1970s.

The early 1980s witnessed a heightening of economic crisis in traditional working-class communities in Montreal. The 1981–2 recession took a significant toll, particularly in the south-eastern region of the city. South-eastern Montreal accounted for 22 per cent of all plant closures in the city, while representing only 11 per cent of total employment. From 1981 to 1987 this area saw 7444 lay-offs, 4983 of which were permanent. This culminated in an unemployment rate of 12.4 per cent for the region in comparison with 9.6 per cent in 1981. These rates are even more dramatic when local spatial communities are examined. In Hochelaga-Maisonneuve, for example (one of the south-western neighbourhoods) it is estimated that at least 10,000 people are at present out of work, or 40 per cent of the active resident population.

The community of Point Saint-Charles in the south-west of the city has experienced a similar drain, though beginning quite a few years earlier. Prior to the 1960s Point Saint-Charles had an economic base that supported more than 20,000 jobs, both for its residents and for those of the neighbouring communities of Saint-Henri and Verdun. The 'Point', as the community is familiarly called, now ranks as one of the poorest regions in the Montreal area. The degree of social assistance, often a measure of the number of people who have given up looking for work and hence are no longer tallied in the official unemployment statistics, is roughly three times the average for Quebec as a whole.

Economic decline has been the stormcloud from which a host of political initiatives from senior levels of government have rained down. The eastern sector of the city was the first to attract sustained attention from the state, as a result of highly publicized plant closings. This led to the creation of several non-partisan committees charged with the task of bringing together representatives of the three levels of the Canadian state (federal, provincial and municipal) and key community groups, in order to sort out an agenda of priorities for economically depressed inner-city regions.

In the eastern sector of the city the Comité de survie de l'est de Montréal was formed. This committee was composed of politicians for whom it was politically expedient to raise the profile of eastern Montreal within their own provincial and federal party caucuses. Their agenda consisted largely of stop-gap measures geared to the attraction of private capital reinforced by federal inducements. The Comité de survie itself survived for about a year. Its mandate laid the groundwork for the next step in the management of the local crisis by the Quebec and federal governments.

The Comité pour la relance de l'économie et de l'emploi de l'est de Montréal (CREEEM) was founded in April 1986. This group was supported by the federal Ministry of Labour and Immigration and the Provincial Ministry of Manpower. The mandate of the

CREEEM group was to identify economic areas experiencing difficulty as well as expansion. The CREEEM report was particularly supportive of community groups working on employment issues in the community of Hochelaga-Maisonneuve. The community economic development corporation, Programme action revitalisation Hochelaga-Maisonneuve (PAR HM) was cited by the CREEEM report as being the best-placed agent for delivering a support system geared towards local entrepreneurship and employment counselling. This early support for PAR HM was later institutionally extended to include various programmes related to federal and provincial ministries. Of the three Corporations de développement économique et communautaire (CDECs) in the Montreal region at the time, PAR HM clearly pursued the most conventional view of local economic development, pointing to the private sector as a key player in the planned revitalization.

With the electoral victory of the Montreal Citizens' Movement (MCM) on 9 November 1986, the local development corporations initially enjoyed great hope of airing their grievances at City Hall. However, the importance the MCM would subsequently accord to the democratization of economic decision-making was far removed from the progressive proposals which first motivated the party.

Although the MCM even in its early years saw itself as a central actor in the strategic development of the Montreal economy, this was to be matched by a programme of decentralization based on local participation. This approach, as outlined in the MCM party platform, was meant to integrate economic debates into public life and municipal politics. Since its election in 1986 however the MCM has been far from enthusiastic about implementing its own programme for democratization. In fact, the bureaucratic fortress surrounding economic decision-making has become more impregnable. And, since the re-election of the MCM on 4 November 1990, the prospects for instituting any measure of local control pertaining to economic matters has become ever more slight.

Within months of coming to power the MCM embarked upon a series of public consultations and commissions, integrating them into the ongoing administrative framework. The new administration created six commissions that have since become permanent fixtures at City Hall, though most power is still held by the Executive Committee of the City Council, as has traditionally been the case in Montreal. The Public Commission for Economic Development held hearings throughout the disadvantaged inner-city core in 1987. The CDECs, which until then had had difficulty inserting themselves into an ongoing municipal political process, clearly emerged as central interlocutors in these hearings. The final report of the

Commission reflected their newly acquired status. Although the report favoured conventional remedies and modes for restructuring, the importance of the CDECs as legitimate representatives of the interests of their communities was clearly acknowledged.

The report suggested that the city pursue closer ties with the development corporations, particularly through establishing investment funds and small 'business incubators', a policy that ultimately pitted communities against one another in the scramble for limited resources. Little of this support, however, was translated into power for these groups to decide on economic priorities for their communities. The Commissions themselves have been criticized for their largely ineffective mediation between local government and community groups; indeed they have become the front line of discontent with the restrained democracy at City Hall under the MCM. As mediational processes have recently become more localized with the development of the district advisory committees (DACs), the Commissions have become listening devices for local government, an exercise in formality that urban movements undertake in order to maintain their status and legitimacy.

Community development corporations throughout Montreal have several different outlooks. Their views range from conventional economic strategies, as in the Corporation de développement de l'est (CDEST), to the local empowerment and entrepreneurial design of the Regroupement pour la relance économique et sociale du Sud-Ouest de Montreal (RESO), to the Corporation de développement économique et communitaire/Centre-Sud (CDEC/Centre Sud) and the contestatory nature of the Centre d'innovation en développement économique local-Grand Plateau (CIDEL-GP).

The differences that exist between the practices of these corporations are substantial. This ultimately moulds their politics as well. The CDEST group (formerly PAR HM) while having accomplished the grassroots political work of regrouping local forces in the eastern sector of Montreal, has largely been influenced by a growth model of development in which community control aspects have diminished. Its social agenda has in this regard come to resemble the needs of more formal institutions, particularly regarding manpower allocations.

While RESO (formerly Programme économique Point Saint-Charles, PEP) has remained committed to its communitarian approach, it too has assumed a pragmatic stance in its relations with the local state. Interestingly this stance allowed it to become a launching pad for innovation. In spite of the substantial differences between CDEST and RESO, both have achieved a new political status as the political processes at City Hall become more modernized. The outcome has been strengthened legitimacy for these groups, within their own communities as well as in the eyes of local government bureaucracies. This also deepened their dependent relationship with state structures, mostly through funding practices. As we shall see, this attribution of status has become a double-edged sword for urban movements and the local state.

CIDEL-GP was formed by ten community organizations; their clientele is composed of women, immigrants, refugees, welfare recipients and jobless youth. Apart from job creation its priorities include a loan circle, daycare services, housing and health care. CIDEL-GP has maintained a relatively autonomous attitude in its relations with the local state, by establishing clear social priorities and receiving support from its community base.

This was most evident in the resistance by CIDEL-GP to a reorganization of development corporations by the city, on the basis that it did not meet the needs of citizens in the Grand Plateau. Over the last year, the Montreal City Council has devised new rules forcing CDECs to merge in order to qualify for further funding. The new constituencies for the development corporations were decided in an arbitrary fashion, without heed to the priorities of various groups and the different needs of the resident populations.

One of the characteristics of development corporations in Montreal is their different views and ideologies: some are oriented towards small business development whereas others address social issues. The stated logic of the city was to avoid having 40 corporations, each with a separate budget requirement. By rationalizing this process, the local state has obscured the geographic and social concerns behind the different development corporations. The new planning designations have separated neighbourhoods with similar problems and combined other districts with opposing socioeconomic and class interests. The initial city plan attempted to merge CIDEL-GP with CDEC/Centre-Sud. This met with strong resistance from CIDEL-GP. Indeed the plan lost its funding due to the geographical overlap with Centre-Sud. Significant support from community organizations in the area however forced the city and the CDEC/Centre-Sud to devise a way to continue supporting the CIDEL-GP initiative. This was recognized as a victory for CIDEL-GP, one which would have been impossible without local support.

Several elements are of considerable concern to activists in the CDEC movement in Montreal. Primarily, the political process for financing these initiatives plays down the enormity of the structural unemployment problem within the respective community and beyond its parameters. There is a feeling that massive responsibilities have been transferred to local groups with few decision-making powers, and that these groups then have to compete for scarce resources.

The scramble for resources, and the concomitant desire on the part of the CDECs to be self-sufficient have also, in some cases, created conditions for the growth and insertion of the private sector into the relationship between community groups and the state. This has occurred in the eastern sector of Montreal, where private capital concerns have an increasingly equal voice in the CDEST group. As the federal and provincial states leave labour issues more and more to the regulation of the market, community economic development appears to have become a way to create a parallel low-wage labour market, in the name of job training for the poor (Shragge, 1990). The CDECs, by engaging in the 'he who pays the piper calls the tune' approach to economic development, have become ambivalent if pragmatic actors, caught between the Scylla of a cold market rationality, pursued by the city, and the Charybdis of the growing social needs of a large proportion of the inner-city population.

Politics and legitimation costs

CDECs have become risky business for local groups *and* for the local state. The recent push to insert CDECs into each of the nine geographical districts of Montreal is being led by municipal authorities. The rationale of the city is to provide businesses already in place with new sources of expertise. While this may indeed be a large part of the agenda for certain neighbourhood groups, others clearly perceive the social goals that inspired their initial emergence as being threatened.

For groups concerned with urban poverty, alternative economic models and escalating unemployment there is little solace in the administration's plan. The corporations are now facing not only resource allocation problems, in their relationship with the local state, but also issues of fundamental purpose as they become more service oriented. Here the stakes are high. As the community corporations lose their political vocation, they are easily transformed into thinly disguised municipal anti-poverty programmes, reaching out to the marginalized in their localities with little hope for any larger democratic transformation or effect.

Yet, in spite of these caveats, community corporations have added an innovative discursive dimension to the realm of local economic development (Favreau, 1989). In part, the very presence of CDECs challenges dominant economic ideologies, but their more global democratic import is considerably harder to assess. The

CDECs over the last few years have built a base of legitimacy in economic matters, strategically positioning themselves as credible agents. To accord public status to these groups, however, presents some attendant problems for the state. Though the CDECs in part represent constellations of interests they are not as narrowly based as traditional interest groups, in that they still maintain vibrant contestatory practices within institutions.

While status and authority place obvious constraints on development corporations, they also up the stakes for the local state, given that these groups have a tradition of militancy which is constantly renewed in their interaction with the community base. The city in this sense buys into relationships that it cannot unimpededly control, but nevertheless needs. This was perhaps best demonstrated in the support received by CIDEL-GP, regardless of the restructuring logic used by the city. The control of funding became, in this case, the strategic mechanism by which City Hall re-established its relative position vis-à-vis the self-asserted autonomy of community groups.

Our question is how the social and political practices of CDECs will adjust to the sociopolitical conjunctures in which they find themselves, and to the opportunities these circumstances offer. There is an indication that a new strategy for local economic development is rapidly emerging in the south-western sector of the city. Activists there are speaking of creating a parallel local economic institution, funded by RESO but more attentive to the marginalized segments of the population.

As a relatively new development in re-establishing the sociopolitical dimension of CDECs this contains several possibilities. Primarily, it short-circuits the perennial funding problems faced by new initiatives. Secondly, it places a now legitimate community actor, the CDEC, between more militant initiatives and the city, opening up the frontier for new alternatives. Thirdly, it points to the ongoing radicalization of community groups and urban movements within increasingly legitimate coalitions and partnerships, which spread contesting ideologies and conflict-laden practices to still untouched spheres. And these spheres are cultural and cognitive in nature: arenas in which modernity is constructed and experienced.

Community resources and collective action

What are the principal theoretical lessons that can be drawn from the recent experience of the CDECs in Montreal, with a view to furthering our understanding of the relationship between social movements and politics as well as more global social issues? The relationship between social movements as constituted actors and social movements as analytical constructs is critical to an understanding of our case study. As collective actors the CDECs have been institutionalizing themselves, in a sense, within and against the institutional order. Their practices are best explained through many approaches. No one approach in and of itself is sufficient.

Resource mobilization theory, political opportunity structures and status attribution approaches are all models of analysis that capture some truth or reality about everyday strategies faced by movements. The dynamics of political regulation also have consequences for the manner in which political domination unfolds on the local level, where local authorities are often much more accessible and accountable to popular discontent or mobilized pressures.

The institutionalization of collective action has important implications here. Social movements penetrate the political field, becoming involved not only in interest mediation processes, but also in issues of political domination. These issues pertain to the building of regulatory structures, articulating higher levels of the state with local state-building, as well as to struggles centred around their bases of legitimation.

But the institutionalization of collective action has other conflict-laden characteristics. CDECs, as social movements, constitute collective actors in a host of cultural and cognitive fields. They contest the institutional ordering of these fields by questioning the nature of work, the types of jobs created, and most crucially the ethical basis for reconstructing local communities. Institutions have indeed become critical and reflexive sites where issues of autonomy, authenticity and risk articulate to produce new repertoires of collective action.

As the welfare state 'deconstructs' the institutional basis of social citizenship, and as more and more groups take on new responsibilities and rights, social groups confront issues of inclusion and exclusion in new citizenship configurations. The experience of the CDECs represents these varying late modern dynamics of collective action as they balance crisis and innovation within economic, political and social institutions.

But let us first look at the way they interact with the formal political field. We should recall that CDECs emerge in areas that have experienced long-term problems of structural unemployment. Usually, these are also sectors which have been identified by governments as strategic for capital restructuring. As new actors on the local scene, the CDECs advocate both market capacity and social welfare on issues of community control and social needs.

Community development corporations are therefore wedded to

an emerging political terrain bringing together all three levels of the state. They have come of age in a period of restructuring heightened by the expanding agendas of municipal government, and the growing importance of urban politics which foresees for itself a greater role in economic planning.

Resource mobilization theory offers a framework within which to locate some of the processes that take place between social movements and a political system. This theory argues that constraints, inequalities and levels of domination cannot in and of themselves explain collective action and its impact on political systems. Collective action has to do with access to resources. Resources and means of intervention are functions of institutional conditions and social forces that characterize a given collectivity. The accent here is less on normative orientations than on particular capacities to mobilize social forces through the management of political opportunities (Tilly, 1984). The social and political impact of grassrooots groups, and their claims upon the larger polity, are mediated by their organizational aptitudes.

There is an explicit success criterion at work here, related to opportunities of an inclusive and exclusive nature. Kitschelt for example has argued that political opportunity structures, combined with inclusive mechanisms for political decision-making, and social policies, explain specific strategic elements of new social movements. As Kitschelt explains, this generally results in medium levels of mobilization within specific groups. It also makes grassroots strategies openly accommodating rather than adversarial. Because of these factors, social movements have had some measurable impact on public opinion, political institutions, policies and social programmes (Kitschelt, 1989).

Resource mobilization theory is mostly focused on the output dimensions of a system of political action. Social movements here display tendencies which resemble the strategic conducts of pressure groups and interest groups. The CDECs have in fact shown a great deal of acumen in their strategic and organizational levels of intervention. And, as noted in our case study, there have been concrete results in terms of funding and political resources. The CDECs have benefited from a complexity of inclusive mechanisms, which has given them visibility in relation to the provincial, federal and, most importantly, local state levels.

At the same time CDECs do not follow the singular route of an interest group. They are not passive agents in these political institutional orders. Their constituency has a contestatory character that challenges these orders, creating a climate of uncertainty for all actors involved. However, an analysis of opportunity structures related to inclusionary mechanisms is not the only way to explain practices of the social movements. Crisis itself presents an opportunity for grassroots groups to position themselves strategically vis-à-vis the local state and political institutions.

Regulation and the frontiers of the political

As an empirical demonstration of the relationship between social movements and politics, CDECs sway to rhythms different from those tapped out by the resource mobilization theorists. To understand this it is necessary to look beyond the policy side of a given system of action. It is important to examine processes through which both claims-making and institutional reform seek to adjust the functioning of a political system. There are two factors at work here: first, there is a sociopolitical strategy by which social movements redefine the intrinsic boundaries of political systems through contesting their legitimacy. Secondly there are institutional strategies of modernization pursued through state-building.

Analyses of new social movements that emphasized direct action tended to target the input dimensions of a political system. These analyses unfolded in the following way: if a political crisis exists, and if social movements in their relation to political systems are features of this crisis, it is because of the impregnability of the political system. The crisis of the political therefore becomes crystallized at the input end of the system. Paying attention to the input side allowed for an analysis of social practices prior to their insertion into an institutional field of action. Early analyses of the peace and ecological movements were indicative of these approaches.

More contemporary approaches would argue however that the input side already contains the traces of the early institutionalization process. Claus Offe, in a text tracing the evolution of the modern welfare state, directs our attention to the state's changing functions in the management of social life (Offe, 1984). He argues that the state systematically conditions the input dimension of the political system. This is accomplished by according a legitimate status to actors outside formal political parties. This same analysis is at the root of the neo-corporatist explanation of the representation of key socioeconomic agents in society. It emphasizes the input dimension of a system of political action as integral to the problem of regulation and modernization.

The state's conditioning of the input side is evident in the practices surrounding the CDECs, particularly in their relationship with the municipality. Over and above the fruits of their labour, measured at the output or policy end, the CDECs have obtained a sociopolitical status of some credibility. This means they have enough standing to present their claims formally, defend their interests, initiate actions and in some cases actually apply social programmes.

The city of Montreal has gone through a process of significant structural and political transformation in the last ten years. The burgeoning of local bureaucracy, the uncertainty of the Canadian nation-state, and the changing global context within which this is occurring is pregnant with instability. The city faces a double-edged sword concerning the type of legitimacy it has given to the CDECs. In according the mantle of public status to CDECs local authorities have aligned themselves in a special relationship with community organizations. The accordance of legitimacy to CDECs, particularly in regard to job creation, allows the local state to play honest broker. Through such bodies as the Comité d'harmonisation de la Ville de Montréal, which distributes funds from all three levels of the state, the city incurs an intriguing 'legitimacy cost'. (In fact, mechanisms such as the Comité narrow the playing field for CDECs in that they can no longer appeal directly to federal or provincial ministries.)

This legitimacy cost is evident in the higher levels of unpredictability in the day-to-day functioning of the municipality. As we have seen, the political allegiance of some of the more progressive CDECs is unsure and transient. Added to this, there has been a maturing of CDECs in Montreal whereby they have become quite skilful in manoeuvring the political field, as well as in instituting internal and autonomous funding procedures to pursue new projects.

These processes bring to the foreground a key theoretical problem in the study of social movements and politics – the tension between political regulation and collective social practices. The CDECs have entered a political system marked by significant constraints and regulations. This however only attests to one part of their collective experience. Receiving legitimacy, for example, allows grassroots groups to 'deliver the goods'. It also allows them to restate their own independent position outside state-sponsored structures. Beyond their strategic conduct CDECs expand the deeper structures of the political system by challenging its legitimacy, while at the same time contributing to local state-building. This underscores the institutional and non-institutional dialectic so many scholars have referred to as being central to the analysis of social movements.

Some commentators have pointed to new middle-class factions and new social movements in conflict with dominant social and hegemonic forces (Inglehart, 1977). The collective practices of the CDECs do not substantiate or disprove this claim. Rather, they point to the complexity of new class alliances in the inner-city core. CDECs, because of their 'clientele' attachment to place and neighbourhood, deal with a substantively reinvented cultural and material politics mediated by the recurring problem of scarcity.

In this regard, they rekindle class issues and combine them with more contemporary concerns around local cultural practices, democracy as well as a reinvigorated social citizenship (Marshall, 1977), rather than the quality of life concerns of the new middle classes. And yet the CDECs have registered themselves within the local political system, which is very much the lair of progressive and reformist factions of the new middle classes, factions that remain at the centre of the restructuring of the local state.

From flexible institutions to reflexive modes of collective action

When urban social movements enter a field of political regulation, are the social issues they bring with them reduced by the formal political grid? Our case study shows that this is not so, even if we assume there to be an effect in terms of how conflict is mediated within communities. Most of the literature on the statist regulation of community groups would argue that political regulation pre-sages the decline of social practices and in some cases community politics.

We find this unconvincing, or at least insufficiently nuanced. Our case study clearly shows a tendency in the CDECs to assume positions that are as much geared towards the social adaptability of their clientele as towards challenging the formal structures of the political and social system. Much is now being written about the powerful regulation function of these types of community organiza-tion across Canada. It would be negligent however to ignore the role they play as counterweights to conventional views of local economic planning.

In an economic environment geared to the interests of developers and property entrepreneurs and interlocked with growth machine politics, the CDECs offer a countervailing voice. Arguing that wider sections of the population need to be involved in economic choices is not a discourse likely to be heard from the private sector. CDECs are therefore present on the ideological battlefield, through their social and discursive practices. They contain a counter-hegemonic challenge to the ruling orthodoxy. The task (as recognized by community activists themselves) is to link this discourse to visible mechanisms of social and political transformation.

We can then say that CDECs institutionalize themselves as collective actors in a conflict-laden cultural and cognitive field. They pursue social experiments and, through them, produce new expressions of authenticity, a new culture of contestation. Authenticity emerges in the very nature of claims-making within modern institutions, underscoring issues of control over the means of representation. It is through this type of cultural struggle around authenticity that we can formulate further critical dimensions in the institutionalization of collective action.

The constituted character of collective experience, subjectivity and agency, as forms of cultural struggle embedded within authenticity, occurs in a contest of power relations. This sets the stage for posing problems of autonomy and risk. Autonomy emerges in struggles to secure a relationship with the state, and state largesse, which allows for critical political distance. Autonomy, nurtured by the fusion of thought and experience, inserts a radical component within institutions. The problem of risk takes shape in the shifting political contexts of actual citizenship statuses, as new terrains of inclusion and exclusion are negotiated, not only in the political order but throughout the social fabric.

This brings to the foreground a revivified understanding of social citizenship that Maurice Roche argues, in Chapter 8 of this book, to be at the very core of social movement practices (see also Roche, 1987). The theoretical notion of social citizenship can be particularly helpful when resituated at the intersection of political regulation and flexible institutionalization outlined here. Indeed, social movements are at the new frontier of new social citizenship statuses, in the sense that they involve more than struggles for social membership.

New issues of citizenship raise questions regarding legal statuses (Turner, 1986) as well as struggles to gain degrees of autonomy in the face of numerous forms of stratification, hierarchy and political oppression (Held, 1987). This implies, as Roche suggests, the likely emergence of political conflicts around the two axes of 'rights versus duties' and 'state regulation versus state enablement' (citizen self-reliance). It must be recognized, however, that these conflicts are themselves products of more encompassing struggles constituted in the social and cognitive order, through the political framing of social experience and the rationalizing of the many cultural fields in late modernity.

The institutionalization of collective action is therefore a multi-dimensional process, articulating new social citizenship statuses and the actual practices of community groups and social movements. If the new citizenship statuses are the motor behind modern forms of claims-making, their field of struggles is clearly at the intersection of state regulation and autonomous collective actions.

It is here that the triadic problem of authenticity, autonomy and risk acquires a special significance. Together, they represent subject-positions that do not surrender their discourse to the state, or the power structures of civil society, but instead use their understanding of social action for new collaborative and collective engagements. In this process a substantive version of citizenship is carved out of a host of institutional practices and linked anew to wider questions of community and social responsibility. In this sense, we take some distance from the viewpoint expressed by Pierre Hamel, in Chapter 10 of this book (see also Hamel, 1991). Rather than focus attention on the individual, post-liberal dimension of modernity we point to the late modern fusing of thought and experience as a subjectively collective endeavour. This finds its expression in new citizenship struggles and the cultural institutions through which sociability is expressed.

This is a good point at which to reconsider both the partial explanations of interest group models and the political crisis of representation approaches. Both these perspectives give too much weight to the distinction between the institutional and non-institutional spheres. This dichotomous positioning makes the formal political sphere appear falsely impenetrable to community strategies. Our case study of the CDECs in Montreal has shown that these processes are considerably more intertwined, complex and rooted in political and social behaviours than either of these 'institutional/non-institutional theories' would have us believe.

Urban social movements do play by the rules of the formal political game. Yet to understand the dynamic of their contingent actions means not only to view urban movements as state-sanctioned mediators between social practices and a political system, but also to see how they enlarge the frontiers of the political. This also means to recognize that their institutional practices interrelate with cultural struggles around authenticity, autonomy and risk.

The strategies of the more progressive CDECs not only affect mediational processes between themselves and the state, but also nourish new forms of counter-hegemonic and radical democratic practices within local communities. They do this by encouraging the participation of citizens in collective projects. In the final analysis this is the most authentic level of social citizenship, the nurturing of the 'citizens' world'. What contemporary social movement theory needs to trumpet loudly is that this 'world' is deeply imbricated in

168   *Space, Power and Collective Action*

institutions as an experiential field. It is here that actors renegotiate their identities in the midst of Others, creating new public spheres as they reveal the hidden structures of exploitation and domination.

References

Bahro, R. (1984) *From Red to Green*. London: Verso.
Cohen, J. (1985) 'Strategy or identity: new theoretical paradigms and contemporary social movements', *Social Research*, 52(4): 663–716.
Favreau, L. (1989) 'L'économie communitaire des quartiers populaires d'un grand centre urbain du Québec: le cas de Montréal', in *L'Autre Economie*. Montreal: Presses de l'Université du Québec.
Gamson, W. (1975) *The Strategy of Social Protest*. Chicago: Dorsey Press.
Giddens, A. (1990) *The Consequences of Modernity*. Cambridge: Polity Press.
Giddens, A. (1991) *Modernity and Self-Identity. Self and Society in the Late Modern Age*. Cambridge: Polity Press.
Hamel, P. (1991) *Action Collective et Démocratie Locale*. Montreal: PUM.
Held, D. (1987) *Models of Democracy*. Stanford, CA: Stanford University Press.
Inglehart, R. (1977) *The Silent Revolution: Changing Values and Political Lifestyles among Western Publics*. Princeton, NJ: Princeton University Press.
Kitschelt, H. (1989) 'Explaining contemporary social movements: an exploration in the comparison of theories'. Paper delivered at the 1989 annual meeting of the American Political Science Association, Atlanta, Georgia.
Lash, S. (1990) *The Sociology of Post-Modernism*. London: Routledge.
Lustiger-Thaler, H. (1992) *Political Arrangements: Power and the City*. Montreal: Black Rose Books.
Maheu, L. (1991) 'Identité et enjeux du politique', in L. Maheu and A. Sales (eds), *Recomposition du politique*. Paris: L'Harmattan; Montréal: Presses de l'Université de Montréal.
Maheu, L. (1992) 'Mouvements sociaux et politique: les enjeux d'une articulation entre grandes problématiques du politique', in G. Boismenu, P. Hamel, G. Labica (eds), *Les formes modernes de la démocratie*. Paris: L'Harmattan; Montréal. Presses de l'Université de Montréal.
Maier, C.S. (1987) *Changing Boundaries of the Political*. Cambridge: Cambridge University Press.
Marshall, T.H. (1977) *Class, Citizenship and Social Development*. Chicago: University of Chicago Press.
Offe, C. (1984) *Contradictions of the Welfare State*. Cambridge, MA: MIT Press.
Offe, C. (1987) 'Challenging the boundaries of institutional politics: social movements in the sixties', in Charles Maier (ed.), *Changing Boundaries of the Political*. Cambridge: Cambridge University Press.
Roche, M. (1987) 'Citizenship, social theory and social change', *Theory and Society*, 16: 363–99.
Shragge, E. (1990) 'Community based practice: political alternatives or new state forms?', in L. Davies and E. Shragge (eds), *Bureaucracy and Community*. Montreal: Black Rose Books.
Taylor, C. (1992) *The Politics of Recognition*. Princeton: Princeton University Press.
Tilly, T. (1984) 'Social movements and national politics', in C. Bright and S. Harding (eds), *State Making and Social Movements*. Ann Arbor: University of Michigan Press.
Turner, B.S. (1986) *Citizenship and Capitalism*. London: Allen & Unwin.

7
Rethinking Class

John Urry

In analysing social class, a number of conceptual innovations have
begun to transform our thinking. In this chapter I shall consider five
'innovations': the concept of causal powers; the 'strategic' character
of collective action; the need to examine the 'resources' available
to social classes; the dialectic of class structure and struggle; and
the significance of space and place to the formation and reproduction of class actions.

These innovations involve a significant break with elements of
conventional Marxism. Marxism has traditionally held that social
classes are generated by the economic base of societies, in particular
by their dominant form of exploitation; that such classes have a
relatively unambiguous 'interest', either to preserve or to destroy
existing social relations; that there is a once-and-for-all establishment of classes-for-themselves which are nationally (or even
internationally) unified and which have a clear class interest; that
such classes generate forms of politics and culture which, except at
the point of revolutionary transformation, cannot reflect back upon
the class structure; and that the only social forces of real significance
within capitalism are the bourgeoisie and the proletariat, meaning
that other social classes and forces do not possess significant
transformative powers.

In this chapter I argue that 'social class' has now to be
investigated differently and that Marxists and indeed non-Marxists
are having to rethink their basic categories and typical modes of
explanation. Nothing of what I say should be taken as an attempt
to reinstate Weber over Marx, since the Weberian tradition is no
more successful at coping with these necessary conceptual transformations.

I begin with some assertions of social ontology. In general I argue
against an event-ontology, namely that the natural or social world
is to be viewed as sets of discrete, atomistic events (actions, interactions, personality characteristics, social phenomena, and so on)
which happen to be distributed in time and space. I would argue in
favour of a 'thing-ontology': that there are persistent and enduring
structures located within time-space, and that they persist because

of the causal powers which they possess and which are in part realized (Harré and Madden, 1975). However, particular sets of events cannot generally be explained in terms of a single such entity: in other words, a given entity does not possess of itself the causal power to produce a whole set of empirical events and its conditions of reproduction. Rather, it is necessary to investigate the conditions under which such causal powers are in fact realized. This fundamental *inter*dependence of such entities means that the causal powers of some entities constitute the conditions necessary for the realization of the powers of other entities. Hence, empirical events generated, such as the spatial distribution of households or factories in a society, are the product of highly complex *inter*dependent processes. That is roughly what Marx was alluding to when he argued that the concrete object is concrete not because it exists or is 'empirical', but because it is the effect of the specific conjuncture of many diverse forces or processes, of – in my terms – entities with specific causal powers. Furthermore, these processes are not to be seen as simply listed, or added up, but as *synthesized*. Their combination qualitatively modifies each constitutive entity (see Sayer, 1992, for further elaboration).

Capital and labour

I have so far talked generally about social entities and their powers. I now turn more directly to two particular social entities: capital and wage labour. Key features of much Marxist social science have involved the following claims: that the causal powers of capital and labour are relatively clear-cut and easy to establish; that an enormous range of empirical phenomena within capitalist societies stems from the causal powers of capital; and that the causal powers of labour arise, through capitalism's unfolding contradictions, to transform societies from within, and ultimately to establish a classless society.

Each of these claims is deeply problematic. That this is so can be seen by considering the distinction between those relations between social phenomena which are external to one another and which are therefore 'contingent', and those relations which are necessary and hence internal to the phenomenon in question (see Sayer, 1982, 1992). The former consist of relations where the objects in question do not stand in any necessary relationship with each other, and where they can exist independent of each other and of the relationship between them. The latter, by contrast, consist of relations which are necessary for the very existence of the objects; such objects cannot exist without such relations. An example of the former would be the employment by a firm of workers from one particular town; an example of the latter would be the relations between capital as a class and wage labour as a class, neither 'object' being able to exist without those connecting relations. I will now set out some minimal characteristics of capital and wage labour, in terms of the mix of necessary and contingent relations, considering in particular the degree to which certain spatial patterns necessarily *or* contingently follow from such relations.

1. Capitalist relations of production are *necessary* or internal, but particular agents *contingently* bear one such relation or the other.
2. Given that particular agents will function as labour power or as capital, then it is *necessary* for at least some of these agents to be spatially proximate.
3. No necessary spatial division of labour (e.g. geographical concentration) will develop, since the industrial and commercial capital appropriates space in different ways; which division develops is partly *contingent* on location of raw materials, physical constraints, relative transport costs, changes in labour supply, skill, organizational levels and so on, and on the changing importance of these different factors.
4. There are *necessary* laws of the capitalist economy which constrain the possible form taken by the spatial division of labour; but the recent development of these necessary laws, especially a putative globalization, means that it is a relatively *contingent* matter as to where capitalist relations will in fact be located, and hence which particular labourers in which particular localities will be employed by capital.
5. Since it is *necessarily* the case that individual sellers of labour power act as subjects possessing a consciousness or a will, there have to be social practices within which those subjectivities are developed and sustained, practices which are also putatively global.
6. It is *necessarily* the case that these practices are structured by the commodity relations generated from the overarching capitalist relations; but the form taken by those practices depends upon various *contingencies*, such as the degree to which pre-capitalist associations and structures persist, the location and the nature of the housing stock, the struggle by individuals and groups to extend or protect those practices, the relations of gender domination and racial oppression.

The causal powers of capitalism are highly complex and mediated, and cannot in a simple sense be reduced to a single interest or a set of necessary social and spatial patterns. Nor can labour be reduced to a single interest, nor can it be claimed that labour has insignificant causal powers. One relatively underexamined feature of labour is that its growth and organization have profound effects upon capital and upon the more general workings of each capitalist society.

Elsewhere Lash and I have investigated the character of 'organized capitalism', especially the different ways in which such organization came to be established in different Western societies in the first two or three decades of this century (Lash and Urry, 1987, 1994). In particular, we show just which social force had been so dominant that it had been able, through the realization of certain powers, to draw 'its' society into an organized capitalist pattern. In the US it was capital which was strongly organized 'at the top' and key to the organization process. In France it was the state itself which was significant in especially promoting organized capitalist forms of collective bargaining. But in Sweden it was labour which became strongly organized at the base of the society, and this (partly together with finance capitalism) developed the most systematic and articulated organized capitalism. Labour played a considerable role in Britain too, particularly because of the peculiarly fragmented character of British capital, its failure to develop modern managerial forms, and its lack of development of the new organized capitalist industries of chemicals and electricals. The British and Swedish cases demonstrate that labour can indeed make the most significant difference to the trajectory of a given capitalist society, whose contours are by no means simple reflections of capital.

It is most important to note how Marx's analysis of capitalist production is seriously deficient because he did not concern himself with the process of *producing* wage labour or labour power. The text *Capital* is concerned with analysing the production of capital, where labour power is a mere presupposition of that process. Marx never completed the volume which would have involved analysing the production of the commodity, labour-power though so-called domestic labour, and its modifying consequences on the wider society.

Class

One term which so far remains unexamined is that of class. I have used the term mainly in the sense of a set of causal powers and have suggested that such powers are diverse and contingently realized. In the US, for example, the powers of labour have been substantially unrealized, so organized capitalism was very much a creature of rampant American capital, with the result that no socialism emerged in the US. However, there are clearly more 'levels' to class than this, and much of the confusion of debates around class stems from an inability or unwillingness to determine which level is being analysed. There are at least five levels in the analysis of class:

1. Class as the basic relation of *exploitation* which characterizes a whole society or type of society. One class here presumes its opposite, since there are necessarily antagonistic relations between them.
2. Class as *causal powers*, that is, the specific sets of transformative consequences which would follow were that social force to be conjuncturally able to realize its structurally defined powers.
3. Class as a specific set of *social organizations* which are organized around a particular project, which may be hegemonic or counter-hegemonic. Two examples would be the conception of the 'English working class' as a set of trade unions, friendly societies, mutual support organizations and so on in the late nineteenth century; or of the 'American service class' as a set of professions and occupations, universities and colleges, business schools and foundations, which came to occupy the middle ground of American society in the early years of this century.
4. Class as a set of *places* within organizations which involve particular kinds of asset, that is, of capital, of skill, and of organizational knowledge (Wright, 1985; Savage et al., 1992). Different places depend upon particular combinations of assets. Over time there are changes in the relative importance of different assets (recently, for example, the heightened importance of 'skill' and reduced significance of 'organizational knowledge').
5. Class as a set of *people* with common social characteristics, which may include past, present or future membership of the social organizations identified in (3) and (4). There is necessarily a complex relationship between class as 'places' and class as 'persons', since over a lifetime people may occupy places within different classes, and the social composition of such places will affect the degree to which, and the forms in which, the powers of a given class come to be realized.

To illustrate the importance of these different notions, I will consider briefly an example just mentioned: the making of the American service class (Lash and Urry, 1987: ch. 6). One feature of 'organized capitalism' was the growth of substantial occupational groups located between capital and labour. Hence, although such societies are pervasively structured in terms of the social relations of capital versus labour, an increasing proportion of the employed population occupy places which are only marginally either 'capital' or 'labour'. Much theoretical labour has been expended trying to 'reduce' these emergent groups to the side of capital through conceptualizing them as functionaries of capital necessitated by its depersonalization, and/or to the side of labour through seeing them as experiencing proletarianization. I would not want to deny these analyses but would maintain that these emergent groups cannot be explained without investigating the way in which a causally powerful 'third force', the service class, is generated and developed within the interstices of organized capitalism, in particular *out of* the exploitative relationship between capital and labour. There are six points to note about such a 'service class' (see Goldthorpe, 1982; Savage et al., 1992):

1. It consists of dominant places which are within the social division of labour but do not principally involve the exploitative ownership of capital, land and buildings.
2. Service-class places are located within a set of interlocking social institutions that 'service' capital by meeting three functions: conceptualizing the labour process; controlling the entry and exercise of labour power within the workplace; and orchestrating the non-household forms under which labour power is produced and regulated.
3. The service class possesses important causal powers: powers to restructure capitalist societies so as to maximize the divorce between conception and execution, and to ensure the elaboration of highly differentiated and specific structures within which knowledge and science can be developed and sustained. These powers thus involve the deskilling of productive labourers; the maximizing of the educational requirements of places within the social division of labour, along with the minimizing of non-educational/non-achievement criteria for recruitment to such places; and the enhancement of the resources and income devoted to education and science (whether privately or publicly funded).
4. Such places enjoy superior work and market situations: incumbents thus exercise authority within each institution; typically, but not necessarily, enjoy well-defined 'careers' in which work and market situations improve side by side; and enjoy medium to high levels of trust and discretion, often stemming from professional control and closure. Careers may be defined bureaucratically or in terms of skills.

5. Entry into such places is generally regulated by the differential possession of credentials, which are either organization-specific or general. Such credentials serve as the main demarcation between the service class and other non-manual workers, although where the demarcation is to be found may change.
6. The relative size, composition and powers of the service class vary substantially, depending upon class conflicts between capital and labour; gender conflicts, especially over attempts to professionalize/masculinize occupations; struggles to extend educational credentialism; attempts to 'professionalize' particular sets of work tasks; conflicts over the size, functions and organization of the state; sectoral changes in the national economy, such as growth in smaller workplaces; increased pressures to flexibilize the labour force, and so on.

The development of this service class was bound up with the social relations between capital and labour in particular societies, but it is *not* to be reduced to that relation (see Lash and Urry, 1987). The development of the service class was initiated by the emergence of modern management in the US in the early years of this century. The growth of such management involved a substantial break in the logic of capitalist development, and was by no means inevitable. Until it emerged, employers used a variety of other means to control their workforces. It was in the US that there was a major shift in these techniques with the growth of modern management. There was, in effect, something of a 'class struggle' in American society around the turn of the century, a struggle which existing capital lost. Complex managerial hierarchies developed in many American companies, leading to the extensive growth of white-collar employment. Such processes meant that the causal powers of the service class came to be more generally realized, as an interlocking complex of new institutional developments emerged – colleges and universities, private foundations, professionalizing occupations in both the private and the public sector, and large corporate and state bureaucracies. They developed and extended between labour and capital, constituting a kind of wedge or third force in American society. There was then a process of 'the making of the American service class', a process which began with the initial development of modern management in the years before the First World War. Paradoxically, then, the archetypal capitalist society, the US, is that whose structure has been *most* transformed by the development of an influential third force apart from those of capital and labour. It is the growth of this American service class which in part accounts for the character of American capitalism.

More generally, the apparent success of the American service class was not due to any sustained sense of 'class consciousness' as such, although American Progressivism could be seen as a form of class consciousness in the early years of this century. Rather, the pursuit of individual interests led to the formation, throughout the US, of collective organizations aimed at pursuing strategies of professionalization via the universities, which then had the mainly unintended consequence of realizing the causal powers of the service class. The availability of two sets of resources were crucial in this process: first, the strategy of *professionalization* via the university, initially pursued by industrial engineers and then available for imitation by other newly emergent white-collar occupational groups; and secondly, the *decentralized system of colleges and universities* which meant that there was relatively little central control (at the federal level) over the content of courses and schemes of study, so that higher education institutions throughout the country could compete to provide professionally relevant credentials for each newly emerging occupation. (Many chapters in this volume highlight the links between resources and various social and cultural opportunities on the one hand, and collective action on the other.)

Working class

I will now turn to the 'working class', noting those points relevant to the issues I have been addressing. First of all, class should be viewed as something that is not pre-given, but fought for (Przeworski, 1977). Part of this class struggle consists of efforts to establish the salience of class as opposed to other basic categories of social division, such as national vs. national, gender vs. gender, generation vs. generation, ethnic group vs. ethnic group, religion vs. religion, and so on. It is not sensible to characterize all of these as status groups, but they are without doubt non-class forms of social division. There is no reason to imagine that they are or will become increasingly irrelevant; indeed, the opposite is in most cases more likely.

Furthermore, there is no single pattern of working-class action that in some sense *is* class struggle in a pure or unmediated form. Three particular patterns can be usefully distinguished (Savage, 1987). They are 'mutualism', in which workers struggle to establish their own independent provision of jobs and services, such as cooperatives, friendly societies, Sunday schools, housing through building clubs, working-class adult education, popular health care through medical aid societies, and so on; 'economism', in which workers seek to struggle against capitalist buyers of labour power in order to reduce or to transform its freely disposable character; and 'statism', in which workers seek to use the state to reduce working-class insecurity through a range of social welfare measures, and to de-commodify labour by providing employment directly or by providing financial support to those in the labour market who thus become less dependent upon it. There is no reason to suppose that there is any necessary historical ordering to these forms, or that any one of them is the *real* form of working-class action.

The 'rational choice' literature has correctly pointed out that the formation of one or another of these forms of collective action does not follow automatically (see Chapter 5 by Pickvance in this volume for a review of this literature). The identification of the interests that would be served if collective action were established does not mean that such action will be pursued. Solutions may well be sub-optimal. In order to overcome the 'free rider' problem, certain kinds of resources must be made available to putative collective actors through the structures of the society in question. These can be classified as follows (Lash and Urry, 1984; Savage, 1987; Calhoun, 1982): (a) *cultural* resources, such as particular conceptions of justice and languages of opposition; (b) pre-established *organizational* resources, such as parties, strikes, riots, unions, and so on; (c) *production* resources, such as large mass-production factories without major social cleavages around, say, gender or ethnicity; and (d) *community* resources, such as well-established and relatively undisturbed patterns of face-to-face interaction.

Moreover, these resources are unequally distributed through time and across space. Indeed, they are often only to be found within particular neighbourhoods or localities for a given period of time. The analysis of how and why such resources are to be found depends upon an investigation of the changing nature of both the economy or the spatial divisions of labour, and of civil society. The spatial division of labour may take many different forms, depending upon technical change, and/or the reorganization of production, and/or spatial relocation, and/or product development within the industrial sectors present within a given local area (see Bagguley et al., 1990: chs 2–3). Civil society varies on a number of dimensions: the degree to which the existing built environment can be transformed; the degree to which the social relations of civil society are integrated within the wider capitalist economy; the degree to which the social relations of civil society are based on face-to-face interaction rather than commodified relations or the state; the degree to which class experiences are culturally specific; the degree of spatial concentration of different social classes; the degree to which a local civil society is vertically organized, i.e. that diverse social groupings and voluntary and informal associations are specific to particular social classes and there is relatively little independent organization; and the degree to which local civil societies are long-established, with intergenerationally reproduced and sedimented cultural forms (for an application of this to different collective action processes, see the chapters by Roche, Hamel, Lustiger-Thaler and Maheu, and Pickvance in this volume).

Putting these sets of arguments together, we find that there is a complex of conditions necessary for working-class action. These are more likely to materialize the more the following conditions hold:

1. There are a number of spatially specific but overlapping class-based 'collectivities-in-struggle', in which there are shared and long-established experiences based on work, residential propinquity, kinship, generation and so on, which facilitate the establishment of 'dialogue', so that workers are able to express, to debate, and to form collective identities that would minimize the costs of individuals' engagement in collective action.

2. The spatially separated experiences of different groups of workers can be viewed as representing the experiences of the whole class within a given nation-state. This depends upon a wide number of local 'civil societies' (often within a region) being structured by class division between capital and labour, rather than by more complex class/status divisions or by the division between the people and the state. Minimally, this implies that there is in each locality a degree of residential differentiation between classes, and that those residentially differentiated classes are nevertheless spatially adjacent.

3. Other collectivities within local 'civil societies' are organized in ways which either reinforce these class divisions or are at least peripheral to them. Collective action is thus more likely the more civil society is organized on a 'vertical' basis in which there are fewer social groupings, and other social practices which are non-class-specific.

4. Gains and benefits (such as higher incomes, lower prices, more consumer goods, increased educational and other opportunities, better services, improved housing, better work conditions, and so on) are thought to be, and in fact are, mainly unavailable except through collective action of a broadly class-based sort. This condition is more likely to be met where social inequalities result from a nationally based system of class relations which produce what are seen as the major divisions of social inequality.

Conclusion

There is a considerable sociological interest in the concept of 'strategy'. All sorts of social entities apparently act strategically, such as ruling elites, employers, employees and unions, households, housewives, carers, social researchers, as well as perhaps social classes, genders, generations, ethnic groups, and so on. Crow (1989), however, has noted that such a viewpoint is incapable of analysing large-scale structural inequality. To consider social groups as 'competing players' may often be to use inappropriate or misleading terminology. But the so-called theory of structuration is meant to overcome this difficulty by suggesting that strategic conduct and institutional analysis are not incompatible sides of a dualism, but interrelated parts of the 'duality of structure' (Giddens, 1984). Crow argues that Burawoy's *The Politics of Production* (1985) and Willis's *Learning to Labour* (1977), for example, show that structures constrain subordinates so that they actively participate in and strategize their own subordination. He insists that there is no analytical incompatibility between severe structural constraint, on the one hand, and strategic action on the other. However, although this reformulation is of interest, it fails to develop the issues sufficiently. In this chapter I have attempted to bring out three further points.

First there are causal powers of a variety of major social institutions and groupings, which in a sense inhere *within* social structures. As a result of strategic actions by various social groups, these causal powers may over time come to be realized. Giddens states but does not fully develop the claim that structures are enabling as well as constraining. This must mean in part that the causal powers of institutions and groupings inhering within social structures can be released as a consequence of initiating strategic actions by a variety of small-scale groups. Structures are thus enabling because there are *powers* inhering within them.

Secondly, structures are enabling in another sense: in providing various kinds of resources to social groups contemplating collective action – cultural, organizational, production and community resources. Structures are not to be viewed as merely constraining. Pickvance clearly shows the enabling character of social movements by pointing out the differences between state socialist Russia and the more market-oriented Hungary (see Chapter 5 in this volume).

Thirdly, social structures are not merely economic, political and cultural, but are also geographical. Both causal powers and resources for collective action are thus spatially variable, and the different *places* which are socially organized (neighbourhoods, localities, regions) are themselves crucial objects in which strategic actions occur. They structure collective actions by providing constraints, powers and resources, but they are also the objects of much collective action. Much of the so-called class struggle is a struggle about *place* in which all sorts of different social groups compete to impose or to prevent others from imposing different transformations of place. Places are not merely reducible to large-scale social processes. They are important in their own right, and they represent much of what is in fact fought for in so-called class struggles (see Urry, 1995, for much more analysis of this).

More recently we have come to appreciate that even further large-scale social processes are singularly important for place. Elsewhere it has been shown that there are a number of different kinds of global flow, not just of capital and of immigrants seeking work, but also of ideas, images, information and visitors that transcend place, region and nation (Lash and Urry, 1994). But it is also important to note how these flows happen to join together in particular ways in particular places, occasionally further disrupting the kinds of 'spatial conditions' for class outlined above. Global flows of images, people and information seem to undermine most of the conditions for class action analysed above, while inequalities of income, wealth and citizenship rights seem increasingly pronounced. Classes dissolve as inequality becomes more apparent. The new regime of the 'global flow' will lead us to rethink class in even more complex and profound ways. Elsewhere I have shown how it is the access to and the significance of information and communication structures which determine both class position and the respective size of different classes (Lash and Urry, 1994: 319–20). We have travelled a long way from base and superstructure models of class.

References

Bagguley, P., Mark-Lawson, J., Shapiro, D., Urry, J., Walby, S. and Warde, A. (1990) *Restructuring Place: Class and Gender*. London: Sage.

Burawoy, M. (1985) *The Politics of Production*. London: Verso.

Calhoun, C. (1982) *The Question of Class Struggle: Social Foundations of Popular Radicalism During the Industrial Revolution*. Chicago: Chicago University Press.

Crow, G. (1989) 'The use of the concept of "strategy" in recent sociological literature', *Sociology*, 23: 1–24.

Giddens, A. (1984) *The Constitution of Society: Outline of the Theory of Structuration*. Berkeley: University of California Press.

Goldthorpe, J.H. (1982) 'On the service class: its foundation and future', in A. Giddens and G. Mackenzie (eds), *Social Class and the Division of Labour*. Cambridge: Cambridge University Press.

Harré, R. and Madden, E. (eds) (1975) *Causal Powers*. Oxford: Basil Blackwell.

Lash, S. and Urry, J. (1984) 'The new Marxism of collective action: a critical analysis', *Sociology*, 18: 33–50.

Lash, S. and Urry, J. (1987) *The End of Organised Capitalism*. Cambridge: Polity Press.

Lash, S. and Urry, J. (1994) *Economies of Signs and Space*. London: Sage.

Przeworski, A. (1977) 'Proletariat into class?', *Politics and Society*, 7: 343–401.

Savage, M. (1987) *The Dynamics of Working-Class Politics*. Cambridge: Cambridge University Press.

Savage, M., Barlow, J., Dicker, P. and Fielding, T. (1992) *Property, Bureaucracy and Culture*. London: Routledge.

Sayer, A. (1982) 'Explanation in economic geography: abstraction versus generalization', *Progress in Human Geography*, 6: 68–88.

Sayer, A. (1992) *Method in Social Science*. London: Routledge.

Urry, J. (1995) *Restructuring Place*. London: Routledge.

Willis, P. (1977) *Learning to Labour*. Farnborough: Saxon House.

Wright, E.O. (1985) *Classes*. London: Verso.

PART III
COLLECTIVE ACTION: FROM POLITICS
TO DEMOCRACY

Introduction

Do we accord undue attention to the relationship between collective action and the realm of politics? Is the 'political' too often the only level that fully absorbs, or best reflects, the effects of collective action? Is it the most privileged site from which to gauge the causal powers of social movements and the collective action of classes?

Indeed, popular movements over the last 25 years have left their mark on the public sphere by openly contesting the existing social order. These movements are in effect historically extended symbols and social metaphors documenting the evolution of collective action. And they represent a process whereby more and more movement activities openly contest the social order.

The literature of social movements has been in the forefront of recording these exchanges. It has traced the impact of collective action on the transformation of political agendas, the evolution of public opinion and the emergence of political elites, to name but a few. The literature has of course also paid attention to the political style movements have cultivated in the public sphere. Though one immediately associates 'direct action' with social movement practices, we know it has not always been the best indicator of their political style.

We need to know more about the insertion of movements into politico-institutional and non-institutional networks. Social movements interject a specific dynamic into the web of political institutions, entering with the option of opting-out.

Two interrelated observations can help us track the complex practices of contemporary movements. The first is concerned with the way social issues penetrate the public sphere, both locally and globally. Emphasis is therefore placed on the innovative input of social movements in their relationship to politics rather than on changes brought to the institutional system of interest mediation.

The second observation underscores the profound ambiguity of this input and exposes the following characteristics of collective action: there are practices which will necessarily remain outside the political sphere as such, because of contingent strategies or solidary commitments. This constitutes, to a certain extent, the self-limiting quality of movements in their relationship to politics, and more importantly their embeddedness in social struggles.

The chapter by Chris Rootes gives us an indication of the delicate mix of the social and the political in modern movements. Echoing Pakulski, Rootes argues that the new social movements are carriers of moral ideals, or a 'moral impetus', that shake up and disturb the political agenda. Libertarian and egalitarian values, through the channel of protest movements and alternative political attitudes, have found a place in the realm of formal electoral politics and political activism. This has certainly been the case in Britain, as well as in Germany and Belgium, as their Green parties attest to, but is less illustrative of the North American political scene. Again, the structural conduciveness of a political system is crucial here.

Rootes argues that the political input of new social movements cannot be explained by Pakulski's analytical model. Generational agents are less important than socialization within libertarian and egalitarian values. Their interiorization, as well as fealty to ideological and symbolic resources, becomes a new site for collective expressions. This site has links to universities, human service sectors and cultural industries.

The innovative impact of social movements on politics also points to a new field of citizenship struggles, according to Maurice Roche. Roche insists upon a merging of two hitherto separate problematics: that of new social movements and the new politics of citizenship. He also identifies those social issues, ideological struggles and new social obligations upon which the claims of the new citizenship rights are founded. This approach gives us a view of the different forms of political inclusion sought out by social movements, enlarging what T.H. Marshall called the 'citizen's world'.

But this political input is also profoundly ambiguous: it points to inclusion but is in a sense already beyond it, because of its social nature. Roche concludes that the new rights are themselves a social entity, a social product. These rights are linked to the development of collective action and the forms of consciousness it engenders. They originate in progressive as well as anti-progressive movements. New social movements, much like their counterparts in anti-movements, are agents of structural transformation in a post-industrial, post-national and postmodern world. The new generation of citizenship rights constitutes an important component of this field of conflicts and struggles.

The ambiguity of these innovative political inputs is also examined by Pierre Hamel. Hamel explores the many traits of modern collective action embedded in individual identities, as well as the motivations of collective actors. He particularly looks at urban movements. These pragmatic and proactive forms of collective action are crystallizations of the local political scene. They bear demands which bring together individual autonomy and collective solidarity.

Hamel emphasizes innovative inputs, to tease out the significance of other forms of struggle. He contrasts his approach to that of Maheu and Lustiger-Thaler, who occupy the same empirical terrain. These social struggles, he argues, are in fact too expansive to be contained in one single register of the political sphere. They reflect structural conditions of late modernity where subjectivity and individualism become twin elements of analysis. Social movements, in this regard, seek a broadening of individual liberties which reflects the needs of subjects. This form of claims-making, based on daily life and global issues, illustrates the importance of cultural domination as a factor in the constitution of collective identity.

The final chapter, by Alain Touraine, focuses on the problem of democracy. Touraine fashions this problem for us by explaining the interplay of social forces and forms of collective action, which sustain different images of democracy. The world today, he argues, is confronted with a crisis that is not only political: it is a crisis of democracy, an unravelling of the traditional ideals of democratic utopia. The social movements of industrial society have disappeared, and with them the vision of industrial and social democracy. For Touraine what has been lost is the context-specific historical field of democracy. Democracy once pointed to and indeed celebrated a reduced gap between work and citizenship, as well as social restrictions on state power. Also now absent is the system of interest representation which affirmed the unity of political society, regulating the diversity of civil society.

Nowadays, the crisis of democracy is most evident in the dualization of the world: a liberal universe increasingly embedded in instrumental rationality and a communitarian *Lebenswelt* focused on cultural experiences and subjectivities. Collective action and social movements are today confronted by new forms of social integration, presaging a profound recomposition of democracy.

As a closing statement to this book, Touraine argues that collective action and social movements, as an expression of the subject in society, are constructing a new totality. This totality requires the passage from a 'politics of citizenship' to a 'politics of recognition'. Touraine, reformulating Charles Taylor's notion of a 'politics of recognition', argues that a modern notion of totality must unveil the new cultural signifiers of democracy.

This definition of democracy, framed by its cultural components, is therefore synonymous with institutional conditions that can assure the development of autonomous subjects. Contemporary social movements may well constitute the modern expressions of these subjects. They herald a new cultural democracy. This cultural democracy, Touraine argues, would highlight life projects based on personal freedom and rational action projects which would be democratically linked to human rights, cultural pluralism, the limitation of state power and the process of rationalization.

8

Rethinking Citizenship and Social Movements: Themes in Contemporary Sociology and Neoconservative Ideology

Maurice Roche

In this chapter I aim to explore the nature of citizenship, particularly social citizenship, in contemporary society. The chapter develops themes in the new sociology of citizenship (section II) and considers these themes in the context of a case study of the reconstruction of social citizenship proposed by American Neoconservatism since the early 1980s (section III). In addition, since Neoconservatism is viewed here as an ideological movement, it is necessary to begin by considering the general relationship between the sociological study of citizenship and of social movements in modernity (section I).

Social citizenship refers to those rights and duties of citizenship concerned with citizens' welfare, broadly understood to include work, income, education and health. In the mid-twentieth century, and certainly throughout much of the post-Second World War period, its meaning came to be intimately bound to the project and structures of the welfare state – particularly in Western Europe, but also in North America and elsewhere. In this chapter I refer to this meaning of social citizenship as the dominant paradigm. However, in the late twentieth century the welfare state is being significantly reconstructed in most Western societies, and the dominant paradigm is under assault from two sets of social forces: structural and ideological changes.

The structural changes involve globalization and technological transformation in the capitalist economy, together with the global and sub-national political dynamics associated with these economic changes. The ideological changes involve the rise of various new social movements, especially ecology and feminism, and of various forms of New Right conservatism, particularly the traditionalistic Neoconservatism which we will consider at greater length later in this chapter, as well as pro-market libertarianism. These changes, both individually and in their confluence and conjuncture since the early 1980s, are restructuring the dominant paradigm of social citizenship on contemporary societies, whether intentionally or not.

Given this background, there is an evident and pressing need, felt across the political spectrum, to rethink the nature of social citizenship. Elsewhere, I have surveyed and analysed these background changes and also developed some proposals about the future nature and prospects for social citizenship (Roche, 1992a). My major aim in this chapter is to summarize some of the main points contained in that study, focusing on the background changes that have restructured social citizenship rather than on the prospects for social citizenship in the future. A secondary aim is to outline the relevance of social movements for a sociological understanding of contemporary citizenship, its political dynamics and its process of reconstruction in Western society in the late twentieth century. In section II we will review some of the structural changes affecting the dominant paradigm of general and social citizenship. And in section III we will consider one ideological movement's (contemporary American Neoconservatism's) conception of how the dominant paradigm needs to be rethought and reconstructed. First, however, we will consider the relationship between citizenship and social movements, or more specifically, the relationship between two important and lively themes in contemporary sociology: the sociology of social movements and the sociology of citizenship.

I Citizenship and social movements: sociological perspectives

Background

My analysis in this chapter is part of a programme of work (e.g. Roche, 1987, 1992a, 1994a, 1994b) which aims to make a contribution to the sociology of citizenship in modernity. This relatively new branch of sociology has been developing strongly since the mid-1980s, especially in recent years (e.g. Culpitt, 1992; Brubaker, 1992; Pixley, 1993; Coenen and Leisink, 1993; Turner, 1993; van Steenbergen, 1994). It has developed in response to a number of contemporary social forces and ideological movements since the early 1980s, not least those connected with the globalization of the capitalist economy, the permeation of markets into all areas of social life both in the West and in the post-communist world, and the resurgence of pro-market and pro-conservative political movements, parties and governments.

Mainstream sociology, as we now realize in retrospect, had unwittingly allowed its thinking and its vision to become limited by the conventional wisdom of its traditional theoretical paradigms (e.g. liberal and Marxist functionalism) and its traditional empirical concerns. These simply failed to provide it with the tools needed to anticipate and explain the historical social changes which have overtaken Western societies since the late 1970s. There was clearly a need for the discipline to begin to address the emergent debates about the nature of and prospects for the social, the public, civil society, and the citizen community in the 1980s in both East and West. In particular, there was a need to understand the new politics of citizens' rights and duties against the background of new and renewed social problems of long-term poverty and unemployment – social problems particularly associated with structural changes and crises in the modern economy and in the role and powers of the modern state, especially the welfare state. The new sociology of citizenship, then, animated as it is by these sorts of issues, has developed as a leading aspect of sociology's more general attempt to reorient itself to the realities of social life, politics and history in the late twentieth century. As such, the new sociology of citizenship could be said to have much in common with the sociology of social movements. Although the latter pre-dates the sociology of citizenship by a decade or more, the former's interest in the theory and practice of the various forms of new social and political movements – which have developed outside conventional post-war parties and their social class bases and worldviews – is implicitly and explicitly connected with the social development and politics of contemporary citizenship. Since this chapter is part of a collection concerned with the sociology of social movements, it is appropriate to outline some of the main differences and points of contact it may be said to have with the sociology of citizenship.

Social movements and citizenship: diversity and commonality

From my perspective, and setting aside some of the more restrictive definitions of the field, the sociology of social movements consists of a collection of distinctive sociological projects. The main projects are as follows: (a) the long-established sociological attempt to understand the old working-class movements (the labour movement, trade unionism, etc.) and the growth of the welfare state and social citizenship rights in response to this; (b) the relatively long-established sociology of new social movements which, since the 1970s, has attempted to understand the nature of such movements as the anti-nuclear, ecological and anti-communist movements (such as Solidarity), and their significance for modernity; (c) feminist sociology and its concern with the women's movement, the critique of sexism and patriarchal power, and the affirmation of female rights and identity/difference; and (d) the sociology of ethnicity and its concern with movements oriented to ethnic politics and immigrants' problems, the critique of racism and dominant/host culture power, and the affirmation of ethnic/immigrant rights and identity/difference.

The Marxist theoretical voice of the old social movements – labour and trade unionism – tended to evaluate the notion of citizenship negatively as compared with conceptions of social membership and collective identity, such as comradeship in the movement, or worker in (the building of) the Communist state. From this point of view, citizenship in the allegedly liberal and democratic state – a state seen as run by and for capitalism – was little more than another weapon of mystification and falsification in the armoury of bourgeois/ruling-class ideology.

Nonetheless the waves of growth of civil, political and social rights in modern Western history, no doubt through long, divisive and discontinuous struggles, can be seen as the extension and intensification of citizens' rights and status. Sociologists of various theoretical persuasions have reasonably analysed old and, more recently, new social movements in terms of the historical development of citizenship (e.g. Marshall, 1964; Parsons, 1970; Turner, 1986; Scott, 1990). In addition, the sociology of social movements has always tried to retain a critical/normative dimension in its analysis, that is, it has always maintained an interest in assessing the social justice and progressiveness both of social movements and of the states and conditions which they oppose and try to transform. Given this, the universalistic notion and language of citizenship (together with its normatively laden implications for rights, duties and so on) is always likely to provide, explicitly or implicitly, a theoretical and normative conceptual foundation within the sociology of social movements.

Each of the new social movements noted above (ecology, feminism, ethnic movements) advocates, in one way or another, the creation or renewal of some set of citizen rights (whether against the state, against other citizens or both), and in some cases argues for the recognition and acceptance of new or renewed responsibilities for citizens as well. So, although it typically casts its net wider in the social and political theory of modernity than a focus on social movements alone would allow, the sociology of citizenship nonetheless must recognize and address the phenomena dealt with by the various social movement sociologies mentioned above.

There are, however, clear differences between the various new social movements with respect to self-understanding, aims, constituencies, and the nature of their struggles. Such fragmentation of

190   *Collective Action: From Politics to Democracy*

the general social movement field, and of the salience within it of the old labour movement, seems to confound attempts at analysis in terms of any singular theme. Certainly the traditional Left's view that ecology and feminism could simply be included in its conception of the movement for the apparently unitary ideal of socialism was always artificial and questionable, given, for example, the trade union movement's traditional patriarchal and pro-industrial assumptions, and the effective absence of feminist and ecological themes in Marxist theory. The potential for dialogue between new social movements and the various sociologies that address them initially appears to be limited to the extent that the particularism and fragmentation of the movements is reflected in these sociologies.

However, contemporary post-communist Left thinking (e.g. Mouffe, 1992) attempts to take a more positive view of this kind of particularism and fragmentation, seeing it as exemplifying common themes and radical ideals of difference, pluralism and democracy. Taking a cue from this political approach to new social movements, sociologists might use the common theme of citizenship to explore and monitor social movements – by developing a 'citizenship reading' or hermeneutic of individual social movements and of the social movement field in general. Such an approach would investigate intra-movement, inter-movement and extra-movement democratic and citizenship issues: it would explore (a) the nature of democracy and members' rights and responsibilities practised within each movement; (b) the tolerance for and linkages between each movement, and their conceptions of citizenship, rights and responsibilities; and (c) the democratic nature of the state and of the citizen community context in which they operate, as well as the ways of and prospects for furthering the development of democracy, citizenship empowerment and civil society autonomy. In each of these respects, social movement analysis could use common citizenship as a way to construct potential common ground, purpose and political language within the diversity of contemporary social movements.

Redefining the political: social movements, post-industrialism and post-nationalism
Post-war social movements, as is often noted, have stretched the boundaries of what can reasonably be deemed political (that is, a matter of public interest, of power struggle and of rights, and thus of potential concern to all citizens) beyond the sphere constructed by the nation-state – its decision-making apparatus, parties, laws and public institutions. The anti-nuclear movement and the ecology

movement have addressed and politicized the problems of nature and history – the global and intergenerational scale of the human threat to plant, animal and human species survival. Traditionally, these problems were seen as outside the public sphere simply because they raised issues beyond the scope of the nation-state. New social movements, however, urge modern societies to treat these as political problems. Comparably, the women's movement addresses and politicizes problems in the most private and personal spheres – those of male power and violence in the spheres of sexuality, intimacy, parenting and domesticity; and it presses modern society to reconstruct the national public domain to include these sub-national dimensions also.

Conversely, on the one hand the anti-nuclear movement and the ecology movement have also pursued a highly particularist and sub-national politics of place – for example, neighbourhood cleaning and recycling initiatives, and NIMBY ('not in my back yard') opposition to the location of nuclear or waste sites in threatened neighbourhoods. On the other hand, the politics of the women's movement contains strong transnational themes, in that patriarchy is a global and historical phenomenon (albeit institutionalized in different ways and to different extents, and thus differently contested) in all societies. In these and other senses, while they undoubtedly continue to operate largely at a national level and in nationally constructed political spheres, these social movements are essentially post-national phenomena calling for a theory and a practice concerned with the trans- and sub-national levels in addition to the national level.

Social movements can thus be said to address the problems of politics in a post-national era. Indeed, new social movement sociology has engaged in a continuing dialogue with the self-understanding of the ecology movement, which has tended to present itself as a fundamental practical and philosophical critique of industrial society. Thus new social movement sociology has begun to analyse social movements in terms of the structural changes involved in the emergence of post-industrialism and post-industrial society (Touraine, 1977).

Social movement sociology, as much as the new citizenship sociology, can be said to address the problems of politics in a post-industrial stage of the development of the capitalist economy. This is a stage in which one of the central institutions of industrial capitalism – the welfare state – is in crisis; and states feel compelled to explore and experiment with moralistic, individualistic and market-based solutions to capitalism's problems of poverty, unemployment and welfare. In each of these respects, the sociology of social movements is concerned with the same problematics and forces of social-structural and societal change that interest writers and researchers in the contemporary sociology of citizenship. There is clearly a basis here for dialogue between these perspectives, and indeed the work of some notable contemporary sociologists overlaps both fields (e.g. Offe, 1985a: chs 9, 10; 1985b; Turner, 1986: ch.4; Habermas, 1987: Pt.VIII; 1994).

Cities, social movements and citizenship
Another important basis for dialogue is connected to this common interest. Some social movement analysts (see Hamel's and Lustiger-Thaler and Maheu's contributions to the present book) argue that post-national and post-industrial structural dynamics, and their responses in social movement politics, can most realistically and instructively be observed and explored by a sociology which takes the urban level and sphere as its main point of reference. It is in this sphere that most modern Western people encounter and respond to the problems and politics which animate the various contemporary social movements: problems of individualism and statism, of sexuality and parentalism, of neighbourhood and ethnicity, of trade unionism and welfare, of housing and the physical environment. Even though many of these social problems may be experienced concretely by the same people, they are usually somewhat abstractly distinguished from each other. This abstraction allows the existence of distinct organizations which reach beyond the city level to the national, international and transnational levels.

Lustiger-Thaler and Maheu, reviving a somewhat underplayed theme in the sociology of social movements (e.g. Castells, 1983), argue that it is in the real-world lived density of the city that social movements are what they are and become what they can become. It is in the city that they communicate and interact with each other, the public, the media and the state. And it is in this urban context in particular that social movements need to be studied as well as practised.

This kind of urban social movement sociology necessarily has much to say about the lived experience of urban politics and urban-level citizenship. In principle it shares much common ground with the contemporary sociology of citizenship. The latter recognizes and addresses the national, sub-national and transnational levels of citizenship as a complex of sites where the structural problems of post-nationalism and post-industrialism are being struggled with (Roche, 1992a). In these struggles, pre-national conceptions of citizen community and civic identity (in the case of Europe, ancient and medieval models from city-states to empires) are being revived to inform the new conceptions of citizenship which need to be constructed in a post-national era. In the national era, the national state centralized and institutionalized itself, objectifying and symbolizing its modernity and progressiveness, in its capital city. It thereby tended to relegate all of its other urban formations to a provincial and peripheral status. In the post-national era, as in some respects in the pre-national era, a multi-polar economy and world order exists, involving a global network of world-cities/capital markets, and giving new political prominence to sub-national and transnational regions and their cities. In this context both the sociology of social movements and the sociology of citizenship (e.g. Roche, 1992a: ch.7; 1992b; see also Gyford, 1990; Jacobs, 1992) have a common interest in paying special attention to the urban level.

Social and ideological movements: progressive and non-progressive types

This is not the place to attempt to consider the similarities, differences and relationships between the sociology of citizenship and the various sociologies of social movements (indicated earlier) in any great detail. I hope that enough has been noted here, in general terms, to indicate the potential for a fruitful dialogue between them. However, from the point of view of this chapter it is necessary to further clarify the aims of the sociology of citizenship as I see it.

Clearly, the sociology of citizenship must be concerned, along with the sociology of social movements, with what might be understood in critical/normative terms as progressive social move-ments (e.g. citizen-organized movements and/or movements promoting the extension of citizenship and the empowerment of citizens) together with their relationship to the state and to institutionalized political processes. However, as part of the task of understanding the political environment, and thus the field of obstacles and opportunities within which new and progressive movements operate, it is also necessary to study other types of socially and politically relevant movements of ideas, ideals and actions, movements and organizations. Whether they are recent or not, in critical/normative terms these other types may be regarded as non-progressive or, in some cases, as anti-progressive or reactionary. Furthermore, they may or may not be explicitly connected with the state and the formal political process; in many ways they may be based, as much as progressive social movements are, in civil society, albeit in the uncivil regions of that political territory.

In some cases, such movements may be identified by their antagonistic stance to new social movements. So it is necessary, when attempting to understand the nature and dynamics of ethnic and anti-racist movements and organizations, to address the problem of understanding both self-consciously racist organizations and racism as a general ideological movement (so-called institutionalized racism, racism as a form of collective consciousness and popular discourse). The same sort of observation could be made about explicitly sexist/patriarchal organizations, together with sexism/patriarchy as a general ideological movement in relation to understanding the obstacles and opportunities facing feminism. And the same thing could be said about explicitly polluting and animal/habitat-destroying industrial states and corporations, together with the wasteful and polluting aspects of mass consumerism seen as a popular ideological movement.

These examples illustrate the point that both the sociology of social movements and the sociology of citizenship need to conceptualize the political field they address as one which includes non- and anti-progressive movements as well as progressive social movements. Furthermore it is not helpful in attempting to understand the political field in which progressive movements operate to restrict unnecessarily what is to count as a movement. The examples indicate that it is wise to broaden the concept to include both formal or semi-formal organizations (often involving intellectuals and/or senior sectorsss within the media industries) attempting to influence and lead public opinion, and also what can be referred to as ideological movements, namely movements within the collective consciousness or popular and everyday culture, involving widely held sets of beliefs and forms of popular discourse.

This way of approaching social movements is to a certain extent illustrated in the case study of American Neoconservatism, together with its project to reconstruct the meaning and practice of social citizenship in contemporary American society and polity, which we consider in section III of this chapter. This is an ideological movement which is evidently non- or anti-progressive, which combines both a degree of formal organization through the activities of social policy analysts and intellectuals, and which is also resonant with themes in American popular culture, collective consciousness and public discourse.

Anti-political and anti-social movements

From the point of view of the new sociology of citizenship, then, the relevant sociological approach to the analysis of social movements needs to be fairly broadly based, open to non-progressive as well as progressive formations, and open to ideological and discursive as well as practical forms of collective action. With non-progressive movements, moreover, in order to be relevant to an understanding of the modern political field facing citizenship politics, the sociology of citizenship needs to be open to what might be called, provisionally and provocatively, anti-political and anti-social social movements.

The concept of an anti-political movement refers to organizations of common ideas, ideals and actions among the powerful (for example politicians and senior state officials at national, regional and urban levels; corporate owners and senior managers; media owners and senior managers) to defend and extend elite power and control, and at best to co-opt, and at worst to ignore, bypass and override democracy and accountability processes. Classic examples include traditional early and mid-twentieth-century forms of corporatism. Contemporary examples include the important wave of movements among elite groups in many North American and West European cities in the 1980s and early 1990s: new forms of urban corporatism involving formal or quasi-formal partnerships among private and public sector leaderships in order to promote economic growth and regeneration. These are as important for sociological study as movements among the relatively less powerful or the powerless, because they often use the language of citizenship and help to structure and constrain the ideological and material sites and contexts in which citizens live and citizens' movements emerge and operate (e.g. Roche, 1992b; Jacobs, 1992).

The concept of an anti-social movement refers to anomic and other-destructive and/or self-destructive patterns of collective attitudes and behaviour (such as violence, addiction or abuse). These may, unlike fully-fledged social movements, involve action which is recurrent but unpredictable. Activity may appear to be organized (via gang and criminal networks and subcultures) or disorganized and in the long term is usually demoralizing and demobilizing – in that it works against whatever potential for social movement organization a community may possess. Anti-social movements are typically connected to the structural situation of poverty and multiple deprivation, as in the urban black underclass in many cities in the US.

This kind of movement is important for the sociology of citizenship in that it indicates something of the exclusive (Lister, 1990; Brubaker, 1992) as well as the inclusive nature of full citizenship. The status and fate of those with second-class citizenship, or with little or no effective citizenship at all, is often that of mere denizenship (Hammar, 1990). Denizenship as a ground for anti-social movements represents an internal division and limit within a society's operational conception of its citizen community. It poses real threats to the quality of the civil society which can exist in that community, and it provides motivating interests and targets for anti-political movements among the powerful.

The sociology of social movements acknowledges these sorts of phenomena mainly in its treatment of the emergence of new social classes, particularly new sectors (state- and market-based information and service-sector professionals and workers) within the middle class. However, in their model of a social movement, some sections of social movement sociology have been more restrictive. They appear to search for a successor to the working-class/labour movement and thus require evidence of comparable opposition-unifying and social transformative potential from any pattern of collective protest before crediting it with the status of being a genuine, fully fledged social movement (Scott, 1990: ch. 3). The anti-democratic and anti-social forms of movement indicated above would not qualify according to this criterion. Interestingly, though, in a reformulation of the theory of social movements, Touraine has proposed that 'Holders of economic or political power must be analyzed as a social movement . . . I would consider management a social movement in exactly the same way as labour' (1985: 775). And more recently Stewart has argued that 'The underclass is the structural equivalent of today's social movements' (1989: 201).

These positions are more consistent with the perspective required in the sociology of citizenship. The latter is concerned, among other things, with the fact of structural social change in modernity, with the effects of this on the whole community (and thus on the most universal status constituting the community and membership of it, namely citizenship), and with citizens' responses to these effects. The types of movement we have considered here are intimately connected with the attempt to control and steer structural social change on the one hand (i.e. elite/anti-political movements), and with reactions to structural social change by groups of people suffering their effects on the other (i.e. underclass/anti-social movements). They are thus of central importance for the contemporary sociology of citizenship.

The rest of this chapter is concerned with a number of themes and debates in the sociology of citizenship. The discussion is divided into two main sections. In section II I outline what we may refer to as the dominant paradigm of citizenship in the post-war West. The focus is on T.H. Marshall's version of this paradigm and on the structural changes in Western societies since the mid-1970s. These changes require us to rethink our conception of citizenship so that it fits the transitional and in some respects postmodern condition (Harvey 1989) of the late twentieth century.

In section III I consider a major ideological challenge to the dominant paradigm's assumption about social citizenship. This has taken the form of a distinctive kind of revival of conservative thinking among political elites and across the political spectrum of popular politics about the nature of social citizenship. This ideological movement, Neoconservatism, needs to be distinguished from other popular contemporary right-wing ideologies such as simple nationalism and the pro-market neo-libertarianism of the New Right. Neoconservatism stresses citizens' family and work obligations as opposed to their work, income and welfare rights. I focus on the tensions and contradictions within this ideological movement and within the policies it promotes, especially those policies intended to address the problem of poverty and the underclass in contemporary societies.

II Citizenship and modernity: the dominant paradigm and structural change

The sociology of citizenship

The sociology of citizenship is derived, to a considerable extent, from the seminal formulations of British sociologist T.H. Marshall in his 1949 lecture 'Citizenship and social class' (Marshall, 1964). In the 1960s and 1970s, leading American sociologists used and developed Marshall's analysis in the context of their studies of nation-building (Bendix, 1964), of the modernization process (Parsons, 1970), and of the growth of welfare states (Rimlinger, 1971). In the 1970s, British social analysts applied Marshall's framework to the analysis of social policy (e.g. Parker, 1975; Room, 1979).

The sociology of citizenship really began to take shape in the 1980s, however, in response to structural and ideological changes during that period. British social and political theorists (e.g. Giddens, 1985; Turner, 1986; King, 1987; Hall and Held, 1989) began to review and reopen debates about the nature of modern citizenship, particularly in the context of the welfare state and social citizenship (e.g. Jordan, 1987; Plant, 1988). By the early 1990s the field had been revived in American sociology (e.g. Brubaker, 1992) and was developing in European sociology (e.g. Coenen and Leisink, 1993).

In my approach to the sociology of citizenship I have suggested (e.g. Roche 1987, 1992a) that any substantial sociological analysis of citizenship needs in principle to give an account of at least three interlinked dimensions of citizenship. Briefly these are (1) the nature of the citizen and the citizen community; (2) the social-structural context underlying citizenship and the citizen community and influencing (both enabling and limiting) their capacities for development; and (3) the history of change in the nature of both citizenship and its structural context.

The first dimension requires attention to such things as the typical forms of experience, typical actor prerequisites, and the typical ideals and values of citizenship and of a community of citizens. These (respectively) phenomenological, ontological and moral aspects of citizenship I will refer to here as the citizen's world, for the sake of brevity. The second dimension requires sociological and political economic analysis of the relation between industrial capitalism and the nation-state as both enabler and disabler of the liberties and equalities, the rights and the duties of citizenship. Finally, the third dimension refers to the historicity of citizen ideologies, communities and structural contexts. It requires an account of the evolutionary or revolutionary character of citizenship's change and development in the modern period.

In the discussion that follows I will use these concepts as a framework for outlining and analysing social citizenship and the contemporary ideological and social forces pressing for its reconstruction. The rest of the chapter then deals with some of the main aspects and debates about the citizen's world and about citizenship's structural context in the dominant discourse on citizenship, in the implications of contemporary social-structural changes, and in an important, contemporary conservative discourse on social citizenship. Due to the range of issues which it aims to cover, the discussion here of the citizen's world and context is intentionally and necessarily schematic and selective. For the same reasons, it does not aim to explore the history of citizenship. (Fuller discussions of the three dimensions are available in Roche, 1987, 1992a.)

Modernity and citizenship: the dominant paradigm and national functionalism

In much of the sociology of citizenship, and implicit in everyday commonsense understandings of citizenship in modern societies, there is a set of assumptions about the citizen's world, citizenship's structural context, and its history. This loose set of assumptions can be referred to as the dominant paradigm or discourse of citizenship. As an intellectual construct, it is probably most clearly expressed in T.H. Marshall's (1964) classic discussion. But in one form or another – and with due acknowledgement of the inevitable oversimplification of complex ideas involved in this claim – the paradigm underlines the consensus on post-war British social policy (Roche, 1992a: chs 1, 2). Moreover this paradigm, and the debate over it, permeates much of the sociology of citizenship (e.g. Turner, 1986; Barbalet, 1988; Lister, 1990; Coenen and Leisink, 1993).

In Marshall's (1964) analysis the citizen world consists of three types of rights – civil, political and social – with corresponding state institutions servicing rights claims (respectively the law, democracy and the welfare state). Social rights are distinct from civil and political rights, but they continue and complement such rights. Social rights enable participation in civilized society and include the rights to welfare, work and income, and to health and education. While the notion of citizens' social *duties* is noted in passing, the main emphasis is on their social *rights* and on the (welfare) state's duties to service the social dimension of citizenship (see also Marshall, 1981). This strong emphasis on rights has been characteristic of the dominant discourse on citizenship throughout the post-war period.

In addition, Marshall's relatively apolitical formulation of social citizenship as distinct from civil and political citizenship is characteristic not only of the dominant discourse but also, in modified form, of the recent Neoconservative alternative, as we shall see later. The main concern of the dominant discourse has been to use state power to overcome inequality in the distribution and realization of citizens' rights within a structural context which is, nonetheless, generative of multiple forms of inequality.

In Marshall's analysis the structural context of citizenship is generally modernity or modern society and, more specifically, what can be called 'national functionalism' (Roche, 1992a: chs 1, 2). This is the complex formed by (1) the nation-state; (2) an industrial capitalist economy, in particular a national capitalism capable of management by Keynesian state economic policy; and (3) a common and functional culture and value system (containing ideological, familial and other such elements functional for the reproduction of the nation-state and national capitalism).

As far as social citizenship and welfare rights are concerned, Marshall and the subsequent dominant discourse tended to focus on one dimension of the modern social complex: the modern state and its welfare role and services. Such a focus tends to take for granted and to make hidden assumptions about modern culture and economic life. First there is the existential fact that in all human societies, including modernity, it is the culture, particularly the family system, which supplies the bulk of welfare services. Secondly there is the historical fact that, since the rise of industrial capitalism in the nineteenth century, a great and increasing share of welfare services have been provided through the economy – through capitalist markets, involving goods and services produced by capitalist producers, consumed by consumers using income derived from capitalist labour markets.

Marshall (1964; 1981:ch. 6) considered the conflicts over inequality which occur between the democratic polity and the economy, between the welfare state and capitalism (see also Titmuss, 1963: ch. 2). However, along with William Beveridge, Richard Titmuss and other proponents of the welfare state, he assumed that in practice a mixed economy (capitalism and state-controlled economic sectors) was viable and that welfare state relations with capitalism could be functional, mutually reinforcing and capable of supporting minimally unequal citizen relations. Many others have subsequently made similar but more explicit arguments from neo-Marxist and critical social theory perspectives (e.g. Gough, 1979; Doyal, 1983; Turner, 1986, etc.), albeit with varying *evaluations* of this functionality and of the possibilities for equality.

Overall, in its analysis of the politics of welfare and of social citizenship, the dominant paradigm has, on the one hand, tended to overemphasize the role and capacity of the state and its officials to produce and distribute welfare *per se*, and to do so on an egalitarian and citizen-respecting basis. On the other hand, the dominant paradigm has tended to underestimate the actual and potential role of markets, the family and voluntary organizations both to produce and to distribute welfare, and to do so not only on an egalitarian and citizen-respecting basis, but on a participative and mutual basis beyond the capacity of the state apparatus. Evidently, the possibilities available in the non-state sectors can be exaggerated, and Neoconservatism typically greatly exaggerates the role of labour markets in terms of welfare and citizenship. In the light of this the dominant paradigm tends, when it explicitly addresses them, to adopt a critical stance towards the inadequacies and inequities of the non-state sectors as welfare providers.

But there are important hidden assumptions in this stance. The dominant paradigm – usually reluctantly and *sotto voce* – is usually well aware that the non-state sectors are in actual fact providers of welfare both on a massive scale and in ways quite beyond the capacity and competence even of totalitarian states to take over or replicate as a whole. It may be that in some areas and on some occasions state welfare provision is superior in quantity or quality to that provided in non-state sectors. But it is important to understand the necessary condition for such welfare state success and superiority as there is: that the state explicitly or tacitly recognizes its *limits* vis-à-vis civil society and non-state sectors. So the resources necessary to support welfare state achievements and successes, such as they are, are only available because they are *not* required to be dispersed in pursuit of grandiose projects of substitution for non-state-sector provision. Ironically, in this analysis the condition of success of the welfare state is the conservation of resources which the effectiveness of the non-state welfare sectors allows it. The hidden assumption of the welfare state, and of the dominant paradigm which supports it, is that of the existence, persistence and success of a plurality of non-state welfare systems understood as functionally related to each other and to the national society as a functional whole, with the state largely in a regulatory as opposed to a provisory role (Jordan, 1987).

Finally, there is the question of the history of citizenship. Marshall offers a picture, based on Britain, of the successive growth of each of the three types of citizenship and relevant state institutions. Thus it is possible to assign the formative period in the life of each to a different century – civil rights to the eighteenth, political to the nineteenth and social to the twentieth (1964: 73). Bendix and Parsons took over this rough evolutionary account in their studies of nation-building in countries such as Japan, India, Germany and Russia (Bendix, 1964) and of Western modernization (Parsons, 1970). A related evolutionary/revolutionary image of successive waves in the growth of citizenship appears repeatedly in a recent study of the intimate relationship between citizenship and the modernization process and between citizenship and its capitalist structural context (Turner, 1986).

Overall, though, the dominant paradigm's conception of the history of citizenship in general is that of long-term growth, formation and coalescence between processes of nation-state democratization on the one hand and the development of industrial capitalism on the other, while its conception of the history of social citizenship is that of the long-term growth of a conflictual but contained and ultimately functional relationship between the welfare state and industrial capitalism.

Recent history and critical reflection give us many reasons to question the assumptions of the dominant paradigm and to rethink its conception of social citizenship. The following sections will examine some of the main contemporary incentives for doing so and their implications for social citizenship. We will look first at the incentives provided by changes in the structural context of citizenship, and then at ideological challenges, especially those of Neoconservatism.

Citizenship and structural change: the postmodern condition
The dominant paradigm of social citizenship – with its associated discourse of welfare rights, its politics of welfare state provision,

and its relative silence on family-based and market-based welfare systems and provision – held sway throughout the early post-war period, the period of post-war reconstruction and the long boom from the 1950s to the mid-1970s. Since then, for a variety of reasons (see Roche, 1992: Part III), the structural base of the dominant paradigm of citizenship has been subject to stresses and to significant change.

In particular, the welfare state and the concept of social citizenship it sustains have been subjected to two sorts of critique. First there is the economic critique that the growth of state welfare spending damages economic growth and thus the tax base on which it depends. Secondly there is the moral critique that the welfare state tends to perpetuate the dependency of its clients, that it disables rather than enables them, and even that it increases the poverty it was set up to abolish. We will consider the moralistic conservative criticisms later (section III).

The problems of the welfare state, whether real or perceived, are symptomatic of deeper problems in contemporary society. These problems are associated with social change and a period of historic transition away from the modern social formation of the nation-state, industrial capitalism and a common and functional culture and towards an unfamiliar, uncertain and unclear future. There can be little doubt that, certainly by the late 1980s, the advanced Western societies had begun to part company with the modern formation in many important respects. This drift (with some exceptions such as Japan) involved no clear vision of the likely shape or alternative profiles of a future social formation, even assuming that the pace of social change would never ease sufficiently for stable formations to develop in the early twenty-first century (Toffler, 1970, 1980, 1985).

Without any wish to get detoured into the Byzantine world of postmodernism, I will nonetheless use the terms 'postmodern' and 'postmodern problematic' to refer to this process of significantly unpredictable and apparently irresistible structural change in the main elements of the modern formation. This usage is consistent with other contemporary conceptualizations of the postmodern condition (e.g. Harvey, 1989) and postmodernization (e.g. Crook et al., 1992). It is also consistent with the view that postmodern institutional configurations are continuous with the dynamics of modernity and modernization and represent a new stage within a modernization process which has already gone through a number of qualitatively distinct stages since the pre-industrial period.

The postmodern condition involves the emergence of new orders of transnational and sub-national complexity in the politics, economics and cultures of modern societies. This complexity is potentially disorienting in ideological and normative cultural spheres, and disintegrative and disorganizational in economic and political economic terms (Urry and Lash, 1987) for modern formations. To counter its anomic effects requires a continuous labour of ideological reorientation and of restructuring (i.e. integrative institution-building) from all members, and from social organizations at all levels, in these formations.

The new complexity distinctive of the postmodern condition is clearly visible in the modern polity in the shape of (a) the emerging web of transnational political organizations managing global and world-regional affairs; (b) the emergence of continental/world-regional economic and political alliances, of which the European Community is the leading example; (c) the persistence and development of sub-national nationalist and regional autonomy claims; and (d) the persisting difficulties in realizing the claims of modern societies to be effectively multicultural rather than simply hopelessly politically fragmented along ethnic lines. The new postmodern complexity is equally clearly visible in the modern economy in the interconnected processes of globalization and flexibilization in contemporary capitalism.

Globalization (e.g. Hall and Jacques, 1989: Part III) refers to the rapid development of a multinational structure and role in large corporations and of a genuinely global level of capital movement, production organization and marketing. Flexibilization (e.g. Piore and Sabel, 1984; Hall and Jacques, 1989: Part I) refers to the introduction of computerization and automation into goods production and distribution and into financial and information services for producers and consumers. This is at the heart of the currently much debated shift from industrial to post-industrial or post-Fordist capitalism. Capital equipment and labour are having to become more flexible and skilled, capable of rapid adjustment to changing and segmented markets.

These two processes have operated to profoundly undermine conventional economic policy assumptions. First there is the notion that economies can be national and hence that their labour markets and general price levels can be significantly influenced by national governments. The breakdown of this assumption has profound consequences for the ability of states both to service social citizenship claims to (full) employment and to control inflationary tendencies in consumer (welfare) goods and services markets.

Secondly the flexibilized post-industrial/post-Fordist economy (unlike the mass production/mass consumption Fordist economy it replaces) continuously reduces the demand for labour relative to output (i.e. it increases labour productivity). This presents a permanent threat of structural unemployment (Gorz, 1982, 1985, 1989; Keane and Owen, 1986) as well as increasing pressures for national economic growth and for improvements in national labour supply and training systems to sustain employment (Robins and Webster, 1989; Freeman and Soete, 1987). This comes at the very time when the possibility of economic regulation at the national level is being seriously undermined by globalization. There are serious structural problems of either structural unemployment or at least of underemployment and of a labour market segmented between full-time and part-time or temporary workers. These problems challenge one of the hidden assumptions of the dominant paradigm of citizenship, namely that a great bulk of welfare can be distributed through the market system via consumption based on employment income (Dore, 1987).

Finally, there are significant trends in modern culture towards postmodern complexity. Among other things, these challenge the other hidden assumption of the dominant paradigm. This assumption, as noted earlier, is that the greatest bulk of welfare can be distributed through a standardized family system and mainly through women's labour as those who care for young children, the sick and the elderly. The main development relevant here is the long-term and accelerating breakdown of the standardized family pattern of patriarchally based gender roles and division of labour, and of commonly held and legitimized norms regarding such matters as divorce, incest, violence and illegitimate births (e.g. Wicks and Kiernan, 1990). Since this particular dysfunctionality of postmodern culture for the modern formation is one that greatly worries Neoconservatives, we will return to it again in the next section.

There are evidently many other cultural developments towards postmodern complexity which challenge the functionality of the modern cultural system for both the polity and the economy. Not least is the development of an individualistic, privatistic and hedonistic consumer culture (Lasch, 1979; Featherstone, 1991). As regards the polity, consumerism tends to contribute to ecological problems and to undermine politics based on the legitimacy of notions of the public sphere and the public good. As regards the economy, it has been argued that consumerism constitutes one of the basic cultural contradictions of capitalism (Bell, 1976) in that it tends to undermine both the work ethic and also the incentive to save, thereby also undermining labour productivity and investment resources.

Each of these late twentieth-century shifts away from the modern social formation towards the transitional postmodern condition outlined above carries problems and potential fuel for movements challenging the dominant paradigm of citizenship, particularly its assumed structural context and its welfare-state-based version of social citizenship.. The next section will consider some of the main challenges to the dominant paradigm in the contemporary period from ideological movements, especially American Neoconservatism. These challenges respond to some of the social problems generated by the structural changes which have been reviewed in this section.

III Citizenship and ideology: the dominant paradigm and Neoconservatism

Duty discourses: ideological and social movements in modernity

The dominant paradigm of citizenship, in addition to its structural and historical assumptions, contains assumptions about the nature of the citizen world, as suggested earlier. This latter sphere is the main focus of various ideological movements and challenges which have arisen in the late twentieth century. I have suggested that the paradigm's picture of the nature of citizenship and of the citizen community is one which emphasizes the priority of citizens' rights, together with the continuity and complementarity of social rights vis-à-vis civic and political rights. Certainly the struggle for rights has been a central and recurrent theme in nineteenth- and twentieth-century politics. But there is another side to citizenship which has been relatively neglected by the dominant paradigm: citizens' duties.

Duties have stimulated a considerable amount of political conflict in the post-war West (e.g. the anti-conscription/anti-Vietnam war movement, tax-payers' revolts against welfare state spending and recently the British anti-poll-tax movement). But it is notable that they have been relatively little analysed in the social and political theory of citizenship (for an exception see Walzer, 1985). This neglect is all the worse in that late twentieth-century popular politics seems to be accumulating duty discourses, particularly in the field of new social movements, namely such areas as internationalism, environmentalism and the anti-nuclear-weapons movement. That is, there is a certain popular recognition in the West – albeit one which has yet to find expression through organized national and international politics and policy-making – that rich nations have duties to poor ones, and that all nations and individuals have duties to nature and the environment, as well as to future generations regarding the conservation and transmission of humankind's environmental and sociohistorical heritage (Roche, 1992a: chs 2, 9).

Besides this radical new social movement wing of the new duty discourse in contemporary society, there is also of course (as there traditionally always has been) a right-wing discourse about citizens' duties and responsibilities in Western politics. In the 1980s and 1990s in the US, Britain and elsewhere, interest groups, parties, movements and governments on the Right have developed and deployed a duty discourse, a repertoire of rhetorical and policy strategies focusing on individuals' personal responsibility for themselves and their (as against the community's, the public's, the state's) dependants (children, aged parents, unwaged partners, etc.), and generally upon the social obligations of citizenship. This discourse has been developed and deployed in particular with respect to the underclass, and more generally with respect to the poor and those dependent for some or all of their income and/or welfare services on the state, and thus indirectly on the employed and taxpaying sectors of any society's population. The discourse has achieved considerable popularity and support among skilled working-class and the lower middle-class sectors of societies like the US and Britain, and to a significant extent it authentically formulates and expresses important elements of their ethico-political worldview. Given its orchestration by politicians, parties and sectors of the media, its continuing popular appeal, and the challenges it raises to the welfare state and to the dominant paradigm of social citizenship, I will refer to the development and diffusion of this discourse as an ideological movement.

This ideological movement was most clearly expressed in the early and mid-1980s in the development of American Neoconservative social thinking (to be distinguished from other more economistic and neo-libertarian forms of New Right thinking) which dominated social policy debates and policy-making during the Reagan and Bush presidencies. However, before we consider American Neoconservatism further, it is worth underlining the point that this distinctive movement in the language and assumptions of everyday politics in the US in the 1980s has had a popular and intellectual appeal and resonance beyond the traditional spheres of right-wing politics and beyond the US. Aspects of it, predictably, have appeared on the Right in Britain, in the post-Thatcherite Conservative Party's and government's thinking and rhetoric on social issues and social policy. For instance, inspired by examples in the repertoire of American Neoconservative family policy measures, the Conservative government created the Family Support Agency in 1992 to enforce absent/divorced fathers' child-support duties. Inspired by comparable examples of American Neoconservative work policy, the Conservatives have begun the gradual introduction of workfare-oriented reforms to the state's provision of income for the unemployed. In addition, familist rhetoric and policy (pro-family values, pro-two-parent and anti-one-parent families, etc.) has become a popular theme in Conservative Party think-tanks and at the Conservatives' annual party conferences in recent years.

But these elements have also appeared in the discourses of Centrist and Leftist parties and movements in a number of Western countries, particularly Britain, in the late 1980s and 1990s. Many of the Neoconservative themes we will outline here are connected with a rethinking of social citizenship away from a pure focus on rights towards giving full weight to social obligations as well. These elements have also appeared in recent years in such Centrist and Leftist political spheres as American communitarianism (e.g. Etzioni, 1992); British ethical socialism (Dennis and Halsey, 1988); and President Clinton's social policy agenda. Such themes are evident, too, in the British Labour Party's, and associated Centre/Left think-tanks', continued rethinking of a range of issues bearing on the idea and ideal of citizenship, and of citizens' rights and responsibilities (issues such as the proper relation between the market and the state in welfare, the proper balance between individual freedom and the goal of equality, the nature and importance of the enabling state ideal and constitutional reform: e.g. Andrews, 1991; IPPR, 1993).

An ideological movement: American Neoconservatism and social citizenship

Neoconservatism is to be found in the pro-capitalism and pro-individual-liberty writings of a number of notable American sociologists and policy analysts, and also in journals such as *The Public Interest*. It is a loose label for a relatively diverse group ranging from sceptical liberals such as the sociologist Daniel Bell and the influential Democratic Senator Daniel P. Moynihan on its Left, to New Right anti-welfare state libertarians such as Charles Murray (Ehrenreich, 1987; King, 1987; also Karger, 1991; Lasch, 1991).

What are some of the main preoccupations of Neoconservatism relevant to understanding its conceptions of social citizenship? As far as the *structural context* of citizenship goes, Neoconservatism recognizes the importance of some structural changes comparable to those discussed above, particularly the changes in the cultural (family and value system). But in general (and with due recognition of the federalist sub-nationalism of some Neoconservatives, e.g. Butler and Kondratas, 1987; Murray, 1984), it tends to operate within the dominant paradigm's structural context assumptions of nation-statism, national (here US) capitalism and national functionalism.

But Neoconservatism's main contribution to the ideological challenge to the dominant paradigm of citizenship bears on the paradigm's conception of the nature of citizenship and of the citizen world. On this issue Neoconservatives are forthright and blunt, if also, as we shall see, self-contradictory and at odds with themselves. They set out to counter the dominant paradigm's arguably unjustified overemphasis on rights and on the role of the state in welfare provision and in social citizenship. So their emphasis (or rather their arguably equally unjustified overemphasis) is on duties and the role of the non-state sectors of employment and family in welfare and social citizenship. Neoconservatism undoubtedly makes a general case for the importance of having a conception of duty as a vital part of any conception of social citizenship. However, there are conflicts and contradictions at the heart of the perspective on the relative priority, and indeed the very compatibility, of family duties as against employment (capitalist labour market) duties. (For fuller accounts and critiques of Neoconservatism's approach to social citizenship, family and work policy see Roche, 1992a: chs 4–6; Coenen and Leisink, 1993).

For the sake of this discussion we will assume that social policy helps to demarcate and constitute the political field in which the world of social citizenship exists. On social policy, then, Neoconservatives are united in a belief that the post-war state has failed, that (in the words attributed to Ronald Reagan) in the 1960s we fought a War on Poverty, and Poverty won. They are united also in going further and seeing the liberal welfare state as being the major contributor to the social problems it was ostensibly designed to solve, namely long-term poverty and unemployment. The persistence of these problems has, in the view of Neoconservatives (e.g. Murray, 1989; Mead, 1986) and many liberal commentators (e.g. Auletta, 1983; Wilson, 1987) led to the growth of an underclass of variously incompetent, disturbed and alienated people, often women, mainly in inner-city black ghettos, prone to crime and maintained in their marginalized position by the welfare benefits they usually depend upon (Roche, 1992a: ch. 3).

Neoconservative work policy and social citizenship
Beyond their shared diagnoses of the problems, Neoconservatives differ considerably among themselves about the best prescription for solving them. There is much agonizing and agnosticism about whether any solution exists, together with a distinct difference of

view between a liberatarian wing (e.g. Murray, 1984, 1988), which would abolish much of the welfare state and its custodial democracy, and an authoritative state wing (e.g. Mead, 1986), which would retain the welfare state but would seek to transform the alleged permissiveness of its professional culture and its effects on clients.

The main debate within American Neoconservative social policy, however, is one which is also often heard in current British conservatism. It concerns the relative priority to be given to distinct and possibly competing types of social obligations of citizenship. On the one hand there are the duties enjoined by the (once-Protestant) work ethic, while on the other there are the duties enjoined by traditional family values. The work ethic wing in the US (but also increasingly in Britain, for example current Restart employment policy) is most concerned with workfare policy. In the US it is represented particularly well in the writings of the policy analyst Lawrence Mead (see 1986, also Roche, 1992a: ch.6) among others. The familist wing is most concerned with various pro-family policies. In the US it is represented by notable sociologists (e.g. Peter and Brigitte Berger, 1983; George Gilder, 1986) and policy-makers (e.g. Senator Daniel P. Moynihan, 1989). In the UK it is strongly represented in Prime Minister Major's government. We can now briefly look at the workfare and familist positions within Neoconservatism and at the issues they raise for social citizenship.

Workfare is the policy of making welfare benefits conditional upon employment or training and effectively treating benefits as a loan to be paid off by work. Its implementation has been patchy, covering many but by no means all US states. In practice it has taken a variety of forms ranging from the punitive to the supportive, few of which save public expenditure (rather the reverse), and with a variety of effects, none of them very spectacular in reducing welfare dependency, poverty or unemployment. While the policy threatened to take a more punitive and national (federal) form under the Reagan presidency, Congress was largely able to stall this line of development.

Lawrence Mead is probably the leading academic spokesman for workfare in American social policy and for the view that the importance of work duties is best communicated and legitimized in terms of the discourse of citizenship and its duties. His major study of workfare policy, significantly entitled *Beyond Entitlement* (1986), provided a thorough account and defence, in citizenship duty terms, of the drift towards the more authoritative form of workfare in the 1970s and 1980s. However, in recent years US workfare policy has begun to take on a more benign, even supportive, appearance. For instance, the biggest single group of able-bodied unemployed in the underclass consists of young single black mothers on welfare. In recent years Congress has acknowledged that involvement in workfare for these women requires the provision of child care and other support services, and that what they arguably need is skill training in preference to coercion into unskilled and low-paying jobs.

Nonetheless, with some qualifications, Mead has continued to argue for just such coercion (e.g. Mead, 1988a–d). He argues that the alleged barriers to the welfare poor finding employment such as racism and inner-city deindustrialization and economic decline are largely illusory. He points out that there is a strong and continuing demand for workers in urban areas, albeit in low-skilled and low-paid dirty and menial jobs. He concludes that much contemporary long-term unemployment must be seen as largely voluntary and the product of a lack of job skills and an unwillingness to accept employer authority, not to mention laziness. This produces a vicious circle of personal and social incompetence among the underclass, including a lack of self-respect as well as respectability in the eyes of mainstream American society. For Mead, the only hope to break such circles is through a virtual resocialization of underclass members into the social obligations of citizenship, particularly the work ethic, by an authoritative national workfare policy.

Neoconservative family policy and social citizenship
For other Neoconservatives, however, the primary social obligations of citizenship are family duties – duties to contain the satisfaction of sexual desire and also procreation within the space of legitimacy provided by the institution of marriage; to honour the parental role and to care for children; to honour the dutiful son or daughter role and to care for elderly parents. In the familist view, family duties and work duties are complementary only if traditional patriarchal assumptions are made (and maintained in reality) about the sexual division of labour. Work and family are complementary only if males seek employment and act as breadwinners while females provide child care, elderly relative care and care for the breadwinner (Gilder, 1986).

But, as noted earlier, the traditional institution of the family is clearly changing and is arguably in a deep long-term crisis in contemporary Western society (Berger and Berger, 1983; Wicks and Kiernan, 1990). Rising rates of divorce, male desertion of children, male unemployment and female employment, male violence in families, child neglect and abuse, and finally illegitimacy are all indicators of the severity of the problems here. The family is in crisis not only as a system of regulating gender relations but also as a system of intergenerational relations and as a (indeed *the*) basic non-state welfare system. In particular it is in crisis as the basic system of child care and of childrens' primary socialization. These social systems are changing and/or breaking down generally in contemporary societies, but especially among the poor and the underclass.

The familist wing of Neoconservatism is greatly exercised by these crises. From their perspective, the problems of poor families headed by women, of welfare mothers and their children, are not addressed but exacerbated by a tough workfare approach such as Mead's. Workfare encourages women to attempt to be breadwinners and undermines their mothering role and their performance of its duties. From this perspective, these women need a long-term stable relationship with a male breadwinner, ideally marriage, and their children need a father (Gilder, 1987).

Of course, familism does not suggest that the state can supply husbands and fathers to poor single mothers. But, on the one hand, the state can legitimately enforce the duty of poor unemployed fathers to support their families, by means of authoritative forms of workfare. It can also enforce the paternal duties of deserting fathers by determined efforts to establish paternity and arrange maintenance payments. On the other hand, the state should support motherhood and child care, without providing *incentives* to single parenting. For this familist wing of Neoconservatism, the tough Meadian approach to enforcing workfare on poor single mothers is, to say the least, not the obvious way to support motherhood and family values and may even be damaging to them (Butler and Kondratas, 1987: ch. 5; Gilder, 1986: ch. 8, 1987).

However, in the late 1980s Neoconservatives began to attempt to construct a new consensus of the family (Novak et al., 1987) and on social policy (Glazer, 1988) while Congress advocated a more supportive approach in workfare policy (Moynihan, 1989). It is possible that the underlying tensions between work and family duties will turn out to be relatively manageable for Neoconservatism at the political level and less divisive than they appear when considered at the level of principle.

In this section I have concentrated on outlining some of the internal inconsistencies, tensions and contradictions within Neoconservatism as an ideological movement. To conclude on this theme, we can now note some further problems within this political perspective. The work ethic wing of this ideological movement clearly has a number of major blind spots. For instance, despite appearances to the contrary (for instance the presence in their ranks of the doyen of post-industrial theory, Daniel Bell), proponents of the work ethic approach seem to have little grasp of the negative structural trends in the development of global and high-technology capitalism noted earlier. They wrongly underplay the implications of these trends for labour markets and employment opportunities, particularly for the underclass (e.g. Dore, 1987; Roche, 1992a). Neither do they appear to have grasped one of the messages of the women's movement: that there is more to work than employment (e.g. Oakley, 1974; Pahl, 1988: Parts III, IV etc.). They seem oblivious to the notion that child-care and other care work, so-called women's work, actually *is* work.

In the late twentieth century it is clear that the gendered division of labour implicit in and legitimized by the Protestant work ethic needs to be challenged and reorganized between men and women. Given this, in the agenda of the new politics of citizenship, care work obligations have as much, if not more, right to be understood as social duties of citizenship as have duties to participate in labour markets, particularly cheap labour markets.

By contrast, the familist wing of this ideological movement appears to grasp the latter point, but totally rejects any feminist interpretation of it. Thus it rejects the preceding point about the need to rethink the sexual division of labour, and the fact that the promotion of citizenship ideals requires a new politics of employ-ment and care work distribution.

In this section we have reviewed some of the main contradictions in one of the main ideological movements currently pressing for a rethinking of social citizenship. From this case study we can now return to the broader picture of the theoretical and practical rethinking of social citizenship and social movements required by social change in Western societies in the late twentieth century.

Conclusion

This chapter has explored developments in the sociology of citizenship relevant to an understanding of the contested and changing nature of social citizenship in modernity. Its primary purpose has been to explore the research agenda of what can be called the new sociology of citizenship. As part of this inquiry it was necessary to consider the nature of the long-standing modern post-war rights-based and welfare-state-based paradigm of social citizenship, referred to here as the dominant paradigm, and also the articulation of this paradigm in the work of T.H. Marshall and others in the more traditional sociology of modern citizenship.

In section II we outlined this paradigm, together with the problems posed for the national functionalist societal configuration on which it rests, by structural change in Western soceity since the mid- to late 1970s. These changes involve post-industrialism, post-nationalism, and generally the development of a postmodern configuration within and between culture, economy and polity in modernity. In sections I and III we outlined something of the range of political responses to, and articulations of, this structural change and the postmodern condition. In various ways these political developments, from Left to Right, raise questions about the viability, effectiveness and legitimacy of national functionalism, the dominant paradigm of social citizenship and its institutionalization in the welfare state.

In section I we briefly surveyed the field of social movements and their sociological analysis. The latter has tended to prioritize the study of progressive (new) social movements such as the anti-nuclear, ecological and feminist movements. Progressive movements undoubtedly pose important challenges to the conventional structures and assumptions of post-war Western society and politics. It was suggested, however, that in order to understand how structural and ideological forces are currently conspiring to undermine and restructure the dominant paradigm of social citizenship, we must study and take full account of contemporary non- and anti-progressive organizations and movements.

In particular it was suggested that formal organizations, such as neo-corporatist projects among urban political and economic elites, and the entrenched potential for disorganization, such as that visible in the underclass and the urban ghetto, should equally come within the purview of social movements analysis. The former could be seen as anti-political movements, interested in the management of popular acquiescence and consent, and uninterested in the development of local democracy and governmental accountability, while the latter could be seen as anti-social movements parasitically draining the capacity of the communities which host them to develop even self-defensive and functional forms of organization, let alone more progressive types of collective action and social movement.

In the context of this kind of conceptualization of the progressive and anti-progressive range of contemporary urban social movements, the proposal by social movement analysts in the present volume (e.g. Hamel in Chapter 10 and Lustiger-Thaler and Maheu in Chapter 6) that the urban sphere needs to be given special attention within the general sociology of social movements was welcomed. It was also acknowledged that the sociology of urban social movements, understood in this spirit, overlaps with and is of central importance to the new sociology of citizenship, in so far as sub-national as well as the national and transnational levels of society, politics and structural dynamics in modern social formations.

In addition, it was suggested that the national and transnational levels of citizenship formation and social movement operation required that a central position be given to actions and processes involving collective consciousness (and thus involving collective beliefs and commonsense knowledge, public discourse and communication), as well as collective behaviour. Thus it was proposed that social movements analysis, to be relevant to the interests of the new sociology of citizenship, needs to clarify the nature of its address to what might be termed ideological movements. Whether or not they are strongly linked to organizations and to social and political practice and behaviour, ideological movements contest the field of social values and ideals, and promote normative versions of collective social and political consciousness, at national, international and transnational levels.

In recent years American Neoconservatism has emerged as a particularly important non-progressive, indeed often explicitly anti-progressive, ideological movement which has been influential on British Conservative governments and on politics in other Western countries. In section III we reviewed some of the main themes in Neoconservatism bearing upon its critique of the welfare state and the dominant rights-based paradigm of social citizenship. Its own ideal of social citizenship involves prioritizing obligations over rights, and familial and market sources of welfare over the welfare state. We considered Neoconservative views on citizens' obligations, social ethics and government strategies in relation to the spheres of employment policy and family policy in particular. It was concluded that, among a number of intellectual weaknesses in Neoconservative ideology relating to its underemphasis on structurally generated conditions and problems, there is a fundamental weakness in the tension which exists between its supporters of family values and its supporters of the work ethic. These weaknesses and contradictions were argued to be especially evident in Neoconservative approaches to the various social problems experienced, and posed to the rest of society, by the poor and the underclass.

Nonetheless it was also observed that, to a certain extent, Neoconservatism is currently influential in Centre and Left parties and political movements, in setting the agenda for the reform of the welfare state and more generally for the future development of social citizenship. At the very least it is clear that the political problems caused by a recognition of the existential fact of citizens' ndividual responsibilities for their choices and for their own lives, and the social fact of citizens' responsibilities for their dependants i.e. their children, elderly parents and unemployed partners), can no longer be avoided by, or submerged within, conventional Centrist and Left rights-based politics. Nor can they be ignored or avoided in the social and political thinking of the new social movements.

Indeed it is possible to argue that progressive social movements tend to operate in a moral and political discursive sphere which understands the limitations of purely rights-based politics and which promotes, whether explicitly or implicitly, important new conceptions of citizens' responsibilities. Ecology, for instance, promotes strong conceptions of personal, national and corporate-capitalist responsibilities for the environment, plant and animal life, and the quality of life of future generations. Feminism promotes equally strong conceptions of the responsibilities of men for making their rhetoric of equal opportunities a reality in the sphere of employment, for controlling their violence, and for parenting their children (Roche, 1992a: ch. 3).

However, the structural changes in the national functionalist context underpinning the welfare state and the dominant paradigm of social citizenship outlined in section II indicate the emergence of severe problems of social exclusion involving the poor and the underclass. Generally the post-industrial capitalist labour market, which is a market in increasingly flexibilized forms of labour, while it remains capable of generating aggregate economic growth, is becoming increasingly inefficient and inequitable as a distribution system for income, employment and market-based welfare, and as a servicing system for citizens' rights claims in these spheres.

These problems suggest that we need to work for a new generation of social rights, particularly rights to employment (e.g. Gorz, 1982, 1985, 1989; Keane and Owen, 1986; Coenen and Leisink, 1993; Pixley, 1993) and/or rights to income (Parker, 1989; Roche, 1992a: ch. 7; Van Parijs, 1992). But they also suggest that such rights are needed from the point of view of any reasonably objective sociological analysis. If nations and their market systems are to be sustained in the long term, albeit within new globalized and multinational settings and configurations, then some such new generation of citizens' social rights is likely to be produced by the working through of systemic imperatives, interpreted through the politics and power struggles, the collective consciousness and collective actions, of progressive and anti-progressive citizens' ideological and sociopolitical movements. In this respect it will be important to monitor the European Union, as a working model of a new transnational level of societal organization in modernity, in terms of the new levels of organization of new social movements it makes possible and also in terms of the new forms of transnational and social citizenship which come to be constructed within it (Roche, 1992a: ch. 8; Meehan, 1993).

The discussion in this chapter suggests that two important aspects of the practical agenda facing each of the progressive social movements in contemporary Western societies are intimately bound up with the problems of the meaning of citizenship in modernity. First there is the problem, which ecology, feminism and each of the movements needs to address, of how best to understand and to promote democratic citizenship, that is citizenship within and between social movements, within national civil societies and their states, and at all levels from the urban to the international. Secondly there is the problem faced by each movement – to understand and balance the social rights and obligations implicit in and/or relevant to their particular movement's overall goal and programme together with the problem of how best to achieve that balance in their struggles to develop their vision of social citizenship. Finally the discussion suggests an important aspect of the new research agenda facing both the sociology of social movements and the sociology of citizenship. Both fields in contemporary sociology now need to set themselves the task of understanding social movements struggles with these problems of democracy, rights and obligations seen as set within the new politics of citizenship which is developing in late twentieth-century society.

References

Andrews, G. (ed.) (1991) *Citizenship*. London: Lawrence & Wishart.
Auletta, K. (1983) *The Underclass*. New York: Vintage.
Barbalet, J. (1988) *Citizenship*. Milton Keynes: Open University Press.
Bell, D. (1976) *The Cultural Contradictions of Capitalism*. London: Heinemann.
Bendix, R. (1964) *Nation-Building and Citizenship*. New York: John Wiley.
Berger, B. and Berger, P. (1983) *The War over the Family*. London: Hutchinson.
Brubaker, R. (1992) *Citizenship and Nationhood in France and Germany*. Cambridge, MA: Harvard University Press.
Butler, S. and Kondratas, A. (1987) *Out of the Poverty Trap*. New York: Free Press.
Castells, M. (1983) *The City and the Grassroots*. Berkeley: University of California Press.
Coenen, H. and Leisink, P. (eds) (1993) *Work and Citizenship in the New Europe*. Aldershot: Edward Elgar.
Crook, S., Pakulski, J. and Waters, M. (1992) *Postmodernization*. London: Sage.
Culpitt, I. (1992) *Welfare and Citizenship: Beyond the Crisis of the Welfare State*. London: Sage.
Dennis, N. and Halsey, A.H. (1988) *English Ethical Socialism*. Oxford: Clarendon.

Dore, R. (1987) 'Citizenship and employment in the age of high technology', *British Journal of Industrial Relations*, 25(2): 201–25.

Doyal, L. (1983) *The Political Economy of Health*. London: Pluto.

Ehrenreich, B. (1987) 'The New Right's attack on welfare', in F. Block, R. Cloward, B. Ehrenreich and F. Piven (eds), *The Mean Season*. New York: Pantheon. pp. 161–96.

Etzioni, A. (1992) *The Spirit of Community: Rights, Responsibilities and the Communitarian Agenda*. New York: Crown Publishers.

Featherstone, M. (1991) *Consumer Culture and Postmodernism*. London: Sage.

Freeman, C. and Soete, L. (eds) (1987) *Technical Change and Full Employment*. Oxford: Basil Blackwell.

Giddens, A. (1985) 'Class sovereignty and citizenship', in his *The Nation-State and Violence*. Cambridge: Polity Press. Chapter 8.

Gilder, G. (1986) *Men and Marriage*. Gretna, LA: Pelican.

Gilder, G. (1987) 'The collapse of the American family', *The Public Interest*, 89.

Glazer, N. (1988) *The Limits of Social Policy*. Cambridge, MA: Harvard University Press.

Gorz, A. (1982) *Farewell to the Working Class*. London: Pluto.

Gorz, A. (1985) *Paths to Paradise*. London: Pluto.

Gorz, A. (1989) *Critique of Economic Reason*. London: Verso.

Gough, I. (1979) *The Political Economy of the Welfare State*. London: Macmillan.

Gyford, J. (1990) *Citizens, Consumers and Councils*. London: Macmillan.

Habermas, J. (1987) *The Theory of Communicative Action*, Vol. 2. London: Heinemann.

Habermas, J. (1994) 'Citizenship and national identity', in B. Van Steenbergen (ed.), *The Condition of Citizenship*. London: Sage.

Hall, S. and Held, D. (1989) 'Citizens and citizenship', in S. Hall and M. Jacques (eds), *New Times*. London: Lawrence & Wishart.

Hall, S. and Jacques, M. (eds) (1989) *New Times*. London: Lawrence & Wishart.

Hammar, T. (1990) *Democracy and the Nation-State: Aliens, Denizens and Citizens in a World of International Migration*. Aldershot: Gower.

Harvey, D. (1989) *The Postmodern Condition*. Oxford: Basil Blackwell.

IPPR (1993) *The Justice Gap*. London: Commission on Social Justice, Institute for Public Policy Research.

Jacobs, B. (1992) *Fractured Cities: Capitalism, Community and Empowerment in Britain and America*. London: Routledge.

Jordan, B. (1987) *Rethinking Welfare*. Oxford: Basil Blackwell.

Karger, H. (1991) 'The radical right and welfare reform in the United States', in H. Glennerster and J. Midgley (eds), *The Radical Right and the Welfare State*. Hemel Hempstead: Harvester-Wheatsheaf. Chapter 4.

Keane, J. and Owen, J. (1986) *After Full Employment*. London: Hutchinson.

King, E. (1987) *The New Right: Politics, Markets and Citizenship*. London: Macmillan.

Lasch, C. (1979) *The Culture of Narcissism*. London: Abacus.

Lasch, C. (1991) 'Right-wing populism and the revolt against liberalism', in his *The True and Only Heaven*. New York: W.W. Norton. Chapter 11.

Lister, R. (1990) *The Exclusive Society: Citizenship and the Poor*. London: Child Poverty Action Group.

Marshall, T.H. (1964) 'Citizenship and social class' (1949), in his *Sociology at the Crossroads*. New York: Doubleday.

218   *Collective Action: From Politics to Democracy*

Marshall, T.H. (1981) *The Right to Welfare*. London: Heinemann.
Mead, L. (1986) *Beyond Entitlement: The Social Obligations of Citizenship*. New York: Free Press.
Mead, L. (1988a) 'The new welfare debate', *Commentary*, 86: 44–52.
Mead, L. (1988b) 'The potential for work enforcement', *Journal of Policy Analysis and Management*, 7(2): 264–88.
Mead, L. (1988c) 'Jobs for the welfare poor', *Policy Review*, Winter: 60–9.
Mead, L. (1988d) 'The hidden jobs debate', *The Public Interest*, 91: 40–58.
Meehan, E. (1993) *Citizenship and the European Community*. London: Sage.
Mouffe, C. (ed.) (1992) *Dimensions of Radical Democracy: Pluralism, Citizenship, Community*. London: Verso.
Moynihan, P. (1989) 'Towards a post-industrial social policy', *The Public Interest*, 96: 16–27.
Murray, C. (1984) *Losing Ground*. New York: Basic Books.
Murray, C. (1988) 'The coming of custodial democracy', *Commentary*, 86: 19–24.
Murray, C. (1989) 'The underclass', *Sunday Times Magazine*, 26 November: 26–45.
Novak, M. et al. (1987) *The New Consensus on Family and Welfare*. Washington, DC: American Enterprise Institute for Public Policy Research and Working Seminar on Family and American Welfare Policy (US).
Oakley, A. (1974) *The Sociology of Housework*. Oxford: Martin Robertson.
Offe, C. (1985a) *Disorganized Capitalism*. Cambridge: Polity Press.
Offe, C. (1985b) 'New social movements: challenging the boundaries of institutional politics', *Social Research*, Winter: 817–68.
Pahl, R. (ed.) (1988) *On Work*. Oxford: Basil Blackwell.
Parker, J. (1975) *Social Policy and Citizenship*. London: Macmillan.
Parker, H. (1989) *Instead of Dole*. London: Macmillan.
Parsons, T. (1970) *The System of Modern Societies*. Englewood Cliffs, NJ: Prentice-Hall.
Piore, M. and Sabel, C. (1984) *The Second Industrial Divide*. New York: Basic Books.
Pixley, J. (1993) *Citizenship and Employment: Investigating Post-Industrial Options*. Cambridge: Cambridge University Press.
Plant, R. (1988) *Citizenship, Rights and Socialism*. London: Fabian Society.
Rimlinger, G. (1971) *Welfare Policy and Industrialization in Europe, America and Russia*. New York: John Wiley.
Robins, K. and Webster, F. (1989) *The Technical Fix*. London: Macmillan.
Roche, M. (1987) 'Citizenship, social theory and social change', *Theory and Society*, 16: 363–99.
Roche, M. (1992a) *Rethinking Citizenship: Welfare, Ideology and Change in Modern Society*. Cambridge: Polity Press.
Roche, M. (1992b) 'Mega-event planning and citizenship (on the politics of urban cultural policy)', *Vrijetijd en Samenleving (Leisure and Society)* [The Hague], 10(4): 47–67.
Roche, M. (1994a) 'Citizenship and social change: beyond the dominant paradigm', in H. Lustiger-Thaler and D. Salee (eds), *Artful Practices: The Political Economy of Everyday Life*. Montreal: Black Rose Books.
Roche, M. (1994b) 'Citizenship and anomie: contemporary political ideology and the counter-anomie thesis', in S. Edgell et al. (eds), *The Future of the Public Sphere*. Aldershot: Avebury.
Room, G. (1979) *The Sociology of Welfare*. Oxford: Martin Robertson.

Scott, A. (1990) *Ideology and the New Social Movements*. London: Unwin Hyman.

Stewart, R. (1989) 'Farewell or fair wage? Australian labour as a social movement', in C. Jennett and R. Stewart (eds), *Politics of the Future: The Role of Social Movements*. Melbourne: Macmillan.

Titmuss, R. (1963) *Essays on the Welfare State*. London: Allen & Unwin.

Toffler, A. (1970) *Future Shock*. London: Pan.

Toffler, A. (1980) *Third Wave*. London: Pan/Collins.

Toffler, A. (1985) *Previews and Premises*. London: Pan.

Touraine, A. (1977) *The Voice and the Eye: An Analysis of Social Movements*. Cambridge: Cambridge University Press.

Touraine, A. (1985) 'An introduction to the study of social movements', *Social Research*, 52(4): 749–87.

Turner, B. (1986) *Citizenship and Capitalism*. London: Allen & Unwin.

Turner, B. (ed.) (1993) *Citizenship and Social Theory*. London: Sage.

Urry, J. and Lash, S. (1987) *The End of Organized Capitalism*. Cambridge: Polity Press.

Van Parijs, P. (ed.) (1992) *Arguing for Basic Income: Ethical Foundations for a Radical Reform*. London: Verso.

Van Steenbergen, B. (ed.) (1994) *The Condition of Citizenship*. London: Sage.

Walzer, M. (1985) *Spheres of Justice*. Oxford: Basil Blackwell.

Wicks, M. and Kiernan, K. (1990) *Family Change and Social Change*. London: Family Policy Studies Centre.

Wilson, W.J. (1987) *The Truly Disadvantaged*. Chicago: University of Chicago Press.

9
A New Class?
The Higher Educated and the New Politics

Chris Rootes

Changes in the occupation structure: the making of a new class?

The transformation of the occupational structures of advanced societies since 1945 has been dramatic: the agricultural workforce has contracted sharply as a consequence of the industrialization of agriculture, and the male industrial proletariat has contracted, at first relatively and, more recently, in absolute numbers. Much the most significant change, however, has been the growth in the service occupations, especially professional, managerial, administrative and technical occupations.

These changes in the occupational structure have complicated the orthodox sociological discussion of class and class structure in advanced societies. Managers, professionals and technical and scientific workers have been identified as members or potential members of a new class or, in some versions, a new middle class, but it is the political implications of such developments which have attracted particular attention. It could scarcely escape notice that men and women employed in or training for such occupations were prominent in the new social movements: the anti-war, student, feminist, anti-nuclear, environmental and ecological movements of the past three decades. No less marked was their susceptibility to the adversary culture which developed in the wake of such movements. The combination of these developments with evidence from electoral studies and attitude surveys, which appeared to show a qualitative change in the way mass publics in general and this section of them in particular related to established political institutions, aroused speculation about the nature, sources and prospects of the new politics.[1]

In order to make sense of these developments and to advance prognoses, both left- and right-wing versions of the new class thesis were developed. Barbara and John Ehrenreich (1979) delineated a professional-managerial class which, sandwiched between bourgeoisie and proletariat, was inherently politically ambivalent, generally inclined to conservative deference to its bourgeois paymasters but, out of dissatisfaction with its subordination, at least contingently prone to outbursts of radicalism. Alvin Gouldner saw much the same sorts of people as the constituents of an emergent new class which was 'the most progressive force in modern society and . . . a centre of whatever human emancipation is possible' (Gouldner, 1979: 83). Neo-conservatives such as Irving Kristol and Norman Podhoretz were altogether less enchanted, seeing, in a manner reminiscent of nineteenth-century anarchist critiques of the pretensions of socialist intellectuals, these developments as the making not of a new emancipatory class but of a new *dominant* class, and one profoundly subversive of the entrepreneurial capitalism which they believed to be the foundation of liberal democracy (see Ashford, 1983; Bruce-Briggs, 1981).

However, before the question of the political proclivities of this putative new class can be settled or even sensibly examined, the question of whether it *is* a class requires an answer. The proposition that changes in the occupational structure entail the development or emergence of a new class might be lent plausibility by evidence that such changes are not merely quantitative and economic, but that they are accompanied by other changes giving the members of the putative new class what might reasonably be seen as shared socialization experiences and bases of easy and frequent social interaction. Gouldner, amongst others, saw in their common experience of higher education the cement which binds the new class together.

Higher education: the tie that binds?

Professional, managerial, administrative and technical occupations increasingly, and now typically, require higher educational qualifications as a condition of entry but, because the expansion of higher education is, especially in Europe, a relatively recent phenomenon, there are still many older non-graduates in such occupations. In Britain, where it is only recently that professions such as law and accounting have begun to demand a degree as a qualification for entry, only a minority of professionals (30 per cent) and managers (12 per cent) are graduates (*Social Trends*, 1989). Nevertheless, even in Britain, the effects of the post-war expansion of higher education are striking: whereas in 1971 only 5 per cent of men in England and Wales had attended university, 20 years later some 10 per cent of men and 6 per cent of women were graduates of a university or college.[2] Since the proportion of younger people with degrees is even higher (over 15 per cent of those in their twenties), even if the recent dramatic increase in student numbers in higher education is not sustained, the proportion of the population who are graduates is bound to continue to increase.[3]

Thus, not only has the proportion of the workforce employed in professional, managerial, administrative and technical work expanded, but the people so employed are increasingly likely to have shared the formative experience of higher education. Yet even casual acquaintance with the diversity of cultures among the tribes both of academe and the professions must nurture doubts that there is much basis for social solidarity among the higher educated as a whole; the rivalries and mutual incomprehension between the 'two cultures' of science and technology and the humanistic disciplines and professions may be especially great in Britain but they are, to a greater or lesser extent, universal. Gouldner, who recognized the internal differentiation of the new class of 'intellectuals',[4] insisted, quite reasonably, that such differentiation did not compromise their status as a class because *all* classes were internally differentiated.

For those of us interested in the political significance of these developments, the internal differentiation of the putative new class is, however, a crucial question, because if there are good reasons to believe that the ties which bind the diverse groups of the higher educated together are stronger than the cultural differences which divide them, then the possibility of their developing a solidary and self-interested class politics is enhanced, and the fears of neo-conservative and anarcho-socialist theorists of the new class are well founded. If, on the other hand, the heterogeneity of the higher educated is so great that it is difficult even to imagine solidary class-consciousness and action among them, then the prospects of new class domination are diminished and we must look elsewhere for the political implications of the transformation of the occupational structure and the expansion of higher education.

To address these questions, I propose to review recent empirical evidence of the political proclivities of professionals and the higher educated, particularly in Britain. But first let us consider the theoretical grounds for supposing that the higher educated may comprise, actually or potentially, a solidary class. Is there some general principle which subsumes the apparent heterogeneity of the higher educated, or are there secular tendencies of development which may in future produce greater homogeneity?

Toward the homogenization of the new class?

The attempts to find a general principle subsuming the particular interests of sections of the intelligentsia cannot be said to have been very successful. The leading contender is Gouldner's concept of

cultural capital, but neither it nor recent attempts to refine it (e.g. Martin and Szelenyi, 1987) are entirely persuasive. The best defence of the culture of critical discourse as the basis of new class cohesion is Disco's (1987) insistence that higher education cultivates in the practitioners of even the most technical and applied branches of knowledge an awareness that they are ultimately dependent upon theoretical knowledge and those who produce it. The trouble is that the lesson seems to be very easily forgotten and it must be wondered whether, if the present trend continues towards ever more narrowly instrumental and vocational higher education, any such lesson will in future even be widely taught, let alone sympathetically received. Nor is it obvious that the awareness of technicians of their dependence on theory gives them a community of interest with the theorists on whom they depend. The division between the technical and humanistic intelligentsias shows no sign of diminishing and seems unlikely to be bridged by systems of higher education in which pure theory is the luxury indulged in by the few, while the vocational and the applied is increasingly the experience of the many.

In some respects, however, the present heterogeneity of the new class may in future be reduced. John Goldthorpe (1982), in his discussion of the development of what he terms the service class, suggests that its present social and political heterogeneity simply reflects its novelty. Most particularly, the growth of service-class positions has been so rapid and from such a relatively small base that many of them have necessarily been filled by upward social mobility. However, as the service class grows and consolidates its position, so it is likely increasingly to be reproduced by endogenous recruitment as service-class parents strive to transmit the advantages of their social position to their children. Goldthorpe expects both the social and the political heterogeneity of the service class to diminish as the proportion of service-class positions which are filled by upward social mobility declines.

The politics of the higher educated in Britain

Goldthorpe suggests that political radicalism among the service class in Britain is likely to decline as fewer of its members are recruited from working-class, Labour-voting families. At present only about 25 per cent of the service class are graduates of universities or colleges, but as older non-graduates retire and are replaced by younger graduates, the proportion is steadily rising. To test Goldthorpe's proposition, it would seem reasonable to focus on graduates, since it is they who will increasingly determine the shape of the service class and its politics.

Voting for or identifying with the Labour Party may not be regarded as an especially demanding test of political radicalism, but since it is more frequently encountered than any other of the activities that might be described as politically radical in Britain, it is an obvious starting point. Nevertheless, the level of support for the Labour Party among British graduates is not especially high (22 per cent in 1987). More remarkable is the low level of support among graduates for the Conservative Party: if we partition the British population according to their highest educational qualifications, in 1987 it was amongst graduates that there was *least* support for the Conservatives, less even than among those (mostly working-class) voters who had no educational qualifications at all.

Goldthorpe's thesis might be thought to derive some support from the fact that, within the salariat or service class, it is graduates (the sub-category amongst whom newcomers to the salariat might be expected to be concentrated) who are least likely to support the Conservatives and most likely to support the Liberal-Social Democratic Alliance and the Labour Party (Heath et al., 1991: Table 6.5).

Yet the evidence is that such radicalism as there is amongst the higher educated in Britain is *not* overwhelmingly a product of the recruitment into higher education of students from Labour-voting working-class backgrounds. Data collected by the 1983 and 1987 British Election Surveys suggest that fewer than a third of university graduates who identified more or less closely with the Labour party had working-class, Labour-voting fathers; just over half of Labour identifiers had fathers who voted Labour, and of these Labour-voting fathers only about half were working class. Clearly, identification with the Labour Party amongst the higher educated is not simply a residuum of upward social mobility: if Labour-voting working-class backgrounds account for less than a third of Labour identification amongst the higher educated, and other Labour-voting family traditions account for another third, a further third remains unaccounted for in such terms. There must then be other sources of identification with the Labour Party amongst the higher educated and there is no reason to suppose that the importance of such sources will diminish merely because the service class becomes increasingly socially homogeneous.

If we consider the attitudes of the British population, the distinctiveness of the higher educated is again striking. Data from the 1983 and 1987 British Election Surveys and the 1986 British Social Attitudes Survey show that British graduates are much more libertarian than the rest of the population on a wide range of moral and cultural issues. The evidence about economic and welfare issues is more ambiguous, but recent survey data suggest that the higher educated are now the most economically egalitarian section of the British population as well (Evans, 1990). Indeed, it is highly educated Labour-identifiers among the salariat who are the most libertarian on moral and cultural issues *and* the most egalitarian on economic issues (Heath and Evans, 1989) and it is they (and almost only they) who are the ideologically committed socialists (Robertson, 1984). In so far as it is possible or prudent to identify a trend on the basis of just three surveys, it appears that, far from the higher educated having become more conservative during the 1980s, they have become both more radical and more distinctive in their social and political attitudes.

It is probable that some of this increased radicalism is essentially conjunctural rather than deep-rootedly structural. Since 1979, Britain has had a Conservative government committed to a radical assault upon the welfare state, the public sector and, latterly, the professions in which the majority of graduates are employed. Support for the Conservatives among university teachers, school-teachers and health service professionals, in particular, has fallen to unprecedentedly low levels.

Nevertheless, the fact that the economic egalitarianism (though not the moral and cultural libertarianism) of the higher educated in Britain in the 1980s was to a significant extent probably conjunctural rather than structural does not weaken the general point that there is no evidence, so far, to support the contention that the higher educated will become increasingly conservative as the new class becomes more consolidated and socially homogeneous. Not only is there no clear evidence of any consistent political effects of such a structural tendency but, more importantly, there is evidence that political conjunctures may continue to stimulate radicalism among the higher educated.

New social movements

There is, however, one dimension of radicalism – participation in new social movements – where, if the outbreaks have been conjunctural, the consistency of the pattern is such as to encourage speculation about its structural roots. Two decades of research on activists in the Campaign for Nuclear Disarmament and environmental movements in Britain reveal a remarkably consistent pattern: participants in these manifestations of the new politics are disproportionately, indeed overwhelmingly, drawn from amongst the highly educated members of the new middle classes, with a particular concentration among those employed in teaching, caring and welfare professions in the non-market sector of the economy. These surveys include:

- Parkin's (1968) study of active members aged over 25 of CND local branches and a 10 per cent sample of marchers aged 18–25 who took part in the 1965 Aldermaston march;
- Taylor and Pritchard's (1978) survey of a self-selected sample of former, mainly core CND activists, more than half of whom were supporters of the Committee of 100 and 75 per cent of whom had joined CND in 1958–9 (Taylor and Pritchard, 1980);
- Cotgrove's (1982) study of environmentalists, nature conservationists and others;
- Day and Robbins's (1987) study of a local peace group in West Wales;
- Byrne's 1985 survey of members of the *national* CND, only half of whom were also members of the local CND branches that provided CND with two-thirds of its total membership (Byrne, 1988);
- A 1987 survey of members of Friends of the Earth which found that 87 per cent worked in senior managerial, administrative, professional, educational, technical or scientific occupations, 15 per cent of them as teachers or lecturers, and that 70 per cent had tertiary-level education (Porritt and Winner, 1988: 182);
- A 1990 survey of over 4000 members of the British Green Party, 87 per cent of whom were also active in environmentalist organizations (mainly Friends of the Earth and Greenpeace), which found that they were, like their continental European counterparts, disproportionately younger, highly educated professional people: two-thirds were university graduates or students and nearly half were employed in professional or technical occupations, with a notable concentration in teaching and the caring professions; the lower end of the occupational structure, which comprises 55 per cent of the British population, accounted for just 21 per cent of Green Party members (Rüdig et al., 1991: ch. 3).

This consistency, despite the fact that the sample frames are so different, is the more remarkable because since Parkin conducted his surveys in 1965, the proportion of the population who have received higher education and are employed in such occupations has increased so considerably. Save for the increased participation of women to a position of parity with that of men, the social profile of participation in the new social movements in Britain has scarcely changed at all in more than 25 years. The consistency of this pattern casts doubt upon any suggestion that their elite social base was simply a reflection of their novelty and that as the novelty of these movements wore off and the social costs of joining them fell, so their social base would broaden. Clearly this has not happened: the new politics remains as peculiarly rooted in a particular section of society as it was when it first appeared.

These findings are entirely consistent with the evidence of the 1987 British Election Survey that it is employment in the welfare and creative occupations that, amongst the salariat, is the best predictor of preference for the Labour Party over the Conservatives (see Heath et al., 1991: Table 6.10). They are consistent, too, with Kriesi's (1989) conclusion, based on Dutch data, that the notion of the rise of an oppositional new middle class as an explanation of the new politics is both too narrow and too broad. The new middle class is not the whole of the social base of the phenomenon, and some sections of the new middle class are better disposed than are others. It is the social and cultural specialists and human service professionals amongst whom support for the new politics is concentrated. Analyses of attitudes in the United States have come to broadly similar conclusions (see especially Brint, 1984, 1987; McAdams, 1987).

The implications of all this for the theory of the new class are several. First, if new class theory is designed to explain or to predict the new politics, then it is at best a very limited success: among the various categories proposed as candidates for inclusion in the new class, only social and cultural specialists and human service professionals appear to have the expected political attitudes and orientations. Yet it would seem unduly to complicate the map of class structure to identify these groups alone as the whole or even the core of a new class. More fundamentally, it must be questioned whether what gives these categories their distinctive political colour derives from their class position or any other class-like characteristic. In other words, is the language of class being employed to explain a phenomenon that might be better explained in some other, non-class terms?

Alternatives to class

Jan Pakulski, in Chapter 2 of this volume, argues that support for mass social movements is less a matter of class than a product of generation, social situs, autonomy and mobility. Whilst these concepts may be useful – indeed, *have been* useful – in explaining the incidence of support for social movements, each is itself problematic and, more importantly, even in combination they are not by themselves enough. Moreover, analyses employing them may be as determinist and reductionist as those of the class analyses which Jan Pakulski and I consider to be unsatisfactory.[5]

Generation is clearly a factor in the development of movements, but it is, like class, a disconcertingly stretchable concept. Where it has been used to analyse conflicts *within* movements, generation has often – as in the case of student movements – been used to refer to what are in effect birth cohorts only a year or two apart. But Pakulski refers to the 'post-Second-World-War generation', a generation which by now comprises more than half the populations of the advanced societies. Situs may indeed be important, but it is surely a mistake to reduce situs to sector; equally, autonomy is not simply a benefit of favourable situs but, more importantly, is embedded in the ethics and practice of certain professions (Rootes, 1983).

Pakulski's emphasis on mobility as an essential facilitator of movement growth seems to me a major step backwards and one that runs directly counter to his focus on the positive role of values in social movements, containing as it does undertones of status discrepancy and mass society theories. It may indeed be the case that mobility plays a positive role in making the contradictions, injustices and irrationalities of conventional practice more transparent (the salience of migration in the biographies of German sociologists or American and Australian social critics is evidence enough of that), but there is a great deal of research on social movements which suggests, contrary to mass society theorists' emphasis on deracination as a precondition of mobilization, that social *ties* are very important in giving people the psychic as well as the social resources necessary to sustain at least initial mobilization (cf. Pinard, 1969). Pakulski's stress on mobility places too much emphasis upon the activist's escape from the constraints of tradition and too little upon the continuing influence of traditional values even after they are removed from the security of unreflective institutionalized expression.[6]

Generation, social situs, autonomy and mobility may help explain who has the opportunity to give practical expression to moral values, but they are not of themselves sufficient to explain the existence of those values nor, unless we lapse into a rather crude reductionism (see, e.g., Bürklin's [1987] explanation of the rise and inevitable decline of the German Greens),[7] why it is that some people rather than others are the bearers of such values. Moreover, although Pakulski and I share a conception of social movements as movements of moral protest (cf. Rootes, 1980) and although we both insist upon the centrality of values to the character of social movements, it seems to me that Pakulski is insufficiently attentive to the specific *contents* of the values to which he attaches such importance.[8] Klaus Eder, in Chapter 1 of this volume, is similarly indifferent to the contents of education and treats education as a demographic variable, a matter of educational *level*. It is my contention that we will better understand the politics of the higher educated if we pay less attention to the forms and more to the content of their values and their education.

Value, professionalism and higher education

I suggested earlier that it is higher education that best discriminates libertarian moral and cultural attitudes and economic egalitarianism in Britain. Yet it is clear that higher education itself is too broad and inclusive a category adequately to predict political party identification or involvement in the new politics of social movements. A combination of occupation/profession and higher education fares much better: it is among higher-educated social, cultural and human-service professionals that the activists in and sympathizers with the new politics are overwhelmingly concentrated.

How then are we to explain this? McAdams (1987), finding that a new class worldview is concentrated among professionals and those with high levels of education, interprets his results as demonstrating that there exists in the United States a new class that is consistently more liberal than either the traditional middle class or the working class, and which has a class interest in the expansion of government. He gives a series of reasons why professionals *and* the higher educated should hold attitudes favourable to the expansion of government and hostile to business. These, he suggests, constitute the class interests of the new class. What he neglects to consider, however, are the *values* inculcated in the professions and developed by higher education, and the possibility that it is the values of professionals and the higher educated that are directly expressed in their attitudes and behaviour rather than that their attitudes and behaviour are the reflection of class interests.

As McAdams himself recognizes, professionalism is not simply an ideology screening the self-interest of privileged practitioners; it is also a set of ethically bound, client-centred practices. It is thus scarcely surprising that human-service professionals will often, in the interests of their clients as well as their own autonomy, be critical of the arbitrariness and authoritarianism of existing arrangements as well as hostile to a market philosophy which makes money the measure of all things and treats people as mere factors of production.

In Britain, perhaps more than in most other advanced societies,

the self-interest of many professionals and (professionals' percep-
tions of) the interests of their clients have, in the face of
Conservative government policy and practice, become virtually
impossible to disentangle, and it would be pointless to deny that the
sectional self-interest of such professionals is a major source of their
antipathy to the present Conservative government. It is, however,
much more doubtful that their more general social and political
attitudes or their involvement in new social movements can be
attributed to sectional self-interest, much less to class interest.

The values inculcated in and by the cultural and human service
professions and, indeed, the values which lead people to seek
employment in such professions, are a more obvious source of the
political attitudes and involvements of their practitioners than is any
class or other sectional interest.

But where do such values come from? Clearly, a major source is
family socialization, which is, of course, profoundly shaped and
differentiated by class. But families are also, relatively independently of class, repositories of cultural and ethnic traditions, religious or
secular, that are directly relevant to the formation of an individual's
values, attitudes and career choice.

Education, and especially certain kinds of higher education, is
another likely source of such values and attitudes. The impact of the
pre-professional socialization of students in such professional/
vocational courses as medicine and law is well documented. But the
less vocational or non-vocational higher education in the humanities
and social sciences that is, especially in Britain, still the experience
of most graduates who make their careers in the creative and human
service professions, may also have a socializing effect, if perhaps a
more subtle and ambiguous one.[9]

Nor should despondency about increasing attempts to subordinate education to the demands of the economy blind us to the extent
to which higher education is concerned with the development of the
intellect and remains – and is likely in the future to remain – a
relatively critical and enlightening process. One does not have to
imagine that all higher education initiates students into the
priesthood of the culture of critical discourse to recognize that much
of it (still) has the function of upsetting old prejudices, imparting
knowledge, broadening social experience, developing skills of
critical analysis and enhancing the self-confidence of its benefi-
ciaries so as to make them more tolerant of the diversity of others,
to imagine alternative futures and, sometimes, to act to translate
that imagination into reality.

It is, of course, the case that the people who hold and act upon
these attitudes are concentrated in a particular class, but class seems

a peculiarly blunt instrument to explain values that are more obviously the products of professionalism, socialization within families and higher education.[10]

Conclusion

The effort and ingenuity expended in order to reconstruct the concept of class and the theory of class struggle so as to accommodate the awkward phenomena of the new politics and the new social movements is impressive, but it seems to me to be fundamentally misguided. Once sociologists overcome their embarrassment at believing in the critical and emancipatory value of what they do, as teachers and researchers, once they cease to regard education as a demographic variable which is merely a more or less adequate surrogate for class or component of socioeconomic status, and once they permit themselves the luxury of taking seriously the values by which most of the world, external constraints permitting, attempts to live, then we shall discover that class is all very well in its place, but that its place in the analysis of the new politics and the new social movements is really very limited.

Notes

The present paper is a product of research undertaken in the course of a collaborative project on the Politics of the Higher Educated in Western Europe. Work on the British Part of that project was made possible by grants from the Economic and Social Research Council and the University of Kent at Canterbury.

1 For a fuller discussion, see Rootes (1986). I have argued elsewhere (Rootes, 1992b) that the new social movements are a contingent rather than an essential manifestation of the new politics; whether and how they develop in a particular country depends upon the pattern of opportunities and constraints presented to them by social and political institutions and the prevailing balance of political competition.

2 The British figures are not as atypical of Western Europe as might be supposed: because of their higher non-completion (drop-out) rates, West European countries such as France, Italy and West Germany, which have until recently admitted a higher proportion of young people to higher education, do not produce many more graduates than does Britain; indeed, Italy produces many fewer.

3 Since 1989 the numbers of students enrolled in British higher education has risen dramatically, with the result that one in three 18-year-olds now enters higher education. The government announced in 1993 that it planned that 40 per cent of 18-year-olds should be in higher education by the year 2000.

4 In what follows, I avoid using the term 'intellectuals', because I think it is quite misleading so to characterize all graduates of higher education, let alone all occupants of professional and managerial positions. The term 'intelligentsia' is preferable but, to avoid all possibility of misunderstanding, I shall employ the term 'higher educated' to refer to graduates of universities and colleges.

5 Reductionist strategies, although they risk arbitrarily imposing upon actors definitions they would not apply to themselves, may be justified where they serve some clear heuristic purpose; actors, after all, are not always fully conscious of the nature of their action, especially where their action is collective. But sociologists still seem to be prone to leap to reductionist conclusions even before they have carefully considered the phenomenal evidence, let alone the expressly articulated reasons of actors themselves. This is always problematic, but it is especially so when the phenomena to be explained are political, when it is conceded that politics, more than many other areas of human activity, is *especially* heavily freighted with value and meaning. Sartori's (1969) strictures against the (reductionist) sociology of politics and *for* a political sociology which takes ideas and values seriously remain as pertinent today as they were 25 years ago. For a similar argument, this time from a professed Marxist, see Miliband (1977). I have discussed reductionist explanations of the politics of the higher educated at greater length elsewhere (Rootes, 1992a; see also Levy and Rootes, 1987).

6 This, incidentally, is the major weakness in Pakulski's discussion of Fascist movements; he underestimates the extent to which Nazism was, as a movement of nation above class, an extension of *traditional* German nationalism which flourished most in precisely those social milieux in which pre-war nationalism was most strongly rooted.

7 Bürklin purports to explain the rise of the Greens by reference to the social marginality of their supporters. Yet, *pace* Bürklin, the fact that many of the supporters of the Greens were not, in 1984, permanently employed, did not attend church, did not have children in the household, did not own a house or apartment, were unmarried and were disproportionately concentrated in big cities seems less to demonstrate that they were poorly integrated into society than simply to correlate with the fact that they were overwhelmingly young and highly educated, many of them still students. There is little evidence that Green supporters are chiefly youthful idealists whose idealism will increasingly be tempered by realism as they age and assume the responsibilities of work and family; on the contrary, in Germany as in Britain, it is now not the youngest age cohorts which are most over-represented amongst the members and supporters of the Greens, but people already approaching early middle age and established in professional employment.

8 Pakulski asserts that value-conflicts do not have such an instrumental character, organizational format and sectional/class basis as conventional politics does. Value preferences, he continues, make compromises difficult; lack of programmatic coherence and organizational discipline make settlements unlikely. For this reason movement politics cannot be accommodated within the conventional, highly bureaucratic, political idiom. The problem is, however, that movements differ and they differ not least in the values they espouse. I accept that the values about which movements are oriented impose constraints upon their political practice and upon the possibilities of their accommodation to conventional politics, but different values imply different forms of organization and different potentials for compromise and accommodation. Scrutiny of the variety of movements Pakulski himself considers – Fascist movements, Polish Solidarity, and the eco-pax movements – provides ample evidence. Consider, too, the case of the New Left of the 1960s and early 1970s: Breines (1982) does an excellent job of illuminating the constraints which the values of American New Leftists imposed upon their political and organizational practice but, as Bouchier (1979) demonstrates, *within* the New Left the different theories and values of different groups had profound consequences for the political practice and

ultimate fate of those groups. A similar story could be told about first-wave feminism in Britain, or the contemporary environmental/ecology movement. Moreover, as Levitas (1977) has shown in her study of the Christian socialist movement, it should not be presumed that the values around which a movement is constructed are immutable; movements are constantly engaged in a dialectical transaction with other actors in their environments, and one possible consequence of that transaction is the modification of the values as well as the practice of the movement. In short, some movements – and some strands within movements – are more readily accommodated to the conventional political idiom than are others; the values to which movement activists subscribe are a principal but not necessarily temporally invariant source of constraint.

9 This question remains surprisingly under-researched, especially in Britain, although generations of surveys, particularly in the United States, have shown that students in the technical subjects are more politically conservative than those in the humanities and social sciences. One British study (Marsh, 1977: esp. 202) appears to show that whereas the attitudinal differences between science and arts students are small at university entrance, the attitudes of science students change little during the course of their studies whereas those of their contemporaries in the arts become progressively more radical. It is not clear whether this should be attributed to the radicalizing impact of arts subjects or whether it is simply that the more flexible conditions of study usual in arts subjects permit the continuation of a trajectory of development embarked upon before university, whereas the more restrictive conditions of science education do not foster, or perhaps positively impede, such developments.

10 I have focused in this discussion upon values as they are transmitted through higher education and sustained or developed in the course of subsequent professional practice. What I have not done – because it would enormously have extended the scope of this chapter – is to consider the ways in which values are developed in the course of *political* practice. A partial justification of my neglect of this lies in the distinctly infrequent incidence, even among the higher educated, of political participation of any kind more demanding than voting or signing petitions (Parry and Moyser, 1990; Parry et al., 1992). Nevertheless, the way values are developed and transmitted in and through the mobilization of social movements is an important topic.

In so far as I have dealt here with *knowledge* as distinct from values, I have treated it too as a product of education or professional practice, but I readily concede that political action is also a cognitive process. I find congenial and stimulating Eyerman and Jamison's (1991) treatment of social movements as complex collective cognitive processes and their argument that it is cognitive practice that is the essence of social movements. I can best justify my failure to emulate their example by my concern, on this occasion, to encourage sociologists to take values, education and professionalism seriously.

References

Ashford, N. (1983) 'The new class: the neo-conservative analysis', *mimeo*, Department of Politics, University of Strathclyde.
Bouchier, D. (1979) *Idealism and Revolution*. London: Edward Arnold.
Breines, W. (1982) *Community and Organization in the New Left*. New York: Praeger.

234   Collective Action: From Politics to Democracy

Brint, S. (1984) 'New class and cumulative trend: explanations of the liberal political attitudes of professionals', *American Journal of Sociology*, 90(1): 30–71.

Brint, S. (1987) 'Classification struggles: reply to Lamont', *American Journal of Sociology*, 92(6): 1506–9.

Bruce-Biggs, B. (ed.) (1981) *The New Class?* New York: McGraw-Hill.

Bürklin, W. (1987) 'Governing Left parties frustrating the radical non-established Left: the rise and inevitable decline of the Greens', *European Sociological Review*, 3: 109–26.

Byrne, P. (1988) *The Campaign for Nuclear Disarmament*. London: Croom Helm.

Cotgrove, S. (1982) *Catastrophe or Cornucopia: the Environment, Politics and the Future*. Chichester: John Wiley.

Day, G. and Robbins, D. (1987) 'Activists for peace: the social basis of a local peace movement', in C. Creighton and M. Shaw (eds), *The Sociology of War and Peace*. London: Methuen. pp. 218–36.

Disco, C. (1987) 'Intellectuals in advanced capitalism: capital, closure and the new-class thesis', in R. Eyerman, L.G. Svensson and T. Söderquist (eds) *Intellectuals, Universities and the State in Western Modern Societies*. Berkeley: University of California Press.

Ehrenreich, B. and Ehrenreich, J. (1979) 'The professional-managerial class', in P. Walker (ed.), *Between Labor and Capital*. Brighton: Harvester. pp. 5–45.

Evans, G. (1990) 'Changing political values?' Paper delivered to the Sociology Seminar, Nuffield College, Oxford, 31 January.

Eyerman, R. and Jamison, A. (1991) *Social Movements: a Cognitive Approach*. Cambridge: Polity Press.

Eyerman, R., Svensson, L.G. and Söderquist, T. (eds) (1987) *Intellectuals, Universities and the State in Western Modern Societies*. Berkeley: University of California Press.

Goldthorpe, J. (1982) 'On the service class, its formation and future', in A. Giddens and G. Mackenzie (eds), *Social Class and the Division of Labour*. Cambridge: Cambridge University Press. pp. 162–85.

Gouldner, A.W. (1979) *The Future of Intellectuals and the Rise of the New Class*. London: Macmillan.

Heath, A.F. and Evans, G. (1989) 'Working class conservatives and middle class socialists', in R. Jowell, S. Witherspoon and L. Brook (eds), *British Social Attitudes: The 5th Report*. Aldershot: Gower. pp. 53–69.

Heath, A.F., Jowell, R., Curtice, J., Evans, G., Field, J. and Witherspoon, S., (1991) *Understanding Political Change: the British Voter 1964–1987*. Oxford: Pergamon.

Kriesi, H. (1989) 'New social movements and the new class: the class base of the mobilization potential of Dutch new social movements in 1986', *American Journal of Sociology*, 94: 1078–116.

Levitas, R. (1977) 'Some problems of aim-centred social movements', *Sociology*, 11(1): 47–63.

Levy, C.J. and Rootes, C.A. (1987) 'Disoccupazione Intellectuale e Mobilitazione Politicà', *Bibliotecca della libertà*, 22(97): 139–69.

McAdams, J. (1987) 'Testing the theory of the new class', *Sociological Quarterly*, 28(1): 23–49.

Marsh, A. (1977) *Protest and Political Consciousness*. London: Sage.

Martin, B. and Szelenyi, I. (1987) 'Beyond cultural capital: toward a theory of symbolic domination', in R. Eyerman, L.G. Svensson and T Söderquist (eds.),

Intellectuals, Universities and the State in Western Modern Societies. Berkeley: University of California Press.

Miliband, R. (1977) *Marxism and Politics.* Oxford: Oxford University Press.

Parkin, F. (1968) *Middle Class Radicalism.* Manchester: Manchester University Press; Melbourne: Melbourne University Press.

Parry, G. and Moyser, G. (1990) 'A map of political participation in Britain', *Government and Opposition*, 25: 147–69.

Parry, G., Moyser, G. and Day, N. (1992) *Political Participation and Democracy in Britain.* Cambridge: Cambridge University Press.

Pinard, M. (1969) 'Mass society and political movements', in H.P. Dreitzel (ed.), *Recent Sociology No. 1.* London: Macmillan.

Porritt, J. and Winner, D. (1988) *The Coming of the Greens.* London: Fontana.

Robertson, D. (1984) *Class and the British Electorate.* Oxford: Basil Blackwell.

Rootes, C.A. (1980) 'Student radicalism: politics of moral protest and legitimation problems of the modern capitalist state', *Theory and Society*, 9(3): 473–502.

Rootes, C.A. (1983) 'Intellectuals, the intelligentsia and the problem of legitimacy', paper presented at European Consortium for Political Research Joint Sessions, Freiburg-im-Breisgau.

Rootes, C.A. (1986) 'The politics of the higher educated', *Melbourne Journal of Politics*, 18: 184–200.

Rootes, C.A. (1992a) 'Higher education, labour markets and politics in Western Europe', paper presented at British Sociological Association annual conference, Canterbury.

Rootes, C.A. (1992b) 'The new politics and the new social movements: accounting for British exceptionalism', *European Journal of Political Research*, 22(2): 171–91.

Rüdig, W., Bennie, L. and Franklin, M. (1991) *Green Party Members: a Profile.* Glasgow: Delta.

Sartori, G. (1969) 'From the sociology of politics to political sociology', in S.M. Lipset (ed.), *Politics and the Social Sciences.* New York: Oxford University Press. pp. 65–100.

Taylor, R. and Pritchard, C. (1980) *The Protest Makers: the British Nuclear Disarmament Movement of 1958–1965 Twenty Years On.* Oxford: Pergamon.

10

Collective Action and the Paradigm of Individualism

Pierre Hamel

Over the last few years, the interpretation of collective action seems to have been enhanced by an important addition which research in the 1970s had tended to neglect or ignore: a new concern for the place and role of individual actors. A certain number of recent sociological studies (Ferry and Renaut, 1987; Piotte, 1987; Melucci, 1989; Ion, 1990) have focused on a phenomenon previously overlooked by researchers: namely, what individuals gain from their involvement in collective action, what motivates them, their need for self-assertion and a recognition of their differences. In other words, these recent studies emphasize that in order to grasp the scope or meaning of social movements, researchers must take into account the ways in which individuals become involved, the concerns that motivate their involvement, and what they as individuals derive from their participation in a collective project.

Consequently, as will be seen, it is possible to differentiate several approaches within the sociology of social movements. Researchers have studied different dimensions of the participation of social actors – their individual and collective identities, their intention to become involved in the political realm, and the meaning of their actions. They have thus tried to make sense of the changes that occur within social movements, bearing in mind that these changes are also influenced by the interactions of movements and institutions.

This critical shift in orientation is the result of several factors: a political crisis, a readjustment in the discourse and the representations posited by the actors in the social movement themselves, and the critique, both direct and indirect, formulated by the proponents of methodological individualism with respect to structural-Marxist-type analyses. In fact, the sociology of social movements can no longer ignore the complexity of collective action. Thus, in conjunction with the values of identity and solidarity, the deeper motivations of individual actors are questioned, as is the issue of their personal choice and their concern for authenticity.

Moreover, these studies further a basic reflection on an old problem that liberal democracy has confronted throughout its history: the reconciliation or harmonization of conflicts between individual and general interests or, at another level, the articulation of the contradictory principles of equality and liberty. There is apparently no political model which has both reconciled individual and general interests and also guaranteed everyone equal opportunities of access to the exercise of individual freedoms without, paradoxically, threatening these freedoms.

Wrestling with this problem throughout its own history, liberalism has been more successful in asserting the equality principle in theory than in confronting real social inequalities (Sayer, 1993). Despite periodical reviews and corrections, modern institutions, and especially the welfare state, have never been able to analyse these inequalities satisfactorily nor provide a convincing model of intervention.

In considering and integrating individuals identities and interests, the social movements of the 1980s – and, to a certain extent, the interpretations which highlight this dimension – have modified the representations and forms of collective action, helping in their wake to reformulate the social relations to the political realm. Thus, to the question posed concerning the resolution of the liberal paradox, the actors in social movements suggest possible practical solutions which call on individuals' initiative and creativity.

To clarify this development, let us compare the response proposed by the social movements with that advanced by the political class. Within the context of the welfare state, and up to the present, the latter have preferred to support forms of institutional integration and domination, hoping to maintain state control over society. By the early 1980s, a number of studies had already revealed this radical opposition between the state vision of social management and that advocated by social movements. Katz and Mayer (1983), among others, pertinently recalled that the self-help movements which focus on the question of housing had, through their mode of action and organization, developed mechanisms for resisting the state policies. In the same spirit, others have spoken of the struggles against 'state appropriation of the social fabric' (Maheu, 1983), or have emphasized the tendency and ability of social movements to take over from the parties and other institutions of the political system which have become unable to pursue the goals of democratization (Cohen, 1983).

From a historical point of view, it is mainly with respect to the theme of individualism and its expression in the development of modernity that political thinkers have proposed regulatory models of transitory social contracts within Western societies in order to harmonize the contradictory principles of liberty and equality within a liberal democracy. Experience has shown, however, that the underlying social consensus often remained fragile and so had to be constantly reviewed, despite the supremacy that the lawful state has attained over civil society.

Within this general context, the theme of individualism is by no means the sole prerogative of the actors in social movements. Its explicit emergence in the latter's concerns during the 1980s – in so saying, I am thinking in particular of urban movements and their expression in Montreal – nonetheless reveals a maturity of collective action. From this perspective, I am not interpreting what others have described as 'the return of individualism' as a factor of demobilization. On the contrary, I maintain that individualism is a necessary detour which reunites certain currents within the liberal democratic tradition and permits the renewal of our conception of democracy and politics. In this sense, as others have pointed out, citing the French student movement as an example, the defence of individualism and the pursuit of solidarity are in no way antinomic (Ferry and Renaut, 1987). This is also true of the recent Montreal urban movements. It may be hypothesized that in bestowing greater importance on individual identities and interests, the actors in urban movements define the limitations of the political realm and the concrete possibilities of mediation that it preserves. This has been achieved, however, on the condition of active participation in the definition of the political scene and its major issues.

The chapter is divided into three parts. First, I present the main characteristics of the Montreal urban movements in the form in which these have mainly been expressed since the mid-1980s. Secondly, after a succinct consideration of the principal debates which marked the development of liberal democratic thought, with particular reference to the critical contributions of several studies in the field of philosophy and sociology, I consider certain elements which allow us to identify the principal dilemma of liberal democracy. Finally, to emphasize the way in which these movements concretely formulate possible solutions to the aporiae of liberal democracy, I return to the recent urban movements and to the importance they grant to individualism.

Principal characteristics of the urban movements of the 1980s

In order to respond to the problems of economic deterioration which were becoming increasingly acute in the districts surrounding the Montreal urban core, numerous community actors and various urban movements became involved, from the mid-1980s onwards, in the setting up of *Corporations de développement économique et communautaire* (CDECs)[1] with the purpose of stimulating entrepreneurship, participating in job creation, and training local manpower – in short, of contributing to local development. To an extent, these corporations (like some other community groups) were shifting the focus of the urban movements of the 1960s and 1970s, which had primarily struggled for an improvement in living conditions, towards public services and issues related to social reproduction (Hamel, 1991). Furthermore, these struggles were often characterized by an ideological approach which proved to be one of the determining factors in the form taken by popular movements.

Nevertheless, it is important to mention that these CDECs were built upon the communitarian and participatory democratic tradition of Montreal urban movements going back to the early 1960s. There is, in a sense, a continuity within these movements. The social vision of local development elaborated by CDEC actors grew from a humanitarian vision of the city and from urban development proposed by previous urban movements in Montreal. Their capacity to deal with local politics in a more pragmatic way was the result of a learning process which evolved from the previous struggles and interactions with the state.

It is important to underline the fact that movement activists were involved in a dynamic learning process during the 1960s and 1970s. This process was not, however, exclusive to movement activists but concerned all of the actors involved in local politics. Yet until the 1980s, the viewpoint of urban movements tended to be marginalized by the political class and state institutions. The crisis of the welfare state, the process of the movement's institutionalization, and the new strategies of collective action elaborated by urban movements' leaders by the 1980s had all assisted in modifying the position and legitimacy of the urban movements.

Through close study, it is clear that what characterizes recent urban movements is often related to the question of individualism. The actors in the Montreal urban movements today are less involved in defending a cause that is external to them – democratizing the welfare state or defending an abstract conception of social justice – than the militants of the 1970s were, even though they are still concerned with those issues. Instead, they choose to act in the public arena with a view to changing a situation which affects them directly in their daily lives. If, from time to time, they press for changes or reforms which are likely to improve living conditions, they do so pragmatically. There is no longer any question of fighting exclusively in terms of ideological principles: what ultimately count are the improvements obtained.

Consequently, it also appears, as Bruno Jobert (1988) has shown in the case of home care for the aged in France, that public action and civil solidarity are no longer antinomic. This is partly due, paradoxically, to a more centralized and a stronger integration of community organizations within the institutional networks, but also to the fact that collective action is more pragmatically defined. As Jobert shows, public action is no longer necessarily opposed to private solidarities that are expressed in the sphere of civil society, although the latter retains its specific nature.

Within the Montreal urban context, collective action constructs similar compromises, especially on socioeconomic issues such as manpower training and entrepreneurship for job creation. Concerning these, the urban movements have begun to experiment with various patterns of private–public partnership. They have agreed to play the collaboration game, especially at the municipal level, by developing tools and strategies of negotiation with the authorities, and very often taking the initiative. On this point their approach is characterized both by pragmatism and by the elaboration of a proactive perspective.

The pragmatism of collective action, in this case, comes less from the application of formal principles than from a realistic adjustment following previously conducted experiments during the 1970s as well as a consideration of the nature of the social problems experienced in the districts surrounding the urban core. Moreover, it should be noted that this pragmatism is not only directed at the authorities. A twofold process can be witnessed. On the one hand, the state tends to define its role differently in the management of the social sector: it appears less as the party mainly responsible for this management and more readily assumes the role of partner. On the other hand, the actors in the urban movements no longer necessarily consider the state as their principal interlocutor.

Choosing to rely primarily on their own resources or means of action, the actors in the urban movements initially define their projects in relation to themselves, their vision of the city and their requirements in terms of quality of life. If we accept Charles Tilly's definition that proactive collective action introduces claims 'which have not previously been exercised' (1978: 147), it may also be said that these actors increasingly channel their action through proactive processes.

In their chapter on the role of the CDECs in local politics, Henri Lustiger-Thaler and Louis Maheu also affirm the innovative aspects of these groups. They recognize the fact that the CDECs' ability to raise economic issues pertinent to their communities gives them a strong legitimacy on the political scene. Confronted by a socioeconomic crisis, they have mobilized diverse categories of actors. As Lustiger-Thaler and Maheu underline, however, the CDECs main target remains the social integration of their neighbourhood citizens instead of the 'formal structures of the political system'.

By proposing new claims or by occupying material as well as symbolic spaces that they formerly neglected, the urban movements and especially the CDECs have been innovative on several levels. One may in fact interpret their actions and strategies from the viewpoint of the new relationships that they propose between space and society.

Thus, one may speak of a deepening or widening of local democracy. No longer restricted to the traditional spheres of political representation, local democracy extends to *all conditions* of production and control that the citizens of urban districts may experience over the development of their local environment. Moreover, in such a situation the questions of development and land-use planning appear to be closely related.

The vision of mechanical solidarity mediated by the state, whose financial limitations are constantly recalled by the political class and the state bureaucracy, is no longer adequate. This is not because of a desire to substitute organic solidarity in its place, but because mechanical solidarity remains incapable of providing people with the certainty of the freedom of action essential to their individual and collective self-development.

The recognition of individual interests within the collective action of urban movements is ultimately expressed by the position that is henceforth accorded to private life and its specific demands. The actors in the 1980s urban movements no longer sought to lose their identity in a cause which transcended them, as was the case with the militants of the 1970s. As Jean-Marc Piotte puts it, the 1970s 'militant lives in terms of the other through the organization to which he has devoted himself' (1987: 115). Today, participants in urban movements maintain sufficient space and freedom of action in their private life, defined in terms of time and intimacy, to allow them frequent opportunity to test and measure the reasons for their involvement in collective action.

Although the participants in urban movements express autonomy and independence and accept collaboration and recourse to private–public partnerships, urban movements are still fragile, precarious and vulnerable. They are always subject to what might be described as the danger of institutional integration, with the consequences that this implies for individual and collective freedoms as well as for their articulation within a lively and dynamic local democracy.

These dangers have been clearly revealed by several studies (see, for example, Katz and Mayer, 1983; Maheu, 1983; Craig, 1987; Gagnon and Rioux, 1988; Wolch, 1989). These authors emphasize the shift in political contradictions and the consequences of this closer integration of private and public, the institutional and the communal, the political sphere and the civil society. Within this context, social problems – an increase in social inequalities and poverty, less integration of young people into the labour market and the banalization of jobs – have not lost their importance. If the configuration of class relations has been modified, it is by no means dissipated. Faced as they are by the urgency of finding economic solutions to the divorce between employment and growth or the inappropriateness of the existing structures, and by the need to define the processes of mediation and collaboration in the political arena, urban societies must engage in restructuring efforts. The action of urban movements occurs at the heart of these efforts.

Liberal democracy and the question of individualism

In order to understand the issues related to the main dimensions of individualism, it seems useful to recall some debates that have marked liberal democratic thought. In other words, to grasp its meaning, one must locate the question of individualism within its main theoretical and political context. As we will see, the problems raised by liberal thinkers converge with some of the preoccupations of social movements research.

Liberal ideology is not univocal. Although initially it corresponded with an effort to represent, within the context of the break-up of medieval society, the people's legitimate aspirations to emancipation, and although it was then defined around the principles of equality and liberty – legal recognition that all men are born free and equal – it was thereafter destined to become diversified (Vachet, 1988). Nonetheless, let us say that the two main components of liberalism, which converge in the pursuit of equality of conditions, clearly delineate the theme that best characterizes liberalism, namely individualism. This is particularly so in Tocqueville's vision of democracy.

For Tocqueville, if society in essence no longer gains priority over each of its members taken separately, then individuals should not at the same time gain a logical priority over society. What should prevail is a contract of association between equal individuals (see Gauchet, 1980).

This reversal of the 'social order' required, for its pursuit, the existence of political mediation. As a consequence, the liberal ideology was very early on articulated with the democratic revolutionary project and thereafter with the recognition of the necessity – or with the creation – of a lawful state. As C.B. Macpherson observes, liberalism, in pursuing the project of freeing individuals from 'antiquated institutions', proposed to build democratic forms for social mediation (Macpherson, 1985: 27).

This union of liberalism and democracy, though providing guarantees for the protection of civil liberties, did not completely solve the discrepancy between the irreducible character of private interests and the legitimacy of the public good. The entire history of democratic liberalism may be summed up as the retracing of the various conceptual formulations or intervention models that have proposed solutions to this problem. In this regard, for example, Macpherson (1985) identifies four major models as stages in this history. It should be noted that while recognizing the demands of universal suffrage, these models do not bestow identical weight on the market, the regulatory function of the state, the government and popular participation. They also differ with regard to the central values of liberal democracy.

Even though a re-examination of the terms of these debates has no place here, it should be noted that the thinkers of liberal democracy, when not themselves involved in theoretical reflections,[2] have called on and appropriated the outcome of philosophical debates concerning the central themes which nourish their vision of the political sphere. Above all, it is the political philosophers of liberal thought who have tried to find a solution to the political problem of social mediation between individual and general interests (Dupuy, 1988).

Within this framework, many authors have recognized the era of modernity and the emergence of individualism as concomitant phenomena (Gauchet, 1980; Dumont, 1983; Heller et al., 1986). Later, in political discourse and representations, despite the ambiguities that remain associated with the word, individualism retains a fairly explicit meaning in relation to the sociopolitical phenomena of modernity.

Regardless of the qualifications that might be applied to this statement, it is a starting point for recognizing what Western society seems to have attained in this shift to modernity, namely a break with transcendency as an axiological system. This proposition is clearly conveyed through the formulation of a principle of immanence, confounded with the values of humanism, regarding the role and sovereignty of the subject in the modern era. This precedes the advent of individualism in philosophical thought.

However, by participating in a liberating movement – the assertion of the sovereignty of man over reality through knowledge – humanism nonetheless has a reverse side. On the social level, it gives free rein to the forces of destruction and, as regards knowledge, it prevents the conception of parameters of an acceptable limitation, or 'common norms', for individual and collective action (Renaut, 1989: 61).

Alain Renaut's *L'ère de l'individu* attempts to respond to the problem of reconciling this twofold demand for autonomy and for a definition of social constraints. Renaut questions modern philosophy about its conflicting visions of subjectivism – which is expressed through humanist thought – and individualism. The author traces not so much a straight course as a series of high points which have allowed Western philosophical thought to advance towards a critical conception which escapes both what he calls the 'individualistic digressions of humanism' and the spectre of totalitarianism (Renaut, 1989: 288). Renaut's approach shows that the restoration of the contemporary autonomous subject cannot be achieved, however, without an essential conquest of individual independence. It is principally the 'Leibnizian moment' (1989: 112), as he calls it, which permits modern individualism to be grounded ontologically, through the monadological model.

Without entering into the philosophical arguments, let us recall that the practical or ethical consequences of the definition of the monad in Leibniz – for whom individuality is constitutive of the substance itself – are decisive. Indeed, for Leibniz the individual acquires an unprecedented capacity for freedom by becoming an element which no longer has to obey external laws even though they may be immanent. For Leibniz, liberty coincides with each monad's accomplishment of its own constitutive law, the law of his being: 'self-deployment' of his own determinism instead of 'self-determination' (Renaut, 1989: 138). With his monadology, Leibniz thus permits us to conceive of autonomy without recourse to an extrinsic rational principle. Henceforth, individuals need no longer respond to anyone but themselves for the choices they make.

This conquest of rationality for the individual does not, however, solve every problem. How can we envisage, for example, the possibility for individuals to escape their 'monadic individuality' and of communicating with the 'multiplicity of subjectivities', the world around them, their communities? This question will subsequently be posed in a multitude of ways, not only within philosophical circles but also by sociologists.

From the perspective of Alain Touraine (1992a, 1992b), a perspective shared by, among others, Eyerman (1992) and to a certain extent by Eder (1993), this question must be contextualized with a specific view of modernity – a modernity which is no longer based on a rationalist exclusive paradigm. Rather, it is based on a bipolar vision and a tension between the process of rationalization and the process of 'subjectivation', which encompasses the idea of individual freedom (Touraine, 1992b). Above all, subjects are defined here by their capacity to become engaged in action with others and to be recognized as actors by others. Touraine establishes a distinction between an individual and a subject. For him, 'the idea of subject is both linked and opposed to the idea of individual' (1992a: 65). The individual remains related to the logic of the economic or political system, while the subject is related to the capacity of a particular actor to oppose cultural and political domination, and to become involved and to transform his or her own material and social environment.

For Touraine, the threat that modernization brings to the social fabric has achieved a new stage with the emergence of post-industrial society. Defining themselves in that context and in opposition to the culturally dominant logic, the new social movements give to individual and collective actors the possibility of expressing their autonomy and subjectivity. However, as mentioned by Haferkamp and Smelser (1992), in this Touraine does not share the perspective of Eyerman for whom the 'new sense of self' or of subjectivity goes back more than 100 years and is related to the upheaval of traditional society and to the early problems of modern life.

The contrast between the two interpretations raises the question of our capacity to read historic reality correctly. What was at stake at the beginning of the modern era is related to an objectivity limited by the relativity of the interpreter's values. Nevertheless, beyond this divergence, the two authors agree that modernity has made an important impact on the nature of social movements. The fact remains that if these aspects of modernity are useful in an understanding of the context of individual participation, they do not explain the profound motivations of specific individuals.

In their work on the forms of expression of individualism in daily life, Robert N. Bellah and his team (1985) have examined the factors at play behind the personal choices made by American citizens with regard, first, to their professional career and their private life and, secondly, to their community. There is no doubt that individualism constitutes one of the central themes of American culture and identity. The researchers tried to pin-point, in the daily practices of their fellow-citizens, the way in which the latter perceived the individualistic values as well as the traditions – biblical, republican, modernist – which motivated them.

The initial aim of their study was to produce a more accurate understanding of the most urgent social problems. Situating the choices of individual actors within their social and historical context, they thus opted for a study of these actors' basic motivations with regard to the forms of both public and private involvement that they espouse.

Nevertheless, as it emerges from the representations, existential choices and social practices of the citizens of the United States, individualism is not exempt from ambiguities and conflicts. If it is fair to associate it on the cultural level with the spirit of innovation and entrepreneurship as well as with the ability of individuals and communities to count first and foremost on their own means, it also comprises another aspect which threatens withdrawal or the assertion of a retrograde vision that ignores social needs and the public good in favour of an exclusive defence of limited personal interests. In brief, suffice it to say that Bellah and his team describe these tensions by speaking of two forms or two traditions of individualism: a 'utilitarian' individualism mainly focused on material success and an 'expressive' individualism capable of assuming a certain civic responsibility and more open to communication and to the basic needs of the 'self' (Bellah et al., 1985; see also Bellah et al., 1992).

Even though the spectre of narcissistic individualism remains present, these researchers did not find that this constituted the greatest threat to a redefinition of social solidarity. Nonetheless, considering, first, that the socioeconomic changes of the last few years have had the effect of banalizing work activities in many sectors, and secondly, that participation in public affairs does not appear to be an obvious solution to solving existential doubts, individuals tend rather to seek a meaning for their existence by turning towards their 'lifestyle enclave' (Bellah et al., 1985).

Finally, this study reveals that involvement in private life and involvement in public life are not necessarily antinomic realities. It would be more accurate to view them as the two sides of a coin, or as two aspects of a dialectical reality. Participation in public affairs does not seem to be necessarily opposed to the search for 'private' happiness, even though it assumes a certain degree of wealth or material security. Furthermore, contrary to certain altruistic views of social involvement, individuals do not seem to sacrifice themselves or their interests when they choose to become involved in associations or community groups. It is rather the contrary that can be seen (Bellah et al., 1985: 167).

Despite these remarks, the threat remains of a narcissistic or exclusively utilitarian withdrawal into the lifestyle enclave. This danger once again raises the difficult problem of reconciling private interests and the public good. A certain legitimacy is granted to the political sector and its institutions, a legitimacy which is, in fact, needed by the political class for its intervention in the public arena. We know, however, from claims made by contemporary social movements that the limitations and precariousness of the social consensus prevails in this respect.

If it is true, as Terry Pinkard (1987) writes, that the liberal democratic state must in principle permit the creation and establishment of conditions that guarantee respect for the dignity of individuals, we in fact observe distortions or contradictions which limit their application. These contradictions include conflicts between private interests that are hard to contain, such as differences of sexuality and ethnicity, as well as the misdirection of the aims pursued by public policies. These problems have been extensively studied, from both the empirical and the theoretical perspectives. Numerous currents of political philosophy have, moreover, proposed formulas which focus either on acceptance of an external constraint – through a social contract (Rousseau) or through a political contract (Rawls) – or on reasserting the defence of basic individual freedoms (J.S. Mill).

Theoretical and political attempts to formulate a satisfactory model for reconciling private interests and the public good on the basis of external constraints have largely been failures. It seems wise, therefore, to consider approaches which place greater emphasis on the defence of individual freedoms. Throughout the history of modern thought, attention to freedom of choice has been paramount. At the same time, concerned with the need to offer a wide range of possible solutions and with the external conditions allowing people to decide for themselves, the thinkers of modernity have ultimately paid very little attention to the subjective validity of individuals' choices (Ignatieff, 1986).

The quest for certainty regarding individual choices must be pursued according to a perspective which, if it recognizes that individuals may misjudge their own interests, still allows them to progress towards a recognition of their 'essential self' and their deep-seated aspirations. It seems that individuals are confronted here above all with their own authenticity. This criterion has been suggested by the existentialist tradition from Kierkegaard to Sartre: the ultimate guarantee which individuals give themselves through the experience of authenticity is the only valid element of control left for them to verify that they have made the right choice. In this perspective, individuals are faced with assuming 'full responsibility' for their choices.

However, an authentic choice in private life lies, to a certain degree, within a public space which determines the limits or possibilities of individual action. Access to authenticity thus leads to a need for independence that can only be offered by a liberal democracy which integrates a dynamic vision of popular participation.

Here it is useful to draw upon the work of Samuel Bowles and Herbert Gintis (1986). In formulating a critique of both Marxist and liberal conceptions of collective action, and in proposing a perspective of 'becoming-through-action', they elaborate a vision of action which takes into account individual differences, social mediations and personal choices.

Within the dominant tradition of liberalism, a distinction is usually made between the 'choosers' and those who remain 'learners'. This instrumental vision of action gives individuals no choice other than to leave if they are not satisfied. Neither does it recognize that individuals become what they are mainly through the decisions they make. Apart from reproducing the relationships of power, the instrumental conception of action does not favour access to information. Nor does it favour individual and collective learning geared towards the extension and renewal of democracy.

The Marxist view, for its part, succeeds in overcoming the limitations of the liberal tradition only by evacuating the question and determining its orientation. In the end, this perspective leads to a denial of the legitimacy of individual action – even its conceptual pertinence – in favour of class solidarity, with the consequence that individual rationality can no longer be explained (Bowles and Gintis, 1986).

These critiques parallel those advanced by methodological individualism which, as Przeworski (1986) points out, have revealed a serious weakness in Marxist analysis relating to the origins of class action regarding both the links between elements of a single class and the structural foundations of collective action. Marxist explanations of historical changes have thus set aside the problem of individuals' basic motivations and behaviours. By contrast, the 'becoming-through-action' approach permits the expression and recognition of actors' identities. It also obviously contributes directly to individuals' personal development by giving them the opportunity to enhance their autonomy and independence. Individuals' choices, both private and public, are thus related to a principle of freedom open to social and political communication based on a challenging recognition of individualization processes.

If individuals decide to act with others, it is not always to realize a specific goal. Collective action is a constructive process: ends are not always 'pre-given'. Individuals define themselves as social beings through their direct involvement in action with others (Bowles and Gintis, 1986).

In recent years, the sociology of social movements has paid more explicit attention to individual actors. It has done so in three ways, excluding the rational choice model: the construction of individual – and collective – identity; the production of meanings by movement actors; and the cognitive practices of these actors. Through their complementary concerns, the approaches usually associated with these models tend to emphasize the importance of the issue of individuality in relation to collective action.

The first model has mainly been used by Alberto Melucci. Like Touraine (1992a, 1992b), Melucci (1989) focuses on the main features of modernity with its contradictory social effects in order to describe the contemporary social movements context. From this perspective, collective action is a process constructed by actors who choose to become involved in action with others in order to define their individual and collective identity. In 'complex societies', where contemporary movements take place, participants focus on the defence of their identity, since they continually need to redefine themselves. The notion of collective identity appears to be the key factor in explaining the process of mobilization.

In Melucci's view, the collective identity resolves neither the differences between individual actors nor the diversity of goals pursued by the participants in a social movement. Melucci presents the Italian movements of the 1980s as networks characterized by a multiplicity of groups. In these fragmented organizational forms, individuals tend to participate in an informal manner, but at the same time they must define more clearly the terms of their personal involvement. This is why the need for individual 'self-realization' is one of the principal characteristics of contemporary social movements (Melucci, 1989).

Melucci underlines the role of meaning in the construction of collective action, yet he tends to relate this process exclusively to the internal life of a movement's organizations (Klandermans, 1991). In contrast, Snow and Benford (1992) locate this aspect within a broader context. Recognizing the fact that the production of meaning is central to the life and evolution of movements, Snow and Benford stress the relations with previous social movements and take environmental constraints into account. In order to define their legitimacy and to mobilize participants, the leaders of a movement must produce significant meanings which can be shaped

by a 'master frame' able to highlight a specific issue. This frame
proposes an articulation of events and experiences which are
significant to movement actors. It also suggests an innovative vision
of comprehension and action. For these authors, the 'failure' of
mobilization can be explained by 'the absence of a resonant master
frame' (Snow and Benford, 1992: 144).

Even if the production of meanings through a 'resonant master
frame' is seen as a contextual and dynamic process, Snow and
Benford do not specify that these meanings are part of a learning
process which leads the individual actors to transform themselves
through their participation in collective action. It is this aspect that
Eyerman and Jamison (1991) have considered. Their approach
emphasizes the role of individuals at a cognitive level in the creation
of new social identities. It is by the elaboration of 'cognitive praxis'
that social actors reconstruct their world vision and redefine their
cognitive identity, transforming their action through social movements. These processes are influenced by political factors and result
from the interaction of movement actors with their opponents.

These three aspects – identity, meaning and cognition – and the
approaches that have elaborated them, lead us to pay more
attention to the role of individual actors and their personal
motivations for collective action. Here we are moving away from
the 'rational choice model' (Olson, 1968). However, one must
recognize that this model has raised a fundamental dilemma
concerning the interpretation of collective action.

According to Olson, rational actors will not become involved in
collective action unless they are personally motivated to do so.
Rational actors are spontaneous 'free riders' who gain from others'
actions without themselves being involved in action. This model
deals with the costs and benefits of participation for individual
actors who normally need personal incentives to become involved
in collective action.

Though this model has been taken seriously by resource
mobilization theorists, many critiques have commented on its
limitation in regard to concrete conflicts and mobilizations (among
others see Hirschman, 1982; Klandermans and Tarrow, 1988;
Ferree, 1992). All of these critiques agree that Olson's analysis
conveys an instrumental and abstract view of the individual as a
'pseudo-universal' actor. Yet Olson does not provide us with an
answer to the question of why people mobilize when there are no
specific incentives to do so.

For Olson, individual interests are rational in a very limited
instrumental and economic sense. By contrast, the approaches
dealing with personal identity, meaning and cognition see individuals

as much more complex than the rational choice model suggests. Their participation involves self-determination and self-definition, which become possible through their authenticity and their interaction with others. In that regard, their interests are not opposed to their choice to participate in collective action, as Bowles and Gintis (1986) also remind us.

The 'widened' conception of choice and freedom which underlies these approaches bestows great importance on individual interests. At the same time, these models reassert a confidence in individuals' ability to solve their problems in cooperation with others, assuming personal and collective responsibilities. Henceforth, the paradoxical twofold demand of liberty and equality, or what was described above as the contradiction of liberal democracy, may be considered on a practical level. This is, moreover, the only ground where it seems possible to find a solution. And it is precisely this spirit that has recently characterized the action of urban movements in Montreal.

Urban movements and the assertion of individualism

In resorting to a pragmatic and proactive approach, the participants in urban movements have made a radical break with the 'revolutionarist' perspective (Lefort, 1981). This last conception, which had prevailed in the 1970s, was based on the implicit demand for the abolition of the conditions of domination at the highest level of the political apparatus. Within such a representation, as many authors have shown (see for example Castells, 1983; Lowe, 1986; Melucci, 1989), the actors ultimately had little responsibility, and the significance of the action was usurped by structures or forces which escaped them.

Through the concrete forms of collective action advocated by the actors in the Montreal urban movements of the 1980s, recognition of individual needs and interests permitted the space of the political realm to be anticipated and defined differently. Beyond certain humanist universalizing trends of modernity, through the defence of authenticity and self-determination, individual and collective identities have proved convergent. It is also important to emphasize the fact that once one accepts the sovereignty and independence of individuals, the relationship between these two types of identity cannot in any way be a relationship of subordination.

Keeping ethnic, cultural and sexual differences in mind, how can individual and collective identities be harmonized if we can no longer accept the solution of authoritarian control through a repressive form of collectivism? Though they raised it in a specific way, this problem was not exclusive to CDEC actors: it has preoccupied urban militants since the mid-1970s.

Many conflicts have arisen in the organization of collective action. Citizens have conflicted with militants; professionals working for community groups have conflicted with those making use of the groups' services, over how these groups should be managed. However, it was mostly impossible to understand these conflicts, sometimes covert, sometimes manifest, because the representational image constructed by the leaders, and reinforced by militants and professionals, harmonized the diversity of interests in the name of solidarity and in the interest of the organization's survival.

Women initially started to raise difficult questions concerning the male-dominated hierarchical patterns of the movements' organization. By the mid-1970s some community workers, especially in popular day care centres, started to discuss and to organize unions for themselves within their community groups to improve their working conditions. For the first time, these actors acknowledged openly that they had specific interests which were different from those of other participants, mainly administrators and users of group services.[3] They saw that even though workers and users of community group services could share a mutual vision of local democracy and join their efforts to gain resources from the welfare state, they could also have specific interests of their own which were sometimes difficult to reconcile. An acknowledgement of the differences between participants contributed to the recognition of diversity and specificity of individual interests.

The attempts at unionization within community groups had an impact on the way collective action was perceived by movement sympathizers and leaders. It was no longer possible to ignore the fact that mobilization and popular participation are built on diverse motivations and conflicting interests. CDEC leaders, now aware of the need to respect the diversity of individual interests, did not ask their sympathizers to sacrifice themselves in the name of a superior cause. Instead they proposed a project which, from the beginning, respected local community tradition and the individuals involved in it. At the same time, the proposal addressed the new socioeconomic problems that the deprived urban neighbourhoods were facing. Thus, leaders suggested the possibility of combining the strengths of various community groups and economic actors on the basis of a shared vision of local development, despite their specific or particular interests. The idea of a partnership to foster local development within a communitarian perspective led them to define the kind of relations among the participants of the groups that were invited to join the CDECs.

The responsibilities of each participant were made clearer than they had tended to be in community groups. Yet, in order to work, the CDECs themselves and their numerous projects required a strong commitment from all participants as individuals.

In addition, by recognizing the importance of entrepreneurship in local development, the CDECs moved away from the Marxist idea of a collective subject which had influenced the vision of collective action in the 1960s and 1970s. Local economic development was no longer seen as something which was carried out by historical and external forces. Instead it was defined as a social and political process. If local actors did not control it, they were at least able to influence its course.

This perspective also implied a more pragmatic, but no less critical, vision of the state. CDEC actors no longer waited for solutions for local social problems to come from above, although they were still willing to use the resources provided by the state. Above all, they wanted to participate in the discussion concerning investment priorities in local economic development.

At different levels, all of these elements converge and imply recognition of the individualization process and its contribution to the redefinition of collective action. This is not an abstract consideration but a social and political one which is contextualized by the learning process of urban movements. It is possible to interpret these movements as cognitive practices. Concerning the perspective of participants and the definition of political space, which is central to the CDECs' vision of local democracy and development, two aspects are noteworthy: that the recognition of political space is, first, a legitimate field of expression for conflicts and negotiations; and second, a social reality with objective limits.

With respect to legitimacy of the political space, the urban movements have reasserted the validity of representative democracy which, though it may have been used occasionally by the political class or state bureaucracy to support particular interests, preserves the autonomy of the private sphere and civil society. Thus, the actors in the urban movements came to recognize the importance of the bonds between the individual and the collective in their oppositions, but also in their convergence – bonds which the 'romantic' visions of revolutionarism or direct democracy had tended to ignore (Miller, 1987). They express this, for instance, by participating in and challenging the various forms of private–public partnership.

In just as meaningful a way, moreover, the actors clearly define the frontiers of politics itself and of the political arena. But this occurs not only because past struggles have eventually brought to light the negative effects of the welfare state's bureaucratic management of the social sector. Nor is it simply because the financial crisis is now known to affect the higher levels of government, nor because the nation-states have an increasingly narrow margin in which to manoeuvre in the era of the globalization. Rather, these clear definitions of politics and political space come about as a result of the belief that not everything takes place in the arena of institutional politics. Whether we refer to the affective sphere, to interpersonal interaction, or to the space necessary for individual freedoms in the expression of personal daily needs, all these aspects, in the end, have very little to do with political regulation. Yet they are essential to the expression of individual freedoms, and even to their development in both private and public life.

Nevertheless, the limitation of the political arena resulting from the diversity and breadth of social practices does not undermine the importance of political regulation in which CDECs have become involved at the local level. In their analysis of CDECs, Henri Lustiger-Thaler and Louis Maheu argue that these practices are characterized above all by their relationship to politics. Although it is easy to agree with this assertion, it is nevertheless important to understand what it hides: how individuals have been involved in interrelations with others and how they have challenged and redefined institutions. It is necessary to consider the subjective dimension of collective action. Moreover, CDECs have acted in continuity with previous urban movements, yet their leaders have simultaneously been able to renew the movements' vision.

Questioning the bureaucratic vision of separating economic development from social development, CDECs have suggested a more comprehensive understanding of the social problems faced by citizens in deprived Montreal neighbourhoods. They have challenged local representatives and the political class connected to other levels of the state, concerning their perception of urban and social problems. They have become involved in public–private partnerships and, at the same time, have used the community tradition as a way to transform top-down policies. In this approach it is essential not only to recognize the specificity of individual actors – and the diversity of their identities and interests – but also to value and encourage their creativity and their entrepreneurship.

We have come a long way from the worrisome vision of the dangers of narcissistic individualism and from the spectre of the 'free rider'. As the actors in urban movements are making more and more clear, social emancipation is necessarily mediated through individual emancipation.

Notes

1 These corporations were set up in the districts surrounding the urban core of Montreal by the mid-1980s. Challenging the traditional division between the sectors of production and reproduction, they proposed a social conception of urban development. To do so, they acted simultaneously on a number of fronts: support for local entrepreneurship and job creation, manpower training and the improvement of urban design. For a more detailed presentation of these corporations and their socioeconomic context, see Chapter 6 in this volume by Henri Lustiger-Thaler and Louis Maheu.

2 At the same time, it is important to remember that 'political thought and political life are, in the modern era, linked by an immediate and intimate bond' (Manent, 1987: 8).

3 The term 'users' refers here to that sector of the population served by social service networks, or increasingly by community groups, a sector referred to in Quebec as *les usagers*.

References

Bellah, R.N., Madsen, R., Sullivan, W.M., Swidler, A. and Tipton, S.M. (1985) *Habits of the Heart*. New York: Harper and Row.
Bellah, R.N., Madsen, R., Sullivan, W.M., Swidler, A. and Tipton, S.M. (1992) *The Good Society*. New York: Vintage Books.
Bowles, S. and Gintis, H. (1986) *Democracy and Capitalism. Property, Community and the Contradictions of Modern Social Thought*. New York: Basic Books.
Castells, M. (1983) *The City and the Grassroots*. Berkeley and Los Angeles: University of California Press.
Cohen, J.-L. (1983) 'Rethinking social movements', *Berkeley Journal of Sociology*, 28: 97–113.
Craig, G. (1987) 'L'action communautaire et l'État', *Revue Internationale d'Action Communautaire*, 17: 161–71.
Dumont, L. (1983) *Essais sur l'individualisme*. Paris: Seuil.
Dupuy, J.-P. (1988) 'L'individu libéral cet inconnu: d'Adam Smith à Friedrich Hayek', in *Individu et justice sociale (autour de John Rawls)*. Paris: Seuil.
Eder, K. (1993) *The New Politics of Class*. London: Sage.
Eyerman, R. (1992) 'Modernity and social movements', in H. Haferkamp and N.J. Smelser (eds), *Social Change and Modernity*. Berkeley: University of California Press. pp. 55–77.
Eyerman, R. and Jamison, A. (1991) *Social Movements: A Cognitive Approach*. Cambridge: Polity Press.
Ferree, M.M. (1992) 'The political context of rationality: rational choice theory and resource mobilization', in A.D. Morris and C. McClurg Mueller (eds), *Frontiers in Social Movement Theory*. New Haven: Yale University Press. pp. 29–52.
Ferry, L. and Renaut, A. (1987) *Itinéraire de l'individu (68–86)*. Paris: Gallimard.
Gagnon, G. and Rioux, M. (1988) *A propos d'autogestion et d'émancipation*. Québec: Institut Québecois de la Recherche sur la Culture.
Gauchet, M. (1980) 'Tocqueville, l'Amérique et nous', *Libre*, 7: 43–120.
Haferkamp, H. and Smelser, N.J. (1992) 'Introduction', in H. Haferkamp and N.J. Smelser (eds), *Social Change and Modernity*. Berkeley: University of California Press. pp. 1–36.

256   *Collective Action: From Politics to Democracy*

Hamel, P. (1991) *Action collective et démocratie locale*. Montréal: Presses de l'Université de Montréal.

Heller, T.C., Sosna, M. and Wellbery, D.E. (eds) (1986) *Reconstructing Individualism: Autonomy, Individuality, and the Self in Western Thought*. Stanford, CA: Stanford University Press.

Hirschman, A. (1982) *Bonheur privé, action publique*. Paris: Fayard.

Ignatieff, M. (1986) *The Needs of Strangers*. Harmondsworth: Penguin Books.

Ion, J. (1990) 'Les trois formes de la sociabilité associative', in R. Levasseur (ed.), *De la sociabilité. Spécificité et mutations*. Montréal: Boréal. pp. 169–82

Jobert, B. (1988) 'Action publique et solidarité civile: le cas du maintien à domicile des personnes âgées', *Revue Internationale d'Action Communautaire*, 19: 89–93.

Katz, S. and Mayer, M. (1983) 'Donnez-nous un toit: luttes d'auto-assistance domiciliaire au sein et contre l'état à New York et à Berlin-Ouest', *Sociologie et Sociétés*, 15(1): 93–119.

Klandermans, B. (1991) 'New social movements and resource mobilization: the European and the American approach revisited', in D. Rucht (ed.), *Research on Social Movements: The State of the Art in Western Europe and the USA*. Frankfurt am Main: Campus Verlag; Boulder, CO: Westview Press. pp. 17–44.

Klandermans, B. and Tarrow, S. (1988) 'Mobilization into social movements: synthesizing European and American approaches', in B. Klandermans, H. Kriesi and S. Tarrow, *From Structure to Action: Comparing Social Movement Research across Cultures*. (International Social Movement Research, Vol. 1). Greenwich, CT: JAI Press. pp. 1–38.

Lefort, C. (1981) *L'invention démocratique. Les limites de la domination totalitaire*. Paris: Fayard.

Lowe, S. (1986) *Urban Social Movements: The City after Castells*. London: Macmillan.

Macpherson, C.B. (1985) *Principes et limites de la démocratie libérale*. Montréal: Boréal Express.

Maheu, L. (1983) 'Les mouvements de base et la lutte contre l'appropriation étatique du tissu social', *Sociologie et Sociétés*, 15(1): 77–92.

Manent, P. (1987) *Histoire intellectuelle du libéralisme: dix leçons*. Paris: Calmann-Lévy.

Melucci, A. (1989) *Nomads of the Present: Social Movements and Individual Needs in Contemporary Society*. London: Hutchinson Radius.

Miller, J. (1987) *Democracy is in the Streets*. New York: Simon & Schuster.

Olson, M. (1968) *The Logic of Collective Action: Public Goods and the Theory of Groups*. Cambridge, MA: Harvard University Press.

Pinkard, T. (1987) *Democratic Liberalism and Social Union*. Philadelphia: Temple University Press.

Piotte, J.-M. (1987) *La communauté perdue. Petite histoire des militantismes*. Montreal: VLB.

Przeworski, A. (1986) 'Le défi de l'individualisme méthodologique à l'analyse marxiste', in P. Birbaum and J. Leca (eds), *Sur l'individualisme*. Paris: Presses de la fondation Nationale des Sciences Politiques. pp. 77–106.

Renaut, A. (1989) *L'ère de l'individu*. Paris: Gallimard.

Sayer, A. (1993) 'Liberalism, Marxism and the city', in *Ninth Urban Change and Conflict Conference*. Sheffield: University of Sheffield.

Snow, D.A. and Benford, R.D. (1992) 'Master frames and cycles of protest', in A.D. Morris and C. McClurg Mueller (eds), *Frontiers in Social Movement Theory*. New Haven: Yale University Press. pp. 133–55.

Tilly, C. (1978) *From Mobilization to Revolution*. Reading, MA: Addison-Wesley.

Touraine, A. (1992a) 'Two interpretations of contemporary social change', in H. Haferkamp and N.J. Smelser (eds), *Social Change and Modernity*. Berkeley: University of California Press. pp. 55–77.

Touraine, A. (1992b) *Critique de la modernité*. Paris: Fayard.

Vachet, A. (1988) *L'idéologie libérale*. Ottawa: Presses de l'Université d'Ottawa.

Wolch, J.R. (1989) 'The shadow state: transformations in the voluntary sector', in J.R. Wolch and M. Dear (eds), *The Power of Geography. How Territory Shapes Social Life*. Boston: Unwin Hyman. pp. 157–67.

11
Democracy: From a Politics of Citizenship to a Politics of Recognition

Alain Touraine

The growth and decline of a democracy of citizenship

Republican views of democracy

The word democracy was seldom used at the end of the eighteenth and at the beginning of the nineteenth centuries to name regimes. This was clearly the case whether these regimes were called parliamentary, republican, liberal or constitutional in Western Europe and in the United States. During the French Revolution the term was almost never employed, and in France it became common only after the events of 1848, when, for the first time, all male citizens, above a certain age, received political rights. In Britain where the historical roots of democracy are deeper than in any other country, the predominant political view during most of the eighteenth century was more oligarchic than necessarily democratic, especially between the 1832 and 1867 electoral reforms.

Nevertheless, this liberal era, which had begun with the Glorious Revolution and would end with the formation of mass parties and of a politically active labour movement, represents a major period in the history of democracy. It corresponds to a definition of democracy which has been in many ways predominant until very recently.

Democracy was synonymous with people's sovereignty and citizenship. It referred to an idea which had first been expressed by Hobbes, then by Locke and later by Rousseau. This was that legitimate political power is based not on tradition or on God's will but on the expression of a general will. Hobbes called this *covenant*, Locke *trust* and Rousseau of course *le contrat social*. The Republic, to use the most common name of this regime, was the standard political form of a modern society defined in terms of achievement instead of ascription, of production instead of reproduction, and of progress instead of tradition.

This general will was identified with individual interest and rational behaviour because it was in everybody's interest to avoid violence and unlimited competition and to build what Durkheim much later, would call organic solidarity. When Benjamin Constant contrasted the freedom of the Ancients to the freedom of the Moderns, he considered this revolutionary view of freedom as the last expression of the Greek or Roman concept of democracy. This was because the Republican spirit implied the identification of man with citizen: freedom was based on civic spirit and democracy was the creation of a realm of liberty above the realm of economic needs and interests.

The people's sovereignty or democracy, as Lincoln defined it in his *Gettysburg Address* (as the government of the people by the people and for the people), meant the triumph of a political vision of social life which corresponded much more directly to Hobbes and Rousseau than to Locke and Montesquieu. The Jacobin spirit, during the French Revolution and its heir, the Republican spirit, which has prevailed over social democracy in French political history, represented an extreme expression of this subordination of social to political categories. This extended itself from classes to parties, social movements to revolutionary or reformist political programmes and organizations.

Liberal challenges to the Republican ideology: democracy as a political market

This Republican ideology has been challenged from the beginning by liberal thinkers. The French Terror and the Bonapartist and the Napoleonic regimes convinced them, especially in Britain and France, that a Republic must be governed by an enlightened elite which could protect it from what the Federalist papers in America had called the 'tyranny of the majority'. Tocqueville himself expressed two conflicting views of democracy. He considered it as the expression of a basic social trend towards more equality, that is towards the destruction of traditional hierarchies and statuses – *Stände*. He also opposed the tyranny of the majority and was not very far from the British Whigs who limited democratization to a free choice between two competing elite groups. In the United States, from the beginning, Hamilton, Madison and Jefferson as well, tried to create a well-balanced regime in which the *major pars* would be countervailed by the *sanior pars*.[1]

The more democracy seems to pave the road to mass mobilization and to populist or nationalist authoritarian regimes, the more neo-liberals identify it with an elitist view of government. British political elitism has been far more conspicuous than French Republican elitism, linked as it was with the upward political mobility of the so-called 'new strata'. In both cases, however, democracy has been conceived of as much as a defence against mass movements as a liberation from traditional hierachies and barriers.

In the eighteenth century, the growing economic role of govern ments provided the elitist school with new arguments. The voter of course must be free to choose between two or more political teams. They cannot however directly transform their social de mands into political and economic programmes. Nevertheless, the predominant evolution of liberal thought was different. It gave more and more importance to the limitation of voluntaristic o ideological political programmes, by international markets o transnational companies, and by consumption patterns. All of them limit the role of national governments and of political systems.

The new version of the liberal or Marxist ideal of a withering away of the state reduces democracy to a competitive and open political market or even to a set of largely autonomous political markets. Freedom means little more than tolerance in societies where more and more areas of social behaviour are no longer regulated by norms. This occurs in a context where a well-tempered multiculturalism gives wide autonomy to communities, which must only respect general laws, public order and other communities interests or values.

Here, we are very far from the traditional goal of social integration and citizenship which defines the much sought after democratic utopia, especially in the United States. Politics was supposed to dominate and even create social life; it is now only one of the systems which regulate constantly changing flows of goods and information. Political life becomes instrumental, and freedom is defined more by absence of control and repression by public authorities than by solidarity, equality or participation.

This liberal-libertarian concept of democracy seems to be prevailing today because of the downfall not only of authoritarian regimes but more deeply of social movements in general, which are accused of opening the way to totalitarian or simply bureaucratic or neo-corporatist regimes. All over the world, in the communist world as in social-democratic Western countries, in the nationalist post-colonial regimes as in the Latin American national-populist universe, we are observing the general defeat or exhaustion of voluntaristic regimes. From revolution to planning, from welfare state to state redistribution of foreign resources, all aspects of the control of social life by political forces or ideas are being replaced by a rapidly growing autonomization of economic activities which is generally labelled the market economy.

In Latin America, for example, after 30 years of a development pattern which was oriented towards the national market – *hacia adentro* – almost all countries, from Chile, Bolivia and Mexico to, more recently, Argentina and even Peru, have accepted, sometimes enthusiastically, the opposite mode of development which gives a central role to external demand – *hacia afuera*. Everywhere, positive freedom, to use Sir Isaiah Berlin's (1969) words, appears to be an indirect way of imposing upon the economy non-economic criteria of resource allocation and an ideological way of justifying the growth of an authoritarian or totalitarian state.

Some people are so impressed by the simultaneous crisis or explosion of different kinds of voluntaristic regimes that they consider liberal democracy, market economy, cultural tolerance and secularization to be interrelated elements of a general type of society. And this society prevails everywhere, not only in the industrial countries of the Western world. They think, in an Hegelian way, that this general pattern of organization of modern society means the end of History.

Labour movements and democracy: the introduction of class conflict

This liberal image of the limited role of the state in societies which function to a large extent as a series of loosely connected markets is quite meaningful. However, it corresponds to only a limited part of the world and of each national society. From the beginning of industrial society to today's world, the instrumental use of political power has existed side by side with expressive social and political movements. Unions and the labour movement in general, through strikes, solidarity, and their image of a society divided by class conflicts and cultural barriers, have defended an image of democracy which is very far from the liberal one. It is equally dissimilar to the Republican image I mentioned earlier.

The central idea here is that society is dominated by selfish interests which transform instruments of possible economic or social progress into weapons against the working class. Against the capitalists' domination, the legitimation of workers' action was based on moral and historical criteria more than on political arguments. This was especially true when a high proportion of workers had no political rights or were submitted to an unfair electoral system. The central category of Marxist political thought was totality. The institutional as well as violent action of the workers should overcome social contradictions and create a rational, almost natural society. The working class itself was defined more as a force than as a political subject; workers were more often defined as pro-letarians, deprived of ownership and influence, than as producers or craftsmen. Clearly, Marx was more influential than Proudhon.

The Enlightenment and the Philosophy of Progress led to a naturalistic or positivist image of social action. The goal of working-class mobilization was not to obtain a fair participation in political processes, or an open political debate; it was to create a society which would be a totality in which a rational development of productive forces would be associated with mass self-government. But in the unfolding of these events political freedom was no longer defined as an expression of a general will; it was defined as the political expression of an historical necessity, of the natural laws of historical development. The guiding logic here was that irrational interests and privileged minorities would be eliminated by a workers' government. This regime was not really defined by social values or political ideas but by the destruction of social contradictions and workers' exploitation.

In some countries, where absolutism was strong and traditional forms of domination and social control still powerful, this general orientation led to revolutionary action; in others, and especially in the most advanced industrial country, Great Britain, it gave birth to an autonomous social movement, unionism. We know the lasting consequences of this opposition between social processes in which social movements are subordinated to political action, and situations in which political leaders control social actors. But the labour movement in its general nature was not preoccupied with limiting state power and intervention; it introduced a new dimension in political life – class conflict – and dreamed of a society which would overcome it and create a totality whose concrete political expression would be workers, the people, the nation and the governments which serve their interests.

There is a great variety of political orientations within the labour movement. The distance however between a class- and conflict-oriented concept of democracy, and the institutional and procedural theory of democracy (libertarian) is so striking that it is reasonable to conclude that neither liberal theory nor the idea of class conflict is necessarily democratic. Liberal theory expresses the elimination by a modernist bourgeoisie of a holistic, hierarchical or traditionalist image of society. This society legitimized a feudal order or absolute monarchies. But the free choice of political leaders is not democratic by itself if these leaders are selected from a limited elite and if the choice is not extended to political programmes themselves. This is particularly the case if the elected leaders are not representative of the interests and ideas of the majority of the citizens.

The triumph of the working class over the bourgeoisie can lead to a social revolution. There is, however, no reason to believe that it will always increase political participation and the respect of fundamental rights. Market economy, or liberalism, and social revolution represent opposite views of social organization. It seems impossible to identify democracy with either of them, although both defend ideas which appear to be basic elements of a democratic political life.

This simple idea brings to our attention the fact that democracy in modern societies has almost nothing left in common with the democratic ideology of the general will, which was historically the first component of democratic political thought and action. Instead of observing the extension of a political democracy into a social and then a cultural sphere, we have lived through the rapid disintegration of the last vestiges of democratic utopia. What we now experience is an almost complete separation between social movements and institutional rules, each of which corresponds, in its own way, to one aspect of a democratic political system but eliminates or marginalizes other aspects. If this is the case, then our process of social change can hardly be called democratic.

During the Western process of industrialization there took place a deepening and now almost complete separation between limited, largely oligarchic political processes and social conflicts. It is impossible here not to speak first of all in class terms: the bourgeoisie limited the power of the state; the working class, which suffered harsh social domination, opposed it and transformed the ideal of citizenship into a naturalistic or populist image of progress. But the same dualization is evident in contemporary societies which no longer conceive of themselves in class terms.

Nationalism and the disintegration of a democratic society

The positive result of this decomposition of the democratic utopia is to recognize that there is no central unifying principle of democratization, and consequently, that there is no perfect democratic society. Democracy is a combination of largely conflicting elements: the limitation of state power, the representation of conflicting or competing interests, and the political participation of fully fledged citizens. This last element introduces a principle of unity and social integration; the latter two require political pluralism and an open debate; and the former refers to a non-social principle of social organization, extending to the idea of natural or fundamental rights. There is no democracy without a combination of these three components: democracy must be liberal, popular and participatory at the same time, but these orientations are largely contradictory.

During the first half of the eighteenth century, when Benjamin

264 Collective Action: From Politics to Democracy

Constant, Tocqueville and John Stuart Mill defined the liberty of
the Moderns, they were interested in criticizing absolute monarchies and in fighting against nationalist or populist regimes. But
their liberal democracy was soon challenged by organized labour
and by national movements which became violent in many
dependent countries, from Ireland to Bohemia. Our West European experience leads us to consider that this decomposition and
the internal contradictions of the idea of democracy characterized
the first stage of industrialization. The formation of mass political
parties, after the creation of the Birmingham Caucus, rapidly
allowed at least some European countries to follow the American
example of mass democracy. This prevailed in Britain after the 1867
and 1884–5 reforms, in France with the victory of the Republicans
after 1875, and in Germany after Bismarck.

But before considering this well-known political model that we have
come to call industrial democracy or social democracy, we must
clearly state that the process of decomposition of the Republican
model – the democratic utopia – in spite of the achievements of
industrial democracy and of the welfare state, has not been stopped.
On the contrary, if we look back over the last hundred years, we
see that social democracy has been weak and limited, while authoritarian nationalisms have prevailed in most parts of the world since
the end of the nineteenth and throughout the twentieth centuries.

Instead of citizenship, the predominant idea has been nationalism, first political and more recently cultural. If we accept for a
moment the oversimplified opposition between the French and the
German definitions of the nation – the first presenting the nation
as an everyday plebiscite or, to use Renan's expression, as a
collective will to live together, and the second defining the nation
as a community of destiny (*Schicksalsgemeinschaft*) – we must stress
that the influence of the second has prevailed over the influence of
the first. The cultural concept of nation has been more prevalent
and enduring than the political image of the nation from the end of
the nineteenth century on. The identification of the nation with the
Republic and the general will, which was the core of the ideology
of the French Revolution, has been replaced by a definition of the
nation as a homogeneous community.

Today, when the Soviet Empire crumbles and when the Titoist
Yugoslav federation bursts at the seams, new nations are born
which refer to national, not to democratic or political, rights. They
are often either divided by internal national wars or dominated by
the monstrously anti-democratic policies of 'ethnic cleansing' which
had already been introduced by Pakistan after the division of the
British Empire in India. Caught between economic difficulties and

nationalist ideologies, democratic processes have been given little space to expand. It is true that Poland and Hungary, on the whole, have built pluralist political systems and that the Czech republic, Slovakia and Bulgaria no longer live under authoritarian regimes, but why should we consider that their evolution is the only meaningful one? Can we say they represent the rule when non-democratic nationalism triumphs in ex-Yugoslavia and in the Caucasian area, when Russia has only now succeeded in building a party system and organizing pluralist elections, and when China, Vietnam and Cuba welcome foreign capital but retain authoritarian control over their populations?

Social movements, defined as actors in conflicts dealing with the social use of patterns of cultural orientation in a given society, are more and more separated from political action, and the idea that central social conflicts are also political conflicts is replaced by a tolerant multicultural view of society. The 'working class' was at least potentially a political majority; today minorities are satisfied with a political and cultural *laissez-faire* attitude and cannot identify themselves with a general, all-encompassing view of a democratic society. Social integration limits itself to respecting a few basic rules of the game.

This extreme disintegration of the image of a democratic society is accelerated by the relative decline of the nation-state. This British, French and American pattern of political organization allowed for a direct correspondence between society, culture and politics. Citizenship was closely linked with representative democracy, and economic and social problems were complementary aspects in a *Nationalökonomie*. Liberalism was based on Montesquieu's idea that virtue is the principle of a Republican government. This idea has been widely accepted in the United States, from Tocqueville to Robert Bellah. Both believe in the central role of civic religion in societies where private interests must be combined within general moral rules and institutional patterns.

Today, on the contrary, we live in a segmented social world, where markets, communities and mass culture are no longer politically related to each other in a national society. Markets combine interests with minimal social and political integration; communities, on the contrary, are defined by differences and specific cultural features more than by social relations, conflicts and negotiations; mass culture or global culture is defined independently from social or political patterns of organization.

This general tendency towards a declining integrative role of politics, the almost complete disappearance of the concepts of *politeia*, *civitas*, or even nation in the French revolutionary sense, is even more present in the breakdown of voluntaristic regimes. If we emphasized only the downfall of communist totalitarian regimes, we could interpret it as a triumph of democracy. But why should we forget that social-democratic regimes are disappearing too? This is the case in Sweden, Austria and France, as in Spain or Australia under the rule of Labour parties. In much the same way as, after the short revolutionary period of the end of the eighteenth century, a liberal but non-democratic regime triumphed, now, after a much longer and universal period of social revolutions and national liberation movements, we are entering a new liberal era. This phase of history is more tolerant, less oligarchic, than the European bourgeois domination of the nineteenth century. This era is also more and more indifferent to democracy, even if a much larger proportion of the population actually participate in all forms of mass consumption, from economic goods to political elections to sex symbols.

A post-democratic world

This is not meant to suggest that democracies are unable to react positively to such negative trends. The welfare state is alive and its crisis stems in many countries not from its decline but from a too rapid growth. It is of interest to note that the Americans are currently trying to improve their social security system and make it more similar to the European pattern. But the central fact is that the democratic movement, which, in the past, has integrated economic progress, political freedom and social justice, has declined and even disappeared. Some people try to breathe new life into the republican utopia, but most people no longer accept the leading role of a state which was supposed to represent the interests of the majority against the economic interest of an oligarchy or of a bourgeoisie.

The decline of the republican image of democracy is not the result of the triumph of authoritarian or revolutionary regimes but rather of an evolution which could be labelled post-democratic. It could very well be part of a much more general transformation of a modern progressive democratic society into a postmodern, partly communitarian, partly market-oriented and liberal post-social situation. Should we accept the idea that democracy was just part of a modern societal type which is now waning? Just at the very moment that we imagine democracy has triumphed over totalitarianism, should we recognize that both have lost the same battle, after the First World War, for common world hegemony?

One of the most visible symptoms of this decline of democracy is the crisis of political representation, and, consequently, participation. This crisis does not always mean an absence of interest in political choices or in elections, but the growing separation of private and public problems, and an absence of cognitive and emotional involvement in political life.

At the end of the eighteenth century in the United States and in France, we spoke of the rights of men and citizens; this expression meant that a human being is first of all a political being, *politikon zôon*, a citizen. Today, on the contrary, we define ourselves by our needs, our interests, our values or by the communities and traditions we belong to. We no longer define ourselves primarily as citizens, and governments appear to be above all managers defending the interests of Japan or British Inc. on international markets. We live in a more global and at the same time more local universe, and in a considerably less political and national world. That is especially true of the richest and the poorest parts of the world population. It is somewhat less the case for new industrial countries which are mobilizing their resources to reach modernization. But even in this category of countries democracy is particularly weak, as it is in Japan and even more in Mexico or in Indonesia.

The conclusion of this first part of my analysis is that there is no natural trend towards democracy. On the contrary, we observe a growing separation between a liberal universe and a communitarian world. In the first instance, the distance between economic and political liberalism, which appeared so important during the first half of the nineteenth century, is disappearing. Democracy is identified with a mobile society where hierarchies and rigidities are constantly challenged by the changing equilibriums of the market. In the second instance, meanings, values and traditions are used to build nationalist, culturalist or ideological power elites. This separation between flows and meanings or instrumental rationality and expressive mobilization is contradictory of democracy, and it is easy to observe that the 'instrumentally oriented world' corresponds to the centre of the world system while the communitarian values are stronger in its periphery.

We are now, at the world level, in a situation which is comparable to the West European situation during most of the nineteenth century: the world and most national societies are dualized. One part of them participates in global markets, the other is either closed into its own subjectivity or abandoned to chaos and violence. The first sector represents 80 per cent or more of the population in the United States or in Western Europe, Canada and Australia, but it represents only 40 per cent in Latin America. In spite of a strong economic recovery in this area, this proportion is decreasing in most countries. In rich countries, the excluded part of the population does not generally live in extreme poverty and most of it is still attracted by patterns of mass consumption, but its political influence is almost non-existent and its political participation is very limited. Almost everywhere, the vast middle class feels threatened by poor immigrants, jobless youth or drug addicts, and philanthropy is substituted for political action.

Democracy as a politics of recognition

From social democracy to cultural democracy
The preceding remarks are not intended to demonstrate the unavoidable decline of democracy as if it had been a pure utopia, unable to transform itself into patterns of political organization. We do not mean to suggest that after the historical weight of a series of revolutions, British, American, French or Latin-American, the dream of a new political order which combines liberty and equality had been dropped so completely that the free world is full of inequalities and the neo-communitarian regimes are inherently hostile to political freedom. There is no reason to accept *a priori* the lasting incapacity of modern societies to overcome these contradictions.

But it is necessary to define democracy not only as a type of political regime, as a set of institutional rules and procedures, but also as a voluntary action to recombine trends and processes which tend to drift away from each other. Democracy is not just a regime. It is a political movement and it exists inasmuch as it finds a way of combining the limitation of state power, representation of conflicting or at least diversified interests and citizenship.

For a long period the solution to this difficult problem was called industrial democracy or, with different orientations, social democracy. It recognized the central importance of conflicting class interests, but believed that legal reform could better the living and working conditions of wage-earners who were becoming a majority of the electorate. New political programmes, supported by labour or socialist parties, aimed at creating new forms of solidarity and integration. This was marshalled against the negative consequences of anomie and of pathological forms of the division of labour, to use Durkheim's words, who, himself, was near the French 'solidarists' and opposed to a Spencerian liberalism.

This synthesis of the representation of interests, citizenship and the limitation of the power of the state, which appeared to be closely linked with the ruling class, rapidly became a central element of European democratic systems. Large parts of the industrial bourgeoisie accepted this general frame of analysis.

They became favourable to what the Germans, later on, would call *soziale Marktwirtschaft* and industrial relation systems which were based on direct bargaining instead of the state's legal intervention. This would lay the groundwork for an integration of class relations into the system of institutional democratic rules, and for the combination of universalistic principles with particularistic interests.

Much later, Keynes discovered that economic policies should be directly united with goals of social integration. Industrial democracy, as the Fabians and T.H. Marshall defined it, meant the extension of general democratic rules to labour relations. Social democracy, on the contrary, gave priority to political action, either because industrialization was still in its incipient phase or because conservative or nationalist political or religious forces were still more powerful than the industrial bourgeoisie.

Some of the social democratic parties became revolutionary, but in the Western world, social democratic parties, in spite of strong bureaucratic and neo-corporatist tendencies, became the most active agents of industrial democracy. Our present-day image of democracy has still much more to do with the post-war development of the welfare state than with the principles of the seventeenth- and eighteenth-century revolutions. Many people have criticized the diminishing returns of the welfare state and its bureaucratization, but these attacks are largely misleading.

It is more realistic to state that if the social problems that have become associated with industrial societies have been dealt with in a democratic way, new problems, more cultural than social, have not yet found democratic political expression in societies based on mass consumption and mass communication.

The main danger for democracy today is the growing distance between market-oriented privileged categories and community-oriented underprivileged groups. Democracy was able to find a solution to capital–labour relations. Is it equally able to find new solutions to the growing segregation in our cities, as much as on our planet, of those who participate in global markets from those who obsessively and aggressively defend their threatened identity? The most important problem for democratic thought now is not a theoretical but a practical one. Nevertheless, defining new practical uses of democracy requires a general analysis and a deep transformation of the concepts which have been elaborated by the intellectuals, politicians and unionists who created social democracy.

The central feature of industrial society was the separation of work from culture, economic activity from social life. The main problem of industrial democracy, then, was to create new links between working conditions and citizenship or the 'citizens' world'. In our society, which is largely dominated by mass consumption, mass communication and mass migration, there is a growing separation of instrumental action from culture; not only tradition but all aspects of cultural experience. Daniel Bell in *The Cultural Contradictions of Capitalism* (1976) underlined the conflicting norms of production, consumption and politics in our society. Bell argued that the expression 'American society' is almost meaningless if we do not identify and defend common moral and legal values.

What is especially important for us in this analysis is the fact that our activity is no longer the central element of our culture. Most people are defined more accurately by their geographical and cultural origin and by their consumption patterns than by their job. This is the most concrete definition of a post-industrial society, because the social rupture between work and citizenship was not – at least not to the same extent – a cultural rupture. Today, on the contrary, both mass communication and mass migration confront us with experiences and problems which are no longer linked to our occupation.

We live in a Babelian world: we receive images and emotion from all parts of the world, and in our own country our neighbours and fellow citizens often belong to different cultures. And we, European intellectuals, can no longer elaborate our ideas within one original national experience. We cannot live within one national intellectual tradition even if we happen to live in the most powerful country, because no hegemony can last long.

The classical image of modernity was a unilinear one: a movement from beliefs to knowledge, from particularism to universalism, and the most enthusiastic defenders of modernity were eager to destroy traditions to build a rational world, to develop science, rational-legal authority, secularization and market economies. Today, we use space- more than time-based metaphors. Our problem is no longer to accelerate the pace of modernization but to reconstruct – Marcel Mauss (1971, 1983) said to recompose – our world, to recombine its elements. That is what we did during a long century of social democracy. We must now invent a cultural democracy, a way to recombine universalism with particularism, instrumental rationality with personal life projects and inherited collective identities. If we do not succeed in integrating, in combining these highly differentiated elements of our culture we shall accept a segmented and necessarily non-democratic society. This will be a society in which citizenship will become a meaningless word, where the diversity of interests and values will not be recognized and will be replaced by the brutal opposition between a dominant mass culture and marginalized subjective experiences. It will be a society where nothing will be able to limit the absolute power of the market and of the decision-makers who control it. This segmented world would be a tightly hierarchized one, too, with an upper class which busily accelerates the flows of goods, services and information, a middle class of individualistic consumers and a lower class of communities which try to protect defensively or aggressively their endangered identities.

Combining unity and diversity in a politics of recognition
The main question then is: what are the democratic forces, what are the principles of democratic action in our society? Democracy was closely identified with institutions during its first period, which was both liberal and revolutionary. Social or industrial democracy depended on mass mobilization and social conflicts. What are the main agents and the main forms of action of a cultural democracy? To answer this question, it is necessary first to be more specific about the nature of the democratic process we are describing.

The pure tolerance of a growing cultural diversity, the ability to accept various types of family organization or of sex life, to tolerate a great diversity of food or clothes, to let all churches, sects or ideological groups organize themselves and publish or broadcast their ideas is not necessarily democratic. It can indicate the reduction of society to an open cultural and political market, in which there is no agreement on commonly accepted practices and values. This could make social life actually impossible. It is impossible to drive cars on both sides of the road and to use different languages in the workplace or in the post office. If there is no longer a majority, who is going to respect minorities?

Yet there can be no respect for cultural diversity if everyone is simply allowed to have free access to a culture which considers itself as the only universalistic one. How is it possible to combine unity and diversity? The nation-state provided its citizens, over a long period of time, with a practical answer. Unity was at the top, diversity at the bottom of the social pyramid. Local life was extremely diversified, while science and laws shaped a limited public life. This solution is impossible in our internationalized, mobile and mass-consumption-oriented society. The sole possible answer is to recognize that personal freedom and responsibility is the only way of combining instrumental action with cultural identity.

I would like to bring forward the possibility of integrating personal values and cultural heritage with instrumental rationality or with scientific and technological activities. This process of integration is possible inasmuch as, on one side, rationality is more instrumental than substantive, more subjective than objective, to use Horkheimer's (1974) words, and, on the other side, culture is not identified with a social or political organization. It is not impossible for example to combine science with religion, but it is impossible to combine a rationalist ideology with participation in a fundamentalist movement which is more political than religious. An autonomous life history or life project is necessary to integrate various elements of one's own life experience, combining instrumental rationality with cultural values.

This image of a life project is built on a combination of three elements: individual freedom, cultural identity and instrumental rationality. These correspond directly to the analysis of democracy I presented earlier as combining three basic principles: limitation of state power by fundamental human rights; representation of diversified interests; and citizenship. Human rights are a concrete expression of individual freedoms, while rationalization is an element both of a democratic society and of an active citizen. Cultural identity introduces a principle of pluralism which was expressed in more social terms by the idea of a representative democracy. Democracy from this view can be defined as the institutional setting necessary for the development of autonomous subjects.

Democracy is not necessary for individuals to pursue their interests; open markets are sufficient for that. But democracy is necessary to protect people against the logic of power and profit which uses individuals as instruments. Freedom is more than free choice; it is the capacity to protect a personal territory from conquest by economic, political or cultural powers.

Some philosophers like to conceive of a democratic society as a Parliament. The image here is one of a forum where free individuals discuss with each other, accept a certain diversity of interests and succeed, through debate and argumentation, in discovering the authenticity and the meaning of different opinions and tastes. But our society is not made up of free-floating individuals, and communication is not just an exchange of ideas. We live in a society where mass media control most of the information that is diffused and where we are used as objects by what Adorno (1950) called cultural industries or by administrative interventions. Habermas (1987) gives a central role to intersubjectivity. I think, on the contrary, that individual subjects become visible and self-conscious through their fight against forces which transform them into objects. Individuals or groups become subjects not because they express ideas, but because they free themselves; they disentangle themselves from categories, regulations and influences which reduce them to elements of systems which they do not control.

But democracy cannot be reduced to the defence of individual subjects. To speak of human rights means claiming for everyone the right to act or speak freely. Public life, in that sense, always deals with communication. But what kind of communication does democracy require? If we accept a total diversity of opinions and behaviour, social life is ultimately threatened through flows of exchange of goods or information regulated only by formal rules. This corresponds to what Habermas (1987) calls 'patriotism of the constitution', *Verfassungspatriotismus*.

Yet, if we are convinced that all human beings are rational beings and will agree on the basis of rational forms of social life, we are ready to accept an enlightened despotism. I said repeatedly that democracy required both unity and diversity. *E pluribus unum.* Such a combination assumes that instead of opposing modernity to tradition and reason to irrational beliefs, we must try to recombine what has been separated, whether personal, cultural or psychological motivations and rational strategies, memory and project, rationalization and freedom or cultural heritage. This would parallel what occurred in industrial society, where social democracy meant the recognition of both management and labour as actors of economic progress.

I am using the word 'recognition' following Charles Taylor's definition of democracy, in his 'Princeton Lecture' (1994). He described democracy as a politics of recognition. This is the best expression I know to define the new image of democracy which corresponds to our political culture. It shifts the emphasis from unity to diversity, from citizenship to recognition. But recognition is as ambiguous as communication and it must be clear that recognition cannot be reduced to simple toleration of differences.

It must mean conceiving of a totality which is the synthesis of a wide variety of partial contributions. These combine various elements of human experience, but they can never succeed in integrating all of them in a concrete individual or collective experience. We are all limited, imperfect citizens of the human condition. We cannot find our own truth without finding it in others as well.

Such a concept of democracy does not limit it to pure tolerance. Diversity cannot be separated from solidarity: everyone must have the opportunity to build their own life story. This assumes a constant fight against political or cultural homogenization. This fight assumes the formation of new social movements, which defend first of all the rights of certain categories to equality and to the preservation of their identity but which at the same time directly oppose the domination of new centres of political or cultural power. That reminds us of the impossibility of opposing negative and positive freedom.

A new definition of democracy

It therefore stands to reason that we can no longer believe in a self-governing community in which all citizens would be free. This is because those citizens would identify with the general will, and this image of a direct democracy appears more like a totalitarian regime than like a free society. So we are tempted to satisfy ourselves with a negative freedom, that is with a regime in which nobody can reach or keep power against the majority's will. We have to come to define democracy by its procedures and not by any image of the good society or by the satisfaction or happiness of its citizens.

I share this view, which has been expressed more often in Britain than anywhere else. But it is dangerous to give a definition of freedom which is too narrow to take into account the existence of dominant or elite groups in all societies and the trend towards concentration of resources which exists even in open societies and, more brutally, at the world level.

We know both that popular democracies are dictatorships and that market economies are not necessarily politically democratic. The best way to overcome the dangers of a positive definition of freedom and the weakness of its negative definition is to define freedom as the capacity to resist pressures and to incorporate actions and attitudes into a life project, into a self-defined or transformed identity. This definition seems to be the most complete expression of what Constant (1980) called the liberty of the Moderns, while the identification of democracy with citizenship was the last form of the liberty of the Ancients.

The old image of democracy was based on the separation of political society, where liberty is proclaimed, from civil society which is subordinated to needs. The new one is no longer a representation of society but the definition of the institutional conditions of personal freedom. Democracy was a political notion; it is now defined in cultural terms, and Charles Taylor has done this very adequately (1994). This transformation was addressed by studies such as *The Authoritarian Personality* (Adorno, 1950). In this study German Marxists, working jointly with American social psychologists, defined the anti-democratic personality and particularly Fascism, by the rejection of the Other, of his physical appearance when he is different from what is considered normal by a given group.

Totalitarian regimes, be they Fascist or communist, can still be defined by their opposition to self-government. New authoritarian regimes, from South African apartheid to ethnic cleansing in Bosnia or in Caucasian new states, must be defined by their destruction of minorities or even majorities which they refuse to recognize, with which they refuse to be integrated. This sort of nationalism, because it dreams of a homogeneous society, is incompatible with democracy, which is the political management of social and cultural diversity and conflicts.

Any definition of democracy is utterly useless if it does not help us identify its main enemies, especially in our own country. In the past, democrats designated as their main enemy the problem of social inequality; today, because we are afraid that equality would require, as in Maoist China, a dangerous normalization, we should consider homogenization the most dangerous threat to democracy. In my country, the slogan of many anti-democratic movements, including the National Front, was and is: France for the French. Exclusion of different people, especially of those who want to be integrated without giving up their specific culture, is a central goal for anti-democratic political activity. A democratic political culture, on the contrary, instead of identifying human beings with citizens, limits political power. It does this not only by asserting fundamental human rights but by recognizing the ability and the right of each human being to combine rational action, cultural heritage and personal freedom.

Note

1 These terms, of Christian origin, were largely used by political philosophers to separate the masses from wise, well-educated 'good citizens'.

References

Adorno, Theodor, with Frenkel-Brunswik, E., Levinson, D.J. and Nevitt Sandford, R. (1950) *The Authoritarian Personality*. New York: Evanston; London: Harper & Row.
Bell, Daniel (1976) *The Cultural Contradictions of Capitalism*. London: Heinemann.
Berlin, Sir Isaiah (1969) *Four Essays on Liberty*. Oxford: Oxford University Press.
Constant, Benjamin (1980) *Écrits politiques* (First published 1819). Paris: UGE.
Habermas, Jürgen (1987) *Théorie de l'agir communicationnel* (2 vols). Paris: Fayard.
Horkheimer, Max (1974) *Éclipse de la raison*. Paris: Payot.
Mauss, Marcel (1971) *Essais de socioologie*. Paris: Ed. de Minuit.
Mauss, Marcel (1983) *Sociologie et anthropologie*. Paris: PUF.
Taylor, Charles (1994) 'Princeton lecture', in C. Taylor and A. Gutmann (eds), *Multiculturalisme, différences et démocratie*. Paris: Aubier.

Index

action systems, 74–5
Adorno, T., 272, 274
agency, 31–2, 47; *see also* collective agency
American Federation of Labor, 92
Anthias, F., 90
anti-nuclear movement, *see* peace movement
anti-political movements, 194–7, 213
anti-Semitism, 87, 90, 92–3, 94
anti-social movements, 11, 94–7, 194–7, 213; denizenship, 195–6
Arato, A., 73
Arendt, H., 55
authenticity, 161, 166, 167, 247–8, 251
authoritarian regimes, 274–5; social movements and collapse of, 134
autonomy, 161, 166, 167, 228, 244
Aycoberry, P., 90

Baker, R., 91
Balibar, E., 90
Benford, R.D., 249–50
Bell, D., 104, 207, 270
Bellah, R.N., 245–6, 265
Bendix, R., 201
Berger, B., 209
Berlin, I., 261
Blossfeld, H.P., 46
Bouchier, D., 232n
Bouglé, C., 89
Bourdieu, P., 42n, 43n, 47n
Bowles, S., 248, 251
Brand, K.W., 48n, 135
Breines, W., 232n
Bund, 102
Burawoy, M., 179
Bürklin, W.P., 46n, 232n
Byrne, P., 226

Campaign for Nuclear Disarmament, 63, 225, 226
Cantril, H., 87
capital, labour and, 170–2, 174, 175
capitalism, 89, 108, 134–6, 199; welfare state and, 200
Castells, M., 127
CDECs (Corporations de développement économique et communautaire), 156–68, 239–41, 252–3, 254
Centers, R., 45

citizenship, 108, 187–97, 197–8, 270; democracy and, 258; ideology and, 205–12; modernity and, 198–201; postmodern, 201–5; and rights, 166–7, 205; social, 161, 166–7, 186–7; welfare state and, 202–4
civil rights, 1, 70, 71, 134, 189, 199, 201
civil society, 177–8, 188; and collective action, 121, 122, 151, 153, 177–8, 193; new social movements and, 71–4, 75
Clark, K., 98
Clark, T.N., 42n
class, 44–5, 66, 172–6; as casual power, 172–6; definitions of, 57–8, 169, 172–6; identity and, 38, 40; Maxism and, 9, 57, 169, 170, 261; race and, 88–91; relations, necessary and contingent, 170–2; in social movement theory, 9–11, 21–6, 29–34, 117–18; and social movements, 55–77, 106; *see also* middle class; 'new class'; new middle class; working class class conflict, 24–5, 31–2, 57, 65–7, 116, 176, 180; institutionalization of, 34; labour movements and, 261–3; new social movements and, 39–40; social definition of, 36–7
class theory, 22–3, 28, 29, 39, 175–6; constuctionist, 31; critique of, 75–7; levels in, 173–4; new social movements and, 37–41
cognition, 250, 253
Cohen, J.L., 5, 73
collective action, 1, 5–9, 11, 107, 111–13, 116–17; ambivalence and, 2, 114–16; as analytical construct, 11–12, 87–8, 153; class conflict and, 9–11, 24–5; as conflictual and structural space, 6, 9–10, 16, 114–16, 121, 122, 180, 182–5; individualism and, 236–54; institutionalization of, 12–14, 161–3, 166–7; and reflexivity, 13, 113–14, 165–7; repertoire of, 124, 135; socially constructed, 12; theories of, 1–5; totality and, 9–11; Touraine and, 126; *see also* civil society
collective actors: classes as, 9–11, 66–7; metaphysics of, 110–13; social movements as, 11–12, 153, 154
collective agency, 11–12, 154
community action, 159, 160–3; conflicts in, 252–3

conflicts, 13, 116, 160, 166, 247, 252–3; *see also* class conflict; culture as a conflictual field; social conflicts
consensual social relations, 38, 39, 40
Conservative Party (UK), 206–7, 209, 224
Constant, B., 259, 264, 274
consumerism, 204
Cotgrove, S., 80, 226
Cox, O., 89
Crow, G., 179
cultural democracy, 270–1
cultural diversity, 271–4
culture: and class, 24, 25, 27, 28, 29; of mobilization, 32, 33; of social movements, 30–1, 67
culture as a conflictual field, 13, 32–3, 34, 38, 66, 74–5, 113–14, 116–17, 120, 121, 165, 166, 167, 194, 268–75

Dahrendorf, R., 62
Dalton, R.J., 2, 14, 15
Danube Circle, 139, 142
Day, G., 226
decomposition thesis, 70, 81
demands, of social movements, 135
democracy, 15, 108, 115–16, 190; crisis of, 153, 184–5; labour movements and, 261–3; nationalism and, 263–6; as a political market, 259–61; and poliics of recognition, 184–5, 268–75; republican views of, 258–9; social movements in Western, 134–6, 143–4
difference, and collective action, 103, 252
Disco, C., 223
Duff, A., 80
Durkheim, E., 268
duties, of citizens, 205–6, 208, 209, 214–15

Eastern Europe, anti-partocratic movements in, 69–71
eco-fascism, 103
ecopax movements, 63–5
ecological movements, 1, 73, 135, 190–1, 194, 205, 215; class and, 42n, 56, 80, 225; under state socialism, 137–8, 140, 141
economism, 176–7
Eder, K., 7, 10, 16, 19, 56, 63, 66–8, 69, 123, 229, 245
education: leadership and, 144; mobilization and, 37, 80; *see also* higher education
Ehrenreich, B., 43n, 220
Ehrehreich, J., 220
elitism, 259–60, 267
environmentalism, *see* ecological movements
Estonia, 140, 142; Green movement in, 138
ethnicity, 203; and social conflicts, 192, 194; and social movements, 101–4, 189
exploitation, 26, 173, 174

Eyerman, R., 233n, 245, 250

family policy, 209, 210–12
family socialization, 230
Fascism, 44, 55, 69, 78, 274; middle class and, 58–61
Featherstone, M., 47n
feminism, 1, 74, 103, 135, 188–9, 190, 191, 194, 215; class and, 56; in Eastern Europe, 140; status politics and, 70, 71; work ethic and, 212
fission/fusion, of an anti-movement, 96–7
flexibilization, 203–4
Foucault, M., 7
framing, by collective actors, 13, 120, 166, 249–50
France, middle-class racism in, 100–1
freedom: democracy and, 259, 260, 272, 274; individualism and, 244, 247, 248
French Revolution, 258, 259
Friends of the Earth, 226

Gamson, W.A., 112
Gans, H.J., 47n
general will, 258–9, 263, 264
generations, social movements and, 19, 68–9, 76–7, 80–1, 183, 228
Giddens, A., 179
Gilder, G., 209
Gintis, H., 248, 251
Glemp, Josef, 93
globalization, 186, 203–4; and citizenship, 186, 191; and planetary consciousness, 114, 116; and social movements, 114, 116, 118
Goldthorpe, J., 223–4
Gompers, S., 92
good life, 38, 40
Gouldner, A.W., 63, 69, 78n, 80n, 221, 222
Green Party (UK), 226, 232

Habermas, J., 7, 48n, 81–2n, 272, 273
Haferkamp, H., 245
Hagtvet, B., 78n
Hamel, P., 10, 16, 167, 178, 184, 192
higher education, 221–4; political affiliations and, 223–7; values and, 229–31, 233
Hirschmann, A., 100
historicity, 10, 88
Hobbes, T., 258
housing movements, 140, 143, 158
human rights, 272, 273; *see also* citizenship and rights
Hungary, 129, 130, 137, 265; environmentalism in, 137, 139, 141; local power in transition from state socialism, 131, 132–3; social movements in, 139–40, 141, 142, 145
hyperghetto, 98–9

identity, 4, 5, 6, 46n, 152–3; class and, 10, 38, 40, 57, 62; collective, 13, 33, 37, 67, 74, 167, 184, 241; individualism and, 248–9, 250, 251; of new social movements, 32, 226; of social movements, 152
identity politics, 4, 152–3, 159–60
ideological movement, 205–7; see also Neoconservatism
Igrunov, V.V., 141
individualism, 32–3, 236–8; liberal democracy and, 242–51; and urban social movements, 239–41, 251–4
industrial democracy, *see* social democracy
industrial society, 21, 28, 108, 263, 264, 269; crisis of, 66, 70, 100; democracy and, 269–70; in Eastern Europe, 129
Inglehart, R., 45, 63, 69, 76, 81n
institutionalization, 21, 73; as an experiental field, 13, 15, 122, 152–4, 161–7; of collective action, 12–14, 115, 118, 125, 241; of minorities, 103–4
integration, 242, 260, 263, 265, 271–2
intelligentsia, 64, 222–3, 231n; role of in social movements, 14
interest groups, 152, 153, 162
interests, shared, 30, 32; democracy and, 258, 263

Jamison, A., 233n, 250
Jobert, B., 240

Katz, S., 237
Keane, J., 81n,
Keynes, J.M., 269
Kitschelt, H., 162
Klandermans, B., 5
knowledge, 113, 115, 116, 118; control of, 66; humanism and, 244
Konrad, G., 79–80
Kornai, J., 129
Kriesi, H.P., 47n, 65, 80n, 127, 227
Kristol, I., 80, 221
Kuechler, M., 2, 7, 14, 15
Kuhnl, R., 78n

labour, capital and, 170–2, 174, 175
labour movements, 22, 30, 91, 102, 188, 189, 190; democracy and, 261–3; racism and, 87, 91–2; *see also* working class
Labour Party (UK), 224–5, 227
Lash, S., 172
Latin America, 260–1
Lefortovo movement, 142
legitimacy, 164, 247
Leibniz, G.W., 244
Levitas, R., 233
liberalism, 242–3, 262–3, 265; democracy and, 242–3; individualism and, 244–51
Lipset, S.M., 42n, 55–6, 58, 59–60, 78n

local democracy, 163–5, 241–2
local power structures and politics, 121, 128–34, 151, 153, 154–68
local state and government, 153, 154, 156, 16
Locke, J., 258
Luhman, N., 78n
Luke, T.W., 48n
Lustiger–Thaler, H., 10, 13, 14, l6, 120, 121, 122, 178, 184, 192, 241, 254, 255n

McAdam, D., 8
McAdams, J., 229
McCarthy, J.D., 8
Macpherson, C.B., 243
Maheu, L., 10, 13, 14, 16, 120, 121, 122, 178, 184, 192, 241, 254, 255n
Mannheim, K., 76
market systems, 215, 260, 265; democracy and, 263
Marsh, A., 233n
Marshall, T.H., 69, 196, 198–201, 212, 269
Marx, K., 6, 30, 43n, 55, 170, 172, 261
Marxism, 9, 71, 78, 89; class and, 2, 19, 57, 169, 170, 261; collective action and, 107; liberalism and, 248; and totality, 9–11
Mattausch, J., 80
Mauss, M., 270
Mayer, M., 6, 237
Mead, L., 209–10
Melucci, A., 7, 10, 12, 16, 19, 45n, 46n, 47n, 74–5, 82n, 136, 137, 146n, 249
Merkl, P.H., 78
Merton, R., 92
middle class, 42n, 44, 63; class theory and, 26–34; Fascism and, 58–61; racism in, 99–101 *see also* new middle class
Milza, P., 87
mobility, 34, 43, 228
mobilization, 37, 40, 97, 144, 249–50, 252; class and, 23, 29, 33, 35; culture and, 32, 33; motivations for, 3; *see also* resource mobilization theory
modernity, 36, 60, 196, 270; citizenship and, 198–201, 216; individualism and, 243, 245, 247; late modernity, 13, 15, 122, 161, 166, 167, 184; social movements in, 205–7
Montreal, urban movements in, 154–60, 164–5, 238, 239–41
Moynihan, P., 209
mutualism, 176

nationalism, 90, 92, 101, 102, 263–6
Neidhardt, F., 7, 13–14
Neoconservatism, 197, 200, 207–12, 214–15
'new class', 64–5, 79, 196, 220–31
new middle class, 27, 29, 44, 47, 196, 227; new social movements and, 10, 20, 34–7, 63–5, 67–8, 164–5

new social movements 2, 19, 22, 47, 135–6, 183; citizenship and, 183, 189–90, 191; civil society and, 71–4, 75; class and, 21, 22, 25, 33, 56; class theory and, 37–41; as distinct from social classes, 22–6, 65, 75–6, 109, 116, 117, 125–6, 135, 227; duty and, 205–6; Habermas and, 81–2; new class and, 220, 225–7; new middle class and, 20, 34–7, 63–5, 67–8, 164–5; participation in, 225–7; status politics and, 69–71; theory of, 4–5, 6–7, 109–10
Nisbet, R.A., 78n
non-progressive social movements, 193–4, 213
norms, shared, 30–1, 32

Offe, C., 48n, 63–4, 72–3, 78n, 163
Olofsson, G., 46n
Olson, M., 3, 250
opportunity structures, 111, 112, 120; cultural, 38–9; and movements, 176, 179; occupational, 220–1; political, 7, 121, 127–8, 161, 162; social, 25, 30, 33–4, 37–9, 40
Orfali, B., 87

Pakulski, J., 9, 16, 18–19, 34, 42n, 43n, 46, 227–8, 232n
Parkin, F., 63, 69, 78n, 226
Parsons, T., 201
participation, in social movements, 115, 225–7
peace movement, 12, 63, 74, 135, 140, 190–1, 205
Pickvance, C., 10, 14, 16, 19, 109, 112, 120, 121, 179
Pinkard, T., 247
Piotte, J.–M., 241
pluralism, 73, 263, 272
Podhoretz, N., 221
Poland, 92–4, 145, 265
political parties, 124, 125, 264; and movements, 124, 125, 138, 139, 145, 183, 223–5, 226; in transition from state socialism, 139, 145; under state socialism, 130, 138
politics; new, 63, 183, 225, 227; social movements and, 112, 117, 152–3, 161, 163–5, 182–4, 253–4; *see also* democracy and politics of recognition
post-democracy, 266–8
post-industrialism, 191–2, 215, 270
post-Marxism, 71–2, 77, 81
post-materialism, 32, 69
postmodernism, 76, 201–5
post-nationalism, 191–2
Poulantzas, N., 90
power, 72, 116, 129–30, 261; class and, 173, 174, 175, 179; *see also* local power structures and politics
Pritchard, C., 226

private interests, and the public good, 243–8, 250–1
professionalism, 221, 229–31
progressive social movements, 193–4, 213, 215
Przeworski, A., 248
public spaces, 6, 9–10, 16, 114–16, 180, 182–5

racism, 87–104, 194; middle-class, 99–101
radicalism, middle-class, 34–41; political, 223–4, 225; youth, 68, 180
rational choice theory, 3–4, 32, 177, 250
rationality, 13, 116–17, 244–5, 272, 273
reductionism, 112–13, 232
regime transition, social movements and, 134, 138, 144, 145
regulation, 164–5
reflexivity, of social movements, 13, 113–14, 165–7
relative deprivation theory, 3
Renaut, A., 244
representation, 115–16, 118
resource mobilization theory, 4, 6–7, 161, 162, 177
resources for collective action, 111, 112, 113, 116, 120, 122, 176–80, 228
risk, 13, 15, 38–9, 161, 166, 167
Robbins, D., 226
Roche, M., 10, 14, 16, 166, 178, 183
Rootes, C.A., 9, 16, 128, 183
Ross, G., 11
Rousseau, J.–J., 258
Rucht, D., 5, 7, 13–14, 147n
Ruderman, A.J., 88
Russia, 137, 139; environmentalism in, 138; local power in, 131–2, 133; social movements in, 139–43 *passim*, 145

Salvatorelli, L., 58
Sartori, A., 232n
Scott, A., 11, 126, 189, 196
self-realization, 74, 249
service class, 121, 173–6, 223
Shavit, Y., 46n
Shlapentokh, V., 141
Shomina, E.S., 129
Smelser, N.J., 245
Snow, D.A., 249–50
social anti-movements, 11, 94–7, 194–7, 213
social change, 2; and collective action, 8; and discontinuity, 18–19, 27; and social movements, 1; structural, 201–5
social conflicts, 18, 32–3, 75–6, 116–18; ethnicity and, 102; *see also* conflicts; collective action
social democracy, 264–6, 268–70
social exclusion, 98–9

social movements, 11, 23, 56–7, 68–71, 123–4;
    as analytical constructs, 153, 161; in
    capitalist democracies, 134–6, 143–4;
    citizenship and, 161, 166–7, 187–97; class
    relations and, 9–10, 24–5, 33, 55–77, 106,
    261–3; ethnicity and, 101–4; in modernity,
    205–7; organizational forms and structures
    of, 57, 72, 74, 108–9, 114, 117, 123–4, 135;
    under state socialism, 136–43, 144–5;
    success of, 124, 162; theories of, 1–16,
    124–8; types of, 12, 137–41, 193–7; *see also*
    collective action; new social movements;
    relative deprivation theory; resource
    mobilization theory
social policy, 206–7, 208–11
social rights, 199, 205, 215
social structures, 23, 35, 179; change in,
    202–3, 207, 215; racism and, 97–101
socialism, 42, 61–3, 71, 190
socio-economic conflicts, 70, 74, 116, 117,
    135; racism and, 98–9
solidarity, 241, 246
Solidarity (Poland), 66, 79, 137, 141, 145;
    racism and, 92–4; working class and, 61–3
Sombart, W., 55, 78n
Sørensen, A.B., 45n
state, 237, 240, 261; public spaces and, 115;
    social movements and, 121, 127–8, 133,
    141–3, 144, 163–4; urban movements and,
    153, 154–68, 240, 253
state socialism: local power and, 129–34;
    transition from, 136–46
statism, 64, 177
status politics, 69–71, 77
Stewart, R., 196
structural functionalism, 14, 125, 127–8
subjectivation, 13, 245
sub-nationalism, 202–3
Szabo, M., 139, 147n
Szelenyi, I., 79–80
Szirmai, V., 141, 147n

Tarrow, S., 5
Taylor, C., 152, 184, 273, 274
Taylor, R., 226
Tilly, C., 135, 162, 240
Tocqueville, A. de, 242–3, 259, 265
totality, 9–11, 184–5, 261, 262

Touraine, A., 10, 20, 46, 125–7, 196; on class
    conflicts, 65–6, 78; on democracy, 184–5;
    and historicity, 10, 80n, 88; and
    modernity, 245; and new social
    movements, 7, 36, 56
transnationalism, 202–3, 216
Turner, B.S., 63, 69–70
Tyomkina, A.A., 132

underclass, 98–9, 196, 208, 210
unity, and diversity, 271–4
United Kingdom: ethnic minorities in, 103;
    ideological movement in, 206–7
United States of America: ethnicity in, 104;
    ghettoism in, 98–9; individualism in, 245–
    6; labour movement in, 91–2;
    Neoconservatism in, 206–12; service class
    in, 173, 175–6
urban politics, 151–68, 239–42, 251–4
urban social movements, 122, 192–3, 213–14;
    individualism and, 251–4; in Montreal,
    154–68, 239–41, 251–4
Urry, J., 10, 16, 120, 121–2, 180

values, 31, 32, 45, 76, 183, 228, 232; higher
    education and, 229–31, 233

Wallerstein, I., 89
Warner, W.L., 89
Weber, M., 6, 30, 55, 57, 69
welfare: ideological movement and, 206–7,
    208, 214–15; non-state sector and, 199–
    201, 204, 208
welfare state, 186, 237, 269; citizenship and,
    202–4; crisis in, 154–5, 191, 266
Wieviorka, M., 11, 16, 19
Willis, P., 179
Wilson, W., 98–9
Winkler, H.A., 44n
Winock, M., 87
work ethic, 209, 211–12
workfare, 209–10, 211
working class, 36, 79, 98, 173, 176–8, 261;
    industrial conflict and, 108; Solidarity and,
    61–3

Yanitsky, O., 129, 138, 141, 143

Zald, M.N., 8
Zelditch, M., 5